D0329295

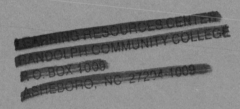

Wilsonian Idealism in America

Wilsonian Idealism in America

DAVID STEIGERWALD

Cornell University Press

ITHACA AND LONDON

First published 1994 by Cornell University Press.

Printed in the United States of America

⊚ The paper in this book meets the minimum requirements
of the American National Standard for Information Sciences—
Permanence of Paper for Printed Library Materials, ANSI Z39.48-1984.

Library of Congress Cataloging-in-Publication Data

Steigerwald, David.
   Wilsonian idealism in America / David Steigerwald.
      p. cm.
   Includes bibliographical references and index.
   ISBN 0-8014-2936-6 (alk. paper)
   1. Liberalism—United States—History—20th century. 2. Wilson, Woodrow, 1856–1924. 3. United States—Politics and government—20th century. I. Title
   E743.S76 1994
   320.5′1′0973—dc20
                                                              94-11847

8.98   320,51
                Ste

In memory of RJS

Not many of you were wise by human standards, not many were power-ful, not many were of noble birth. Rather, God chose the foolish of the world to shame the wise, and God chose the weak of the world to shame the strong, and God chose the lowly and despised of the world, those who count for nothing, to reduce to nothing those who are some-thing, so that no human being might boast before God.

—1 CORINTHIANS 1:26–29

For the modern man who has ceased to believe, without ceasing to be credulous, hangs as it were, between heaven and earth, and is at rest nowhere.

—Walter Lippmann

Contents

Preface

The twentieth century has been hard on liberalism. In the heady final days of World War I, the world seemed poised to embrace democracy, free trade, and social justice. Liberal reason, embodied on its highest plane by the League of Nations, appeared to have prevailed. Thirty years later liberal aspirations were out of reach. In the interval, humanity endured a disastrous depression, the emergence of totalitarianism, and a second total war. Rapid and unpredictable technological change, most dramatically manifested in the production of weapons of mass destruction, undid liberal faith in technological beneficence. By 1950 many people agreed with Arthur M. Schlesinger, Jr.'s terse appraisal of the century. "Nineteen hundred looked forward to the irresistible expansion of freedom, democracy, and abundance," Schlesinger wrote in his famous Cold War tract, *The Vital Center,* "1950 will look back to totalitarianism, to concentration camps, to mass starvation, and to atomic war" (p. 2).

Those American liberals who lived through these calamities would have us believe that the modern crisis was not of their own making. In an immediate sense they were correct—we can hardly blame them for the Holocaust. But what liberals confronted, on a more general level, was nothing less than modernity itself—a modernity, let it be said at the outset, mostly of liberalism's creation. Industrial concentration undermined economic individualism, and the technocratic character of industrial society created cultural and intellectual forms that dissolved the power of the faith, so central to Enlightenment liberalism, that humanity was capable of building the good society because it was endowed with reason. Both industrialization and technocracy had their origins in liberalism:

the first in the liberal defense of the free market; the latter in the liberal affection for science. Twentieth-century liberals have confronted what Thomas Spragens, Jr., rightly describes (in the preface to his book of that name) as the "irony of liberal reason," by which he means that the humane propositions inherent in the philosophy—the defense of individual political rights paramount among them—have had to coexist with the often inhumane traditions, also inherent in liberalism, of scientific rationalism and free-market capitalism.

I have tried to approach this confrontation by looking at the ways that a group of moderate American liberals attempted to sustain the faith in reason, and all the ideological baggage that went with it, through this trying century. My focus is not primarily on philosophers and intellectuals but on people of power and influence, policy makers, leaders of various institutions, and, occasionally, politicians. Modernity's challenges to liberalism resulted not just in liberal self-doubt, after all, but in political and military enemies. The confrontation was sharpest for the American political and cultural elite, who experienced it both as the press of practical events and as a more elusive moral and philosophical decline.

I have called these moderate liberals "Wilsonians." First associated with Woodrow Wilson and the liberal effort of World War I, and thereafter united in the American internationalist movement, they tried to institutionalize and defend liberal reason, embodied in the proposition that enlightened self-interest would lead to political harmony, even in a world that was increasingly irrational and embattled. The group is not self-defining, as are, for example, political parties or professional groups, and so the term has its faults. Some of the liberals included here were well-known domestic opponents of President Wilson who saw themselves as "internationalists" but not as "Wilsonians." Elihu Root and Nicholas Murray Butler considered Wilson a lesser man, not a mentor, and would have cringed at my categorization (though Root willingly accepted the second Woodrow Wilson Peace Prize from the Woodrow Wilson Foundation in 1926). Others, at least for a time, considered themselves to be on Wilson's left. Walter Lippmann, who appears prominently in this book, was variously on Wilson's left and his right and for that matter is usually regarded as an anti-Wilsonian realist. He was not: he probably would have fought the designation as a Wilsonian but he never renounced idealism.

In any case, Wilson became the leader and eventually the symbol of liberals who found themselves moving to the center of American politics, and he brought together a wide variety of liberals during World War I who began to see themselves as ideological allies. All those prominently included here fought for American participation in international organizations and shared Wilson's definition of those organizations. Yet it is not enough simply to call them "internationalists." For when one looks at the ideas that underlie their activism, it becomes clear that they shared much more than their commitment to the League of Nations. Like Wilson, they knew that modern economic relations undermined laissez faire and feared that modern science relegated liberal faiths to the theistic dust bin; yet like him, they could not shake their faith either in the free market or in the notion that free people naturally moved toward political harmony. Like Wilson and for the same reasons, they bitterly opposed interest-group politics, the only antidote to which they believed was the reinvigoration of a sense of disinterested statesmanship devoted to the common good.

They were idealists, in other words, who based their defense of individual rights on the faith that enlightened self-interest would lead inevitably to economic and political progress. They did not draw from a formal philosophical tradition; we cannot speak of Wilsonian idealism in the same way we refer to German idealism. At the same time, I want to distinguish them from mere "do-gooders." They saw themselves as heirs to a coherent Anglo-American political tradition that carried with it certain assumptions. Wilsonian idealists, at the very least, shared a temperament, and the term, whatever its faults, captures the combination of philosophy, political goals, internationalist commitments, and social class better than any alternative.

I intend this book to be the first in a series of studies on the philosophical, aesthetic, and political consequences of the post-Nietzschean assault on reason and faith. It made sense to begin by studying the effects of that assault on liberal WASP men, members of the very group that presumably has been dethroned. It turns out that those men understood the consequences of the repudiation of truth more clearly than many who today blithely disregard the very real public repercussions of the Nietzschean tradition. We live at a moment when accumulating evidence, in the form of intractable economic inequalities, racial and sexual animosities, and institutional disintegration, suggests that the great emancipation from the Enlightenment has exhausted itself. And yet more and more American intellectuals eagerly, faddishly, count themselves among Nietzsche's heirs. There are, of course, many thinkers who, following the likes of Jürgen Habermas and Richard Rorty, continue to rec-

ognize that ideas have consequences. I do not have a strong enough reading on the future to know whether Rorty's increasingly keen disillusionment with cultural politics marks the intellectuals' return to common
sense, or whether, as E. Ann Kaplan has written of Habermas (in the introduction to *Postmodernism and Its Discontents*), it is all merely "a
desperate reaction against postmodern culture." I do know that when
there is no more liberation to gain, no more truths to destroy, no more
ruling classes to unseat, no more regulations to suspend, the poor will
still be poor, the vulnerable unprotected, and the vanquished unvindi-
cated. The intellectuals will still have their tenure and the artists their
government grants. At that point, postmodernism will be only destructive when what we will need is reconstruction.

It is my conviction that we are fast approaching that point, if we are
not already there. The first job of reconstruction, accordingly, will be the
reclaiming of shared moral ideals, and my purpose in this book is to try
to determine which parts of liberal idealism are best left in the past and,
by way of conclusion, which parts continue to hold out some promise. I
do not find much promise in liberal internationalism, or in the vague re-
vivals of universalism that one can see, for instance, in Daniel Patrick
Moynihan's defense of international law or in Francis Fukuyama's Hegelian "end of history." I concede that there are compelling defenses of
universalism, such as the one Orlando Patterson began making in the late
1970s. Patterson insists that universalism must be revived lest ethnic
chauvinism run rampant, but he argues that liberals are inherently incapable of managing such a revival and that an idealist renewal rests on a
socialist commitment to a just distribution of wealth.

My own view is that there is a difference between universal ideals and
universalism and that the political implications of that distinction are vitally important. The universal society is possible only through the expansion of the marketplace; science and technology indisputably bring the
world closer together. Yet those very forces work against the capacity of
people to embrace the sort of universal ideals without which there can be
no genuine unity. Instead of producing the homogeneity that liberals expect, technological interdependence tends to heighten the sense of differences because it offers no common compelling moral goal to which
different people can commit themselves. The only common goal seems to
be abundance, which all the world might want but not all the world can
have, short, of course, of a redistribution of wealth, which in turn would
undermine the processes of capitalism and technological change that
make that abundance possible in the first place. The postmodern dialectic that confronts us promises a universal economy that is possible only

by way of processes that make the acceptance of political, cultural, and moral universals impossible.

This is a well-traveled project. Like any self-respecting vagrant, it has never stayed in one place long enough to owe many huge debts, though it has accumulated countless smaller ones. It seems wisest for me to acknowledge these by recalling them collectively, stop by stop. Friends at Ohio State University, Ohio Wesleyan University, Goucher College, Hobart and William Smith Colleges, and the University of Rochester put up with me as I worked this manuscript over. I want to single out Michael Hogan, William O. Walker, Peter Bardaglio, Mary Young, and Jules Benjamin for their help and advice. I have learned much from Wayne S. Cole's work on isolationism, and I appreciate the advice he offered. The research was undertaken in the archives at Yale, Princeton, the Roosevelt Library at Hyde Park, the Kennedy Library in Boston, and the Library of Congress.

Itinerancy aside, I do have some heavy, probably irredeemable debts. All Wilson scholars depend on Arthur S. Link, whose careful and steady editing of the Wilson Papers has made a tremendous public resource readily available. The Papers are not merely the chronicle of one statesman's life but a resource for an age. Personally Professor Link has never failed to be gracious and accommodating. Jean H. Baker has saved me—I hope—from a simpleminded understanding of Adlai Stevenson, though I doubt she will agree with the result. My real debt to her is less tangible: watching her in action is a lesson in scholarly diligence. Frederick Siegel played an important role in placing this book with Cornell University Press, and it is a better work because he goaded me to consider the subject beyond the Cold War. Finally, the further I have moved from Christopher Lasch, the more I appreciate how great a teacher he is. He understands, as too few people do, that there is no such thing as "teaching," there is only example. As the example of his work continues to unfold before me, he continues to teach, and I hope I continue to learn.

Even a hobo cannot run from family debts. Peg and Larry Woerner have sustained us in many ways, and it looks as if they will finally get a book for their shelves. I dedicate this book to the memory of my father, but everyone who knows them understands that this includes my mother as well. Susan, Drew, and now Stacey, the newcomer, have been fellow transients who have given up the stability and predictability they deserve. I should say more to them, but one can never say enough.

DAVID STEIGERWALD

Delaware, Ohio

PART 1

THE RISE AND DECLINE
OF WILSONIAN IDEALISM

I

Liberalism
between Two Worlds

In the space of one or two generations surrounding the turn of the twentieth century, the fortresses of traditional bourgeois society crumbled across all fronts. Economic man became a factory hand, a corporate manager, or a "professional." The grandiose nineteenth-century conceptions of human potential, contained both in Romantic culture and in positivism's claims that humanity could master nature, caved in to the relativistic tendencies of the modernists. The complacent assumption that people were rational beings who deserved democracy ran up against Freud and the distinct possibility that much human behavior was something other than rational. Even Newton's ordered universe was jumbled after Einstein. The assault on liberalism was more than the "major intellectual reorientation" that Thomas Haskell modestly has described; the conceptions of human nature that had predominated in the West since the Enlightenment became subject to thoroughgoing transformation.[1] These transformations shattered the self-justifying liberalism of the nineteenth-century bourgeoisie but offered no similarly comprehensive way of conceiving political order or public life. Modernity tore down but did not rebuild, at least not systematically.

---

[1] Thomas Haskell, *The Emergence of Professional Social Science: The American Social Science Association and the Nineteenth-Century Crisis of Authority* (Urbana, Ill., 1977), 15. I use the term "modernity" here to include the entire scope of social change associated with the late-nineteenth-century economic transformation, which was peculiarly reliant upon technological manipulation.

The causes of these tremendous shifts in Western life are practically beyond dispute. By 1900 the major European nations and the United States had become fully industrialized. Industrial capitalism was, of course, long in coming, but by 1900 the singular characteristics of economic development were the concentration of capital and of management control, usually in some form of business incorporation, on the one hand, and increasing reliance on systematic invention and technological transformation on the other. In terms of how work was done and how work was controlled, modern capitalism had become a collective enterprise based on technological manipulation.

These characteristics profoundly affected the twentieth-century West. Modern capitalism did away with economic man, the lone, self-seeking, rational individual of liberal lore. Not only did enterprise and work become collective pursuits, but industrial society was collectivized in the larger sense that it created the modern class structure and gathered the classes in cities. In such settings, mass politics emerged in which people organized in pursuit of shared class and ethnic interests.

Because twentieth-century progressives, either in their liberal form in the United States or in European social democracy, long have been proponents of mass politics, it is easy to forget how the emergence of politicized groups ran against prevailing liberal political thought in the late nineteenth century. The momentum of nineteenth-century political development was toward greater political consolidation and homogeneity; the national unifications in Italy and Germany, the American Civil War, and even nineteenth-century imperialism, hailed by liberal supporters as a means for uniting the world, all are cases in point. Liberals justly could take some credit for this movement, and, indeed, for a time, they equated progress with unification in the nation-state. Initially, the emergence of mass politics and, along with it, anti-liberal ideologies of both the left and right undermined the liberal faith in political progress by threatening political unity.

In Western Europe, turn-of-the-century liberalism lost its political and intellectual legitimacy when decadent bourgeoisies fought simultaneously against resurgent aristocrats and insurgent working classes. The fate of liberals in both Germany and England attests to such difficulties. Never potent in Germany in the first place, liberals there, bound together in several different centrist parties, failed to provide a viable middle way between left and right. More often than not they sided with the right, and the German case thus demonstrated that economic might in an industrial age did not rely on entrepreneurial freedom or constitutional democracy.[2] England, meanwhile, had been the veritable birthplace of liberalism and was its nineteenth-century bastion, and yet, by the early 1920s, the Liberal party was dead. The Liberal fate was a vivid example of liberalism's demise on two counts: first, because the party had embodied liberal ideals since its inception; and, second, because the party was unable to shape acceptable appeals to working-class voters or, for that matter, to suffragettes. The Liberal party did not survive the emergence of mass politics because, try as they might, British Liberals could not appeal to the collective will of new constituencies and simultaneously preserve their devotion to individual liberty. In England, the greater the philosophical need to synthesize liberty and positive government, the more irrelevant liberalism became.[3]

If European liberals bowed to political opponents, the most important force for undermining their legitimacy, namely the technocratic impulse, grew out of liberalism itself. As Thomas Spragens has argued, technocracy was deeply rooted in the Enlightenment's devotion to rational thought; reason and "science" were always closely aligned. Reason was the basis of democracy yet was easily blurred into a purely scientific mentality. Technocracy, the institutionalization of science as a social and political force, undermined democracy by elevating "a highly paternalistic secular theocracy" led by an elite that "debunks liberty and justice." Where reason originally undermined repressive authority, the technocracy that evolved out of reason gradually hardened into a repressive regime in its own right.[4]

Liberalism, in Spragen's view, was always dualistic, and that dualism widened, as technocracy prevailed and industrialization proceeded. The prestige of science began to overtake the republican impulses in the nineteenth century; in several of the century's most powerful intellectual movements, positivism particularly, science displaced theology as the intellectual avenue for revealing ultimate truth.[5] The technological changes

---

[2] Gordon Craig, *Germany, 1866–1945* (New York, 1978), especially chap. 3; and Carl E. Schorske, *German Social Democracy, 1905–1917: The Development of the Great Schism* (Cambridge, 1955).

[3] George Dangerfield, *The Strange Death of Liberal England* (New York, 1935, 1961); Trevor Wilson, *The Downfall of the Liberal Party, 1914–1935* (Ithaca, 1966); Roy Douglas, *The History of the Liberal Party, 1895–1970* (London, 1971); Stefan Collini, *Liberalism and Sociology: L. T. Hobhouse and Political Argument in England, 1880–1914* (Cambridge, 1971); and Michael Freeden, *Liberalism Divided: A Study in British Political Thought, 1914–1939* (Oxford, 1986).

[4] Spragens, *The Irony of Liberal Reason* (Chicago, 1981), chap. 4 and 194–95.

[5] See ibid., 125–26.

of the late nineteenth century, furthermore, altered the relationship between liberalism and science in important ways and empowered the insidious side of the liberal dualism. The so-called Second Industrial Revolution rose on the strengths of electricity, synthetic chemistry, and precision manufacturing, which relied on applied science.[6] Industrialists discovered that technological change, like labor, could be commodified, and they relied on the expertise of engineers, laboratory scientists, and universities. The commodification of science undermined science as a form of metaphysics and brought with it the possibility that people could do more than understand and master the environment, as the earlier devotees of science had believed. With applied science, the environment could be manipulated and even fabricated, which meant that nothing defined as "natural truth" was permanent or inalterable, even if "scientifically" proven to be fact. Because applied science produced practical change, the scientists of the Second Industrial Revolution tended to ignore absolute principles as impediments to progress, and in so doing undermined the intellectual infallibility of science even as they helped to institutionalize it as an economic force and, in the bargain, vastly improve their own social status. Instead of high priests preaching constants, turn-of-the-century scientists, along with the technocratic reformers devoted to "efficiency," were increasingly well-paid managers of change.[7] Based on a faith in human reason, political liberalism had confirmed science as the surest foundation of transcendent knowledge and objective truth, and the rise of a commodified science, which thrived on instituting change and denying, thereby, settled truths, threatened the essence of the tradition that had spawned it.

The political impact that widespread uncertainty, constant change, and relativistic notions of truth had on liberalism was profound. In the humane tradition, universal reason, which itself implied the existence of objective truth, was to provide the means to democratic order; the citizen did not need a ruler to explain right and wrong. Liberals conceived the "common good" as that place where the body politic captured objective truth as a means of protecting society against anarchy and avarice. As modernity undermined the faith in objective truth, therefore, it undermined common-good liberalism as well. Modernity began to exert its

<hr/>

[6] See David S. Landes, *The Unbound Prometheus: Technological Change and Industrial Development in Western Europe from 1750 to the Present* (Cambridge, 1969), chap. 5.

[7] See David F. Noble, *America by Design: Science, Technology, and the Rise of Corporate Capitalism* (Oxford, 1977); Samuel Haber, *Efficiency and Uplift: Scientific Management in the Progressive Era, 1890–1920* (Chicago, 1964).

corrosive power just as the emergence of a globalized economy began to convince many Americans that liberalism was the standard of the future, and thus the paradoxical development of universalism and fragmentation is illuminated in the condition of American liberalism.

The Persistence of Liberal Idealism in America

The Great War brought together the two elements, technological advance and social fragmentation, that since have defined modernity. The war's origins lay in technological changes and imperialism, which had brought the world close together, only to generate ethnic and international conflict. The destruction unleashed violated all previous measures of civilized behavior, rendered absurd the claim that nations recognized natural restraints, and confirmed the prevalent doubts about humanity's rationality. The carnage reached from Russia to France and turned large sections of the Western Front into swampy craters. The great battles of the attrition period, the Somme, Verdun, Ypres, were almost wars in themselves, so great were their scope and duration. Trench warfare and increasingly efficient weaponry, as Modris Eksteins writes, "reversed all traditions of warfare," for "defense was turned into offense. . . . The gulf between technology and strategy meant that the attacker, regardless of numbers, was far more vulnerable than the defender." The greatest and most unprecedented horror of all, of course, was the sheer waste of life. The British lost more than a half million men at the Somme, 60,000 on the first day alone; the Germans nearly 800,000 during the Somme and Verdun. In all its frightfulness, the Great War became the pivotal event between the nineteenth century and the twentieth and foretold a century of anti-rational catastrophe.[8]

Liberalism survived, of course, though most obviously in its technocratic form. So too, however, did liberal idealism—a sort of liberalism in which reason, the common good, and objective truth remained essential principles, the foregoing developments notwithstanding. In the United States, liberal idealism not only survived but remained important; indeed, in the broadest sense and to the degree that tradition and rhetoric have had anything to do with political thought, liberal idealism remained the standard against which ideas and programs had to prove themselves before the Cold War.

---

[8] Modris Eksteins, *Rites of Spring: The Great War and the Birth of the Modern Age* (Boston, 1989), 144–45.

It is unnecessary to believe that the United States was unique in order to accept that liberal idealism persisted here while it evaporated elsewhere. In very important ways, the country was at the forefront of modernity. Certainly technocracy was institutionalized more deeply and received more adulation in American than anywhere else, save Germany. The United States had undergone a tremendous national consolidation since its Civil War. It also had more of the elements of political fragmentation than any nation, save none. The ethnic fragmentation for which the first shots of World War I were fired appeared in the United States as an extraordinary mixing of cultures. As Randolph Bourne wrote in 1916, America held out a "trans-national" ideal for the entire world. "In a world which has dreamed of internationalism, we find that we have all unawares been building up the first internationalist nation. . . . What we have achieved has been rather a cosmopolitan federation of national colonies, of foreign cultures, from whom the sting of devastating competition has been removed. America is already the world-federation in miniature."[9]

The staying power of liberal idealism lay not in the "world-federation in miniature," but in more mundane circumstances. The American party system proved more flexible certainly than the British system, and the Democrats and Republicans both accommodated competing groups and contained the challenges to liberalism. America was also relatively insulated from modernist culture: modern art, for instance, arrived here officially only with the 1915 Armory Show, and Freud even later than that. In sharp contrast to the experience of all the European belligerents, Americans were spared the war's insane bloodshed by virtue of their late entry into the conflict.

Two other explanations lay behind idealism's survival. First, many among the American elite—the ethnic, political, and economic elite—almost instinctively embraced liberal idealism. It was part of their heritage. Second, this instinctive idealism was shaped into something less than a movement, but more than just a coherent program of internationalism during the push for American entry into the war and subsequently into the League of Nations. Thereafter, American internationalism embodied the idealist hopes for a homogenous, liberal world. Taken together, the program of internationalism and the value system that generated it are best understood as Wilsonian idealism.

[9] Randolph Bourne, "Transnational America," in *War and the Intellectuals*, ed. Carl Resek (New York, 1964), 117. See also Horace Kallen, "Democracy vs. the Melting Pot," *Nation*, 18 February 1915, 190–94, and 25 February 1915, 217–20.

Wilsonian idealism clearly grew out of a particular class and culture. The Wilsonians were predominantly white, Anglo-Saxon, East Coast, and male, which is a long-winded way of saying that they were part of the traditional WASP elite. There were women within their organizations—Vera Micheles Dean and Virginia Gildersleeve come to mind—but for the most part they were men who had their hands near the reins of power even when electoral politics limited their formal access to it. Perhaps they were naturally elitist, given their backgrounds, but their elitism was usually muted. Wilsonians distrusted mass politics and pluralism because they believed that group politics was a form of self-interest that promoted fragmentation rather than the common good.[10] Members of a shared culture, they lived within restricted geographical boundaries. While many were natives of neither a large city nor the eastern seaboard, the vast majority led their adult lives in the urban East. Some had grown up in small towns—some in the south, some in the midwest—rather removed from the hubs of industrialization, and this background might help explain their attraction to traditional ideals. Still they made their public reputations not as defenders of rural America but as cosmopolitan participants in national life. There is no better example of this character than Walter Lippmann: Manhattan raised, Harvard educated, a frequent visitor to Europe as a child, Lippmann was the essence of Progressive Era cosmopolitanism.[11]

When one considers these origins, it is difficult to avoid the observation that the particular economic needs of the east coast lay behind American internationalism. In various guises, of course, this material connection has encouraged all sorts of charges, including those made in the 1930s by the isolationist Nye Committee, which investigated the in-

[10] We shall note this point in far greater detail below, but see the similar descriptions of internationalists and international lawyers in, respectively, Robert Divine, *Second Chance: The Triumph of Internationalism in America during World War II* (New York, 1967), 18–23; and C. Roland Marchand, *The American Peace Movement and Social Reform, 1898–1918* (Princeton, 1972), 40–51.

[11] See C. H. Cramer, *Newton D. Baker: A Biography* (Cleveland, 1965); Cordell Hull, *The Memoirs of Cordell Hull* (New York, 1948), 2 vols.; William Harbaugh, *Lawyer's Lawyer: The Life of John W. Davis* (New York, 1973); Ronald Steel, *Walter Lippmann and the American Century* (Boston, 1980); D. Steven Blum, *Walter Lippmann: Cosmopolitanism in the Century of Total War* (Ithaca, 1984). I have drawn from various biographies, which I will duly note. Other information comes primarily from the following: Warren Kuehl, ed., *Biographical Dictionary of Internationalists* (Westport, Conn., 1983); Albert Nelson Marquis, ed., *Who's Who in America*, vols. 16 (1930–1931), 17 (1932–1933), and 22 (1942–1943); and Miranda C. Herbert and Barbara McNeil, eds., *Biography and Genealogy Master Index* (Detroit, 1980).

fluence of eastern bankers on Wilson's decision to intervene in World War I. These charges should never have been taken seriously, but it is worth noting that some eastern business leaders were attracted to Wilson's programs and shared his political ideals. World "interdependence," the most fashionable idea of the 1920s, surely appealed to those whose businesses were caught up in the process of trans-Atlantic economic integration. It was not disinterested philanthropy that drove Wall Street bankers and their business companions, James Warburg, Norman Davis, and John W. Davis to name several, to champion Wilsonianism.[12]

In addition to ethnicity and material circumstances, these liberals shared common institutional affiliations. Ivy League universities were homes to and breeding grounds for Wilsonians—so too was Johns Hopkins. Prominent Wilsonians at one time led Princeton, Columbia, and Harvard; and Wilson, Nicholas Murray Butler, and A. Lawrence Lowell staffed their respective schools with like-minded scholars. This is not to say, of course, that America's elite universities constituted centrist bastions. But these schools encouraged the sort of tame cosmopolitanism that Wilsonians at large practiced, and Wilsonianism was, if nothing else, academically respectable before World War II.

Though their cultural origins evoke a picture of eastern gentility, Wilsonians were not mugwumps, a displaced and cranky cultural elite. Their intellectual prestige put them in positions of potentially increasing power. Indeed not only did they readily adapt to the processes of modern government, they helped pioneer what some scholars today call "quasi-public organizations."[13] American internationalism was closely linked to organizations that existed primarily to influence government. The Carnegie Foundation, the League to Enforce Peace, the Council on Foreign Relations, the Foreign Policy Association, the World Peace Foundation, the League of Nations Association, the Williamstown Institute of Politics, all were founded with that intention, and Wilsonians overwhelmingly inhabited them.[14]

They resorted to organized politics—a strategy that forces us to be frankly skeptical of their criticism of interest-group politics—because

[12] See Divine, *Second Chance,* 22–23.
[13] See, for example, Louis Galambos, "The Emerging Organizational Synthesis in Modern American History," *Business History Review* 44 (Summer 1970): 279–90 and "Technology, Political Economy, and Professionalization," ibid. 57 (Winter 1983): 471–93; Ellis Hawley, *The Great War and the Search for a Modern World Order* (New York, 1978).
[14] Robert Schulzinger, *The Wise Men of Foreign Affairs: The Council on Foreign Relations* (New York, 1984); and Ruhl Bartlett, *The League to Enforce Peace* (Chapel Hill, 1944).

they were not instinctive politicians. Though they enjoyed consistent access to formal power and from 1912 to 1944 were never far from positions of national influence, that power was primarily institutional and bureaucratic. The State Department was an important source of their influence, especially because the Republican Henry Stimson and the Democrat Cordell Hull headed the department from 1929 to 1944, even though Wilsonian intellectual influence over the diplomatic corps was never very complete.[15] They were visible and prominent in both major parties but simply were not effective vote-getters. Woodrow Wilson himself was the most successful politician among them, and it is important to recall that even he won skimpy national victories.[16] More interested in the rigors of "statesmanship" than the needs of the modern citizen, they did not make appealing candidates. Electoral shortcomings might have been blessings in disguise. Because there never had existed a strictly "liberal" party in the United States, Wilsonians were not obliged to reshape their philosophy to suit new coalitions of voters, and so they did not go the way of the British Liberal party.

The Philosophy of Wilsonian Idealism

In the simplest terms, Wilsonian idealism was a fairly coherent set of assumptions about political life and human nature. Probably more than other twentieth-century liberals, Wilsonians drew from America's common-sense tradition and defined the common good as the result of enlightened self-interest tempered by human reason; given the freedom to pursue their interests, reasoning citizens would recognize that they had an essential stake in moderation. They had faith in reason, and therein lay their idealism.

[15] The professional diplomatic corps, as Robert Schulzinger has described it, developed an ideology of its own that overlapped with Wilsonian ideas about free trade, but rejected the belief that international harmony was the inevitable product of liberal reason. The professional diplomat's view of the world was more cynical and more given to the narrow pursuit of national interests, a difference which became glaring at the end of World War II. Robert Schulzinger, *The Making of the Diplomatic Mind: The Training, Outlook, and Style of United States Foreign Service Officers, 1908–1931* (Middletown, Conn., 1975), especially chap. 1. C. Roland Marchand makes a similar point in *The American Peace Movement and Social Reform,* 70–73.

[16] Wilson gained the presidency in 1912 when the Republicans split. His victory over Charles Evans Hughes in 1916 was narrow, especially for an incumbent. The Democrats did not even do well in the 1914 off-year congressional races, when they had just finished a session of important reform. Arthur Link, *Wilson: The New Freedom* (Princeton, 1956), 467–69.

But reason was under fire in the modern world, and they knew it. Wilson himself, resolute and strong-willed to the point of dogmatism, confessed to confusion at times and acknowledged that modernity had seeped even into the most cloistered places. He counseled the Princeton graduating class of 1905 that

> the modern world confuses very practiced thinkers, throws very experienced guides out of their way, not because it is so big, or even because it is so multiform and various ... Things new and old jostle one another in our day and live in no peace or concord, arrange no modus vivendi among them. The new do not seem to have sprung from the old. Their lineage and connection seem undermined and accidental. The tendencies which sway them are gathered nowhere into any one great drift or current, but swirl hither and thither in confused and lawless eddies, in giddy hazes which the age despairs of following. The age desires law but does not discover it, would be led but knows not whom to follow.

Wilson, and many other liberals, felt squeezed on all sides and shared the uneasiness that Matthew Arnold had expressed years earlier: they were caught, as they often stated, "between two worlds."[17] Wilson and likeminded liberals suspected that technological transformation and the emergence of corporate capitalism were responsible for modernity's flux but never could bring themselves to forthright criticism of either. If advanced capitalism undermined individualism it also generated unprecedented prosperity and brought the world together. Wilsonians, accordingly, were never more than ambivalent about technology's place in the world.

They were more inclined to blame other developments for modern confusion. Modern group politics, in their estimation, revived habits of political self-interest and produced fragmented and conflict-ridden polities. They accused labor and ethnic groups of factionalism and derided "class politics" and the "hyphenated-American." During World War I, they extended this perspective to the crisis in global politics and interpreted imperialism in general and German policy in particular as nothing

[17] Woodrow Wilson, "A Baccalaureate Address," 11 June 1905, in *The Papers of Woodrow Wilson*, Arthur Link et al., eds. (Princeton, 1967–), 16: 120. Hereafter cited as *PWW*. Note the popularity of Matthew Arnold's "Stanzas from the Grande Chartreuse" among Wilsonians: Raymond B. Fosdick, *The Old Savage in the New Civilization* (New York, 1929); William Smith Culbertson, "Wandering between Two Worlds," *Annals of the American Society of Social and Political Science* (hereafter cited as *Annals*) 174 (July 1932): 81–87; and Nicholas Murray Butler, *Between Two Worlds* (New York, 1934).

more than horrifying examples of political self-interest. They took this line of thinking beyond the war and condemned both the right and the left during the 1930s as self-interested factions bent on returning society to feudalism.

Because they blended right and left together, their perspective is difficult to place on a political spectrum, and it is helpful to understand their view of what constituted a progressive world. The good society was capitalist, individualistic, and yet unified; it promised individual fulfillment and world interdependence.

It was natural for them to expect the world to move toward unity, because such a view was ingrained in their temperament, more deeply than we can appreciate. Most of what this generation and this class of people saw told them that unification and "interdependence" were iron-clad rules of human order the march of which only reactionary perversity could stall. As Thomas Haskell has shown, the notions of biological and social interdependence dominated turn-of-the-century social sciences, and Wilsonians were both students and scholars in these disciplines.[18] Their study of history convinced them that the individual thrived best in a society unified not by state power but by "common habit" and public consensus. What they did not learn from contemporary academics they observed in the seemingly irreversible growth of the international economy. Both theory and practice confirmed humanity's march toward interdependence. They were amazed that anyone would question the fact of global interdependence or doubt that interdependence was good for one and all.

As challenges to interdependence continued after the Great War, Wilsonians seized internationalism as the best hope for sustaining liberal idealism. Internationalism, for one thing, provided the antidote to the worst aspects of technological society; the stronger world interdependence, the less likely people would be to use technology for destructive purposes. The real danger, as far as they could see, lay in a kind of political lag in which nations still mired in the archaic politics of fragmentation got hold of destructive weapons. Thus Raymond Fosdick, Princeton product, Wilson devotee, spokesman for the League of Nations Association after the war, and eventually head of the Rockefeller Foundation, warned in 1926 that the "old savage," the archaic, militaristic nationalist, was alive and well and thriving on the confusion of the masses. The old savage was everywhere, displaying "modes of thought"

---

[18] Haskell, *The Emergence of Social Science*, chap. 2.

that had not changed since Frederick the Great, stimulating the "irrational impulse" toward war, and exciting the "primitive and overpowering" pack instinct. In such an excited state, reality faded and politics became the art of provocation advanced in campaigns where "prejudice and passion take the place of intelligent analysis. For the detachment of the laboratory," Fosdick wrote, presaging Walter Lippmann's more elaborate attempt three years later to find reason's refuge in the laboratory, "we substitute the emotion of the torchlight parade."[19]

The "torchlight parade" was an allusion to mass politics and showed Fosdick's concern that modern confusion made it possible for modern-day autocrats to exploit popular passions. Was the fundamental problem technocracy itself? His appeal to the "detachment of the laboratory" shows his faith in science. But then he worried that the enlightened individual, capable of reason and moderation, was becoming a mere cog in the "great machine" of civilization. Perhaps it was impossible to combine large-scale industry with the "diversity, originality, and spontaneity which are the supreme contributions of the individual to society." On the other hand, "scientific politics" was more in harmony with the interdependent world. It was more modern. "No longer are nations self-contained or self-supporting," and humanity was reliant on science to reinforce the new "world of specialized and dependent parts knit together in a common unity." Scientific politics encouraged a "political internationalism that paralleled economic realities"; it gave rise to "synthetic thinking on a terrestrial scale" and to a "planetary consciousness."[20] Science, technology, reason, and the common good all led, in Fosdick's view, toward internationalism. No good liberal, he believed, no one who believed in both reason and progress, could possibly disagree.

It was a view of the world not without its genius even if it was ambivalent, and it held a powerful attraction for a politically moderate section of American elites largely because it provided the means by which to position themselves between the domestic left and right. They searched for a "positive" liberalism that protected the marketplace and created general security at the same time.[21] Wilsonians accepted the state as an

---

[19] Raymond B. Fosdick, *The Old Savage in the New Civilization* (New York, 1929), 27, 125, 147, 115.
[20] Ibid., 135, 201, 182, 177.
[21] They took pains to distinguish themselves from the social Darwinists of the Gilded Age. See especially Walter Lippmann, *The Good Society* (New York, 1937), and Raymond Buell, *Isolated America* (New York, 1940). Lippmann distanced himself from contempo-

organic result of a body politic bound by common assumptions and goals. They envisioned an adaptable state that permitted reform, restrained big business, and sustained individual liberty. If liberalism were to survive the onslaught of modernity, Wilsonians would have to effect, as Nicholas Murray Butler put it, a "restatement of liberal principles in terms of present-day economic conditions and problems and [develop] a new demonstration of their justice and their adequacy to solve problems. It will not be enough simply to repeat old formulas."[22]

Butler, in his simplistic dogmatism, is generally instructive. From World War I to the 1940s he argued that liberalism was under siege from both left and right, and in both cases the essential foe was political compulsion. Over the course of several centuries, liberals had buried monarchical repression only to see it exhumed by fascists, by communists, and, in more subtle and perhaps less obnoxious forms, by advocates of socialism. "The compulsion which liberty now faces," Butler contended in 1934, "is precisely the same compulsion today as it was in days gone by. It is compulsion through the forms of government, even of democratic government, by a class, whether large or small, which deems itself privileged to rule because either of its number or of its intellectual inferiority." Evidently determined to take on all enemies at once, Butler swung at everyone save those in the liberal center and implicitly lumped together fascists, communists, and populists, both those who advocated concentrated political power and those who hoped to dilute centralization.[23]

To Butler, as to centrist liberals on both sides of the Atlantic, modern political compulsion emerged as an answer to the not reasonable de-

rary conservatives as well. While he carefully acknowledged in 1937 that *The Good Society* showed some influence of Frederick Hayek and Ludwig von Mises, he nevertheless insisted that he could not accept the purely individualistic views of the emerging right. Lippmann to Lionel Robbins, 24 March 1937, in *Public Philosopher: Selected Letters of Walter Lippmann,* ed. John Morton Blum (New York, 1985), 357.

[22] Nicholas Murray Butler, "The World Needs Another Alexander Hamilton," address to the Summer Session Convocation, Columbia University, 7 August 1934, in *The Family of Nations* (New York, 1938), 57; "The Attack on Liberalism," address at the Parish Art Museum, Southhampton, Long Island, 2 September 1934, ibid., 93. Both Stefan Collini and Michael Freeden make clear how similar were the strategies of British liberals and Wilsonians. See Freeden's description of "centrist-liberals" and L. T. Hobhouse's belief that it was impossible to "ever go back to laissez-faire precisely as it was understood by Cobden and Bright. But I do think that economic and political liberty will play a revived and larger part in our political programmes, and that the real problem of the thinker to-day is to find for the term a new and fuller definition suited to the changed structure of our time" (*Liberalism Divided,* 12–14, 131).

[23] Butler, "Attack on Liberalism," 84–85.

mands by the masses for economic security.[24] But he dismissed the value of collective solutions to insecurity and depression—even "the milder form of compulsion which is Socialism"—because a relatively free market, in a broad historical sense, had generated more wealth and provided more general security than any other economic system. The marketplace, in other words, was a practical and proven means to a worthy end, but it was not an end in itself. He distinguished between liberty and laissez faire: the former provided freedom, broadly conceived not just as legal freedoms but as the freedom to realize individual security; the latter allowed certain individuals to stomp on others and close "the door of opportunity."[25]

If laissez faire provided no means of judging between the worthy and the unworthy, if the marketplace was too pernicious to remain uncontrolled, what force was left to order society and protect liberty? The immediate answer was the state, which alone had the "essential function . . . to protect each individual against exploitation by his fellows." But if the state limited individual freedom, what limited the state? The balance had to be found, Butler argued, in internationalism—the "highest task of liberalism today." Prudent measures to increase economic interdependence would do more than any domestic maneuver to provide security on a firm and comprehensive level. More to the point, internationalism simultaneously expanded the realm of individual liberty. Because the nation-state was best suited to protect individuals from exploitation, it thus "has been the ideal political unit . . . for some two thousand years. We have now come to the time, however, when, if liberty is to be preserved and extended, its upholders and defenders must be prepared to lead the way to the next stage of political organization." The next stage was a federated world where nations would check the transgressions of other nations. "If liberty is to survive," he concluded, "it can do so only in a world organized on the principles of liberty, but in terms of present-day needs, conditions, and opportunities. Only so can liberty find air to breathe."[26]

The tremendous attraction that internationalism held for moderate liberals thus becomes clear, appearing not only as a weapon against autocracy but as an antidote to radicalism, fully capable of accommodating, indeed welcoming, technological change and yet designed to protect the enlightened individual. Still it remained an incomplete answer to the

[24] See Freeden, *Liberalism Divided*, 49–55.
[25] Butler, "Attack on Liberalism," 94–95, 90–91.
[26] Ibid., 88–90.

liberal predicament. What could guarantee that nations would act as checks against other nations that wished to bully their own citizens, especially if the marketplace, which allegedly bound nations together, could not be expected to do so? Butler offered the answer that distinguishes Wilsonians from post-World War II liberals and that defines them as idealists: "The effective protection of liberty against compulsion must rest not on force, but on moral principle. . . . Under any other circumstances liberty is doomed."[27]

At bottom, Wilsonian idealism rested upon this adherence to moral principle and on a faith in universalism. Even in their twilight, as they prepared to defend civilization itself against Hitler, Wilsonians maintained the presumption that humanity could discover the grounds for a common life, that society still rested on certain common rules—"moral presuppositions," Raymond Buell called them—upon which modernity might gently be coaxed along.[28]

[27] Ibid., 85.
[28] Buell, *Isolated America*, 31–32.

2

Liberal Idealism
and Woodrow Wilson

In his important book on the professionalization of the American middle class, Barton Bledstein points out that the ministry as a "calling," a divinely inspired obligation, had become essentially a career, which one chose as an occupation, by the mid-1800s. The more secularized it became, the less attractive the ministry was to middle-class men who could realize more money and prestige in other professions. The increasingly technocratic society respected the scientist and the "university man"; theology, as an intellectual discipline with a metaphysical nature, was correspondingly diminished. Mainstream Protestant ministers tried to adapt to these conditions by turning God into a palpable, personal being, an all-loving and accommodating sovereign. They proposed a creed that did to theology what the professionalization of the "calling" did to the ministry: it undercut its social power, and thus its attraction to young minds, by making God a matter of personal choice.[1]

Woodrow Wilson was raised in the midst of these transformations, and we should be clear at the outset about their effects. Every biographical sketch of Wilson is obliged to note the extensive influence of his minister father, but that influence must be understood in the wider light of middle-class change—to do otherwise runs the risk of overestimating the religious influence on the younger Wilson. As John M. Mulder has suggested, Wilson's father, Joseph, pursued his ministerial career with te-

[1] Barton Bledstein, *The Culture of Professionalism: The Middle Class and the Transformation of Higher Education in America* (New York, 1976); Daniel Walker Howe, "The Decline of Calvinism: An Approach to Its Study," *Comparative Studies in Society and History* 14 (1972): 306–27.

nacity and suffered the chronic disappointments that were common in nineteenth-century life. Though he ultimately realized some prominence, he remained unfulfilled, left to live vicariously through his favorite son. However much the son admired him, the father was no great advertisement for the ministry. Joseph Wilson's theology, meanwhile, was a variation of liberalized Protestantism. He preferred God the "loving authority" to the forbidding sovereign of Calvinism. Dr. Wilson taught his son the moral life, but it was an increasingly modern sort of morality.[2]

The father's direct political influence is more obscure. We do not know which party Joseph was loyal to. It is reasonable to assume that, as a good southerner, he was a Democrat; that his son became a Democrat without any question might be taken as evidence of his father's affiliation. But it would not have been out of character for Joseph to have been a Whig, which in the antebellum South was the party of responsibility and moderation. Indeed we do know that Woodrow's paternal grandfather was a Whig.[3]

Regardless of party affiliation, Woodrow Wilson was very much attracted as a young man to the Whig political ideals of nineteenth-century common-good liberalism. His reputation always has emphasized his affection for English liberals, but as a Princeton student he paid much more attention to Daniel Webster and Henry Clay. Webster was, in his view, "the greatest statesman which this country has produced." The Whig leader "was so thoroughly acquainted with the laws of all other countries that he could have legislated for them with the same ease and ability which he exhibited in his masterly guidance . . . of his own country." The young Wilson not only admired the Whig abilities but their self-denial and devotion to the common good. The Whig statesman was no "partisan . . . who follows his own convictions only so far as they coincide with the convictions of his party and with his own interests."[4]

Taken together, the liberal religious creed and the Whig political creed were loose enough to be transmuted into modern forms. Woodrow Wilson played true to his social type, then, when he set out for the secular

[2] John M. Mulder, *Woodrow Wilson: The Years of Preparation* (Princeton, 1978), 19, 26–28, 31–32.
[3] Francis Weisenberger, "The Middle-Western Antecedents of Woodrow Wilson," *Mississippi Valley Historical Review* 23 (1936–1937): 375–84.
[4] "The Ideal Statesman," 30 January 1877, *PWW* 1: 242–44. My understanding of Whig liberalism is indebted to the following: Daniel Walker Howe, *The Political Culture of the American Whigs* (Chicago, 1979); Thomas Brown, *Politics and Statesmanship: Essays on the American Whig Party* (New York, 1985); and Arthur Cole, *The Whig Party in the South* (Washington, D.C., 1914).

professions, going first into law and then academia. He entered Johns Hopkins in 1883, just when the university was pioneering in the development of professional training and the organization of scholarship.[5] The aspiring scholars at Hopkins were introduced to continental political thought, which emphasized administrative management instead of popular rule, and to the reformist economics of the German Historical School, for which Richard Ely had become the national spokesperson. More generally, they were indoctrinated into patterns of thought that, whether drawn from German historicism or contemporary biology, stressed, as David D. Van Tassel has written, "unity and continuity in the evolution of social institutions." The new professional scholars were preoccupied with continuity over change, and, perhaps above all, they learned of the interdependence of institutions and of historical developments.[6] Wilson took much from this environment, and he labored to assimilate these most contemporary ideas. In a revealing journal entry written in the late 1880s, Wilson summed up his approach to his own role in the middle-class transformation: "It was in keeping with my whole mental make-up to interpret the age" because to do so was to "interpret myself."[7]

Democracy as Unity, History as Progress

It is no surprise that someone determined to "interpret" his age would embrace the focus on institutional studies that permeated the scholarly professions. Nor was it surprising that, like his contemporaries, he aimed his attention at informing contemporary politics. In his two most important works, *Congressional Government* and *The State,* he insisted that the political problems of the Gilded Age required improved "lines of authority" and greater "integration" in government. In *Congressional Government,* for example, he argued that the Civil War had upset the balance between state and federal authorities, which in turn demanded that some tinkering with bureaucratic structure be done in the name of

[5] David D. Van Tassel, "From Learned Society to Professional Organization: The American Historical Association, 1884–1900," *American Historical Review* (October 1984): 929–56; Haskell, *Emergence of Social Science,* 169–71.

[6] Joseph Dorfman, "The Role of the German Historical School in American Economic Thought," *American Economic Review* 45 (May 1955): 17–28; Van Tassel, "From Learned Society to Professional Organization," 943–47.

[7] Wilson's Confidential Journal, 28 December 1889, *PWW* 6: 463; and also the editors' note to "The Modern Democratic State," *PWW* 5: 54–57.

governmental efficiency. The "unexciting but none the less capitally important business of every-day peaceful development and judicious administration" had become the essential task of leaders, he believed, who would depend necessarily on social scientists to explain where inefficiency lay.[8]

On the one hand, Wilson set out on the assumption that his work was on the vanguard, such as it was, of the new social sciences, yet nothing in Wilson's administrative studies or German historicism undermined or threatened an inbred, instinctive faith in the commonsense liberalism that prevailed within the middle class of an earlier day: a belief that the good society balanced the state against the individual, relied on the disinterested statesman for leadership, and upheld the common good over special interests. If anything, he synthesized traditional idealism and contemporary theory. The result was a view of liberalism as a continual process of growing individual rationalism and therefore as an irresistible force for progress.

His most important writings of the 1880s, taken as a single body of work, amply show his mediation between traditional ideals and contemporary method. In 1885, he wrote that liberalism had been brought to maturity in the nineteenth century when democratic rights blended with an "organic state." In search of common rules of political structure and development, he diminished the importance of constitutional rule and the social contract. "Would the nation not exist," he asked, "if the Const[itution] and the rest were suddenly swept away?"[9] Whereas constitutions were simply made, organic government was conceived out of the "innate principle of union" between the individual and the state. Speaking at once like a proper Whig and an adherent of contemporary European political science, he called individuals to subordinate their whims to community action, demanded "habitual soberness and temperateness," and insisted "upon a habit of orderly agreement and peaceful authority on the part of the people." Wilson did not take the individualistic view that government rested on the social contract. He believed that organic democracy depended on cooperative action. Because the individual and the state were united, the activities of the organic state were limited: government exceeded its authority when it went beyond that which would secure the common good. To see the state as a product of temporary and

[8] "Congressional Government," ca. 24 January 1885, *PWW* 4: 6–8, 16, 114–16, 36–37.
[9] "The Modern Democratic State," *PWW* 5: 54–58, 61.

contrived agreement, meanwhile, was to invite the abuse of power. "Those who regard the state as an optional, conventional union," he wrote, opened "the doors wide to socialism."[10]

The social contract did have a place here. It was a sign that democracy had matured.[11] Offering a decidedly optimistic interpretation of history, Wilson argued that the momentum of liberal politics came from the increase in popular education and widened suffrage. Where previous societies were built on class privilege, Wilson claimed, the new political order would enjoy "autonomous life in every part yet a common life and purpose." The modern state was "not a head organism with huge dependent parts, but itself a single giant organism with a stalwart, common strength and an abounding life in individual limbs."[12] The role of leaders was to guide the masses into this organic union. "No democracy can live without a learned class capable of thinking on the problems of government and in a position to think in the light of the most catholic learning." The statesman—who in this description bore a conspicuous resemblance to the academician—held the organic democracy together.[13]

It was a complacent view. The newly empowered working class, the previously disenfranchised, the recently educated, all would rush to the common good behind the leadership of statesmen. No wonder Wilson convinced himself that democracy was historically inevitable, a view he took in his most famous book, *The State*. Aside from Wilson's preoccupation with administration, *The State* was a verbose but simple argument about Western political development. Political fragmentation based on class or monarchical privilege characterized both ancient democracies and feudal societies; democratic popular rule destroyed aristocratic privilege and therefore created political unity and the organic state. "The disintegration of feudalism and the specialization of absolute monarchy," Wilson wrote, were supplanted by societies that bound the citizen and the state into "a compact, living whole" in which "common habit" and general will dictated state action.[14]

In this way, then, Wilson struck the balance between old and new influences. But his administrative studies were unsatisfying. He was seek-

[10] "The Modern Democratic State," 67–69, 74–76; "Memorandum," 61.

[11] The belief that the state was to facilitate personal interests "little elevated above merchandising," Wilson argued, was itself the product of a burgeoning democracy. The prevailing view of the state as a mere convenience brought government into the daily concerns of the citizen and bred the impression that government was common terrain upon which all dealt equally. "Modern Democratic State," 79.

[12] Ibid., 71–72, 81–82.

[13] Ibid., 86.

[14] "The State," ca. 3 June 1889, *PWW* 6:256–57, 262–66, 293–94.

ing, after all, a form of government that helped sustain the individual citizen in a time of economic and political centralization, and *The State* overemphasized the technical virtues of administration. This bureaucratized version of the common good seemed less an expression of a public philosophy or the product of natural law than the result of the give and take of everyday administration. He sensed himself that *The State* was top-heavy, and it bored him even before he finished it. "What a job it has been," he wrote his wife. "I am thoroughly tired and disgusted with it. I hope nothing with reference to it now except that it may some day be off my mind."[15]

After completing *The State* in 1889, Wilson returned to Princeton, only to find his salary inadequate and to suffer his first stroke in 1895. Fate, it seemed, had limited him to the obscurity of academia. Unwilling to accept fate's limitations, he tried his hand in various fields: popular history, contemporary commentary, and even literary criticism.

Wilson's popular writings contrast curiously with his administrative studies. Neither institutions nor bureaucracy play much of a role in them. The optimistic, even banal patriotism of his writings exposed a conservative, Cleveland Democrat committed to free trade and the gold standard. As he grew more clearly conservative, he shed the German influences of Hopkins and blended traditional liberalism with still newer ideas, especially the novel ideas about the frontier that Frederick Jackson Turner, once Wilson's student, was popularizing.

His most important book of the period was a general American history, aptly entitled *Division and Reunion* (1894). The most illuminating part of the work is Wilson's treatment of the sectional crisis. One might expect a man whose childhood passed in the South and whose earliest memories equated Lincoln with war to be impressed with human conflict, but he drew the opposite conclusion. The national spirit and economic development overcame, as the Constitution did not, sectional principles, which, he wrote, led to failure "at all points" and to "discord and wasted resources." Wilson honored the man whose election meant war: Lincoln was a hero who at once upheld the Constitution, who encouraged economic growth through prosecuting the war, and who was the symbol of maturing democracy. "He was altogether like the frontiersman with whom he lived," Wilson wrote, "in his coarse, neglected dress, his broad and boisterous humor, his careless, unstrenuous way of life." Lincoln rose from humble origins until he was "vastly above" his peers in "intellectual and moral stature." In an article published shortly after

[15] WW to Ellen Axson Wilson, 9 March 1889, PWW 6: 139.

Division and Reunion, Wilson was even more clear about Lincoln's importance: "Lincoln . . . was the supreme American. . . . He never ceased to be a common man: that was the source of his strength. But he was a common man with genius, a genius for things American, for insight into the common thought, for mastering of the fundamental things of affairs. . . . The whole country is summed up in him: the rude Western strength, tempered with shrewdness and a broad and humane wit; the Eastern conservatism, regardful of law and devoted to fixed standards of duty."[16]

Whatever else he accomplished in these writings—wider recognition, a larger income—Wilson escaped the preoccupation with bureaucracy and found a livelier answer to the problems of democracy in the pioneer spirit. He followed Frederick Jackson Turner closely here; indeed he had helped Turner formulate the frontier thesis.[17] The crude yet democratic frontier spirit, Wilson decided, sustained democracy in the midst of economic and political centralization. The frontiersman matured into the statesman; yeoman agriculture blossomed into industrial power; and the confederated states merged into a nation. Whereas institutions provided the element of continuity in *The State,* liberalism and democracy provided continuity in *Division and Reunion.*[18]

It is important not to misunderstand why Wilson embraced the frontier thesis. Many of his contemporaries, including Josiah Strong and, arguably, Turner himself, believed that when the frontier was exhausted America would fracture along class lines, and the simplest alternative to class conflict was imperialism. It has become a stock assumption that the United States was led into its imperial career during the late 1890s by men who embraced the frontier thesis. Certainly, like Turner, Wilson believed that the frontier spirit was a great source of democratic strength. Unlike Turner, he believed that the frontier's closing removed a source of sectionalism and redirected the pioneer spirit toward national unity.

[16] Mulder, *Woodrow Wilson,* 29–30; "A Calender of Great Americans," ca. 15 September 1893, *PWW* 8: 378. Compare the description of Lincoln as a common man with "a singular genius for getting and using knowledge" with Wilson's very similar self-assessment: "The phrase that Bagehot uses to describe the successful constitutional statesman I might appropriate to describe myself: 'a man with common opinions but uncommon ability.' " Woodrow Wilson, *Division and Reunion* (New York, 1894), 127–29, 44–45, 216; "From Wilson's Confidential Journal," *PWW* 6: 462.

[17] See "The Significance of American History," 9 September 1901, *PWW* 12: 179–84; and Wendell Stephensen, "The Influence of Woodrow Wilson on Frederick Jackson Turner," *Agricultural History* 19 (October 1945): 249–53.

[18] Wilson, *Division and Reunion,* 4.

When Wilson spoke of the twentieth century as a "new era," he expected that the pioneer spirit would inspire internal development rather than expansion.

Wilson's nationalism—and his later internationalism—looked not to expansion but to consolidation. "The old sort of growth is at an end, the growth by mere expansion," he wrote in an 1897 essay, revealing because it was contemporaneous with the Spanish American War. "We have now to look more closely to internal conditions, and study the means by which a various people is to be bound together in a single interest." Much could be left to its own course, for "many differences will pass away" as capital moves to new places, new industry springs to life in the West, and "all the scattered parts of the nation are drawn into a real community of interest. . . . But not everything can be left to drift and slow accommodation. . . . It required statesmanship of no mean sort to bring us our present growth. . . . It will require leadership of a much higher order to teach us the triumphs of cooperation, self-possession and calm choices of maturity."[19] Wilson's view of the frontier and his views on overseas expansion were, then, of a different order than those of contemporary expansionists. He believed that the United States, with the end of continental expansion, was prepared to join the world of mature nations, and it was more important that the nation be united within than spread without.

None of these arguments kept Wilson from supporting American imperialism in the Philippines, though he did so only after the fact. He showed no interest in the Cuban issue, much less in the taking of the Philippines, until at least after the sinking of the *Maine*. In this he was typical of middle-class Americans. He continued to believe well after 1898 that expansion had been "thrust" upon the United States by "surprising circumstances." Wilson did not advocate expansion but insisted that America assume its "responsibilities" once the Philippines had been conquered. If anything, his position was more like that which the Whigs took on the Mexican-American War a half-century earlier—that expansion threatened a dangerous diffusion of national energy—than that which contemporary expansionists took.[20]

[19] "The Making of the Nation," ca. 15 April 1897, *PWW* 10: 230.

[20] "Democracy and Efficiency," 1 October 1900, *PWW* 12: 18–19. Wilson decried jingoism and defended the right of anti-imperialists to criticize expansionism in "An Address on Patriotism to the Washington Association of New Jersey," 23 February 1903, *PWW* 14: 365–78. On the Whigs see Howe, *The Political Culture of the American Whigs*, 93–95; John H. Schroeder, *Mr. Polk's War: American Opposition and Dissent, 1846–1848* (Madison, 1973).

No doubt for the Filipinos, as for the Nicaraguans and Haitians who later endured Wilson's effort to live up to such "responsibilities," there was little difference between paternalism and expansionism. But what is at issue is how Wilson's liberalism shaped his view of the world, and here the distinction helps illuminate Wilson's later foreign policy. Wilson's support for imperialism led him, for the first time, to argue that the processes of political maturation, of growing complexity and unity, were at work internationally. In part, he called on the United States to fulfill its duties as civilizer in order to sustain the momentum of democratic development against the "peril of reactionary revolution" that could accompany the "contest of nations." He worried that America's indifference to imperial competition showed that the nation remained "provincial" and therefore potentially undemocratic. In contemplating the new imperial role of the United States, Wilson connected international duty to domestic unity and, conversely, isolation to domestic conflict. Americans had to understand that "the whole world had already become a single vicinage. . . . No nation could live any longer to itself." The failure to appreciate the new circumstances would perpetuate the shabby political leadership evident in America's own misgoverned cities, deepen the nation's political divisions, and elevate self-interested leaders. If nothing else, governing the Philippines wisely would help renew democratic unity at home.[21]

Wilson in Progressive America

Beginning in 1902, Princeton became Wilson's dutiful concern. His presidential tenure there need not detain us, though the job marked the beginning of his public career. Wilson gained a reputation as an educational progressive by instituting educational reforms and fighting with alumni and university factions over the undergraduate eating clubs and the character of a new graduate school.

Once he emerged as a political figure, Wilson again updated his belief that democracy depended on a unified political life. His relationship to Progressivism was not unlike his relationship to the European academic thought he encountered at Johns Hopkins. He took up the prevalent concerns over concentrated power and industrial strife, indulged in the catch-all criticisms of the day, and yet remained a traditionalist.

[21] "Democracy and Efficiency," 10–19.

His views on labor are a case in point. Class conflict was not the product of an unequal division of wealth or a battle over the control of the workplace but an example of clashing special interests. On the one hand, Wilson blamed unions, rather than mechanization, for the "standardization" of labor and argued that unions "drag the highest man to the level of the lowest" on the job. Such views were not well designed to cultivate the political support of organized labor. Hoping to ward off labor critics, he characteristically explained that he would not support any special interest. "I have criticized some of the things organized labor has occasionally done," he wrote a New Jersey labor leader, "because I thought them harmful to the laborers themselves and harmful to the country. I know of no other standard by which to judge these things than the interest of the whole community." During the 1912 New Freedom campaign he admitted that labor "should have the right to do anything that is legitimate," by which he meant anything not "contrary to the interests of the community." Here was the posture he assumed when he opposed labor's move to include in the Clayton Anti-Trust Act a provision that would protect unions from prosecution for acting in restraint of trade during strikes or boycotts.[22]

Essentially a conservative position, Wilson's view of labor was less interesting than his view of the corporation. Wilson saw the corporation, or at least "the trust," as a symbol of faction and an important force behind political disintegration, as more a political danger than an economic one. The legal mystification of corporate power made him suspicious, for when corporations were defined as individuals they lost any incentive for accountability to the community. He often argued that an adaptation of law could cure corporate malfeasance by finding "the man behind the trust," by insisting, in short, on individual responsibility. He repeatedly said that "there was no such thing as corporate morality" and linked the political divisiveness of the corporation to its feudal nature. Wilson pursued this line of argument persistently, arguing that the word "corporate" referred to virtually independent bodies in the same society. "A modern corporation is an economic society, a little economic state"

[22] A News Report of an Address on Trusts and Labor Unions at New Rochelle, New York, 27 February 1905, *PWW* 16: 15; and Baccalaureate Address, 13 June 1909, *PWW* 19: 245; A Labor Day Address in Buffalo, New York, 2 September 1912, *PWW* 25: 70–71; A Campaign Speech in Newton, New Jersey, 22 October 1910, *PWW* 21: 401; A News Report of a Campaign Address in Elizabeth Port, New Jersey, 29 October 1910, *PWW* 21: 469; An Address at a Workingmen's Dinner in New York, 4 September 1912, *PWW* 25: 98; An Address to Workingmen in Fall River, Massachusetts, 26 September 1912, *PWW* 25: 263–64; Link, *The New Freedom*, 427–33.

that ought to be prevented from "building up bodies economic outside [the] body politic."[23] He was nearly advocating a return to a common-law definition of the corporation as a public trust, but the implications of such a view were too radical. Wilson trapped himself between a defense of community rights and an unyielding support of economic progress. He weakened his stand against "corporate morality" when he insisted that the trust issue was not economic and trivialized the power of the corporation by making it but one special interest among many. Thus he arrived at the truly facile distinction between big business "with a big B and big business . . . with a small b," where the latter "is an unwhole-some inflation created by privileges and exemptions which it ought not to enjoy," while the former grew of its own energies.[24] This lame view reified corporations every bit as much as had the legal slight-of-hand that encouraged their growth. To insist that there is "good" big business and "bad" big business is to imply, after all, that there is a "corporate morality."

Because he took this view, Wilson gives us reason to see the 1912 New Freedom campaign as political posturing, linked as the campaign slogan was to the anti-trust position of Louis D. Brandeis, the leader of "small-is-good" liberalism well through the 1930s.[25] Wilson listened to Brandeis because he needed to court Progressive Democrats, whose support he did not secure during the convention. He also needed a catch-all slogan to distinguish himself from Theodore Roosevelt, who had broken from the Republican Party to run as an advocate of rationalization and a managerial state.

The New Freedom slogan allowed Wilson to denounce Roosevelt's New Nationalism as a dangerous combination of corporate and governmental interests in a regulatory state. He was no free trader, he assured

[23] An Address in Chattanooga, Tennessee to the American Bar Association, 31 August 1910, *PWW* 21: 72–73. Wilson's critique of the corporation can be found in the following: The Authors and Signers of the Declaration of Independence, 4 July 1907, *PWW* 17: 253–58; A Credo, 6 August 1907, *PWW* 17: 336–37; An Address to the Commercial Club of Chicago, 14 March 1908, *PWW* 18: 39–51; Baccalaureate Address, 7 June 1908, *PWW* 18: 325–30; The Man behind the Trust, 3 August 1909, *PWW* 19: 325–27; A Speech in St. Peter's Hall in Jersey City, New Jersey, 28 September 1910, *PWW* 21: 186–87; and A Campaign Speech in Newark, New Jersey, 30 September 1910, *PWW* 21: 208–9.
[24] An Address to Workingmen in Fall River, Mass., 266; A Speech Accepting the Democratic Nomination at Sea Girt, N.J., 7 August 1912, *PWW* 25: 10–11. See also A Campaign Address in Sioux City, Iowa, 17 September 1912, *PWW* 25: 152, and A Campaign Address in Madison Square Garden, 31 October 1912, *PWW* 25: 497.
[25] Arthur Link, *The Road to the White House* (Princeton, 1947), 488–93.

audiences; he was interested in the "relative freedom of trade" and in "laws that will give the little man a start."[26] America needed "regulated competition," which, he insisted, was the only alternative to Roosevelt's "regulated monopoly," on the one hand, and Republican laissez faire on the other. Wilson often defined the "unregulated competition" that created monopoly but never defined "regulated competition" with any rigor. He claimed that "regulated competition" was necessary because "we shall never return to the old order of individual competition." That was precisely the problem. He was uncommitted to Brandeisian liberalism but was unwilling to accede to any plans, such as the one Roosevelt advanced, for accepting into political life the collective forces of modernity, best seen in the corporation and the union.[27] Wilson's solutions to the great problem of concentrated power amounted to nothing more than tame reforms that lowered the tariff, brought some coherence to the banking system through the Federal Reserve Board, and clarified antitrust law.

Its flimsy nature notwithstanding, the New Freedom introduced one important supposition. During the campaign, Wilson intimated that the "little man" could find a place in the modern world so long as big business were free to expand through international trade. In voicing his opposition to tariffs, for instance, Wilson implied that international trade and individual liberty were related, much as were imperialism and democracy. He was not opposed to economic growth, he argued, but growth could lead to one of two conditions. If undertaken in a "provincial" spirit, it first would depend on special favors such as the tariff, later would lead to monopoly, and finally would necessitate regulation. If growth were allowed to take place freely it would destroy provincialism and make Americans international traders. This alternative condition, Wilson argued, "will make a very different country of the United States"; indeed it would do away with the special favors of the tariff and preserve individual liberty at the same time.[28]

[26] An Address at a Workingmen's Dinner in New York; A Campaign Address in Detroit, 19 September 1912, *PWW* 25: 192.
[27] See An Address at a Workingmen's Dinner, 103; A Campaign Address in Detroit, 19 September 1912, *PWW* 25: 192; A Labor Day Address in Buffalo, New York, 74–75; An Address to the New York Press Club, 9 September 1912, 25: 122; A Speech Accepting the Democratic Nomination at Sea Girt, New Jersey, 11.
[28] Address at a Workingmen's Dinner in New York, 104–6. Also An Address on the Tariff in Syracuse, New York, 12 September 1912, *PWW* 25: 137–43; An After-Breakfast Talk to the Commercial Club of Minneapolis, 18 September 1912, 25: 167–68; and An Address to Workingmen in Fall River, Mass., 268.

Wilson never drew this line of reasoning very aggressively in the early years of his presidency. Still, he pushed international trade less as a means for extending American national interests than for unclogging concentrated economic and political power at home. As we shall see, this proposition became essential to Wilsonians after World War I. For his part, Wilson soon conceded that mild reformism failed to restore political civility or respectable statesmanship. Not more than two months after having completed his first-term reforms, he mused that "the longer I occupy the office that I now occupy the more I regret any lines of separation; the more I deplore any feeling that one set of men has one set of interests and another set of men another set." He continued: "What has got to pervade us like a great motive power is that we cannot, and must not, separate out interests from one another, but must pool our interests."[29] The New Freedom, it seemed, had not led to political reunion. Tariff reform, which promised to rid public life of special interests, never had a chance to prove itself before the war in Europe disrupted the international markets. "Regulated competition," along with the reconciliation of individualism and the corporate economy that it was meant to effect, was buried under bitter coal strikes, revolution in Mexico, and the first pains of a widening European war.

The Idealist Critique of Imperialism

Wilson's political ideals generated positions that were conservative in domestic politics but that when taken to the international arena accommodated revolution.[30] There was very little in his foreign policy that was inconsistent with the liberal idealism to which he was committed. The list of enemies changed and the problems broadened: instead of political partisans or self-interested corporate leaders, Wilson faced down imperialists. Where he worried over political factionalization and sectional

---

[29] An Address to the United States Chamber of Commerce, 3 February 1915, *PWW* 32: 179.

[30] This paradox, one way or another, is at the heart of the best writing on Wilsonian diplomacy: N. Gordon Levin, *Woodrow Wilson and World Politics: America's Response to War and Revolution* (Princeton, 1968); Arno Mayer, *The Political Origins of the New Diplomacy, 1917–1918* (New Haven, 1959), and *The Politics and Diplomacy of Peacemaking: Containment and Counterrevolution at Versailles, 1918–1919* (New York, 1967); Lloyd Gardner, *Safe for Democracy: The Anglo-American Response to Revolution, 1913–1923* (New York, 1984); Lloyd Ambrosius, *Woodrow Wilson and the American Diplomatic Tradition* (Cambridge, 1986).

strife at home, in foreign policy he confronted a shattered balance of power. He denounced nations that defied his vision of the liberal future as reactionary; his eye, he believed, was on the progressive future.

He did not back away from pursuing what he believed was the national interest—indeed he was a good deal more flexible than he is usually given credit for. He opposed European imperialism and engaged in imperialism himself with no evident sense of hypocrisy. To Wilson, we might say, there was Imperialism and imperialism. In the years before American intervention in World War I, Wilson's foreign policy was caught up in issues that, in one form or another, were related to the imperialist competition among the western powers, at least as that competition infringed on traditional American interests in the Far East and Latin America. European imperialism, he believed, extended the self-interested qualities of Europe's feudal past to international affairs; imperialism denied democratic unity because it was the product of narrow national interests carried on with no regard for subject peoples, much less for the international common good. The Europeans were doing in international affairs what corporations were doing at home: preventing unity by building up "little economic states." At the same time, this criticism of imperialism presumed that an international common good existed.

Though this connection of corporate power and imperialism grew out of Wilson's idealist craving for unity between state and citizen, it shared much with the contemporary liberal and left-wing critiques of imperialism. However bitterly they may have disagreed about particulars, many of the most prominent commentators on the phenomenon shared the view that corporate capitalism had produced late nineteenth-century imperialism. Wilson's views were not far, for example, from J. A. Hobson's path-breaking argument that modern imperialism was thrust upon western nations by a group of "social parasites": diplomats, importers, arms makers, religious leaders, bigots, and, above all, "a little group of financial kings."[31]

In Wilson's hands, the idealist critique of imperialism encouraged policies that consistently opposed European intrusions in Latin America and

---

[31] The idealist critique of imperialism might even be considered paradigmatic of Western left-liberalism. See Hobson's *Imperialism: A Study* (New York, 1902), 63–64, 132, and the following American variations: Frederic C. Howe, *Why War?* (New York, 1916; Seattle, 1970); *Privilege and Democracy in America* (New York, 1910); *The Only Possible Peace* (New York, 1918); and Thorstein Veblen, *An Inquiry into the Nature of the Peace and the Terms of Its Perpetuation* (New York, 1917).

the Far East and that endorsed democratic revolution. In Wilson's first international crisis, the Mexican Revolution, he opposed the counterrevolutionary government of Victoriano Huerta because it lacked public support and depended on the help of foreign governments; the American intervention at Veracruz in 1914 was designed to pressure Huerta's abdication. Wilson stood his ground against the European governments, especially the Germans and British, who were spurred on by narrow national interests to support Huerta in the face of Mexican popular aspirations. Wilson was not a benign defender of the revolution: his own patience was insufficient for him to await a resolution to the Mexican crisis; he resorted to ample bluster and another, even more pointless intervention in 1916. In his Mexican policy, he translated his belief in insurgent democracy into a hesitant sympathy for contemporary revolution, but only in so far as it seemed that the revolution was moving toward political harmony. He could accept revolutions as necessities but expected them to issue in liberal political development.[32]

Wilson applied the idealist interpretation of imperialism as well against the encroachment of Western economic power in China and the Caribbean. In 1913, the administration refused to lend its support to a group of American bankers who sought approval to participate with European banks in a large loan to the Chinese government. The banking consortium, the administration argued, was insisting on trade and political privileges as security for the loan, and the whole business therefore smacked of special-interest favoritism.[33] In 1914, meanwhile, the German government insisted on the right to participate with the United States in Haitian customs collections in order to protect German investment there. The administration ignored the open door and invoked the Monroe Doctrine on the grounds that the doctrine applied not just to military intervention in the region but to any "foreign influence or interest proceeding from outside the American hemisphere." Financial interests, merchants, bankers, and others, were insinuating narrow interests into diplomacy and thereby "imperiling the political independence, or, at least, the complete political autonomy of the American states." American policy, in contrast, was based, as Secretary of State

---

[32] See Link, *The New Freedom*, chaps. 10–12; Friedrich Katz, *The Secret War in Mexico: Europe, the United States, and the Mexican Revolution* (Chicago, 1981); and Gardner, *Safe for Democracy*, chaps. 2–3.

[33] Daniels Diary, 13 March 1913, *PWW* 27: 174–75; A Statement on the Pending China Loan, 18 March 1913, 27: 192–94.

William Jennings Bryan insisted, on disinterestedness and the disavowal of "exclusive privilege."[34]

Undoubtedly the administration pursued a course that it considered best suited to national interests, and just as clearly Wilson had no objection to the expansion of American commerce. Particularly in Haiti one must see the shallowness of the administration's professed disinterestedness, where the argument used against the Germans was employed to rationalize the long-term intervention that the administration was even then moving toward. The incompetence of Haitian politicians and customs authorities, the administration believed, made that nation an inviting target for unscrupulous European investors and imperialistic European nations. Democratic progress, accordingly, depended on American intervention.[35]

The contradictions in Wilson's foreign policy grew out of the arrogance of liberal idealism as a whole. So long as Wilson took for granted his own disinterestedness, just so long then he assumed that American interventions would clear out the obstructions to progress. In the broadest sense, Wilson fell to the erroneous assumption that interdependence and unity were the same as democracy.

Wilson in the Great War

Well into the period of neutrality, from 1914 to the war declaration of April 1917, Wilson, like so many other liberals, interpreted the Great War as a clash of imperial interests brought on by holdovers from Europe's feudal past. He explained in 1916 that the war was "a competition of national standards, of national traditions, and of national politics." In his well-known condemnations of balance-of-power diplomacy, he maintained that alliance was constructed against alliance only as a means for pursuing "selfish aggression." Peace without victory in Wilson's view would result, "not in a balance of power, but in a community of power; not organized rivalries, but an organized common peace."[36]

---

[34] William Jennings Bryan to Count Von Bernstorff, 16 September 1914, *PWW* 31: 34–36.

[35] Hans Schmidt, *The United States Occupation of Haiti, 1915–1934* (New Brunswick, 1971).

[36] Address to the League of Enforce Peace, 27 May 1916, *PWW* 37: 115; Address to the Senate, 22 January 1917, *PWW* 40: 535–36. See also WW to House, with enclosure, 23 August 1917, *PWW* 44: 34–35.

The neutrality policy aptly symbolized the idealist's place in the world catastrophe, and given Wilson's perspective, the sincerity of neutrality should not be questioned. In the early years of the conflict, Wilson did believe that both sides were guilty of self-interested aggression. Obviously the German U-boat campaign rankled him, and the invasion of neutral Belgium was contemptible. The British naval blockade committed the relatively minor sin of interrupting American trade. As Arthur Link points out in what remains the fairest interpretation of wartime policy, Wilson never would have entered the war over the trade issue, but the German assaults on civilians forced him to consider the possibility.[37] Wilson knew that there was no clear moral imperative at issue. Intervention in April 1917 came, as Link argues, because Wilson had concluded, probably sometime in early 1916, that American interests were best protected through an American-mediated peace. When a year of attempted mediation—during which Wilson presented the United States as the one disinterested nation—produced only recalcitrance from all sides and, when the Germans resumed submarine warfare in early 1917, Wilson concluded that he could influence the future only by intervention. It took a series of events, culminating in the March Revolution in Russia, to convince him that entering the war against the Central Powers would advance the cause of democracy, and even then he brought the United States in as a "disinterested" party, a sort of belligerent neutral, a condition that he hoped to emphasize in America's status as an "associated power."

After American entry, Wilson shifted blame from imperialism in general to Germany specifically. He had to argue that the Prussians were the most stubborn, the most violent of all reactionaries. He called for Americans to take up arms against the "autocratic governments backed by organized force," to fight the "military masters" of Germany whose interest was in nothing but "an immense expansion of German power, an immense enlargement of German industrial and commercial opportunities." It was consistent of Wilson to separate out the German "people" from the military lords, as he did in the War Address, for such a view was rooted in his belief that a feudal political system thrived on the separation of the state and the body politic.[38] Germany was feudalism mod-

---

[37] Arthur Link, *Woodrow Wilson: Revolution, War, and Peace* (Arlington Heights, Ill., 1979), 69–71.

[38] An Address to a Joint Session of Congress, 2 April 1917, *PWW* 41: 519–27; see especially 523.

ernized, its aggressive foreign policy a closely related blend of the mutually expansionistic interests of German industry and the German state. Recalling his opposition to the New Nationalism, he came to think of Germany as a frightening example of what could happen when the state linked its interests to those of big business. The dual motives of economic expansion and political control had led Germany to brutal war. "There is no important industry in Germany upon which the government has not laid its hands to direct it and, when necessary, control it," he explained in late 1917. That relationship had included subsidies to businesses, special favors that reminded Wilson of the tariff and "were the same sorts of competition that we have tried to prevent by law within our own borders."[39]

Wilson's answers to the dramatic conflict, institutionalized in his wartime diplomacy, were as characteristic as his analysis of the war. Just as, in his historical interpretations, the bloody and violent American Civil War resulted in a coherent, democratic nation, so he expected World War I to end in a united, democratic world. The organic society was given grandiose extrapolation: the intimacy between state and citizen became global in the League of Nations and the self-determined state. Wilson insisted, again and again from 1916, that the world stood on the edge of a "new age," as he described it in a campaign letter to Democratic National Chairman Vance McCormick. It has "become at once too big a world and too little a world to submit destinies to the hostile rivalries and ambitions now of this and again of that member of the great family of men. . . . An inevitable partnership of interests has been thrust upon the nations. They are neighbors and must accommodate their interests to one another."[40]

For this accommodation, a postwar league of nations was necessary. Once convinced that the war was the culmination of a global democratic revolution, Wilson advocated the league as the international analogue to the organic state. As he explained it to Edward House, his confidante

[39] Note to the Provisional Government of Russia, 22 May 1917, *PWW* 42: 365–67; Flag Day Address, 14 June 1917, 42: 502; WW to Pope Benedictus XV, enclosure WW to Walter Hines Page, 27 August 1917, *PWW* 44: 57–59; and An Address in Buffalo to the American Federation of Labor, 12 November 1917, *PWW* 45: 13.

[40] The "new age" of interdependence was a recurring theme in Wilson's 1916 campaign, far more important, it is clear, than the slogan, "he kept us out of war." See the following: A Speech in Long Branch, N.J., Accepting the Presidential Nomination, 2 September 1916, *PWW* 38: 136; Address to the Commercial Club of Omaha, 5 October 1916, 38: 337; Address in Omaha, 5 October 1916, 38: 348; and the Final Campaign Address, 4 November 1916, 38: 613. Wilson's letter to McCormick, which was distributed nationwide, can be found in Wilson Day Address, 17 October 1916, 38: 462–63.

and advisor, the league could not be prefabricated: "The administrative constitution of the League must *grow* and not be made." The underlying purposes of political independence and territorial integrity must be insisted upon, but "the method of carrying those mutual pledges out should be left to develop by itself." If the league were to be a genuine organic state, it would be limited in scope and action to what could be agreed upon through "common counsel." Rather than a superstate, the league would depend on unity between the liberated nations and the new administrative body and would create an international polity unspoiled by divisive interests. Moreover, the league could not be simply a formal institution; Wilson did not expect it to work simply because it was founded. Success depended on national leaders who pursued enlightened self-interest; the league would evolve only "when men of good will, of whatever country, come to understand their true common interests."[41]

In so envisioning the league, Wilson continued to hold forth as the one disinterested world leader. Capable of tolerating revolution because he was convinced that the future held improvement, Wilson promoted ideas that incorporated the revolutionary movements for self-determination with his innately conservative, "organic league." This combination was most serviceable and most convincing just at that moment when, by September 1918, the war had become an intensely ideological struggle. By then the war was in its waning season. The Czechoslovakians and Yugoslavians had congealed into formal allies; Bulgaria had surrendered; and the Dual Monarchy was collapsing.

Just then, as other statesmen in other nations plotted out their expansionist intentions, Wilson brought together the many strands of ideas about the future world that he had been developing since 1913. Unlike the other statesmen, he was impressed not by the opportunity for national gain but by the very opposite, and he used the entirely mundane occasion of a Liberty Loan Address in New York's Metropolitan Opera House to make his position clear. The postwar world, the President declared, was to be a democratic one that shunned balance-of-power diplomacy and destroyed imperialism. The forces that had brought war, the militaristic, imperialistic autocracies of Central Europe, were nearly vanquished and Europe's subjugated masses were the victors. The democratic forces were poised to create a world in which independent na-

[41] WW to House, 22 March 1918, *PWW* 47: 105; on the organic evolution of the league see also Frank Lyon Polk to Jean Jules Jusserand, *PWW* 43: 359–60; WW to John St. Leo Strachey 5 April 1918, *PWW* 47: 258–59; A Translation of a Memorandum by William Emmanuel Rappard, 1 November 1917, *PWW* 44: 488.

tions joined in a harmonious order. "The war has lasted more than four years," he asserted, "and the whole world has been drawn into it. *The common will of mankind has been substituted for the particular purposes of individual states.* Individual statesmen may have started the conflict, but neither they nor their opponents can stop it as they please. It has become a people's war," which demanded the end of rule by classes and militarists. Common standards of right were at issue and could be settled "by no arrangement of compromise or adjustment of interests." No durable peace could be built on the recognition of the "special or separate interests of any single nation or any group of nations . . . ; there can be no leagues or alliances or special covenants and understandings with the general and common family of the League of nations." Americans should not mistake what had happened: "National purposes have fallen . . . into the background and the common purpose of enlightened mankind has taken their place."[42]

Here was vintage Wilson. The "people's war" had destroyed the archaic spirit that reactionary classes inherently exhibited. The new world would thrive without class rule and uphold international standards of common rights and obligations. The diplomatic implications of his position, which later critics debunked as naive, idealistic, and even destructive, made sense in 1918. Wilson did not have to invent international analogies to the domestic trusts, for alliances between the European powers smacked of the same conspiratorial methods and pursued similarly narrow interests. The European alliance system did leave the entire continent precariously suspended on a balance of power. It hardly mattered that such analogies might seem obtuse in retrospect. The collapse of the balance of power had led to war, and for a generation of American liberals, the war confirmed the destructiveness of narrow self-interest and the secret machinations of the powerful.

Wilson's basic political ideals provided ready and partially incisive readings of world events. The real problem was that his readings of the war and of the future were one-sided. He did not see that, however old the pursuit of national gain, however archaic the collapsing European political systems, the forces of the past were complemented by an entire array of modern forces. Some of these new forces were objectively just, not least the quest to destroy colonialism; some were basically oppressive, as was the clamor for territorial gain after the armistice. All ran

---

[42] An Address at the Metropolitan Opera House, 27 September 1918, *PWW* 51: 127–33. The emphasis is in the text. Preparations for the speech can be seen in House diary entry, 24 September 1918, 51: 102–3.

against the inclusive, organic vision of Wilsonian idealism. Wilson continued to believe, as he wrote in 1918, "that our own desire for a new international order under which reason and justice and the common interests of mankind shall prevail is the desire of enlightened men everywhere."[43] It was precisely this faith in the compelling nature of "reason and justice" that became problematic as the war ended and the Versailles Peace conference began.

[43] A Draft of an Address to a Joint Session of Congress, 8 February 1918, *PWW* 46: 278.

3

The Idealist Synthesis in American Internationalism

When he described himself in 1889 as an "interpreter" of his age, Woodrow Wilson was presumptuous but not incorrect. As an academic, he borrowed from the intellectual trends around him. As a politician, he traded on his relationship with Brandeis. In both cases he managed to blend current trends with old ideals. As a statesman, he adopted the internationalist agenda and brought together an eclectic group of American liberals who shared an idealist temperament in spite of their differences. There was something in Wilson's internationalism both for conservatives, who saw in it a means of preserving American constitutional values, and for those to Wilson's left, who believed that world interdependence was the logical culmination of the cooperative politics that they advocated at home. Whether one was conservative or progressive meant less during the war than whether one was an internationalist or an isolationist; the former came to define liberalism, the latter smacked of reaction.

Internationalists in Progressive America

To claim that during the Great War a synthesis of political ideals produced a coherent group of "Wilsonians" is not to dismiss the important differences that existed among those who supported internationalism and the Wilsonian cause during the war. Even among those who are usually considered mainstream internationalists, that is, those who had been involved in the halting steps toward international organization since the

First Hague Conference of 1899, there were important differences of emphasis and priority. For some, establishing the World Court or some comparable institution for international arbitration was the single most important cause. The "legalists," as Sondra Herman has called them, were thorough conservatives bent on bringing systematic order to international relations. Well-established spokesmen such as Elihu Root, secretary of war under McKinley and mainstay among New York Republicans, and Nicholas Murray Butler, the president of Columbia University, were hesitant to embrace what they considered visionary schemes for international parliaments or police forces. Convinced, at least before 1914, that the cause of war was the politician who had to answer to nationalist mobs, the legalists hoped to elevate international relations to the austere plane of judicial control and oversight.[1] Their legalistic emphasis brought them into conflict with the League to Enforce Peace, the influential internationalist lobby that sought a postwar league that included some form of police power. The LEP was formed around the idea that international sanction would be necessary to the success of a world league, and it was the demand for this compulsive element that the more conservative legalists objected to. The legalists put their faith in the voluntary compliance of nations with international law; in their view, law itself was sufficiently compulsive, and beyond that, the greatest instrument for controlling international aggression was the sanction of public opinion.

The differences between the legalists and the "sanctionists" were sufficiently important that William Howard Taft and his fellow LEP leader, Harvard president A. Lawrence Lowell, spent the war years dealing rather uncomfortably with Root and Butler, when by all other measures the men were natural allies. They were never antagonists, but Root and Butler declined membership in the LEP and remained lukewarm about the organization even after American intervention led them to soften their stand against sanctions.[2] Nor did their support for the war entail absolute or consistent support for President Wilson. Prominent internationalists were largely Republican, and a good deal of partisan acrimony marked their wartime politics. Taft and Lowell cooperated with the administration after 1916, when Wilson first committed himself to a postwar league while addressing the LEP. Wilson wavered on many things, in their view, but intervention showed that he was willing to use force in

---

[1] Sondra Herman, *Eleven against War: Studies in American Internationalist Thought, 1908–1921* (Stanford, 1969).

[2] Ibid., 44–47.

the service of postwar organization. Hoping to influence the shape of the league, LEP leaders stayed loyal to Wilson through the Paris Peace Conference, and when their own partisan loyalties were tested during the Senate debate on the Versailles treaty in 1919, Taft strained to find a compromise between moderate Republicans and the administration. The more bitterly partisan Root, meanwhile, fell in with Henry Cabot Lodge in the effort to derail the treaty, and he did so by focusing attention on the one point that had rankled him about the LEP, the pledge of collective security in Article X.[3]

In the long run, these conflicts were less important to American internationalism—and to liberalism—than the real similarities that internationalists shared. They debated means, not ends. Even the partisan divisions among them over the Versailles treaty should not be exaggerated. Wilson himself was an aggressive partisan, and Taft, for one, blamed the president for the bitterness of the treaty fight. Root, as we shall see, supported the League of Nations all along; his partisanship and his personal dislike for Wilson dictated his short-term position in 1919 and 1920.[4] More important, American internationalists shared class origins; they were symbols of an increasingly powerful, ambitious America that was coming of age as a world power. It is difficult to avoid concluding, in fact, that American internationalists were drawn into the movement in part because of their desire for continual development in the international economy, and because they, like Wilson, had few doubts that Americans could succeed in an open marketplace. Many internationalists believed that new economic conditions necessitated new international arrangements, and many business leaders no doubt agreed. Few would have dissented against LEP member and Boston department store magnate Edward A. Filene when he maintained in 1916 that internationalist goals made for "sound business policy. A peaceful world makes possible a permanently prosperous America."[5]

---

[3] Ambrosius, *Woodrow Wilson and the American Diplomatic Tradition*, 153–59, 183–84, 148–50; Herman, *Eleven against War*, 49.
[4] Ambrosius, *Woodrow Wilson and the American Diplomatic Tradition*, 183. Root once remarked that "we had weak presidents and wrong-headed presidents, but never until Wilson had we had an unscrupulous and dishonest president." Chandler P. Anderson quoted in David Martin Dubin, "The Carnegie Endowment for International Peace and the Advocacy of the League of Nations, 1914–1918," *Proceedings of the American Philosophical Society* 123 (December 1979): 355, n. 74.
[5] Edward A. Filene, "The League to Enforce Peace and the Soul of the United States," in *Enforced Peace: Proceedings of the First Annual National Assemblage of the League to Enforce Peace* (New York, 1916), 49.

This material element aside, American internationalists were mainly college presidents, constitutional lawyers, and nationally prominent party leaders. Not many were industrialists, the notable philanthropist Andrew Carnegie notwithstanding; they did not comprise J. A. Hobson's "little group of kings." Rather, they were those who had the most at stake in the survival of American institutions because they were institutional leaders. They spent far more energy agitating for the World Court and international federation than in demanding free trade. They craved codification and institutionalization; they sought stability and order. Their main export was American liberalism.

Whatever the material basis of their politics, their view of the world was primarily shaped by domestic conditions. As conservatives, they were on the defensive in an age of widespread reform. Convinced that the United States Constitution was the finest of political conceptions, they were prone to anxieties in an age that included more than a few attempts to amend the Constitution, usually in order to widen popular political power. In an age of revolt, even defenders of tradition had to offer something "progressive." Contemporary politics dictated a curious situation: some of the most powerful Americans, those who were most dubious about domestic reform, rejected nationalism and embraced the idea of an international comity of nations. While other Western ruling classes were vehement nationalists, American elites became ardent proponents of a progressive world order. American nationalism had been captured by the forces of movement, which consequently left the conservatives to champion internationalism.

American internationalism was less a result of Progressivism than a reaction against it, and there was a real ideological consistency between internationalist efforts and the fear of reform. Many internationalists believed that Progressivism would bring anarchy by violating constitutional, representative government; like Wilson, they equated anarchy with the heedless pursuit of self-interest, whether by individuals, political groups, or nations. To the internationalist president of Stanford, David Starr Jordan, reformers threatened to bring anarchy because they had too little respect for institutions. A noticeably defensive Jordan wrote in 1912 that "it is the fashion today . . . to regard civilized society as effete, outworn, tyrannical; to consider the institutions our fathers have built up as mere temporary scaffolding; and the constitution, of which the Americans of the past have been so proud, as a maze of paper agreement, respected only when it favors some man's ambition or gives play to some man's greed."[6] To Jordan and others, Progressive reform had a curious double nature: it was as transient as any fashion; yet reformers seemed driven to their ill-mannered assault on tradition by the vices of greed and immoderation that long had lurked among the depraved. Where many other Progressive Era liberals considered reform an antidote to national debilitation and moral depravity, Jordon and his colleagues saw it as a manifestation of those maladies.

In spite of their frequent misgivings, internationalists were confident that the institutions they valued so highly would survive. In their view, the real strength of American institutions was their flexibility, which meant that reformers could be allowed a hearing without diluting the supremacy of those institutions. Elihu Root conceded that the American way of governing might be improved, that experimentation could be legitimate, largely because he was confident that only those reforms devised in the original American spirit of representative government would take hold. Root at once acknowledged the desirability of reform and rejected those reforms that contemporaries advanced, especially any proposal "which involves the idea that people can rule merely by voting."[7]

The conservative conclusion that Progressivism grew from the immoderate and impulsive mob truly did mark them off from Wilson and others before the war. Root and Jordan belittled the demands for the recall, the referendum, and the direct election of senators, not only because the national government, in their view, had a distinguished record of public service but because the demands themselves issued from haste and imprudence. The recall and referendum were an admission of public incompetence, because there would be no need to recall representatives chosen properly in the first place. If the public elected poor leaders, Jordan wrote, "that is our own fault. Perhaps they represent us too well." The agitation for change exhibited the ancient human weakness that induced people to give into passion and reject the counsel of reason. The modern tendencies of people to form specific groups only made those passions stronger and more prone to the wily manipulation of politicians. Where Wilson linked anarchy to lingering forms of feudalism, the conservatives blamed "mob rule," for, in part, they believed that politicians exploited the public because the public, too often intoxicated, was spiritually weak. "It is the weakness of the weak," Jordan preached, "rather than

---

[6] David Starr Jordan, "Unrest and Progress," *Independent*, 8 August 1912, 310.
[7] Elihu Root, *Experiments in Government and the Essentials of the Constitution* (Princeton, 1913), 8–13.

the strength of the strong, from which spring tyranny and injustice."[8]
They were not social Darwinists, as Sondra Herman has suggested.[9]
They had little taste for the struggle that social Darwinism assumed.
They objected to reform not because it interfered with the natural workings of competition but on the grounds that it overreached the capacity
of law and threatened institutions by diluting their effectiveness. As Root
maintained, "law cannot give to depravity the rewards of virtue, to in-
dolence the rewards of industry, to indifference the rewards of ambition,
or to ignorance the rewards of learning." Life, perhaps, was a struggle,
but rather than welcoming it, these men expected institutions to mediate
or reduce life's antagonisms. Jordan hoped that "in the struggle of life,
there is still a premium placed on faith, hope, charity; on industry, fru-
gality, sobriety, self-denial; on self-restraint and persistence; on self-
devotion and idealism."[10]

Conservative internationalists relied on a tautology—reformers were
depraved because to call for reform was a sign of depravity—that betrayed their own confusion over exactly how to shape a liberalism that
was positive and cautious at the same time. The institutions that they
defended supposedly embodied popular will, arrived at through intelligent discourse, codified in the Constitution, and invested in representative government. They were products of natural law, of the capacity of
citizens, however depraved, to restrain themselves long enough to agree
on what constituted the common good and to protect that agreement
with organized government. But they feared that this measure of necessary self-restraint could no longer be taken for granted, and if change
was necessary, as they reluctantly admitted, then there was no firm basis
upon which to judge what was healthy change and what was not.

Perhaps one of the more complete examples of this conundrum came
from A. Lawrence Lowell in 1913. Lowell, who hailed from one of the
Brahmin Massachusetts families most deeply associated with an antebellum, industrial Whig tradition, attempted to come to terms with Progressive reforms by judging them according to traditional measures. He drew
the old distinction between public opinion, which comes when "a body
of men . . . are agreed upon the ends and aims of government and upon
the principles by which those ends shall be attained," and majority opinion, which amounted to mob rule; Lowell proposed to judge governmen-

[8] Jordan, "Unrest and Progress," 310–13.

[9] Herman, *Eleven against War*, 24–30.

[10] Jordon, "Unrest and Progress"; Root, *Experiments in Government*, 13, and "Tampering with the Constitution," *Independent*, 9 March 1911, 500.

tal reforms according to how likely they were to strengthen the former rather than the latter. On this basis, he agreed with Jordan that the recall should be rejected, for it was nothing more than "an acknowledgment of popular incapacity to choose trustworthy men" and was therefore just "another device for restraining misconduct rather than for improving the conditions under which the legislature works." For the same reason, the direct primary should be avoided, for it relied on majority opinion and avoided altogether the more important need to agree on principles. The referendum had some merit to it, but only when the issue in question was one of general principle; the process of amending the Constitution was an example of just such an exercise in developing consensus on methods of governing, according to Lowell.[11]

This means to consensus was at best problematic. Public opinion, and therefore reasoned consensus, could grow only from an enlightened electorate that had mastered the necessary facts, and Lowell concluded that the nature of modern society made mastery difficult if not impossible. "With the accumulation of human knowledge," Lowell wrote, presaging Walter Lippmann's postwar views on public opinion, "with the growth of man's control over the forces of nature, with the greater complexity of modern transactions and of modern society, the amount of information needed to form an intelligent opinion upon public affairs has been constantly increasing." Modern conditions limited the number of questions upon which the public could employ reason. Rather than expanding popular control over government, reform should be directed at restraining such control.[12]

Anti-pluralism and the Search for Authority

How to order the modern cacophony? Here was the essential question. One way was through the institutionalization of political groups, through, in other words, political pluralism. Lowell considered this avenue. Popular opinion, he thought, was no longer the sum of individual voices; because modern complexities also created organized groups, "cooperative interests have in some measure replaced personal ones." Traditional liberal thought "treated the state as a sum of equal and independent units," but modern liberalism had to account for groups

[11] A. Lawrence Lowell, *Public Opinion and Popular Government* (New York, 1913), 7–10, 147–51, 154–63.
[12] Ibid., 46–50, 39–40.

and move away, at least in part, from the old preoccupation with individuals. In what way should liberalism reconsider its relationship to individuals, and what form should these new groups take? Lowell was not noticeably concerned about reducing the importance of the individual in liberal thought. Nor were he and his colleagues reluctant to praise modern organization, especially business, for bringing economic efficiency. Like Wilson, they gave business the benefit of the doubt and soft-pedaled the issue of the trust by arguing that the logic of business was toward consolidation and economic unity. Root believed that modern business organization permitted "securing through organization the united action, and concentrated action, of great numbers of Americans who have a common purpose." Still they insisted that even corporations measure up to the old standards of individual political behavior. Groups, like individuals, contributed to political consensus only when they were willingly loyal, as Root put it, to "prescribed and established governmental institutions, which work out the ends of government through many separate human agents, each doing his part in obedience to the law."[13]

Root was more optimistic that such obedience could be exacted, at least from corporations. Lowell agreed that modern economic "change was for the better, because it means greater devotion to something higher than purely personal objects[. But] that very fact, whether the body be a bank, a railroad company or a trade union, may cover with a gilding of altruism what is after all only cooperative selfishness." Others more vigorously asserted that politicized groups would center around particular occupations or ethnicity and would represent not a step forward but, as Harry Garfield contended, a "reversion to the trade guilds." Garfield, son of the president whose assassination sparked the mugwump demands for civil-service reform in the 1880s, himself president of Williams College and founder of the internationalist Williamstown Institute of Politics, forthrightly revealed that pluralist politics was one of the concerns underlying the fear of reform. Group politics "would exchange party prejudice for trade prejudice. . . . Groups would combine with groups and in the end we would have class against class." Because pluralism invited selfishness and incited political passion, it therefore threatened consensus, which the liberal state embodied in accepted law. Pluralism was organized anarchy. As Butler argued later in the decade, "to assert that the political state is only one among many forms of hu-

---

[13] Elihu Root, "Individual Effort in Trade Expansion," *Annals* 37 (May 1911): 580; and *Experiments in Government*, 11.

man association, and that it is not necessarily any more in harmony with what some writers are pleased to call 'the end of society' than a church, or a trade-union, or a masonic lodge, or a college fraternity," leaves the individual to "decide which of these relationships and which of his loyalties is at any given time to take precedence [over] the others." Individuals and groups would be prone to ignore law for their immediate gain. It hardly mattered whether such a system were called direct democracy, pluralism, or socialism, for in fact it was "correctly and bluntly described as the gospel of anarchy and disorder."[14]

If these arguments could be marshaled, as Butler employed them, against unions, churches, and those perpetual hotbeds of radicalism, college fraternities, they certainly provided ammunition for use against the "hyphenates" during the preparedness debates of 1915 and 1916. Though their cultural impulses were aroused on the hyphenate issue, internationalists worried less about ethnic heterogeneity than political heterogeneity—that is, that ethnic groups might introduce distinct interests into matters of national interest during the war. They equated ethnic conflict, or, more important, an ethnic group's refusal to put aside provincial loyalties, with the grasping nationalism that drove the Europeans into war. Dual allegiances had to be foresaken for pure loyalty to America. The immigrants "have married this country for better or for worse," remarked Secretary of War Newton D. Baker in 1917. They have "been rebaptized with the American spirit."[15]

The basis of this anti-pluralism was the idealist affection for political unity as embodied in strong institutions, recognized authority, and consensus. Henry Stimson, known as a moderate Progressive Republican in his early days, perhaps put it most clearly. Stimson insisted in 1911 that

[14] Lowell, *Public Opinion and Popular Government*, 46–50, 39–40; Garfield, "Notes for Address on Government and Good Citizenship at Pittsfield," 25 February 1910, Harry A. Garfield Papers, Library of Congress, Washington, D.C., box 141; Butler, "The Real Labor Problem," address to the Institute of Arts and Sciences, Columbia University, 13 October 1919, printed in Nicholas Murray Butler, *Is America Worth Saving? Addresses on National Problems and Party Politics* (New York, 1920), 89–91.
[15] Newton D. Baker, "Problems of the Melting Pot," address to the Annual Convention of Police Chiefs, Washington, D.C., 4 December 1917, printed in Newton D. Baker, *Frontiers of Freedom* (New York, 1918), 168. See also Harry Garfield to Mr. M. O. Von Klock, 3 February 1915, Garfield Papers, box 142; Henry Stimson, "The Basis for Military Training," *Scribner's Magazine* 61 (April 1917): 408–12. When airing his objections to the Versailles treaty, Root argued that by obliging the United States to become involved in every breach of the peace, the treaty would ensnare Americans in nationalist rivalries that, in turn, would excite ethnic rivalries within America. Ambrosius, *Woodrow Wilson and the American Diplomatic Tradition*, 148–49.

"responsibility could not be divorced from authority." The study of government convinced reasonable men that "irresponsibility was a direct result of scattered authority and divided power. . . . The true remedy for American misgovernment would lie, then, in exactly the opposite direction from that indicated by the advocates of direct democracy. The elected officials must have more power, not less." The solution to the political difficulties of the day, according to Stimson, was the reinvigoration of the federal government, for that alone was the expression of political consensus and that alone would thwart class war and personal greed.[16]

In defending centralized political authority the conservative internationalists constructed a bridge to the Progressive left, and the conception of the unified nation-state provided a core belief of the Wilsonian liberals. New Nationalists such as Walter Lippmann, Walter Weyl, and Herbert Croly, the *New Republic* editors who became influential supporters of the American war effort, came to internationalism because of its defense of concentrated authority. Wilson's conception of the nation-state and the internationalists' defense of constitutional government were not far from the sort of political order that Croly promoted in his classic tract, *The Promise of American Life*. All returned to the Federalist-Whig tradition of positive government and agreed that the state was an indispensable feature of political life. Croly was the most famous and intelligent writer to exhume Alexander Hamilton during these years, but the Federalists were enjoying a vogue among internationalists as well.[17]

The ideological overlapping of conservative internationalists and social imperialists took place gradually, largely because Lippmann and Croly indulged in the self-flattering illusion that they were left-wing moderns. To them, the political crisis of the Progressive Era resulted from the lingering influence of individualism in a collective age, the antidote to which was not far from that which the conservatives recommended. They too sought centralized authority. "The national advance of the American democracy," Croly wrote, "does demand an increasing amount of centralized action and responsibility," and there was no mis-

---

[16] Henry Stimson and McGeorge Bundy, *On Active Service in Peace and War* (New York, 1948), 58.

[17] Croly, *The Promise of American Life* (New York, 1909; Indianapolis, 1975). Mainstream internationalist thought is replete with allusions to the Federalist tradition. For example see James Brown Scott, *James Madison's Notes of Debates in the Federal Convention of 1787 and Their Relation to a More Perfect Society of Nations* (New York, 1918), and Nicholas Murray Butler, "The World Needs Another Alexander Hamilton," address to the Summer Session Convocation, Columbia University, 7 August 1934, printed in Nicholas Murray Butler, *The Family of Nations* (New York, 1938), 57.

taking that the enlargement of the federal government "is the natural consequence of the increasing centralization of American industrial, political, and social life."[18]

On the face of things, their quest for centralized reform was at odds with the stodgy, anti-reform instincts of conservative internationalists. Before they became caught up in the war effort the new nationalists did differ with conservatives, but not regarding political centralization. Rather, the new nationalists initially saw no contradiction between centralized authority and pluralism. Lippmann, for example, called for a "redefinition" of traditional liberalism that recognized modern pluralism: "We need a great elaboration of representation of group institutions—that's where semi-legal bodies like unions and foundations come in."[19] Liberals had to accommodate the modern political phenomenon— a welcomed alternative to destructive individualism—that Lippmann and Croly identified as the "expansion of loyalties," and to measure political maturity by the degree to which a people renounced individualism and parochialism. Perhaps a product of the Comtean Positivism that David Levy has described in Croly's political thought, this notion equated complexity with political and ideological progress; they admired industrial complexity and, for the same reason, cultural and political cosmopolitanism.[20]

The New Nationalists welcomed complexity in foreign affairs as well. Just as they excused corporate power in the domestic sphere, so they considered imperialism a progressive force because it incorporated "unorganized territory" and "backward states" into the modern system. Any "real friend of mankind," Lippmann explained tersely in a 1916 article, "would be passionately devoted to the regeneration of those territories which constitute the stakes of diplomacy." Any "real friend of mankind," the argument went, had to be an imperialist. The United States, for its part, was obliged to help backward states—Lippmann pointed regularly to China, Turkey, and the Caribbean states—by putting their finances in order, much as Wilson then was doing in the Caribbean, by leading them to administrative modernization, by developing their "economic resources," and by educating them.[21]

---

[18] Croly, *The Promise of American Life*, 274.

[19] Lippmann Diary, 1914–1918, Walter Lippmann Papers, Sterling Library, Yale University, box 236, folder 1, 43–49, 76.

[20] David Levy, *Herbert Croly of the New Republic: The Life and Thought of an American Progressive* (Princeton, 1985).

[21] Walter Lippmann, "What Program Shall the United States Stand for in International Relations," *Annals* 66 (July 1916): 61, 63.

In 1915 and 1916, the New Nationalists found nothing unpalatable in imperialism. Indeed it was apparently necessary. While conceding the "brutality and bloodiness of colonialism," Walter Weyl maintained that "it at least represents a certain phase or form of an inevitable development, the creation of an economic unity of the World." Pacifists and "dogmatic anti-imperialists," models of muddled thinking, had to face facts, which in the modern world meant that the backward states would be exploited. Modernity, in the guise of export capital, would continue to flood the unorganized world and could not be stopped, Weyl insisted. Capitalist expansion, moreover, involved not just "capital" but the simple "interrelation of peoples," as Lippmann put it, which exported "rum, bibles, rifles, missionaries, traders, concessionaires."[22]

The problem with this argument was that shouldering imperial responsibilities undercut political pluralism. If the status quo was supposed to yield to political multiplicity at home, why should the powers rule over weaker peoples in the international arena?

Lippmann tried to resolve this problem by coaxing to the surface a submerged belief that imperialism was a step toward internationalism, and both were inevitable not because of economic realities but because modern people were gripped by the need for expanding loyalties. Simple loyalty to locale, to one's home, even the patriotic spirit that ran with nationalism, were yielding to loyalties to larger groups. Lippmann hoped that nationalism would draw people from their petty concerns and simple desires into some larger whole, and the internationalist program offered hope that this same process could be extended even beyond the nation. If interest groups could proclaim their mutual regard for the common good at home, there was no theoretical reason why imperialism should snuff the self-assertion of colonial subjects. Indeed there was something about the modest success of harmonizing interests at home that lent credence to his faith that the same process would work internationally. At least Lippmann took heart. "Every time we increase the area of . . . practical loyalty we take a step toward decreasing the friction of man," he wrote in 1916. "We shall learn world-citizenship, if at all, in the school of graded experience when the object of loyalty is constantly being enlarged." From this perspective, imperialism was not a system of domination but the beginning of a process by which political loyalties

[22] Walter Weyl, *American World Policies* (New York, 1917), 149–50, 135–36; Walter Lippmann, *The Stakes of Diplomacy* (New York, 1915), 89–90.

would be brought to a global level. The "surrender of sovereignty" to world government, Lippmann wrote, "will be much easier if it occurs first in outlying portions of the earth" and is initially built on "a number of partial means at the scenes of greatest friction."[23]

The case that imperialism was benign was based on a version of organic political development similar to that of Root and Wilson. Root stressed the organic development of law, Lippmann and Croly the organic growth of human association, and in each the desired end was global interdependence. The New Nationalists believed that interdependence was an evolutionary process of increasing centralization, and like all prominent American internationalists, they thought that the process respected national and ethnic differences. Croly maintained that interdependence did not lead to denationalization. He concurred with Lippmann that those who pressed for the abolition of national boundaries, who considered nationalism and internationalism contradictory, were wrong. Nations associated with other nations after they ventured into the world in pursuit of national self-interest, and those interests would not decompose simply through international association.[24] Working from this assumption, Croly proceeded to defend a postwar league of nations as a means for fostering domestic pluralism. Properly conducted, a league would "liberate within existing states voluntary economic, professional, technical, . . . and religious associations, which could be allowed a larger measure of autonomy, a more explicit license to compete with the state, than would be safe under a condition of anarchy." The league fulfilled the role of the state in domestic reform: it liberated independent groups and nurtured them until they could compete on their own for the loyalty of the citizen.[25]

Croly's efforts notwithstanding, the proposition that separate national interests would not interrupt pluralist development proved impossible to maintain after American intervention. The Allies' refusal to clarify war aims and renounce imperialism, the Russian revolution, and the surge of ethnic demands for self-determination in Central and Eastern Europe all forced the New Nationalists into the mainstream of internationalist

---

[23] Walter Lippmann, "Integrated America," *New Republic,* 19 February 1916, 64, and "Sinews of Peace," 20 November 1915, 8.

[24] Herbert Croly, "The Structure of Peace," *New Republic,* 13 January 1917, 290. See also Weyl, *American World Policies,* 161–62.

[25] Croly, "The Future of the State," *New Republic,* 15 September 1917, 179, 181; and "Counsel of Humanity," 15 December 1917, 175–76.

thought, and as they did so, the defense of pluralism waned. In his post war career, Lippmann saw how contradictory internationalism and pluralism were, but as early as 1917 he had begun to wonder whether it was realistic to expect the citizen to "distribute his available energy between a league of nations, the government at Washington, his state government, his city, his neighborhood, his family, his church, his vocation." He subsequently concluded that it was not.[26]

Interdependence and the Extension of the American Experience

There was much that attracted Lippmann, Croly, and Weyl to internationalism from the first. They shared the belief not only in strong, centralized authority but in global interdependence as well. Their many differences notwithstanding, conservatives, mainstream internationalists, and New Nationalists alike shared the view that the world had become "too small" for nations to go about their own business and that the reckless pursuit of narrow interests was self-defeating. For American internationalists, proclaiming the virtues of interdependence was a way to be practical, to satisfy the liberal thirst for idealistic goals, and to preserve American institutions at the same time.

Interdependence was an indisputable product of modern industrial society, internationalists assured themselves. When he reduced his arguments for a postwar league to "sound business policy," for instance, Edward Filene was suggesting that the modern economy no longer could tolerate the economic isolation of tariffs or large armament programs. Internationalists assumed that industrial technology, international travel, and communications all brought the world closer together. "Our relations with other nations have become so much closer than formerly that our interests can no longer be disassociated from theirs," one member of the LEP Executive Committee suggested. The war was the best evidence of how interdependent the world had become. As the *New Republic* editors wrote in 1915, no nation could afford isolation in a world "where a quarrel between the Magyars and the southern Slavs throws our whole life into a sink of depression, and balks the political and social reforms upon which our hearts are set." The internationalist program became all the more important, because it recognized modern realities and extended

[26] Walter Lippmann, "A Clue," *New Republic*, 4 April 1917, 316–17.

modernity's progress. Clearly, the publisher Hamilton Holt proclaimed, it was time for the world to adopt a "Declaration of Interdependence."[27]

As Holt's proclamation suggests, internationalists conceived of world organization in ways that were so nearly identical to the way they understood American government that internationalism itself became a strategy for preserving American political institutions. In Holt's view, a postwar league should be an international version of the United States, with a "parliament of man" and a "court with jurisdiction over all questions."[28] Root used similar reasoning several years before the war to define what he hoped would be the nature of a world court. The problem with international law as it existed was its vagueness; it was something informally interpreted by diplomats rather than formally employed by jurists. A world court, in contrast, would emphasize clear adjudication over mere arbitration. Root not only encouraged Americans to work for the world court but considered them ideally suited for such work. "The extraordinary scope of judicial power in this country," he advised Theodore Marburg, a Baltimore philanthropist devoted to internationalism, "has accustomed us to see the operations of government and questions arising between sovereign states submitted to judges who apply the test of conformity to established principles and rules of conduct embodied in our constitution. . . . It seems easy, therefore, for Americans to grasp the idea that the same method of settlement should be applied to questions growing out of the conduct of nations." The natural desire of Americans for political consensus prepared them to understand how natural law would work in international affairs: "There is a consciousness that in the most important affairs of nations, in their political status, the success of their undertakings and their processes of development, there is an indefinite and almost mysterious influence exercised by the general opinion of the world regarding the nation's character and conduct."[29]

If nothing else, this simplistic extrapolation of domestic experience provided a useful position from which to batter down critics. Only a fool

[27] Edward A. Filene, "The League to Enforce Peace and the Soul of the United States," in *Enforced Peace*, 49; Thomas Raeburn White, "The League Platform," ibid., 25; and Hamilton Holt, "The League Program, Preparedness, and Ultimate Reduction of Armaments," ibid., 57; "The Deeper Preparedness," *New Republic*, July 1915, 218.
[28] Quoted in Warren Kuehl, *Seeking World Order: The United States and International Organization to 1920* (Nashville, 1969), 182.
[29] Root to Theodore Marburg, 2 February 1910, Theodore Marburg Papers, Library of Congress, Washington, D.C., box 1; Elihu Root, "The Sanction of International Law," Presidential Address at the Second Annual Meeting of the American Society of International Law, 24 April 1908, reprinted in *Addresses on International Subjects*, ed. Robert Bacon and James Brown Scott (Cambridge, 1916), 30.

would dare call the ideal of the United States impractical, and in the unlikely event that a less irrelevant critic made such a point, the very existence of the nation, prosperous and united, was proof that states can be wedded in an effective union. The development of a constitutional order proved, James Brown Scott asserted, that "a Society of Nations is not a theory," nor were the obstacles presented by differing national interests "insuperable." William Howard Taft returned to this position several times while debating the use of international sanctions with the pacifist former secretary of state, William Jennings Bryan. The feasibility of international arbitration and a world court was unquestionable, according to Taft; one could not reasonably dispute the existence of "a court to administer international justice," since "our own Supreme court is one." If the world court was not quite a world federation, Taft maintained, echoing Holt's position, it was still a step toward the final goal: " 'the Parliament of Man and the Federation of the World'."[30]

The international federalism to which internationalists looked was to take the same form, was to be based on the same political beliefs, and was even to enjoy the same historical development as the United States. Theodore Marburg insisted that the American experience was "really an application" of the principle of federation; just as the American states had done, nations in a federated world would surrender sovereignty to the "common good" yet retain the power to "govern themselves with respect to three quarters of the things that touch the public interest." David Starr Jordan agreed that the league would be "similar" to the United States but with "considerable more emphasis laid on 'States Rights'. It will not be easily secured," he added with faithful determination, "but nothing politically worth while can be gained without great effort." Americans could take heart, for the league was to be based on "a group of principles that will work as successfully in world affairs as our own constitution works in our internal affairs," as Simon Patten put the matter.[31]

[30] Scott, *James Madison's Notes of Debates*, 97; and *The United States of America: A Study in International Organization* (Washington, 1920), 467. Taft presumably had some knowledge of the Supreme Court, but his grasp of international law seemed less than profound when he claimed that the relations between Kansas and Colorado were governed by international law. But one did not have to be thoroughly practical to debate Bryan, whose alternative to the LEP's program was "international brotherly love." William Howard Taft and William Jennings Bryan, *World Peace: A Debate between William Howard Taft and William Jennings Bryan* (New York, 1917), 20, 61–62, 119.

[31] Theodore Marburg, "Sovereignty and Race as Affected by a League of Nations," *Annals* 72 (July 1917): 142–43; David Starr Jordan, *Ways to Lasting Peace* (Indianapolis, 1916), 245; Simon Patten, "Peace without Force," *Annals* 72 (July 1917): 36; see also William Hull, "Three Plans for a Durable Peace," *Annals* 66 (July 1916): 13.

Nothing less than an affirmation of American history, this interpretation of the principles of federation hung on a Wilsonian view of the frontier and the Civil War. In the beginning, the typical description held, the frontier was made up of isolated and well-armed individuals who were inclined to take the law into their own hands and to bump off a neighbor if self-interest dictated. Civilization brought these people into greater contact, and their antagonistic interests gradually became entwined. With this frontier experience, American historical development stood as a model of evolving interdependence and, with it, of civilized peace built on enlightened self-interest.[32] As Walter Weyl explained, the indecorous taint of "brutal and bloody" imperialism would not appear if the American model were embraced in the international arena. The "American tradition points to internationalism," Weyl wrote, because the settling of the West was a great adventure in the process of civilization, conducted by immigrants who came to escape "political and religious warfare" and who carried with them "an ideal of peace, internationalism, freedom and equality." Any Native American probably would have wanted to qualify a point or two for the next lucky object of this "broad humanitarian ideal," but to Weyl, Americans, chastened by the "frontier mind," abhorred the "militaristic and excessively nationalistic" nature of European expansion.[33]

The Civil War, even more than the frontier, provided a useful analogy for interpreting World War I. It destroyed slavery, gave reign to individual freedom, and at the same time established unquestioned dominance for the principle of federal union. Order and freedom were simultaneously established, with the economic progress of industrialism the clear result. David Starr Jordan surmised that if America could not endure half-slave, half-free, then Europe could not remain half-democratic and half-autocratic.[34] Lippmann wrote that the Civil War was fought over conflicting claims to the unexploited West. "We were virtually two nations, each trying to upset the balance of power in its own favor . . . ; and until the problem of the West had been settled, peace and federal

---

[32] See Filene, "The League to Enforce Peace and the Soul of the United States," 46.

[33] Weyl, *American World Policies*, 12–13, also 41–42.

[34] Jordan, *Ways to Lasting Peace*, 14–15; also Herbert Houston, "Commerce and the Mailed Fist," in *Win the War for Permanent Peace: Addresses at the National Convention of the League to Enforce Peace, in the City of Philadelphia, May 16th and 17th, 1918* (New York, 1918), 143–44; Lowell, "Safeguarding the Future," in *Win the War*, 39–40; "Who Willed American Participation," *New Republic*, 14 April 1917, 309; and "Lincoln in 1917," *New Republic*, 17 February 1917, 62.

union were impossible." It was not hard to see that "the world's problem is the same problem tremendously magnified and complicated."[35]

The past thus witnessed the steady unfolding of progress toward unity and the common good, and if enlightened individualism led to domestic harmony, so would the enlightened self-interest of nations result in international unity. International authority and national independence could coexist if reasonable nations respected the league as the institutional expression of the common good. As Marburg put it, the "central idea of the League" was that the long reign of "international anarchy" could be ended by the international application of liberal democracy's first principles. The modern democratic state did not give absolute freedom; rather it established institutions of government that provided order and promoted the "general welfare." This system, as Marburg read it, was originally applied to the sovereign states "comprising the American union. . . . There was no suppression of local aspirations and ideals. On the whole the welfare of each made for the welfare of all." Democracy, furthermore, depended absolutely on the willingness of the individual to accept the state and to sacrifice for the common good. "Society implies restraint," Marburg wrote. "We can have no liberty without surrender of license. The one license which has become perfectly clear the nations must surrender is the license to make war at will. . . . That truth is at the bottom of the whole movement for world organization."[36]

Once it was assumed that internationalism was a movement in pursuit of the global common good, it became a simple matter, indeed a duty, to support intervention in the Great War. War for the common good even had an inspiring sublimity for Edward Filene, who exhorted his fellow LEP delegates to commit themselves, body and soul, to the war effort, "since *when war is for the common weal, then war is worship, war is prayer.*"[37] The Great War revealed the promise of the cooperative world, and the wartime alliance made the league of nations an immediate reality. No one "dared to hope" that the league of peace would spring to life so soon, declared the *New Republic*, but America's intervention meant that "the liberal people of the world are united in a common cause." The extensive organization of resources that the war compelled, the editors noted, amounted to "a gigantic experiment in internationalism. For the

---

[35] Lippmann, *Stakes of Diplomacy,* 109–10.

[36] Theodore Marburg, "The League to Enforce Peace: A Reply to Critics," *Annals* 66 (July 1916): 50.

[37] Edward A. Filene, "The War and Insight," in *Win the War for Permanent Peace,* 25; also H. M. Chittenden, "Questions for Pacifists," *Atlantic Monthly* 116 (August 1915): 168.

first time in history the food supply, the shipping, the credit, and the manpower of the nations are all to be put under something like joint administration." Walter Weyl, who in his first book on foreign policy was pessimistic about the prospects of a league of nations, wrote enthusiastically in 1918 that overnight the war "formed, or revealed, a vague super-organization, a partial fellowship of nations united by the same sort of compulsions and attractions as those which cement a nation." Nations at war, Weyl discovered, learn how to subordinate "special interests to the larger group interests of the Alliance."[38]

Permanent harmony depended on the establishment of liberal institutions based on the natural inclinations of self-restrained nations to seek peace. Only democracies, unselfish by nature, by definition committed to the common good, possessed the will to such self-restraint. Where nationalism was "the philosophy of irresponsibility," democracy was the philosophy of constant service. The crucial element for the league's success, therefore, was that it had to draw the allegiance of the liberal nations; and, because it was in their nature, there was every reason to expect that the liberal democracies would rush to such international service. "Just as the evolution of democracy means the gradual purification of the governmental motive," Ralph Barton Perry wrote, "the purging of it from admixture with personal, dynastic, and class interests, so we may expect to witness on the larger scale the gradual evolution of some similarly disinterested agency that shall represent the good of all mankind." When internationalists spoke of the end of American isolation, they spoke of her "duty and obligation" to humanity, the duty that the democrat had to the community. The world needed nations that possessed, David Starr Jordan was certain, "more self-control, more personal responsibility, more willingness to live and let live." Thus internationalists were determined to do nothing less than construct, as Holt put it, "the machinery by which reason can enthrone itself in the world."[39]

War, Democracy, and the Future

By upholding American political development as a model of progress from the wilderness of anarchy to the "enthronement of reason," internationalists advanced themselves as prophets for an inevitable demo-

[38] "The Great Decision," *New Republic*, 7 April 1917, 28; editorial note, *New Republic*, 28 April 1917, 357; and Weyl, *The End of the War* (New York, 1918), 236.
[39] Ralph Barton Perry, "What Is Worth Fighting For?" *Atlantic Monthly* 116 (December 1915): 830–31; Jordan, *Ways to Lasting Peace*, 246; and Holt, "The League Program, Preparedness, and Ultimate Reduction of Armaments," 53.

cratic future. Once convinced that internationalism and human progress
were synonymous, they grew more critical of European nationalism—at
the same time that a strong patriotism underlay their own positions.
Woodrow Wilson was only one of a host of liberals who argued that self-
interested reactionaries started the war, for which the Kaiser and the
Prussian "war caste" shouldered the largest blame. "The primal motive
behind the war was largely international and political," wrote David
Starr Jordan; it was a war begun by "a conspiracy of the privileged
classes" but that had become part of the "age-long struggle against privilege." Those elusive bogeymen—the "interests," "trusts," even "imperialism"—had metamorphosed into "Prussian military domination."[40]

In reducing the political enemies of the day to this single antagonist,
liberal internationalists came to the common ground marked off by Wilson. In coming around to support Wilson and the war effort, the conservatives Root and Butler concluded that the masses were not the great
threat to peace that they had assumed earlier in the decade. In Sondra
Herman's estimation, Butler "completely reversed his interpretation of
the causes of war, or at least the causes of this war." The New Nationalists, meanwhile, who only a short time earlier had prided themselves on
their "realistic" appreciation of balance-of-power diplomacy and had
found the cause of war in "disorganized territories," also came around.
Where he had first maintained that genuine internationalism must be
based on the pursuit of national self-interest, Walter Weyl speculated in
1918 that national interests might be subordinated to some international
"common good" and concluded that a durable peace would look to international cooperation with disregard for national self-interests. "Internationalism" was not the sum of each nation's pursuit of self-interest at
all costs but subordinated "state policy to the larger interests of the
whole family of nations." The contradictory forces in the modern world,
he wrote, perhaps criticizing the very movement of which he had been an
important part, were "the New Nationalism, aggressive, and confident,"
and internationalism.[41]

It would seem that by 1918 American internationalists could look forward to increasing influence and sure success. They had settled into a
fairly coherent political movement, the ends of which were military vic-

[40] Weyl, *The End of the War,* 167–68, 161, 252, 256; Jordan, *Ways to Lasting Peace,*
7, 10; Cosmos, *Basis of Durable Peace* (New York, 1917), 54–55; Theodore Marburg,
"The World Court and the League of Peace," *Annals* 61 (September 1915): 286.
[41] Herman, *Eleven against War,* 44; Weyl, *The End of the War,* 167–68, 161, 252, 256.

tory, the vanquishing of the international right wing, and the construction of a League of Nations. They stood behind a powerful president leading a nation at war. Many contributed what they could to the war effort, usually through some form of government service.

In the midst of the most destructive of wars, though, even the greatest optimists were bound to entertain doubts about the future. Granted, they firmly believed that history was running their way, but the carnage of World War I still gave pause. The entire program of the League to Enforce Peace rested on the premise that some instrument of compulsion was necessary in the postwar league because nations were still not ready to live in complete peace. One of the war's clearest lessons was that nations, like people, were imperfect.

Human nature aside, the war exposed a deeper threat to the idealist reading of history. Whatever one thought about its political structure, it was impossible to think of Germany as a backward, uncivilized state. Germany, as not a few internationalists who had studied there knew, was as sophisticated as any nation, and its technical prowess had made it powerful in the short span of a single generation since national unification. The assault on Belgium, the bloody battles, the wartime jingoism all hinted at the possibility that industrial progress did not bring moral progress with it. Humanity seemed to have turned its industrial genius from "steam, electricity, gas, and many other treasures" to "instruments of destruction," one LEP member put it. If industrial advance was reaching new heights, why did society seem close to "rebarbarization?"[42]

This troubling issue was a theme of Secretary of War Newton Baker's wartime addresses. The Germans, he argued, had become obsessed with "mechanical and industrial supremacy" and had lost their "moral balance." Modern war was total; it had "become a thing of industry and commerce and business," he once said. The old rules that had governed "civilized warfare," in which "restraints were put upon the combatants in the interest of the non-combatant population," had been "cast aside," and the world was left in "a new era of barbarous warfare," as the violation of neutral rights and the killing of civilians showed.[43]

So long as he could focus blame on the Germans, Baker held to the conviction that the war represented a clear choice between democracy

---

[42] R. G. Rhett, "American Business and the League to Enforce Peace," 97, in *Enforced Peace;* Oscar Strauss, "Preparedness against the Rebarbarization of the World," ibid., 28–37.
[43] Baker, *Frontiers of Freedom,* 32–33, 136.

and moral advance, on the one hand, and, on the other, "autocracy, a certain kind of mechanical efficiency, a certain absence of spiritual quality, a completely selfish and ambitious attitude by a favored class." One might even maintain that there were great benefits to total war, particularly as it functioned to bring Americans into a common cause. "The people of America have associated themselves in this great enterprise," he announced, and the nation was "knit together in spirit, more harmonious in its aspirations, more effective in its occupations. We are more of a nation to-day than we have been at any time in the whole hundred years and more of our glorious history."[44]

Baker failed to consider the possibility that this "unity" was artificial or that technological advances, not autocracy, made civilian casualties more likely. But to think through these possibilities would have compelled a thorough reconsideration of his sense of history. At the very least, he would have been obliged to accept the more sensible position that modernity could have more than one outcome. Blaming Germany alone for "rebarbarization," therefore, was more than just an exercise in propaganda, it was necessary to his faith in liberalism. It made it possible for him to assure audiences—and no doubt himself in the bargain—that "no return of the Darker Age is possible."[45]

The same, more generally, can be said of the importance of establishing the internationalist agenda. If "rebarbarization" actually was a threat, then it was all the more urgent to establish the World Court and the League of Nations. "Moral progress" demanded nothing less. Marburg counseled his colleagues against undue pessimism but had to admit that "progress in any direction is seldom without interruption. Moral progress is especially slow. But its general tendency is unmistakable." One had to have faith. If the war blighted the world with indications of human shortcomings, then its legacy could "be eradicated," as Baker concluded. "When the reconstruction of the world takes place; when a finer and better civilization has been worked out; when the human race puts its shoulder to the wheels of industry and begins to spread abroad the incalculably valuable discoveries of science, I can imagine that a new history of the world will be written."[46]

[44] Ibid., 145–46, 80.
[45] Ibid., 78.
[46] Theodore Marburg, *The League of Nations* (New York, 1919), 2: 94–95; Baker, *Frontiers of Freedom*, 60.

They expected this "new history" to begin when Woodrow Wilson traveled to Versailles. Who better to write it than the man who had written of America's own "new history," its development of union over provincialism, the maturation of the national authority, and the ascendance of the common good?

4

Wilson Meets Modernity

According to longstanding wisdom, the Versailles Peace Conference was the scene of a titanic diplomatic battle between historic antagonists. The "old diplomacy" fought the "new diplomacy"; the "forces of movement" battled "the forces of order"; the "realists" struggled against the "idealists"; imperialists working through secret alliances bullied their way against the struggling nations and Woodrow Wilson, who called for "open covenants openly arrived at," self-determination, and, above all, the organic union of democratic nations. To Ray Stannard Baker, head of the Press Bureau of the American Committee to Negotiate the Peace (ACNP), Versailles simply was the struggle between "the two Ideas."[1]

The burden of my argument obliges a different view, one that runs along the lines set out by Howard Elcock and Lloyd Ambrosius. As Elcock has pointed out, Versailles was the first genuinely modern diplomatic event, held as it was under the influence of modern mass politics. Pressure groups attended the conference and pushed their agendas, and the leading statesmen were beholden to their respective domestic constituencies in unprecedented ways. Ambrosius, writing more recently and in a different context, has argued that Wilson's vision of the postwar world

---

[1] For the general lines of inquiry see Ray Stannard Baker, *Woodrow Wilson and World Settlement* (Garden City, 1922), 3 vols.; Paul Birdsall, *Versailles Twenty Years After* (New York, 1941); Arno J. Mayer, *The Politics and Diplomacy of Peacemaking: Containment and Counterrevolution at Versailles, 1918-1919* (New York, 1967); and Klaus Schwabe, *Woodrow Wilson, Revolutionary Germany, and Peacemaking, 1918-1919* (Chapel Hill, 1985).

competed with the "pluralistic" world that was every bit as modern as Wilson's new world.[2]

I share these views. Though Wilson's postwar vision was new among diplomats, it was but one vision of the future and competed with at least three other very modern developments: organized, radical revolution and state building; mass politics played on an international level; and the emergence of nationalistic policies predicated on public support. None of these developments fit the idealist view of history. Radicals put revolution above all other causes, including Wilson's organic league. None of the alleged guardians of the old diplomacy fit the image of the Bismarckian statesman—not Georges Clemenceau, not Vittorio Orlando, not even the Polish reactionary, Roman Dmowski. Nor did they fit the image of the hardheaded realist fighting against Wilson the idealist, for they based their claims to territorial spoils on such vague grounds as "public sentiment" and rebuked Wilson not for being a naive idealist so much as for his dogmatic insistence on solving all questions according to logic and reason. Versailles is best seen not as the "old" against the "new," but rather as a momentous indication that the drift of modern politics was more toward fragmentation than the homogenous, liberal order that Wilson envisioned.

Wilson and Revolution Revisited

The best known example of Wilson's idealism bumping against competing forms of modern politics is, of course, his policy toward the Bolshevik revolution, the complicated details of which, so thoroughly reviewed by others, need not burden us here. For our purposes, there are two points to be gained from a brief examination of Wilson's policy toward the Bolsheviks. First, as Christopher Lasch and N. Gordon Levin pointed out long ago, Wilson, like many other American liberals, badly misread the nature of the Bolshevik Revolution as merely the extreme of a democratic movement against Russian autocracy.[3] Second, Wilson participated in the Allied intervention in Russia as a means of defending emerging nationalities.

[2] Howard Elcock, *Portrait of a Decision: The Council of Four and the Treaty of Versailles* (London, 1972); Ambrosius, *Wilson and the American Diplomatic Tradition*.

[3] Christopher Lasch, *American Liberals and the Russian Revolution* (New York, 1963); Levin, *Woodrow Wilson and World Politics*.

From the outset of the Russian revolution in 1917, Wilson presumed that democracy would emerge to supplant autocracy. He noted as much in the war address and in announcing the Fourteen Points went so far as to insist that the treatment accorded Russia was "the acid test" of Allied good will. He broached the possibility of opening "unofficial" relations with the Bolsheviks as early as January 1918, against the opposition of Secretary of State Robert Lansing.[4] No doubt Wilson hoped to counter Bolshevik diplomacy and dilute Lenin's increasing prestige within the European left. But he also believed that Bolshevism would expire naturally and that, meanwhile, Russian radicalism could be moderated best through diplomacy.

Russia was tricky business, though, for it was so close to anarchy that building a coherent policy was next to impossible. In January 1918, the Japanese already were preparing a unilateral intervention in Siberia. The British and French were aiding counterrevolutionaries even as they made their own overtures to the Bolsheviks. The British were making out a case for intervention on the grounds that it was necessary to reconstitute the eastern front. Wilson recognized that only the northern port of Archangel offered the slightest military rationale, since it lay near Murmansk and various military stores that the Germans still threatened. In March 1918, Wilson agreed to a small, symbolic American participation in the north.[5]

Wilson allowed himself to be coaxed into the much more important and ultimately more disastrous intervention in Siberia for different reasons. He feared that Japanese expansion in Siberia would upset the natural progress of events within Russia, and by June he had concluded that a joint American-Japanese intervention would allow him to limit the scope of the Japanese commitment, protect Russian integrity, and show his concern for "the sufferings of the ordinary man in Russia."[6] The formal American intervention of July 1918 was intended to help the famous "Czech Legion," a footloose group of Czechs seeking to reenter the war

[4] Betty Miller Unterberger, "Woodrow Wilson and the Russian Revolution," in Arthur Link, ed., *Woodrow Wilson and a Revolutionary World* (Chapel Hill, 1982), 48–49, 55–56; Fourteen Points Address, 8 January 1918, *PWW* 45: 435–39.

[5] George Kennan, *The Decision to Intervene* (Princeton 1958), 43–57; Unterberger, "Woodrow Wilson and the Russian Revolution," 58–63.

[6] Jean Jules Jusserand to Stephan Marie Pichon, 6 June 1918, *PWW* 48: 254; and 9 June 1918, 48: 274; Wm. Wiseman to Eric Drummond, 14 June 1918, 48: 315; House to WW, 21 June 1918, 48: 390–91; "Remarks to Mexican Editors," 7 June 1918, 48: 256–57; Peyton March to Newton Baker, with enclosure, 24 June 1918, 48: 418–21; and George Tom Molesworth Bridges to Lord Reading, 18 June 1918, 48: 353.

against the Germans. There was good reason to get the Czechs out, especially because they were causing substantial chaos by fighting Bolshevik authorities along the Trans-Siberian railway. It is necessary to appreciate that Wilson saw the Czech legion, not incorrectly, as a small part of the larger Czech nationalist movement, and to aid the Czech troops was to aid the larger movement against autocracy. Seen in this light, there was no contradiction between intervening to help the Czechs, on the one hand, and protecting the Russian Revolution on the other, because both were part of the same flowering of organic democracy, as far Wilson was concerned.

As Betty Miller Unterberger has argued, Wilson's Russian policies cannot be disassociated from his policy toward the Czechs. He initially had believed that Austria-Hungary in some form was necessary to long-term order and stability in Central Europe, but the decline of the Dual Monarchy, the constant lobbying of able Czechs such as Thomas Masaryk and Edvard Benes, the military dangers facing the Czech Legion, and finally the persuasion of Secretary of State Lansing, forced Wilson to reconsider his stand. Intervention on behalf of the Czech soldiers was linked inextricably to his decision, announced in late June, to extend formal recognition to Czechoslovakia. Stolid liberal revolutionaries, the Czechs would not be obnoxious to Russian sentiment, because, as Wilson wrote Lansing, "these people are the cousins of the Russians," and thus they might provide the basis for a police force to reorder the Trans-Siberian railway and forestall a wider Japanese intervention in the bargain.[7]

Through summer 1918, the situation in Russia only confirmed his idealist expectations, though that confirmation came from the Japanese rather than the Bolsheviks. Wilson believed that the Japanese were bent on traditional, self-interested expansion, and Japanese policy provided evidence in support of that view. By tacit agreement, the joint Japanese-American intervention in Siberia was limited in scope to 7000 troops each and in intent to aiding the Czechs in Vladivostok to return west and meet their fellow soldiers, all the while reassuring "the people of Russia" that the United States intended no political interference or compromise of Russian sovereignty. Because the administration neglected to secure a hard-and-fast agreement on limitations before approving the intervention, the Japanese decided that, while there were "no fundamental dif-

[7] Betty Miller Unterberger, *The United States, Revolutionary Russia, and the Rise of Czechoslovakia* (Chapel Hill, 1989), 226–31; WW to Lansing, with enclosure, 17 June 1918, *PWW* 48: 335–36; Lansing to WW, 23 June 1918, 48: 398.

ferences" between the nations, prudence dictated 12,000 to 14,000 troops. Even before the policy was announced, Wilson complained to Navy Secretary Josephus Daniels that the Japanese were "trying to alter the whole plan," and after several weeks, Lansing passed along reports that the Japanese were moving into Manchuria. His suspicions confirmed, Wilson cut the American commitment. He concluded that saving the Czechs on the interior was beyond the scope of American power, and he reduced the commitment in Murmansk.[8]

For Wilson, the imperialist nations behaved true to form, but the antiliberal character of the Bolshevik revolution mystified him. On the one hand, these revolutionaries proved every bit as committed to party as the most sordid ward boss. On the other, they had internationalized revolution, making appeals to legitimate aspirations across both artificial and organic boundaries. By fall 1918, when the war itself was at an end, Wilson went from tolerating the Bolsheviks to asking himself what allowed Bolshevism to spread, and he concluded that the problem lay with the sheer disorder that the war had wrought. Drawing partly from the arguments of William Bullitt, who insisted that "economic disorganization and famine are the parents of Bolshevism," Wilson continued to anticipate "a sober second thought" to Bolshevik excesses. "I am confident," he told Congress when he submitted the armistice terms, "that the nations that have learned the discipline of freedom and that have settled with self-possession to its ordered practice are now about to make conquest of the world by the sheer power of example and of friendly helpfulness." The "poison of bolshevism," he told the American delegation on its way to Paris, remained what it always had been: a reaction to czarist autocracy.[9]

Wilson faced a moment of truth when he began to understand that the Bolsheviks were not liberals and that they threatened liberalism throughout Central Europe. He met this ideological challenge by reasserting his firmest belief that the superiority of an ordered liberalism would outweigh Bolshevism's immediate allure for the rational "European people." As he continued to seek diplomatic solutions to the Russian crisis, he reiterated his appeals to the Russian people, assuring them of Allied

---

[8] "Draft of an Aide Memoire," 16 July 1918, *PWW* 48: 624–26; "Press Release," ca. 3 August 1918, *PWW* 49: 170–72; Lloyd George to Reading, 10 July 1918, *PWW* 48: 587–89; Balfour to Reading, 22 July 1918, *PWW* 49: 57–60; Reading to Balfour, 23 July 1918, 49: 67–68; WW-Lansing correspondence through August and September in *PWW* 51–53; Kennan, *Decision to Intervene*, 377–80.

[9] Bullitt to WW, 2 November 1918, *PWW* 51: 563–68; "An Address to Joint Session of Congress," 11 November 1918, *PWW* 53: 42; Bullitt Diary, 10 December 1918, 53: 352.

goodwill and beckoning them toward liberalism. Even if he admitted that the Bolsheviks were "poison," he weathered this particular crisis without a loss of faith.[10]

Mass Politics and the Peace

When Wilson faced the Bolsheviks, he confronted modern revolutionaries, committed to party at home and revolution in the world at large, neither of which accorded with his sense of decorous politics. Still there were many indications that the legitimate democratic aspirations that Lenin tapped were alive and well among people who fit the Wilsonian mold. Wilson never doubted the legitimacy of Polish hopes, and once he came to respect Benes and Masaryk, he could support Czech nationhood in good conscience. So too, once the destruction of Central European authority was complete, he accommodated himself to Yugoslavian aspirations. Wilson supported national aspirations when the people in question seemed to conform to, or have some promise of conforming to, his idea of the "organic" state and when the given issue was necessary to a restoration of political order and coherence. All other questions, he believed, could be left to the League of Nations.

He never set these two conditions down as guiding rules, to be sure, but they help to explain what seems like tremendous inconsistency, the cynical suspension of principle, or waffling compromise, depending on the observer's perspective. How else to explain why Wilson could extend the principle of self-determination to the Poles but not, say, to the Irish? How else to explain why Wilson respected China's national identity but refused the same to Egypt? How else to explain why he turned a deaf ear to requests for planks respecting African rights and yet demanded that the Poles and Rumanians agree to respect the rights of their Jewish populations?

Wilson's approach to the nationality problem at Versailles was rooted in his general understanding of self-conscious ethnicity as a form of group self-interest. In domestic politics, this view ensured his unpopularity among organized ethnic groups. During the 1912 run for the Democratic nomination he was forced to eat a steady diet of words from his popular histories that had condescendingly described recent immigrants

[10] Council of Ten Meeting, 16 January 1919, *PWW* 54: 99–102, 21 January 1919, 54: 183; and 22 January 1919, 54: 205–6. John M. Thompson, *Russia, Bolshevism, and the Versailles Peace* (Princeton, 1967), 109.

more or less as lower-class beasts. If Wilson never endorsed the idea, for-
warded in different ways by bigots and Progressives alike, that the war be
used to speed assimilation, to "heat up the melting pot," nonetheless his
characteristic opinion was that ethnic Americans should devote themselves to their adopted nation. "You cannot become thorough Americans
if you think of yourselves in groups," he declaimed to a group of immigrants. "America does not consist of groups. A man who thinks of himself as belonging to a particular national group in America has not yet
become an American."[11] As the war increased ethnic tensions, Wilson
increased his criticism of dual loyalties and vigorously condemned "every group or organization, political or otherwise, that has for its object
the advancement of the interest of a foreign power."[12]

Irish-Americans, particularly organized advocates of Irish independence, made antagonizing Wilson an art form, so frequently and intensely
did they grate on his nerves. Wilson was not an unctuous Anglophile, but
he did stereotype the Irish as sleazy ward politicians. He was predisposed
to be critical of the Irish, though it surprised even him that Irish-
Americans took part in the 1916 Easter Rebellion in Ireland. Because
Irish nationalists conspired with the Germans, Wilson could see nothing
here but sheer group self-interest, and ignoble, treasonous self-interest
at that.[13]

He did not see the Irish as an "organic" movement but as an interest
group, and on that basis he sought to keep the Irish question out of Versailles. Yet his diplomacy invited American advocates of home rule to see
in him the best hope for their cause. When the president reiterated his
strong support of a peace based on self-determination in a 1918 Fourth
of July address, Irish leaders read it as a direct reference to them. Privately, Wilson continued to argue that supporting independence would
amount to "an attempt to outline a policy for the British Government."
Thus Wilson put himself in the peculiar position of supporting a British

[11] Link, *Road to the White House*, 380–89; "An Address in Philadelphia to Newly Nat-
uralized Citizens," 10 May 1915, *PWW* 33: 148; also "Remarks to the Associated Press in
New York," 20 April 1915, 33: 37–41.
[12] Louis L. Gerson, *The Hyphenate in Recent American Politics and Diplomacy*
(Lawrence, Kans., 1964), 64–67.
[13] Ibid., 67–68; Charles C. Tansill, *America and the Fight for Irish Freedom* (New
York, 1957), chap. 6. For general treatments of Wilson, the war, and the Irish question see
John B. Duff, "The Versailles Treaty and the Irish-Americans," *Journal of American His-
tory* 55 (December 1968): 582–98; and Joseph P. O'Grady, "Irish-Americans, Woodrow
Wilson, and Self-Determination," *Records of the American Catholic Historical Society* 74
(1963): 159–73.

policy that ignored basic Irish demands, clamped down on dissent, and brought Ireland to the brink of civil war.[14]

Hoping to keep what he considered a domestic British issue—and by extension, mass politics—out of Paris, Wilson inadvertently left the Irish to internationalize the home-rule issue and to hope that the peace conference might act on their behalf. By Wilson's own declaration, the conference was to see to the self-determination of subject people, which the Irish believed themselves to be. Because they were geographically irrelevant to the central military equation, however, Irish nationalists could only clamor for attention and hope self-determination actually meant something. That lone option, in turn, meant employing strategies of organized pressure, which included pushing the U.S. House Foreign Affairs Committee to consider a resolution calling for home rule.[15]

The Irish issue came to a head for Wilson when, upon returning to the states after the first round of talks, he spurned requests to see an Irish-American delegation. His secretary, Joseph Tumulty, urged hum to receive the delegation in New York after a speech at the Met. An Irishman himself, Tumulty feared that a fight with the Irish would have both domestic and diplomatic consequences, and other members of the admin-

[14] Tansill, *America and the Fight for Irish Freedom,* 268–69; WW to Sen. James D. Phelan, 1 July 1918, *PWW* 48: 471–72; Kenneth O. Morgan, *Consensus and Unity: The Lloyd George Coalition Government, 1918–1922* (Oxford, 1979), 35–43, 125–26; and *The Age of Lloyd George* (New York, 1971), 72–76.
There is real irony in Wilson's predicament. David Lloyd George, after all, was to mass politics what Lenin was to modern revolution. Indeed if Lloyd George were an American politician, he probably would have run as far afoul of Wilson's political ideal as the Irish had. He was, as Bentley Gilbert has recently described him, essentially a political salesman, whose principles were flexible to say the least. As Gilbert writes, Lloyd George "would not be a good man to go tiger hunting with, not for lack of pluck, of which he had plenty, but because, as several of his contemporaries observed, there was always the danger that he might take the side of the tiger." John Maynard Keynes once described him as a "Welsh witch" who "was rooted in nothing ... void and without content." Wilson eventually came to see these qualities during the final crisis of the conference, when Lloyd George appealed in June for a thoroughgoing revision of the treaty. The man "had no principle whatever of his own," Ray Stannard Baker reported Wilson as saying. "He reacted according to the advice of the last person who talked with him: expediency is his guiding star." Bentley Brinkerhoff Gilbert, *David Lloyd George, A Political Life: The Architect of Change, 1863–1912* (Columbus, 1987), 16; Keynes quoted in Elcock, *Portrait of a Decision,* 2; also see Morgan, *The Age of Lloyd George,* chap. 1; Baker Diary, 9 June 1919, *PWW* 60: 329.
[15] Wilson let the matter run its course, probably on the advice of State Department Counsel, Frank Polk, who pointed out that the issue had become essentially partisan, with both sides racing "to get the Irish vote." WW to Lansing, 13 February 1919, *PWW* 55: 149; Lansing to WW, 10 February 1919, 55: 547–48.

istration reenforced Tumulty's warning.[16] He did meet with a delegation, but only after Judge Daniel Cohalan, perhaps the foremost American proponent of Irish independence and a traitor in Wilson's opinion, withdrew. Even without Cohalan he "had hard work keeping my temper," as he later told Ray Stannard Baker.[17]

Wilson was rarely at his most reasonable when it came to the Irish question, though his long-term solution, a future settlement through the League of Nations, was not an unsound strategy for the conference, which surely would have been bogged down even more than it was had the Irish found a place on the agenda. If the League were allowed to function in the manner that Wilson had in mind, then justice would be done the Irish in time. Wilson was appalled to hear the Irish threatening to fight against the League at home unless their cause were taken up at Paris. He wanted to tell them "to go to hell," David Hunter Miller, an American lawyer at work on the covenant wrote, "but he realized that . . . it would not be the act of wisdom or the act of a statesman."[18] When a delegation of prominent Irish-Americans visiting Ireland injudiciously proclaimed American support for independence, Wilson instructed Lansing to inform them that their behavior had given the "deepest offense." Privately he told Ray Stannard Baker that the Irish "can see nothing but their own small interest."[19]

The administration's policy continued to oscillate between domestic considerations and diplomatic ones. Tumulty kept the issue before Wilson and monitored Irish lobbying in the Senate; he also warned Wilson not to tie himself to Lloyd George. The British prime minister continued to press Wilson for support, suggesting privately that his coalition could well fall if the Irish gained a hearing in Paris.[20]

Wilson met his obligations to the English and addressed his domestic political predicament by receiving the Irish-Americans in Paris. It was an important meeting, for the Irish-Americans of course, but also because Wilson made clear his position for the first and only time. The delega-

---

[16] Tansill, *America and the Fight For Irish Freedom*, 302–3; Tumulty to WW, 1 March 1919, *PWW* 55: 348; Creel to WW 1 March 1919, 55: 363–64.

[17] News Report, 4 March 1919, *PWW* 55: 421–22; Grayson Diary, 4 March 1919, 55: 411–12; and Baker Diary, 8 March 1919, 55: 463.

[18] Miller Diary, *PWW* 56:79–80.

[19] Creel to WW, 31 March 1919, *PWW* 56: 486; Grayson Diary, 17 April 1919, *PWW* 57: 426; WW to Lansing, with enclosure, 22 May 1919, *PWW* 59: 394–95; Lansing to WW, with enclosure, 26 May 1919, 59: 513–14; Baker Diary, 29 May 1919, 59: 604; Tansill, *Fight for Irish Freedom*, 312–15.

[20] Tumulty to Grayson, 7 June 1919, *PWW* 60: 291; WW to Tumulty, 8 June 1919, 60: 298; Tumulty to WW, 9 June 1919, 60: 331–32; Grayson Diary, 9 June 1919, 60: 304.

tion's leader, Frank Walsh, appealed for Wilson's help by reading from the president's own addresses. Wilson responded that he never referred to Ireland when he spoke about immanent self-determination: "You must have known . . . that what I said . . . referred distinctly and decidedly to the problems affecting the nations that were involved in the war, and especially the smaller nations that had been the victims of the Central Powers." The conference had time to decide only war-related problems, especially those created by the destruction of Austria-Hungary. The fact was, he maintained, many deserving people would not realize self-determination out of the treaty.[21]

Wilson could not have given a more succinct statement of his position at Versailles. As a diplomatic strategy, it made sense. To hold off all issues that were not directly involved with the urgent tasks of restoring order was a way to limit the scope of the conference. Particularly in the case of the Irish, Wilson's strategy played to the domestic political interests of the one ally he most needed, Lloyd George. As a long-term means for achieving the organic world order, it left something to be desired. Versailles was not just a conference for restoring order, but for establishing a more just world, and Wilson's own speeches and positions over two years, as Walsh rightly pointed out, certainly had created the impression that he intended as much.

It is possible to explore Wilson's view of subject peoples by looking beyond the Irish question into the more obscure issue of the League's relation to minority rights. Clearly he believed that the rights of colonial subjects and the realization of justice were bound up with the establishment of the League and perhaps would constitute the most important long-term business of the League. Wilson dabbled with a means for confirming the League's responsibilities here from the outset. In the so-called First Paris Draft of the League covenant, he included a provision by which member states agreed "to accord to all racial or national minorities . . . exactly the same treatment and security, both in law and in fact, that is accorded the racial or national majority of their people." Exactly what Wilson had in mind with this commendable article is not clear, but there were probably two considerations. Wilson first intended to deal with Eastern Europe. Because the borders of the "new states" (those nations created at the conference) would be so difficult to draw, it was inevitable that dissatisfied populations, racial, and national minor-

[21] Grayson Diary, 60: 383–87; Tansill, *Fight for Irish Freedom,* 319; and Duff, "The Versailles Treaty and the Irish-Americans," 595.

ities would emerge.[22] He also had in mind the protection of European Jews, who as early as October 1918 came to Wilson's attention when Colonel House broached the issue of protecting the Jews in an independent Poland. "If Posen and Silesia go to Poland," House argued, "rigid protection must be afforded minorities of Germans and Jews living there, as well as in other parts of the Polish state." Warnings from the American Jewish Committee that Jews faced pogroms throughout Eastern and Central Europe reenforced House's view, and the committee asked Wilson for a public pronouncement regarding the issue on the eve of Versailles. The president declined to commit himself in public but reassured Louis Marshall, his principal contact with Jewish-Americans, that he would press the issue at Paris.[23]

The article was dropped from the covenant after a number of other nations raised objections. Wilson told Ray Stannard Baker that the Poles, who had minorities to whom they did not care to grant equality, and, even more the Australians, who worried that the clause would interfere with their immigration restrictions, had opposed it. But so too the English objected, and David Hunter Miller, the American counsel on the drafting committee, believed that the article was impractical.[24]

Wilson did not exactly put up a struggle. Evidently he decided that "publicity upon such an acute issue as this would do more harm than good." According to Dr. Cary Grayson, the Americans feared that the article would allow Asians to press for free immigration into the United States and thus would constitute League interference in domestic matters. Though they lobbied on the issue with great caution and settled for an innocuous call for member states to accord equal treatment and rights without racial distinction "so soon and as far as practicable," the Japanese were the article's firmest supporters, and Wilson was apt to read sinister designs in their advocacy. Beyond that consideration, if the League could interfere with the Australians or with immigration matters, it also could call the United States to account for its treatment of African-

[22] See Article VI of the supplementary agreements in the Wilson draft, 8 January 1919, *PWW* 53: 686. For a brief discussion of the issue, see Ivo J. Lederer, *Yugoslavia at the Paris Peace Conference: A Study in Frontiermaking* (New Haven, 1963), 239–40.

[23] House to WW, 29 October 1918, *PWW* 51: 504; WW to Tumulty, 13 November 1918, *PWW* 53: 67; Marshall to WW, 14 November 1918 and 16 November 1918, 53: 79–80, 104–5; WW to Marshall, 20 November 1918, 53: 141.

[24] Baker Diary, 8 March 1919; David Hunter Miller, *The Drafting of the Covenant* (New York, 1928), 2: 91. See also John Philip Posey, "David Hunter Miller and the Far Eastern Question at the Paris Peace Conference, 1919," *Southern Quarterly* 7 (1969): 382–84.

Americans.[25] Whatever his real motives, Wilson cast the issue in terms of his idealist conception of the League. "My own interest," he explained, "is to quiet discussion that raises national differences and racial prejudices. I would wish them . . . to be forced as much as possible into the background." Prejudices, he held, should be permitted "no part in the discussions connected with the establishment of this League."[26] Particularly within the League, he could not support an open invitation to political fragmentation.

Dropping the race article allowed Wilson to withdraw what he no doubt saw as a very troublesome matter. In so doing, he addressed the various allied complaints, held off the Japanese, and eliminated a potential source of trouble. He discovered, moreover, that it was possible to address the specific problem of Eastern European Jews and other national minorities in the new states by inserting racial justice clauses into the treaty that would apply only to the new states, especially Poland, rather than in the League covenant where they applied to everyone. When including provisions on the new states in the treaty with Germany seemed impractical, the powers decided to develop separate treaties, which isolated the issue even more.[27]

Why should Wilson have cared about the Jews? To be sure, the Jews were another racial or ethnic group, but one that had none of the specific liabilities of the Irish. Jewish-Americans were an organized interest at home, but their quest was for assimilation. The international Jewish population endured repression as the Irish had; unlike the Irish, that repression was not a function of a single national policy and could not be construed merely as a matter of "domestic" politics. Unlike the Irish, as Wilson noted, European Jews did not have a country, and their appeals for protection therefore were not soiled with a "narrow" national self-interest. The Jewish issue did not have the potential for creating general problems, as did the race clause. Neither the United States nor Great Britain could be accused of repression, and thus protection for the Jews meant protection for a specific population in Eastern Europe. Not only was the issue isolated, it also met an important standard: it promoted order in the region of upheaval.

[25] Grayson Diary, 11 April 1919, *PWW* 57: 239–40; Miller, *My Diary at the Conference of Paris* 1: 99–100.
[26] "Remarks upon the Clause for Racial Equality," 11 April 1919, *PWW* 57: 268–69.
[27] See John Phillip Posey, "David Hunter Miller and the Polish Minorities Treaty, 1919," *Southern Quarterly* 8 (1970): 163–76.

The protection afforded to Eastern European Jews illuminates Wilson's standards of justice at Paris: the group in question was subjected to repression; it had appealed for relief through moderate means that smacked of no self-interest; and solving the issue promised to promote order in the area of direct concern to the conference. Protecting them was in effect a means of international assimilation. He explained that, while the conference was eager to redress Jewish grievances—the "result of a long persecution," he said—he was also eager to frame articles that did not concede to Jewish demands for some "sort of autonomy for the national minorities." "Remember that, when the Jews were outside the law in England, they acted as people outside the law. Our wish is to bring them back everywhere under the terms of the law of the land."[28]

The new states raised numerous objections, some of which were quite legitimate. They rightly pointed out that the powers had not embraced a race clause; they saw through Wilson's strategy, in other words. They also objected to undue interference in their domestic politics, an objection that defied logical rebuttal. Beneath these sound objections lurked the bitter anti-Semitism of men such as Roman Dmowski, then jockeying against Jan Paderewski for leadership in the new Poland.[29]

Wilson answered these objections, raised during the debate over the Austrian treaty in late May, with illogical eloquence in an address that was reputed to have been among his most vigorous at Paris. The powers were doing their best to be just, he pleaded, but under their actions "lies this fundamentally important fact that, when the decisions are made, the Allies and Associated Powers guarantee to maintain them." By rights, the great powers should insist that the settlements eliminate all of the foreseeable sources of conflict and disorder, and "nothing, I venture to say, is more likely to disturb the peace of the world than the treatment which in certain circumstances is to be meted out to minorities."[30]

It was an absurd position, since it amounted to a fundamental limitation on self-determination and a basic admission that the powers were the powers. When he related the speech to Ray Stannard Baker, the journalist quickly caught its meaning. "Again it appears that the world in future is not to be governed by a democratic society of equal nations," he

[28] Council of Four Meeting, 1 May 1919, *PWW* 58: 284–93.
[29] See Lederer, *Yugoslavia at the Paris Peace Conference*, 239–40; *Foreign Relations of the United States, Paris Peace Conference*, 3: 394–410; and Stephan Bonsal, *Suitors and Supplicants: The Little Nations at Versailles* (New York, 1946), 123–25.
[30] Minutes of a Plenary Session of the Inter-Allied Conference on the Preliminaries of the Peace, 31 May 1919, *PWW* 59: 628–29.

wrote, "but dominated by a powerful group of great powers with benev-
olent intentions!" Wilson was under no illusions. He too understood the
implications of his position. All he could do was retreat to an old and
tested strategy of adopting meaningless distinctions. Much as if he were
speaking about "good trusts" and "bad trusts," he attempted to convince the new states representatives that the policy was not "the intervention of those who would interfere, but the action of those who would
help. I beg that our friends will take that view of it, because I see no escape from that view of it."[31]

Wilson had boxed himself in. He had no taste for championing minority rights. However much basic sympathy he had for the Jews, his real
interest in pursuing the protection clause was that the stability of the new
states seemed to depend on eliminating racial strife. In this case, his diplomatic strategy left him on the side of immediate justice. But it was
shaky ground on which he could not stand confidently, for according to
his reasoning, he could enjoy friendly relations with organized groups today, only to suffer their opposition when interests changed and alliances
shifted. Perhaps this thought was in his mind when a grateful Louis Marshall spoke of how "the oppressed minorities in the world—religious or
political—would be for the League." Wilson responded: "All the minorities except the Irish."[32]

"Public Sentiment" and Modern Nationalism

In her epochal work on totalitarianism, Hannah Arendt argued that
the moral catastrophes of modern politics, embodied in Nazism and
Stalinism, were indirect products of late nineteenth-century imperialism.
As European capitalists grew wealthier from industrial investment, she
argued, they became an increasingly powerful political force in each major nation and forged national polices of imperialism in order to extend
their need for capital expansion. Nations themselves became wealthier in
the process, but expansion eroded the traditional attachments to the
nation-state. When "expansion gave nationalism a new lease on life, and
was therefore accepted as an instrument of national politics," Arendt
wrote, political order came to depend on emotional appeals and a new
alliance between the "mob and capital." This process created a general

[31] Ibid.; Baker Diary, 31 May 1919, *PWW* 59: 646.
[32] Baker Diary, 29 May 1919, 59: 604.

political aimlessness by destroying traditional associations and gave rise to vast populations of people without public identities who were easily drawn into totalitarian movements organized around virulent ideologies.[33]

Her view could not nave been more at odds with the Wilsonian interpretation of Versailles, which blamed reactionary provincialism for the failure of the League and, by extension, for the rise of Nazism. If one looks at the manner in which the powers at Versailles went about making their respective claims, one can hardly resist taking Arendt's side. Allied leaders claimed that "public sentiment" demanded territorial gains as compensation for wartime losses and in so doing spawned one of the great undercurrents of Versailles, ironic and generally unappreciated: Wilson, the defender of the enlightened "common people," found himself dueling with statesmen who got their way by scorning "cold reason" and whipping up nationalist emotions among those very people.

Wilson failed to appreciate this undercurrent, which ran strongly during two of the most important debates of the conference, those concerning the French demands and the Italian crisis. In March, the French began to press their demands for extensive reparations from Germany including control of Saar basin coal, German disarmament, and control of a buffer state in the Rhineland. Along with Lloyd George, Wilson wanted a moderate settlement that would discourage Bolshevism in Germany, and thus he objected to the French claims. The French, moreover, were irritatingly and intentionally evasive—negotiating with them was "like pressing your finger into an indiarubber ball. You tried to make an impression but as soon as you moved your finger the ball was as round as ever." Wilson particularly objected to French demands for outright control of the Saar, which were based on claims so old that the Italian prime minister, Vittorio Orlando, quipped that "it would be rather unfair to go back too many hundred years on a proposal of this kind, ... inasmuch as there was a time when England was a part of the Roman Empire." Wilson wanted to compensate France and still ensure the integrity of the Saar. "Both can be done," he insisted, "without annexation and without violation of our principles."[34]

[33] Hannah Arendt, *The Origins of Totalitarianism* (New York, 1973), 154–55.
[34] Grayson Diary, 25 March 1919, *PWW* 56: 247; Diary of Lord Robert Cecil, 18 March 1919, 56: 81; Council of Four Meeting, 27 March 1919 56: 323–24; Memorandum, 28 March 1919, 56: 371; Mantoux's Notes from the Council of Four, 28 March 1919, 56: 360–71.

Clemenceau answered with a remarkable discourse for someone allegedly dedicated to the old diplomacy, based as his appeals were on French popular opinion. To Clemenceau, Wilson was calling for policy based on "cold reason" and "mathematical justice" without due attention to "sentiment." It was, of course, no answer at all to Wilson's position; Clemenceau did nothing more than imply that French demands should be granted because the French had been wronged. Reason against sentiment: it was an explosive match, since Clemenceau threatened not to sign the treaty.[35]

Never one to be outperformed, Wilson responded with threats of his own. He told Ray Stannard Baker that he intended to "fight to the end," and he recalled his transport ship in order to create the impression that the conference was on the verge of collapse.[36] To leave, of course, would have been to give the whole great business to the imperialists, something Wilson could not allow. Especially when the Italians launched their effort to take control of the city of Fiume, a compromise with France, which left the Saar under an Allied occupation, became the lesser of two evils.[37]

During the Italian crisis, Wilson competed directly with the Orlando government for the support of the Italian people and lost. This was the only time he resorted to the diplomacy of mass politics, even though his popularity in Europe constituted a potentially important tool.

The essentials of the Italian question were these: the Orlando government insisted on gaining the territories that had been promised in the Treaty of London, which included readjustments on her northern and eastern borders; in addition, the Italians sought to extend control far along the eastern coast of the Adriatic sea, including the port of Fiume. They based their claims on national security, but their specific case for Fiume rested on what they considered the "Italian" character of the city. With some backing from Clemenceau and Lloyd George, Wilson objected to the Italian claims on several grounds. First, having been no party to the Treaty of London, he was not committed to its provisions, though he agreed that Italian security merited adjustments in the

---

[35] Grayson, Diary, 28 March 1919, *PWW* 56: 347; House Diary, 28 March 1919, 56: 349.
[36] Baker Diary, 7 April 1919, *PWW* 57: 69.
[37] Mantoux's notes of a Council of Four Meeting, 9 April 1919, *PWW* 57: 161; House Diary, 14 April 1919, 57: 334–35; Elcock, *Portrait of a Decision*, 186–88.

north.[38] The conditions under which the Treaty of London had been conceived, moreover, had changed drastically, and Italian security no longer required protection against Austria-Hungary. Second, Wilson insisted that Fiume was essential to the economic health of the new Yugoslav state and to Central Europe generally. Placing Fiume in the proper hands was essential to sustaining order in that vital region. Finally, Wilson argued that even if many residents were Italian, the surrounding countryside most definitely was Slav. The Italian claims ran against both expediency and principle, and therefore Wilson resisted them.[39]

The Italian claims were so outlandish that Wilson presumed that turning the light of reason on them quickly would leave them dashed. The Italian position was not founded upon reason or logic, as both Lloyd George and Clemenceau pointed out, but on the thoroughly unreasonable view that the Treaty of London should be applied in the north but not around Fiume. Both the French and English rested their positions on the treaty, essentially a moderate position that met their obligations to Italy yet supported Wilson on Fiume. The Allies worried about division within the Council of Four and tried compromise, only to find Orlando obdurate and Sidney Sonnino worse. "After having made concessions right and left to legitimate interests," Sonnino quipped, "[America] wants to recover her virginity at our expense by invoking the purity of principles. How could we accept that?" Certainly not, he insisted, by mustering up faith in the League, a prospect that Sonnino mocked: "So let [the league] go, if it can, and put Russia in order! Let it settle Balkan affairs! He can't change human nature that way."[40]

The Italians may have been committed to the "old diplomacy" in pushing for expansive claims, but Orlando and Sonnino were politically desperate men, statesmen who, far from enjoying that great distance from popular control that the old diplomacy rested on, were quite at the mercy of the mob. Their constant appeals to Italian popular opinion

[38] See Sterling J. Kernek, "Woodrow Wilson and National Self-Determination along Italy's Frontier: A Study in the Manipulation of Principles in the Pursuit of Political Interests," *Proceedings of the American Philosophical Society* 126 (1982): 243–300.

[39] For Wilson's initial positions see WW to Orlando, 13 January 1919, *PWW* 54: 50–51 and Council of Four Meeting, 3 April 1919, *PWW* 56: 562–65. He summed his views up in "A Memorandum Concerning the Question of Italian Claims on the Adriatic," 14 April 1919, *PWW* 57: 343–45. For two good general descriptions of the Italian crisis see Elcock, *Portrait of a Decision*, chap. 10 and Lederer, *Yugoslavia at the Paris Peace Conference*, chap. 7.

[40] Council of Four, 19 April 1919, *PWW* 57: 489–92; Mantoux's Notes of a British-French-Italian Meeting, 21 April 1919, 57: 538; Baker, *Wilson and World Settlement*, 2: 156–60.

made convenient diplomatic tools, but they were under genuine pressure at home. Much as Clemenceau had based French claims for the Rhineland on "sentiment" against "cold reason," the Italians warned, as Orlando put it, "that if Fiume is not granted to Italy there will be among the Italian people a reaction of protest and of hatred so violent that . . . [it] would be extremely fatal just as much to the interests of Italy as to the peace of the world." Sonnino warned that the Italian people had suffered so badly from the war that nothing less than complete satisfaction would mollify them. No doubt the Italian government was doing its part to inflame its constituents, but such manipulation—perhaps the flip side of fear—itself demonstrated the government's attention to public opinion. The American ambassador to Rome, Thomas Nelson Page, sent along his own warnings about the depth of public sentiment of the Fiume issue.[41]

Almost as if to confirm that the fundamental decisions rested with the Italian public, Wilson appealed over the heads of the government. The statement itself was typical Wilson, its tone, as Ivo Lederer aptly put it, "one of explanation, not recrimination." He affirmed his trust in Italy and the ties "in blood" between the two nations; otherwise, the declaration simply asked Italians to recognize and live by the principles of the peace. Wilson believed that reason could win over Italian public opinion. "Those who knew Italian public opinion well," he told Lloyd George and Clemenceau, "thought that this would for the moment inflame Italian public opinion," but gradually Italians would appreciate that it was in their interests to cooperate with the United States and "opinion would probably change." It was a complacent, even cocky move, and Lloyd George, fearing that Orlando and Sonnino would fall, warned that the Allies might find themselves dealing with a new government under hardliner Giovanni Giolitti. When Wilson argued that his declaration would "clear the air," Lloyd George warned that "poor Europe is like a land sown with grenades; if you step on it, everything blows up."[42]

Ever the modern politician, the English prime minister had a better feel for public opinion than his American counterpart did. Where Wilson anticipated a gradual public reasonableness only sharp, pro-expansionist nationalism grew. Wilson was correct enough about the immediately inflammatory response that his message provoked; Page reported back to

---

[41] Council of Four Meeting, 20 April 1919, *PWW* 57: 514; British-French-Italian Meeting, 538; Page to House, 17 April 1919, 57: 434–36.

[42] Statement on the Adriatic Question, 23 April 1919, *PWW* 58: 5–8; Council of Four Meeting, 22 April 1919, *PWW* 57: 610–13; Lederer, *Yugoslavia at the Paris Peace Conference*, 200–201.

the American mission on the "intense anger" that the Italian press displayed and the threats to American nationals. No gradual reasonableness appeared, and whether or not the reaction was worse than Wilson had expected is beside the point. It is more important that the message allowed Orlando to return home to a hero's welcome instead of political death. Wilson misplayed his hand and solidified his opponent's position, mostly because he misread the depth of nationalistic attachment to compensation for Italy; he had fallen prey to what Ray Stannard Baker called the "slump in idealism." Wilson's manifesto of ringing principles did not hearten even the Yugoslavs, since they recognized that such public diplomacy came in lieu of signed agreements.[43]

The Italian crisis remained unresolved. Though Wilson stuck to his principles, he could not boast of success. Ultimately Fiume came to the Italians in the Treaty of Rapallo. There was another failure. Wilson's diplomatic trump card was supposed to be public opinion, the enlightened reason of the "common man." The Italian crisis marked Wilson's only serious attempt to use that weapon, and it failed miserably. The Italian public spurned him and proceeded to prove that Orlando's fears of public opinion were well founded, since his government fell at the end of June.[44] If public appeals and responsiveness to the "common man" made up the "new diplomacy," Wilson was hardly its foremost practitioner.

Reasserting the Faith

In spite of the vast complications that blocked him, Wilson reaffirmed his faith in the future by seeing the conference as a transition to the "new age." Given the very real failure of Versailles, this view was necessary for his own peace of mind. His performance offers tangible evidence that he believed that the new age was exactly as he had described it: an organic world in the making, and therefore one not yet formed. His vision of the treaty as a transitional vehicle to the new age explains his determination to order Central and Eastern Europe. It explains why he saw his com-

---

[43] Page telegrams to American Mission, 24 April 1919, *PWW* 58: 91–93, 25 April 1919, 58: 143–44; Baker, *Wilson and World Settlement*, 168; Charles Seymour, *Letters from the Paris Peace Conference*, ed. Harold B. Whiteman, Jr. (New Haven, 1965), 209–10.

[44] Elcock, *Portrait of a Decision*, 287–88; Lederer, *Yugoslavia at the Paris Peace Conference*, 234, 249–55, chap. 10.

promises not as portents of modern political dislocations but as short-term adjustments that were sure to yield to the development of world order.

This sense of transition was important to sustaining Wilson's faith in the future in regards to the Japanese claims on Shantung. By the standards that Wilson himself had set for judging the immediate issues at Versailles, he should have fought the Japanese claims to the German concessions in China. According to Ray Stannard Baker, the issue vexed Wilson more than any that he faced at Paris. The dispute revolved around a former German colony and therefore required some immediate redress. Here was a case in which the German colony could be remanded over to an emerging state, China—one, furthermore, toward which Wilson and the American mission generally had great sympathy—and self-determination and the peace settlement could be served at once. Shantung was not just of economic importance to China, he argued, but had religious and cultural importance as well. His sympathies lay with China, "and we must not forget," he added with a point that seemed to grow in his mind, "that, in the future, the greatest dangers for the world can arise in the Pacific." To the Japanese, Wilson counseled disinterestedness; principle, he explained, would have to outweigh national interest in the peace settlement, and to show equal good faith, Wilson suggested that the western powers renounce their spheres of influence in China.[45]

Over the course of several weeks in April, Wilson's position unraveled. He understood that Japanese "honor" was a stake, though that impressed him about as much as Clemenceau's appeal to French "sentiment." The hard realities of the issue pressed far more firmly on him. It was a peripheral area; the Japanese were strong there and to oust them would have been inadvisable; and the Allies had already promised to support their claims. Wilson had little leverage to bargain with. Doubtlessly the general atmosphere of the conference, still tense over the Italian claims, encouraged Wilson to compromise, and as a diplomat, he also knew the Japanese had conceded the race-clause issue and would expect compensation.[46]

---

[45] Baker, *Wilson and World Settlement* 2: 223; Posey, "David Hunter Miller and the Far Eastern Question at the Paris Peace Conference, 1919," 374–75; Meetings of the Council of Four, 15 April 1919 and 18 April 1919, *PWW* 57: 358, 452–54.

[46] See Lansing to Polk, 26 February 1919, *PWW* 55: 293–94; Baker, *Wilson and World Settlement* 2: 243–44; and Arthur Link, *The Struggle for Neutrality* (Princeton, 1960), 269–73.

Painted into this corner, Wilson called on the Chinese to recognize that their best "salvation" lay in "uniting in reality with other nations" in the League. Their salvation, in other words, lay in the future, and the future only could be assured through a general world settlement. China's demands may have been just, but Wilson had begun to worry that the Japanese would join the Italians and leave. The Shantung question threatened to undo the conference, compromise the future of the League, create a "chasm between the East and the West," and engender conflict in a troubled and dangerous area. Out of this the Chinese would gain nothing. Through a curious logic, Wilson came to argue that the Chinese threatened to destroy a principled settlement by asking that the basic principles of the settlement be applied.[47]

No wonder Wilson agonized over the issue. "He is at Gethsemane," Baker mused. Indeed there was something about the Shantung issue that included a hint of desperation. Ultimately, Shantung was ceded to the Japanese, though Wilson extracted a Japanese promise to re-cede sovereignty to China at some later date, a renunciation, he claimed, which would "contribute to the peace of the world" and demonstrate that a dignified Japan was willing to bow "before the common ideal of civilized nations." The whole agreement hinged on the hope that the Japanese would embrace Wilsonian ideals somewhere in the future, but Lansing was unable to tie the Japanese down to a timetable for returning sovereignty to China, and a crucial component of the agreement was left unresolved, much as with the size of the Siberian intervention.[48] Baker composed a long, bitter memo on the decision; meanwhile, the American delegation erupted, from Lansing, who suggested that the whole conference be broken up, to the many lower-level members who walked out in protest.[49]

As for Wilson, the Shantung provisions represented a true test, precisely because he had thrust his principles into the crisis as solutions in and of themselves. His sympathies were with the Chinese, but if the Japanese left the conference at that juncture, the whole elaborate structure could collapse. Other nations might even return home and resume arms. He was damned anyway he moved, and he quite understood Chinese bit-

[47] Meeting of the Council of Four, 22 April 1919, *PWW* 57: 622–25. For Lansing's position see Edward Thomas Williams Memorandum, 26 April 1919, *PWW* 58: 165–67.

[48] Balfour Memorandum, 27 April 1919, *PWW* 58: 175–76; Meetings of the Council of Four, 28 April 1919 and 29 April 1919, 58: 178–83, 216–27; WW to Tumulty, 30 April 1919, 58: 272–73.

[49] Williams Memo, 166; House to WW, 29 April 1919, *PWW* 58: 228; Ray Stannard Baker Memo, 29 April 1919, 58: 230–32; Baker Diary, 1 May 1919, 58: 327–38.

terness. All he could do was invest hope in the League and in the future; to do otherwise was to encourage disorder and war. No doubt Baker described the entire debacle best, though he did not appreciate just how accurate his comments were. "The League of Nations," he asserted, perhaps in order to buck up his own flagging hope, "is a matter of *faith:* and the President is first of all a *man of faith*. He believes in the L[eague] of N[ations] . . . , *sees* it, *grasps* it, *feels* it, with the mighty tenacity of a great faith."[50]

No doubt Baker's "man of faith" should be taken as the correct view of Wilson throughout the conference. One has to wonder just where the prophets of the liberal future were to come from after Versailles. When neither the masses that once welcomed Wilson to Europe nor the leading statesmen of the great powers were demonstrating much dependable idealism, it was left to Wilson's American followers, along with a scattering of others, to sustain idealism in an increasingly fragmented world.

[50] Baker Diary, 30 April 1919, *PWW* 58: 270.

5

Barbarians at the Gate

Wilson's debacle at Versailles had an obvious impact on liberal idealists, for, at the very least, the peace conference demonstrated that the "principles of union" were not quite so close to fulfillment as they had believed. The treaty fight at home shook them more. Never in their worst nightmares did they anticipate that their own people, supposedly models of internationalism, would balk at the League of Nations, no matter what the deficiencies of the treaty or the behavior of an ill and embittered President. Disillusionment nonetheless took the better part of the decade to set in. The Versailles Treaty created the League of Nations, which in turn quickly created the International Court of Arbitration, and thus the two main planks of the internationalist agenda were realized. While grand hopes did get the best of Wilsonians during the war, their consistent counsel for patience allowed them to absorb the shock of 1919 and still believe that history was on their side. During the 1920s, Wilsonians became a more coherent group, enlivened by a generation of younger liberals, second-generation internationalists, who had little experience with and less taste for the internal conflicts of the prewar period. Far from receding, the faith in interdependence became synonymous with a liberal view of things. To question the value of interdependence, to question the inevitability of internationalism, to question the monopoly that liberal idealism had on the future, was in effect to be a political reactionary. It took a decade for them to see that, by this definition, the barbarians were everywhere.

Wilsonianism and Party Politics in the 1920s

In the immediate aftermath of the war, American internationalists split into partisan camps. Democrats and Republicans were at odds beginning with the famous Senate fight over the treaty. Many Republicans believed that they could push an internationalist agenda on the Harding administration after 1920 and that, therefore, they could work for party and cause at the same time. Republican internationalists were in the embarrassing position of having been party, quite literally, to the treaty's demise, and they had to undo the damage. Moving as if the treaty battle were but a minor episode, Elihu Root pushed for a plank at the 1920 convention pledging American participation in international peace organizations. He failed, but in the midst of the campaign, he and thirty-one other Republican internationalists, including Charles Evans Hughes, George Wickersham, Herbert Hoover, Paul Cravath, and seventeen college presidents, asserted their support for Warren Harding by claiming that the candidate favored American participation in some unspecified "association" of nations.[1] The "Manifesto of Thirty-One," which reasserted Root's position on the treaty, was hardly a ringing endorsement for the League of Nations or a solid assault against the nationalist tendencies of the party. It injected some internationalism into the Republican campaign, but failed to produce any clear party commitments.

It did not take long for the Republicans themselves to begin dividing over administration policy. Some Republicans were unqualified internationalists who welcomed any sign that their party was moving toward internationalism. They wanted to agree with Herbert Houston, publisher and editor of the colorful internationalist journal *Our World,* who claimed that practically all prominent Republicans saw that "the whole progress of events was toward the existing League of Nations, with the United States becoming a member on a basis satisfactory to the American people." Republicans understood this "eternal truth."[2] The common belief among such optimists was that Secretary of State Charles Evans Hughes would work gradually for entry into the League, and there were

---

[1] *New York Times,* 15 October 1920; Richard Leopold, *Elihu Root and the Conservative Tradition* (Boston, 1954), 153; A. Lawrence Lowell to Arthur Sweetser, 12 May 1921, Arthur Sweetser Papers, Library of Congress, Washington, D.C., box 13.

[2] W. A. White to Arthur Sweetser, 15 September 1920, Sweetser Papers, box 13; George W. Wickersham, "America's Next Step Abroad," *Our World* (May 1922): 13–18; Houston letter to the editor, *New York Times,* 1 February 1921, 10.

even more optimistic expectations that Hughes would resubmit the treaty with reservations in 1921 and thus allow "the whole matter of peace [to] be settled within three months."[3]

Clearly, however, the optimistic internationalists were wrong about Hughes personally and about the attitudes of "prominent Republicans" generally. Instead of gradually institutionalizing the internationalist agenda, Hughes attempted to expand American influence and avoid formal ties with the League. He grew increasingly skeptical about the League's prospects, for it seemed to him that Europe's persistent instability showed that world problems had less to do with administrative machinery than with power politics.[4] In summer 1922, Hamilton Holt and Raymond Fosdick accused Hughes of reneging on the promise he had made when he signed the Manifesto of Thirty-One. When Hughes dismissed his shift as a practical bow to public and congressional opinion, "all hell broke loose," Fosdick gleefully wrote his friend in Geneva, Arthur Sweetser, who worked in the League secretariat and was the American most closely associated with the League itself.[5] Fellow Republicans lost patience with Hughes by 1923. George Wickersham, attorney general under Taft, began to make himself the single most outspoken critic of his party by denouncing the "almost childish" aversion to anything having to do with the League. A. Lawrence Lowell, who had become chairman of the World Peace Foundation, simply warned that the Democrats would gain if the administration avoided large internationalist commitments.[6]

Hoping to strike a middle way on the issue, Hughes and the Coolidge administration decided to recommend American membership on the World Court but in so doing merely revived the factions of the treaty fight. The nationalists, again behind Lodge, argued that they approved of the Court in theory but could not support it so long as it was asso-

[3] Edwin Bjorkman to Arthur Sweetser, 27 April 1921, Sweetser Papers, Box 13; also A. Lawrence Lowell to Sweetser, 12 May 1921. A curious aside: Hughes could not have resubmitted the treaty in these months even had he wanted. He could not find it. The actual treaty was mistakenly packed with the Wilson's belongings when they moved from the White House, which understandably caused some insiders to chuckle about Wilson having taken it with him. See Hughes's correspondence with George Christian, 11–12 July 1921, Warren G. Harding Papers, Ohio Historical Society, Columbus, Ohio, microfilm roll 143.

[4] Betty Glad, *Charles Evans Hughes and the Illusion of Innocence* (Urbana, Ill., 1966), 179–84.

[5] *New York Times*, 17 July 1922, 19 July 1922, and 10 July 1923; Fosdick to Sweetser, 20 July 1922, Sweetser Papers, box 31.

[6] *New York Times*, 25 August 1923; Lowell to Hughes, 24 June 1924, Hughes to Lowell, 14 July 1922, Harding Papers, microfilm roll 144.

ciated with the League. In December 1923, accordingly, they agreed to approve American membership if the selection of judges were taken out of League hands. These so-called Lenroot reservations were obviously a disingenuous attempt to veto Court membership while proclaiming support for the Republican administration, and the pro-leaguers denounced them as the sleazy dealings of "corrupt minds," as one commentator put it. Lodge incited more criticism from fellow Republicans such as Wickersham when, as chair of the Senate Foreign Relations Committee, he let the Court proposal flounder in committee for well over a year.[7]

The Court issue lingered into the 1924 convention, where Coolidge and Root conspired to fight the nationalists. In the interest of party harmony, and, for that matter, the harmony of the Massachusetts delegation that was preparing a favorite son for the nomination, Lodge relented on the issue. The party, according to Arthur Sweetser's optimistic but relatively objective view, thus repudiated the 1920 platform with its platform plank on behalf of the Court. Acceptance of the plank, however, only obscured the continued hostility toward the League that by now was embedded within the Republican Party. Far from marking a decisive step toward the League, the administration's commitment to the World Court reignited the energy of the irreconcilables, who, behind William Borah, ultimately blocked American membership.[8]

Unable to shake out the irreconcilables, the Wilsonians had to admit that their influence in the Republican Party was limited. Even if the Republican administrations were anxious to see that America "take her place in the world," there was really no incentive for the party to be more forthright on the issue of League participation. Its chances of remaining the dominant party hinged on maintaining a coalition of Eastern elites, nationalists, and isolationists, a coalition that the issue of the League would have fractured.

The Democrats, meanwhile, were in no shape to make the League a major issue. Preoccupied with the bitter cultural clash between rural and urban constituents that characterized the decade, the Democrats pushed the internationalist agenda into the background. Wilsonians remained in high places within the party, but only in what might best be described as a shadow wing. Cordell Hull, later Franklin Roosevelt's sec-

[7] *New York Times,* 12 November 1923, 26 December 1923, and 9 April 1924.

[8] *New York Times,* 1 June 1924 and 10 June 1924; Sweetser to Fosdick, 15 June 1924, Sweetser Papers, box 14; Denna Frank Fleming, *The United States and the World Court* (Garden City, N.Y. 1945); L. Ethan Ellis, *Republican Foreign Policy, 1921–1933* (New Brunswick, N.J., 1969), 68–75.

retary of state, chaired the National Committee in the early part of the decade. Roosevelt himself was a prominent member of the Woodrow Wilson Foundation until he contracted poliomyelitis. The 1924 nominee, John W. Davis, was a Wilsonian, and the party's ranks included Raymond Fosdick and Normal Davis as well. Most important, Newton D. Baker remained a steadfast Democrat, committed to the realization of Wilson's vision.

Baker's postwar career helps locate the Wilsonians within the Democratic party fairly well. His quest for American participation in the League began immediately after he left the Wilson administration for a flourishing law practice in Cleveland. As the former Progressive mayor of Cleveland, as a former Democratic cabinet member, and as a prominent national speaker, Baker commanded a certain deference within the party, as well as some positions of marginal importance, such as the one he held on the platform committee in the 1920s. He took every opportunity that national prominence provided to push for internationalism. In private gatherings and public speeches he made but one point: the United States had to immerse itself in international affairs.

The 1924 convention provided Baker his moment. The larger drama of a convention bitterly split between the rural backers of William Gibbs McAdoo and the urban constituents of Al Smith was mostly lost on him. His only interest was with pushing a resolution calling for immediate American entry into the League, an effort in which other prominent Wilsonians such as John H. Clarke and Hamilton Holt joined. When he was voted down within the resolutions committee, his plank replaced with a call for a future plebiscite on the League, he authored a minority report that reiterated his stand. Speaking on behalf of the minority plank, an emotional Baker claimed that he was ashamed of a party that would repudiate Wilson. It was bad enough that the Republicans had thwarted American membership since 1920, but now the Democratic party had "dumped the League into the street." Calling forth Wilson's specter, Baker admonished the Democrats that Wilson was "standing at the throne of God whose approval he won and received."[9]

The convention was not shamed into repentance but did settle on a compromise candidate who had Baker's blessings. John W. Davis was a fellow West Virginian who had gone on to a Wall Street law career and,

[9] Cramer, *Newton D. Baker*, 218–20; *New York Times*, 21 June 1924, 24–25 June 1924, and 29 June 1924.

eventually, the ambassadorship to Great Britain. Steady, politically moderate, and well respected, Davis was also colorless. Baker and others recognized that Davis was bland and conservative, but he was an internationalist, and that virtue was enough. "I like him a great deal," Walter Lippmann wrote to Baker, but "the few times he has appeared in public, the impression has been rather flat. He has far more sheer ability than Wilson, a much wider experience in both industrial and diplomatic affairs and is a man of finer grain." Yet "he lacks Wilson's flair for warming up people he doesn't know, and he has less dramatic sense."[10] Davis appealed to both Lippmann and Baker, notwithstanding his liabilities, because he represented, better than anyone else in the field, political cosmopolitanism: he was cultivated, realistic, and internationalist. Baker conceded the usual complaints about Davis's big-business leanings, but, he wrote to Raymond Fosdick, Davis "does understand the League and is for it. For that virtue I am willing to forgive a lot."[11]

By 1928, as a leading Democrat and a defender of the internationalist cause, Baker inspired friends to consider him a possible presidential hopeful. Lippmann saw in Baker all of Wilson's statesmanship, and concluded that Baker was the "only man mentioned [for the Democratic nomination] fitted in his own right to be President."[12] Baker declined to run for any office in 1928, convinced as he was that he could not support a platform that endorsed the McNary-Haugen farm legislation while it omitted all mention of international cooperation. Public life was so draining, he complained to his closest friend, Ralph Hayes, that he would reenter it only to support a cause in which he truly believed, and the 1928 platform offered no such thing: "McKinley could have run on the tariff plank and Lodge on the one on international affairs." Worse, the platform "did not contain Woodrow Wilson's name from the beginning to the end . . . ,[which] indicated the extent to which he was absent from the minds who drafted the platform." It also indicated how far internationalism had declined in practical influence, and Baker, well aware of that decline, did not fight for a pro-League plank, as he had in 1924, because the opposition was too strong. "It would have been im-

[10] Lippmann to Baker, 27 November 1923, in Blum, *Public Philosopher*, 157; Lippmann to Bernard Berenson, 16 July 1924, ibid., 164–65.

[11] Baker to Fosdick, 15 July 1924, Newton D. Baker Papers, Library of Congress, Washington, D.C., box 99; Baker to Ralph Hayes, 17 February 1925, Baker Papers, box 114.

[12] Lippmann to Charles Howland, 23 April 1928, in Blum, *Public Philosopher*, 215; Lippmann to Baker, 3 July 1928, ibid., 225.

possible," he quipped, "for a minority to have included even the least offensive of the Ten Commandments in the document." If this were true,
then Wilsonians could not stand as prophets in either party.[13]

Wilsonians as Publicists

Denied any real opportunity to shape public policy, Wilsonians became publicists and organized themselves more systematically than the
prewar internationalists had. They were aggressive, some nearly inexhaustible; their efforts were national in scope and so broad that agitation within the party system at times was almost supplemental to their
wider work.

From the outset of the 1920s, they were uncertain of how public opinion, that always vague animal, sat on internationalist issues. At the
height of the 1920 election, supposedly a referendum on the League,
Newton Baker found it "very hard to have any sort of idea as yet about
the sentiment of the people on the League of Nations. Believing in it as
I do, I can not persuade myself that it is not generally believed in." Without the benefit of opinion polls, Wilsonians had to judge the warmth of
public receptions and how well their agenda was treated in editorial
commentary, a method of keeping tabs that begged self-fulfilling readings. Irving Fisher, an eclectic Yale economics professor who wrote on
everything from the money supply to personal hygiene and who was an
active publicist for the League of Nations Non-Partisan Association, relied on personal impressions to conclude in 1924 that "everywhere evidence is accumulating that the American people are growing more and
more restive over the inaction of their government."[14]

Another way to gauge public support was to measure the success of
their propaganda efforts. At the end of 1921, Denys Myers of the World
Peace Foundation reported that "there is a very good and increasing
demand for League publications, and our own are of course regularly
circulated." Myers estimated that nearly 5000 college teachers were

---

[13] Baker to Hayes, 2 July 1928, Baker Papers, box 115; Baker to Norman Hapgood,
Hapgood-Reynolds Family Papers, Library of Congress, Washington, D.C., box 9. For a
description of the platform, see David Burner, *The Politics of Provincialism: The Democratic Party in Transition, 1918–1932* (New York, 1967), 197.

[14] Baker to Arthur Sweetser, 8 September 1920, Sweetser Papers, box 13; Irving Fisher,
America's Interest in World Peace (New York, 1924), 13. Fisher's curious career included
How to Live: Rules for Healthful Living Based on Modern Science, a hygiene primer that
went through twenty editions from 1915 to 1938.

"permanent parts of our mailing list" and added that the foundation encouraged them to use the mailing materials in their courses. "Personally I am absolutely confident that the American people can travel in only one direction and that is toward the League."[15] Hamilton Holt, who traveled the lecture circuit so vigorously in the mid-1920s that he dropped some sixty pounds, found warm receptions. According to Warren Kuehl, "attendance at his addresses was high, and his speeches . . . were widely printed wherever he appeared." Editors were not "universally sympathetic," Kuehl continued, but "most editors agreed that an educational campaign on the League was necessary."[16]

The problem with this imprecise way of measuring public opinion was that it equated public support with the sheer breadth of their efforts. Wilsonians counted those who came to hear them speak as supporters, and they similarly assumed that newspaper coverage of their efforts also translated directly into public approval. Surely many who listened to lectures were supporters, but just as surely others were not. If indeed the irreconcilables faced "the almost unanimous opposition of public opinion," as Irving Fisher believed, than how was one to account for the lukewarm positions of the two parties, which intuitively had a much firmer grasp on the public pulse?[17]

In the years before the 1924 election, Wilsonians seemed generally to believe that the principal problem was not public hostility but lack of information, and the obvious solution was more organization and more publicity. "The American people," Sweetser firmly believed, just "are not getting the facts of the League." It was astonishing, he thought, that public interest in the League should disappear simply because the treaty was defeated, and yet "at that very extraordinary moment [of the treaty's defeat] nine Americans out of every ten took it for granted that because the United States had failed to ratify the Treaty the League did not exist."[18]

Sweetser met the problem in several ways. He published several accounts of the League's work, provided inside information to League supporters, particularly Raymond Fosdick and Norman Davis, for use on the home front, and worked with Fosdick to establish a League of Na-

[15] Myers to Huntington Gilchrist, 28 December 1921, Huntington Gilchrist Papers, Library of Congress, Washington, D.C., box 15.

[16] Warren Kuehl, *Hamilton Holt, Journalist, Internationalist, Educator* (Gainesville, 1960), 169; see also Raymond Fosdick, *Chronicle of a Generation* (New York, 1958), 225.

[17] Fisher, *America's Interest in World Peace*, 47.

[18] Sweetser to George Wickersham, 22 March 1922, Sweetser Papers, box 13; Sweetser, *The League of Nations at Work* (New York, 1920), v–vi.

tions News Bureau in Washington.[19] First established in fall 1920 under the auspices of the League to Enforce Peace, the News Bureau benefited from the talents of Myers, Fosdick, and the journalist Malcolm Davis, among others. Sweetser was a consistently reliable source of information. But the News Bureau quickly ran into funding problems when it fell between the cracks of the many different Wilsonian organizations, none of which wanted to take responsibility for it. Try as he might to convince would-be sympathizers that "the true facts . . . have never gotten over to this country in any regular way," certain as he was that "this situation would seem intolerable to those who really want to know what is going on in the world," Sweetser never managed to ingratiate his bureau with any source of funding, and late in 1922 he gave up his effort.[20]

The leaders of the many other organizations probably believed that they could do the work themselves. They certainly tried. The decade was the high-water mark of Wilsonian organization. The Woodrow Wilson Foundation was established as a nonpartisan organization for encouraging the former president's ideals in 1922. Grown out of the partisan Woodrow Wilson Democracy, the foundation's original intent was to establish an endowment for a peace prize, along the lines of the Nobel, and it managed to raise $800,000 during a two-year fund drive. Though the drive fell $200,000 short of its goal, an optimist might still have read the outpouring of contributions as evidence of popular support. The real importance of the foundation in the 1920s was that it provided a means for coalescing across party lines; what initial partisanship appeared wore away by 1926 when Root was given the Wilson award.[21]

Harmony appeared more obviously in December 1922 with the organization of the League of Nations Non-Partisan association, the group that perhaps best exemplified the situation of the Wilsonians in the early postwar period. Formed in part because of Republican failures and in part because the organizers felt public opinion swinging their way, the Non-Partisan Association brought together that group of prominent

---

[19] See Sweetser, *What the League of Nations Has Accomplished* (New York, 1924). In his autobiography, Fosdick takes the credit for establishing the News Bureau, but the correspondence between the two men makes it clear that Sweetser was doing much to direct the project from Geneva. See Fosdick, *Chronicle of a Generation*, 220–21; Fosdick to Sweetser, 20 July 1922 and Sweetser to Fosdick, 8 August 1922, Sweetser Papers, box 31.

[20] Fosdick to Sweetser, 22 September 1920, Sweetser to Fosdick, 15 December 1921, 24 March 1922, and 31 May 1922, Sweetser Papers, box 31; Sweetser Diary, 3 November 1921 and 29 November 1922, Sweetser Papers, box 1; Sweetser to Wickersham, 22 March 1922.

[21] Kuehl, *Hamilton Holt*, 163–65, 168; Norman Davis to Arthur Sweetser, 31 December 1924, Sweetser Papers, box 31.

moderates from both parties for whom entering the League had become the be-all and end-all of American politics. On one level, it was a reorganization of the prewar internationalist effort. Most of the prominent internationalists of the past joined, including nearly half of the thirty-one Republicans; the defunct League to Enforce Peace even passed on its office furniture. Yet its energy did not come from the old pioneers—the notable exception of Hamilton Holt aside. New leaders emerged, such as former Supreme Court Justice John H. Clarke, who agreed to head the organization, and George Wickersham, who brought Republicans in when he agreed to fuse his own American Association for International Cooperation with the Non-Partisan Association. Fosdick and Sweetser worked in the background, and relatively young advocates such as Manley O. Hudson and James T. Shotwell were active on the lecture circuit. The Association marked the arrival of the second generation of internationalists, most of whom were indisputably loyal to the memory of Woodrow Wilson. Membership grew quickly to 2368 in its first month, further testimony to Wilsonian coalescence. Warren Kuehl put it well when he noted that the association, committed as it was to American membership in the League of Nations, "showed how completely the breach in the ranks of the pro-League forces had been mended."[22]

The Non-Partisan Association was the most general in purpose, for it was both a lobbying and educative body. Other organizations emerged with more specific functions. The Foreign Policy Association (FPA) was reorganized out of the wartime League of Free Nations Association in 1922 with the intention of encouraging original scholarship on international affairs as well as issuing League publicity. Under James G. McDonald, the FPA became one of the most regular sources of Wilsonian propaganda over the next decade, and, as such, it served the purpose of Sweetser's News Bureau.[23] The FPA's blue-blooded cousin, the Council on Foreign Relations, was organized from the start in 1922 as an exclusive body of movers and shakers, but at least it tended toward nonpartisan snobbery. Wickersham, Norman Davis, John W. Davis, and Walter Lippmann were its first members, along with numerous New York lawyers and bankers. These men intended to sway American policy at the highest levels, and they stooped to educate only the high-minded cosmo-

[22] Sweetser Diary, 29 November, 1–2 December 1922, Sweetser Papers, box 1; Kuehl, *Hamilton Holt*, 167–69.

[23] Foreign Policy Association, *Twenty-Five Years of the Foreign Policy Association, 1918–1943* (New York, 1943).

politan through the journal *Foreign Affairs,* a limitation the editors assured when, as Robert D. Schulzinger has put it, they proceeded to produce "one of the dullest magazines in the world."[24]

These were just the most important and most formal of Wilsonian organizations and forums. One could note as well that the World Peace Foundation eagerly joined in the publicity campaign for the League. So too did the Carnegie Endowment, particularly through its principal publication, *International Conciliation.* Harry Garfield's Williamstown Institute of Politics at Williams College became a Wilsonian round-table. Herbert Houston's *Our World* enjoyed only a brief three-year run, but it was the most thoroughly Wilsonian journal of its day. There were those organizations, furthermore, that cannot be thought of as "internationalist" but nevertheless regularly contributed to the Wilsonian cause. The American Academy of Political and Social Science, for example, was led through most of the interwar period by Ernest Minor Paterson, a University of Pennsylvania economics professor, who continued the tradition of using the Academy's journal, *The Annals,* as a forum for both internationalism and moderate liberal commentary on domestic issues.

There were even gimmicks, such as the American Peace Award, established by philanthropist Edward Bok in 1924. Bok offered $100,000 to the individual who submitted the best plan for pushing the United States into the League of Nations. The award committee, which included Root, Colonel House, and William Allen White, offered the award to Charles Levermore, who submitted a simple plan that called for American adherence to the Court and gradual participation in League discussions as a sort of interested observer. Over 22,000 plans were submitted and a half-million Americans allegedly voted their approval of the Levermore Plan, all of which naturally reinforced the optimistic estimates of public support. Ignoring the possibility that the hefty purse might have encouraged more submissions than devotion to the cause, Bok himself concluded "that the people of this country are far more widely and fundamentally interested in the question of the foreign relations of the United States than most of us believed to be the case."[25]

[24] Schulzinger, *Wise Men of Foreign Affairs,* 6–11.
[25] Edward Bok, "The American People's First Step toward World Peace," *Our World* (January 1924): 3. Sweetser and Fosdick conspired on a much more elaborate plan to force a showdown in Congress on League membership. Fosdick's "reliable sources" told him the plan came in a close second. See the undated manuscript, "A Plan by Which the United States May Cooperate with Other Nations to Achieve and Preserve the Peace of the

Isolation as Unreason

The overriding purpose of Wilsonian organizations through the mid-1920s was to advance what proponents considered enlightened opinion. The main thrust of the educative programs was simply to describe the activities of the League. Not only was Sweetser important in this effort, but most prominent Wilsonians regularly recounted the League achievements for American audiences. These educational efforts were generally dry renditions of events that sent out two basic messages: the League worked, and the rest of the world was constructively engaged in far-sighted efforts while the United States remained childishly aloof.[26]

In the main, the efforts at public education restated wartime positions. The war, these arguments had it, had demonstrated that some nations continued to revel in barbarism, which modern technology made considerably more fiendish. The League was more than simply a guard against this lingering barbarism, more than a body for collective security. It was the historic development of a modern sensibility based on systematic conciliation and institutionalized reason. That fifty-five nations had entered the League demonstrated that it was becoming the organic body that Wilson had foreseen and that its real power lay in world public opinion. The League was neither a superstate nor the guarantor of the status quo: it was international liberalism in action.[27]

The dominant consideration in the Wilsonian mind was that world interdependence made the League absolutely necessary. It always had been a basic premise, but in the 1920s world interdependence became the main argument for American entry into the League. To renounce the League was to renounce the reality of global unity, which meant that isolationism was one grand exercise in national self-delusion. Americans seemed determine to fight history, to impede civilization's march, to

---

World"; Fosdick to Sweetser, 7 January and 6 February 1924; Sweetser to Fosdick, 22 January 1924, in Sweetser Papers, box 14. See also Newton Baker to Sweetser, 2 February 1924, Sweetser Papers, box 30.

[26] See the following: Hamilton Holt, "Remarkable Record Set Forth of Achievements in Maintaining Peace in Europe and South America—World Court Functioning," *New York Times*, 20 August 1922; Raymond Fosdick, "The Third League Assembly," *New York Times*, 3 September 1922; and Manley O. Hudson, "Four Years of the League of Nations," *New York Times*, 10 January 1924.

[27] I take the following as representative: Sweetser, *The League of Nations at Work*; John H. Clarke, *America and World Peace* (New York, 1925); Fisher, *America's Interest in World Peace*; and Manley O. Hudson, *Current International Co-Operation* (Calcutta, 1927).

deny that the way of the future was a "systematized method of contact" between nations, as Raymond Fosdick put the matter: "Spreading from the family to the village, from the village to the state, from the state to the nation, the machinery of social contact has been elaborated and widened over countless centuries. The time has come for further extension."[28] There was simply no use wallowing in the old isolationism. All the talk about avoiding "entanglements" and alliances in order to avoid war was merely a "fool's paradise," charged Norman Davis. If the war had resulted from the new facts of industrial interdependence, it also instructed enlightened observers that "the affairs of the world have become so interrelated that what happens in one part affects another."[29]

In an age in which people were allegedly preoccupied with the main chance, Wilsonians believed that this argument had an automatic appeal, because international interdependence was the essence of economic prosperity. Even Babbitt could see that an industrial economy needed both international sources of raw material and world markets to function properly. Surely Americans would understand that the nation's high standard of living could not be enjoyed without international trade and that even the resource-rich United States was dependent. William Redfield, secretary of commerce under Wilson, called it in 1925 "the weakness of our strength. Out of our very conditions of abounding wealth and prosperity has grown a peculiar dependence on other lands."[30] Interdependence benefited both producer and consumer: open international markets allowed Americans to sell whatever they could produce; they would also bring to consumers coffee for their breakfast tables and rubber tires for their autos. "It would be a real misfortune to the American breakfast table," Elihu Root wrote, "if Brazil ceased to produce coffee and Cuba ceased to produce sugar and China ceased to produce tea." Americans had to accept the international division of labor and adopt national policies that encouraged, in textbook form, "the productive processes of the world . . . to locate . . . where the minimum of effort will in the long run result in the greatest material gain."[31]

---

[28] Fosdick, *The Old Savage in the New Civilization*, 205.

[29] Norman Davis, Address to the Bond Club of New York City, 1 April 1921, Davis Papers, box 15.

[30] William Redfield, *Dependent America* (Boston, 1926), 12.

[31] Elihu Root, "Steps towards Preserving Peace," *Foreign Affairs* 3 (April 1925): 351. Democritus, "The Future Tariff Policy of the United States," See also Fred Kent, "The Interdependence of the United States and Europe," *Annals* 102 (July 1922): 169–70. For interdependence and the consumer see also Fosdick, *The Old Savage in the New Civilization*, 201; John Donaldson, *International Economic Relations* (New York, 1928), 68–69;

Economically interdependent, the world had become culturally bound as well through the exertions of modern science, which brought great improvements in transportation and communication. "In the last hundred years," Fosdick wrote, "[science] has given us airplanes, and railroads, and telephones, and steamships, and wireless, and a dozen other inventions, which have . . . bound the world together in a new unity." Interdependence was comprehensive and pervasive; driven by science and industry, it touched, in Norman Davis's estimation, the lives of "countless millions," whose welfare depended on "continuous production and upon the peaceful and uninterrupted exchange of goods and services." It touched every nation, every industry, and every person. Interdependence broke down ignorance, inefficiency, and parochialism, those notorious barriers to human achievement, and in this sense, the cultural force of science, the economic might of mass production, and the political genius of the League of Nations constituted the very strides of civilization.[32]

Given the extent of the efforts at enlightenment and the indisputable interdependence of the modern world, the Wilsonians hardly could help but wonder why their cause suffered more setbacks than successes. As the decade wore on, as their party strength dwindled and the World Court membership, which they believed was the minimal commitment to be expected, met a series of obstacles, they began to admit that their public support was weak. The more obstacles they confronted, the more Wilsonians had to admit that something other than the lack of information was hampering them. There was something deeper at work. As William Redfield put it, although "the process of assimilating another and a larger truth is now progressing there are those among us now who do not comfortably digest the idea that America is one of an international family."[33] There were only two possible culprits behind this national indigestion: either there was a conspiracy at work, or a deep pathology had gotten a grip on the American people.

The first instinct was to blame conspirators. A small group of irreconcilables, after all, had defeated the League in the first place, and these

---

and L. L. Summers, "Economic Relations between Raw Materials, Prices, and Standards of Living: Their International Effect," *International Conciliation* 226 (January 1927): 16; reprinted from the *Proceedings of the Academy of Political Science* 12 (July 1926): 123–34.

[32] Raymond Fosdick, "The World Court," November 1925, Raymond Blaine Fosdick Papers, Mudd Library, Princeton University, Princeton, N.J., box 17; Norman Davis, "Peace and World Trade," an address to the Academy of Political Science, New York, 23 November 1928, Davis Papers, box 15. See also John Clarke's explanation of America's moral, political, and economic interest in the League, *America and World Peace*, chap. 1.

[33] Redfield, *Dependent America*, 427.

same men had only grown in power since the war. Newton Baker thought that Senate isolationists had the "capacity to terrify the Administration quite out of proportion to any breadth of intelligence or elevation of sentiment which those gentlemen have yet displayed." Stupid politicians, rather than a misinformed public, were the foremost obstacles. Baker complained to Fosdick that "the average of human intelligence could never be high until Senator Lodge is taken to his heavenly reward," because, presumably, the Senator's intelligence quotient was so low that he skewed the statistics. The only reason why America had not bowed to the inevitable and joined the League was that "the people," according to Irving Fisher, "were deceived by the little band of irreconcilables." Without naming names, A. Lawrence Lowell had to think that isolationism betrayed a basic "confusion of thought."[34]

The problem with this argument was twofold. First, it could hold only as long as Wilsonians believed the public was on their side, and it therefore grew less tenable as the decade wore on. But there was a more fundamental problem. The logic of their argument held that to deny the clear drift of the world toward international harmony was in effect to be reactionary, a tidy argument that could not account for the troubling inability to find an apt prototype of the reactionary isolationist. Wilsonians needed a national figure who was a defender of private privilege and a practitioner of realpolitick. They needed an American Kaiser.

American isolationists simply did not fit the type. They could not, for instance, claim that William Borah, the leading isolationist, was a pawn of reaction. Not only did Borah prove a reasonable chairman of the Senate Foreign Relations Committee in the 1920s, much to the surprise of many, but he led the congressional fights to extend recognition to the Soviets and to terminate the military occupation of Nicaragua. Unable to lambast Borah as a political reactionary, patronizing Wilsonians scolded him for intellectual and cultural reaction. "He is an honest but a mistaken man," Raymond Fosdick lectured a Princeton audience. Had he been alive in 1787, Borah would have been one of the anti-federalists, for like them, he refused to "see the necessity of moving out to a larger loy-

---

[34] Baker to Sweetser, 26 November 1923, Sweetser Papers, Box 30; Baker to Fosdick, 11 July 1922, Baker Papers, box 7; Fisher, *American's Interest in World Peace,* 19; Lowell quoted in the *New York Times,* 7 April 1923. Fosdick agreed with Baker's assessment but went further: "You are quite right in your theory that Senator Lodge brings down the average of human intelligence—and there are some others, too, that I could mention who are now holding pretty high office in Washington. In fact, I could run off quite a list of such people who hold the B.A. degree (Below Average)." Fosdick to Baker, 13 July 1922, Baker Papers, box 7.

alty." Borah was all the more parochial now, when the struggle was between nationalism and internationalism and when modern science had
tied the world together. Borah's "feet are caught in an ancient tradition.
Part of his brain is living in the eighteenth century. His narrow conception of nationalism no longer fits the facts." Walter Lippmann was more
subtle, and slightly more fair when he described Borah as "an instinctive
conscientious objector" whose "passion is to expose, to ventilate, to protest, to prevent and to destroy." Even in Lippmann's cautious chiding
there lurked the condescending spirit. Senator Borah could exercise enormous power in Congress because he represented the sparsely settled state
of Idaho and had no real electoral concerns. "No wonder his faith in an
appeal to the people is unshaken," Lippmann wrote, "for there are so
few people to whom he has to make his appeal. A loyal following of less
than seventy-five thousand voters in Idaho is enough to make his reelec-
tion certain." Lippmann went on: "Borah was born and bred on the
frontier far from the complexity of modern civilization; it is in his bones
to distrust formality and collective red tape, and to rely upon direct
speech, common knowledge, individual salvation and his own conception of the sovereign power of the moral law."[35]

Here was a new and overtly elitist argument. Unable to reconcile their
ideological expectations with the real nature of American isolationism,
the Wilsonians traded political critique for cultural critique and denounced isolationism as a product of traditional cultures and parochial
attachments. They began to claim that isolationism was not just a product of nationalism but a pathological rejection of modernity itself that
ignored the basic realities of the industrial world. The pathology ran
deep, for it manifested itself not only in the ongoing clamor of special
interests but in the wider cultural conflict between cosmopolitanism and
localism that ran through America in the years after Versailles.

[35] For criticism of Borah's opposition to involvement with the World Court see Manley
O. Hudson, "The Effect of the Present Attitude of the United States toward the League of
Nations," *Annals* 120 (July 1925): 112–14; Fosdick, "A Way of Escape," an Armistice
Day address, Princeton, 11 November 1931, pp. 4–6, Fosdick Papers, box 25, printed as
"A Way of Escape from War," *International Conciliation* 277 (February 1932): 53–65;
Walter Lippmann, "Concerning Senator Borah," *Foreign Affairs* 4 (January 1926):
211–13.
   Some conceded Borah's sincerity. In his travels through the United States in 1922, for
example, Arthur Sweetser found that Borah was "not an absolute isolationist." The senator
"was in sympathy with all the general humanitarian work of the League" and was "perfectly willing to have Americans cooperate in it." Sweetser Diary, 12 December 1922,
Sweetser Papers, box 1. For Borah's push for both see Robert J. Maddox, *William E. Borah
and American Foreign Policy* (Baton Rouge, La., 1969), chap. 7.

Counting themselves as archetypical cosmopolitans, Wilsonians mocked the isolationist impulse. Those who preferred isolation to world engagement, argued Fred Kent, a regular contributor to *Our World* and chair of the International Chamber of Commerce's Committee on the Economic Restoration of Europe, "are content to live an animal life, a mere existence from birth to death, without thought or desire beyond satisfying the physical craving of the moment."[36] Because interdependence came with modern industrialization, it unquestionably was linked to advanced science, modern art, and the best of high culture in general; isolation, conversely, mingled primitive instincts and base physical cravings. The isolationist was the antithesis of the scientist; he ignored the overwhelming evidence of economic interdependence and was blind to "fact." One former member of the American Committee to Negotiate the Peace, for example, wrote in 1926 that the isolationists' inconsistent positions betrayed a slovenly use of evidence. Like a "feudal baron," according to L. L. Summers, the isolationist was "not subject to any ethical regulations." Something of a relic or an intellectual laggard, the isolationist's only legitimate appeal was to the American past, but his grasp of historical fact was no more certain than was his grasp of modern economics. The isolationist often quoted Washington's warning against entangling alliances without quoting the next few lines of the Farewell Address that spoke to the importance of international trade, and Washington himself "resorted to international cooperation" when "expediency dictated" that he seek the aid of France.[37]

When the isolationist managed to make a good case on the strength of historical precedent, then that precedent came in for some revision. The Monroe Doctrine, for example, had to be reinterpreted as an internationalist policy. Monroe had three doctrines in mind in 1823, Princeton professor of politics and government John B. Whitton argued: the first two were aimed at keeping Europe out of the Americas; and the third aimed at keeping the United States out of Europe. But this rule was no more "absolute" to Monroe than to Washington because, in reality, Monroe insisted only on steering clear of internal European politics and never contemplated "absolute isolation." Those who found in the doctrine a precedent for isolation, held Charles Fenwick, a specialist in international law, merely sought security "in terms of isolated action, . . . of getting security by individual effort, not by common action." Unless

---

[36] Kent, "The Interdependence of the United States and Europe," 169–70.
[37] Summers, "Economic Relations between Raw Materials, Prices, and Standards of Living," 16, 19–20.

interpreted with the benefits of such modern insights, the American past could be every bit as limiting and regressive as the feudal past of Europe. "Let us seek new forms of security," Whitton pleaded, "more appropriate than eighteenth-century isolation, and more in harmony with our situation today."[38]

If American isolationism was not the same crazed imperialism that plagued Europe, it was nonetheless anachronistic in its fondness for past ideals, for individualism, and for local attachments. The "isolationist impulse" might not have been of the same quality as its European counterpart, but it was nevertheless the product of a stubborn mentality that refused to accept the rule of science and the benefits of industry. The struggle between internationalists and isolationists, reduced to fundamentals, pitted the city expert against the stubborn peasant. The issue was never made more clear than when Raymond Buell, president of the Foreign Policy Association, exhorted a group at Garfield's Institute of Politics: "Despite what Senator Borah said about experts, despite his statement that experts would sterilize the humanitarian impulse of angels, in a world as complicated as ours you must allow the expert to talk to you."[39] The isolationist might not have lusted for foreign conquest but he was determined, in a quixotic sort of way, to uphold the county seat over Geneva. Much as H. L. Mencken, another famous cosmopolitan of the day, lambasted the Tennesseeans at the Scopes Trial as "gaping primates . . . who sweated freely and were not debauched by the refinements of the toilet," Wilsonians denounced isolationists for their pathological attachments to what used to be. It was no coincidence that a year after the Scopes Trial, William Redfield argued that, "were it possible to detach ourselves wholly from others and become separate, we should, in so doing, fall backwards. Were we to perfectly isolate ourselves, we should descend on the social scale."[40]

While the Wilsonians believed that the distinction between themselves and isolationists lay in their differing grasp of reality, it is hard to miss

[38] John B. Whitton, "Isolation: An Obsolete Principle of the Monroe Doctrine," *International Conciliation* 290 (May 1933): 211–12, and "What Follows the Pact of Paris," ibid., 276 (January 1932): 31; Charles Fenwick, "Security and Understanding Lead to World Peace," *Annals* 114 (July 1924): 153.

[39] Raymond Buell, "The Limitations of Armaments," opening address to the Institute of Politics, 29 July 1932, Garfield Papers, box 119.

[40] Redfield, *Dependent America*, 253. Newton Baker shared Mencken's interpretation of the Scopes affair when he likened it to the trial of Galileo. But where Galileo "had ten Cardinals as his judges, . . . poor Scopes has eleven semi-literate[s] and one illiterate, while the evidence seems to consist largely in the atmosphere created by an agitated but ignorant populace." Baker to Fosdick, 17 July 1925, Baker Papers, box 7.

the elements of geography and class in these arguments. Harry Garfield, one of the few Wilsonians who tried to understand the roots of isolationism, admitted that the impulse appeared mostly among people who lived between the Appalachians and the Rockies, people, Garfield conceded, who "have not needed to look beyond the mountains. Their interest has been concentrated upon the development of their own resources." But it hardly mattered to Garfield that there was good reason for the Midwest's tepid response to the great cause of the League and the World Court; the whole point was that the isolationist refused to see beyond his own interests. "Self-interest can save us, but we must know what is in the interest of the self. . . . Self-interest demands that we find the facts, that the fact finders be trustworthy."[41] Those attributes did not apply to the isolationists, and thus the mountains loomed as metaphors for ignorance, or, worse, social pathology. Christian Gauss, Princeton professor of romance languages and a Wilson loyalist, relied consistently on pseudopsychology to link isolationism and psychological maladjustment. "It is a notorious fact," he explained, "that when an individual is no longer able to adjust himself effectively to the world of men about him, he resorts to withdrawal, creates an escape mechanism. We speak of such an individual as maladjusted and we recognize that he 'compensates' by creating in his imagination a new world in which he can move freely." The "maladjusted" nation, Gauss argued, unable to accept with maturity its dependence on others, is "driven, like the nonplussed individual, to build and wall-in a world of [its] own."[42]

In condemning provincialism, Wilsonians ignored the possibility that, to rural and small-town Americans, abstaining from international involvements was a logical outgrowth of their world. Far from being "nonplussed," they deduced their opposition to internationalism from their own particular and very real circumstances. For the most part, they were farmers, blue-collar workers in mid-western cities, and small shopkeepers, and internationalism offered them no good reason to surrender either their philosophy or their world.[43] For Wilsonians proposed only

[41] Harry A. Garfield, "The Determinant of Advancing Civilization," address to the Naval War College, Newport, R.I., 9 December 1926, 13; "Notes for Address, Western Trip," an address to the Civic and Commerce Assn. in Minneapolis, 27 December 1927, Garfield Papers, box 147.
[42] Christian Gauss, "Can America Live Alone?" *Scribner's Magazine* 72 (August 1933): 71. See also Gauss's "Recovery—A Longer View," ibid. 72 (December 1932): 334.
[43] Such are the characteristics of the isolationist described by Wayne S. Cole, *Roosevelt and the Isolationists, 1932–45* (Lincoln, Neb., 1983), 8.

vague commitments to debt readjustment, tariff reform, or the League, sensible and important in themselves perhaps, but nevertheless distant, transitory, and all too much to the benefit of the East Coast. Even if such programs genuinely did benefit the heartland, the Wilsonians' elitism was bound to raise suspicions. Indeed some Wilsonians were content to dismiss public opinion out of hand. There was no reason, Cordell Hull once insisted, to make foreign policy comprehensible to a public that had only an inadequate "level of intelligence"; better to shape arguments to "convince and greatly arouse the smaller and more intelligent class." There was no use wasting time on irrational primitives when rationality led to only one conclusion about the political and economic course of the world.[44]

In light of this elitism, the educative efforts of the 1920s take on a more insidious meaning than simply a desire to "get the facts out." The efforts had to have been dedicated as well to countering the anxious maladjustment of the allegedly irrational folk. Indeed it is difficult to see how Wilsonians could advance the critique of isolation consistently without appreciating the extent to which it sooner or later would compromise their own idealist faith. How could isolationism have come to predominate, even to the extent of seeping into the minds of otherwise liberal people, when the facts of modern life made it so patently irrational?

At some level, Wilsonians had to begin questioning their basic faith in the capacity of public reason, though the resolute among them put up a brave front. On the eve of the 1924 convention, Newton Baker announced his intention to stick by majority opinion. "Either the people of the United States are for our entry into the League of Nations or they are against it," he wrote Raymond Fosdick. "If the American people want to stay out and take the consequences, I want to make common lot with them." But when push came to shove at the convention, Baker opposed the platform plank that called for a plebiscite on the issue as an insult to Wilson's memory. His faith in the public diminished from there. Walter Lippmann's *The Phantom Public,* which depicted the citizen as poorly informed at best, reenforced Baker's declining faith in public opinion. "I have pretty nearly finished Walter's book," he mused to a mutual friend. "I do not know what to say about it. I have gone about the country . . . telling voters that they were the government for forty years, and now

---

[44] Hull to Norman Davis, 16 March 1927, Davis Papers, box 27.

Walter says that I have been . . . misleading them, all of which I am afraid is true."[45]

For the time being, the depressing logic of their position was warded off, for they continued to invest faith, if not in the common citizen, then in the irresistible power of modern interdependence, which would drag people into the new age of interdependent harmony whether they wanted to come or not. A serious glance about the world in the 1920s should have raised some doubts that the new age was right around the corner, especially among people supposedly dedicated to finding facts. Instead, as the Great Depression approached, the Wilsonians awaited a new age, much as Wilson himself had promised in 1917. All that was necessary, they believed, was some readjustment in political thought. Industrial interdependence had been brought on by "scientific development and economic expansion," Norman Davis explained, "which cross all national boundaries." But in "political thought and ideals among nations" there was mostly "stagnation." Political science simply had not "kept pace" with "economic laws and present necessities." The new age demanded the end of the politics of selfishness and ignorance. "The most stupid or blindly selfish person can scarcely fail to realize we are in a new era," Cordell Hull declared when he condemned American trade policy in the 1920s. "In the face of this outstanding fact," everyone had to admit that "new policies" were called for. The outworn policies of the past had to be discarded. "Salvation" from the "period of transition," Francis Sayre, Wilson's son-in-law, believed, "depends upon creating and formulating new beliefs and a new faith in [the] international solidarity of interest." Anticipating a new age of irresistible universalism, to their true horror, Wilsonians encountered the 1930s.[46]

[45] Baker to Fosdick, 12 March 1924, Baker Papers, box 7; and Baker to Ralph Hayes, 16 October 1925, Baker Papers, box 114.

[46] Norman Davis, address to the Cleveland Chamber of Commerce, 6 February 1923, Davis Papers, box 15. See also address to International Chamber of Commerce, 19 May 1925, ibid. "Extension of Remarks on tariff Reform by Cordell Hull in the House of Representatives," 19 December 1925, ibid., box 27; Nicholas Murray Butler, "A Call to Action," C.B.S. radio address for the League of Nations Association, 13 January 1933, in Franklin D. Roosevelt Papers, Hyde Park, Personal Papers file 445, pp. 4–5; Francis Sayre, commencement address at Fitchburg College, June 1932, in Francis Bowes Sayre Papers, Library of Congress, Washington, D.C., box 15.

6

The Red Decade

It took no distortion of logic for Wilsonians to denounce isolationists as reactionaries, even if it did mean losing faith in the common citizen. So long as they had the support of mainstream liberals they could hold to the complacent assumption that they had a firm grasp of truth. It was stunning for them to discover during the depression that they stood at odds with many liberals—indeed, that they fell to the right of the political mainstream. Through the late 1920s and into the deepest period of American isolationism in the mid-1930s, into the heyday of the Nye Committee, the pacifist Oxford Pledge, and populist radicalism, they gradually saw that progressive liberals were not Wilsonians. Instead of committing themselves to the institutionalized reason of the League, pacifists embraced the platitudes of the Kellogg-Briand Pact. New Deal liberals, with their effort to achieve democratic collectivism through national planning, renounced global interdependence even more brazenly than did isolationists. These new ideological opponents were not country bumpkins; as slick as the most urbane internationalist, accustomed to highly intellectual circles, the pacifists and the New Deal Liberals were comfortable at the Cosmos Club or at Columbia and could not be dismissed with condescending cultural criticism. It was enough to make those who still pined after the Wilsonian world order fear for the fate of liberalism.

Wilsonians and Pacifism

"Some of the friends of the League have been its worst enemies," Arthur Sweetser lamented to Raymond Fosdick in 1926. "They have oversold it. They have made it appear the millennium. Emotional women, long-haired men, baggy-kneed idealists, impractical dreamers—all of them very fine people in themselves—have raised hopes too high." They could not see, Sweetser continued, that "the League is splendidly human. Thank God it's not perfection. If it were, it wouldn't be worth working for."[1]

The League was very human indeed. It had its conflicts—as Sweetser wrote, Brazil was demanding a permanent seat in the League Council—but it had its triumphs too. The Protocol for the Pacific Settlement of International Disputes, the Locarno agreements on collective security for Europe, Germany's long-awaited entry into the League, all had created a guarded optimism. Meanwhile, as Sweetser explained to Fosdick, the real strength of the League was in the slow and imperceptible accumulation of work, "mostly unseen," that involved "thousands of details and unimportant items." The danger was that the more the League widened its breadth, the more it drew in people who tended to be either old-guard statesmen or quirky do-gooders. Despite successes, Sweetser feared that the League was moving into "new and harder days when Right and Left, Stagnation and Progress, Idealism and Selfishness" were locked in struggle.[2]

Sweetser's concerns, privately expressed, give hints of what was looming as a perplexing irony for Wilsonians. Among Americans, the organized peace movement was gaining popularity in inverse proportion to the popularity of the League. American pacifists generally were middle-class, well-educated, urban Protestants, the very sort of people to whom Wilsonians expected to appeal. But they also were "do-gooders" bred on the Social Gospel and given to political utopianism. The movement to outlaw war, the agitation for the Kellogg-Briand Pact, and the general demand for disarmament all were infused with the optimistic expectation that spirit alone would vanquish war.[3] While disarmament was close to Wilsonians' hearts, they shared the statesmen's concern for hard-and-fast agreements that locked nations together by means of intertwined self-interest. They believed that disarmament depended on more than a nation's willingness to unburden itself of defense expenditures. Nations would disarm only when economically and politically se-

---

[1] Sweetser to Fosdick, dated Spring 1926, Sweetser Papers, box 31.
[2] Ibid.
[3] Charles Chatfield, *For Peace and Justice: Pacifism in America, 1914–1941* (Knoxville, 1971); Charles DeBenedetti, *The Peace Movement in American History* (Bloomington, Ind., 1980), chap. 6.

cure, and while world interdependence was the best guarantor of economic well-being, concrete treaties undertaken within the collective framework of the League best provided political security.

Their hopes for disarmament, accordingly, ran toward formality and certainty. Insofar as they defended the Washington Conference of the early 1920s, they did so on the grounds that substantive agreements were realized; within the League itself, Americans were involved early in the efforts at codifying collective security. In spring 1923, David Hunter Miller, James T. Shotwell, Steven Duggan, and several others began meeting at Columbia University to study how best to outline a basis for the League's security system. It had to begin, they decided, with a clear definition of an aggressor, and Miller and Shotwell subsequently suggested that an aggressor was any nation that would not submit its case to or abide by the rulings of the World Court in a conflict. This rather straightforward idea provided the basis for the Protocol on International Disputes, which passed unanimously through the League Council in 1925, and while it failed of general approval, set the legal precedent for the Locarno pacts.[4]

From the point of view of the Americans, the protocol was an important step on several counts. It made the machinery of arbitration open to any nation, which amounted to an open invitation for the United States to cooperate with the League. Because the process depended on the World Court, which Wilsonians assumed the United States would enter, it was all the more probable that the Americans would use the League's collective security machinery at some point. It also provided further evidence that the League was making progress in the most urgent areas. The beauty of the protocol, as well as the Locarno agreements that followed, was that defensive war was distinguished from aggression, which in effect recognized that nations would protect their fundamental interests while tying that protection to the common interests of League members.

Shotwell and Miller boasted that their formula would "outlaw war," and literally they were right, given the definition of an aggressor as a renegade against the World Court. Shotwell used the term rhetorically as well, however, in hopes of exploiting the growing popularity of an ill-defined movement to outlaw war. The outlawry movement was mostly the brain child of Chicago lawyer Salmon Levinson, who had concluded

---

[4] James T. Shotwell, *The Autobiography of James T. Shotwell* (Indianapolis, 1961), 180–83.

that international law ought to prevent war, rather than to regulate it, as existing international law did. Opposed to the League as a forum for the status quo, Levinson enlisted a variety of prominent people in his cause during the early 1920s, including the pacifist John Haynes Holmes, William Borah, and John Dewey. He managed to put the outlawry idea at the forefront of popular ideas about foreign relations, so much so that the movement eventuated in the Kellogg-Briand Pact, in which war was renounced as an instrument for national policy.[5]

In the short run, Shotwell's strategy of linking the Wilsonian agenda to the outlawry movement worked. He spoke to as many as five thousand people at a time while touring under the joint auspices of the League of Nations Non-Partisan Association and Carrie Chapman Catt's Committee on the Cause and Cure of War.[6] Their involvement in the protocol, and in the disarmament movement generally, thus brought Shotwell and his colleagues into contact with the growing peace movement. The public attention that they received increased their sense of the League's popularity, when it was pacifism that was more popular. It is entirely possible that many of those who read Sweetser's literature or attended speeches were more interested in disarmament than in American entry into the League specifically.

Wilsonians accepted public support wherever it seemed to appear, and they were willing to align with the pacifists on the issue of disarmament. In June 1925, the pro-League groups and the peace movement joined together in defense of a single program, the Harmony Plan. Engineered by pacifists Kirby Page and Sherwood Eddy, the Harmony Plan tried to address the concerns of both groups by calling for both participation in an outlawry agreement and American membership in the World Court. Hopes for this union were high at first, and the initial meetings brought together a varied group that included the Socialist leader, Norman Thomas, Shotwell, James McDonald, and Judge John Clarke, and leading pacifists. But the Wilsonians saw the plan as a rejection of the League, and by the end of the year they had fled the group. In Shotwell's view, the pacifists were suggesting that merely joining the Court "absolves us of any further method of cooperation in the organization of international peace."[7]

---

[5] See Robert B. Westbrook, *John Dewey and American Democracy* (Ithaca, 1991), 260–74.

[6] Shotwell, *Autobiography*, 195.

[7] Ibid., 196; Chatfield, *For Peace and Justice*, 104–6.

The collapse of the Harmony coalition exposed the very different ideas that underlay the two groups well before pacifism reached the height of its public influence in the mid-1930s. Some, like Justice Clarke, felt compelled to explain the differences. In his 1925 Colver Lectures at Brown, Clarke explained that he was "not an extreme pacifist. I believe that in the present state of civilization . . . it is possible for any nation at almost any time to become involved in war." War was the underside of advanced industrial society, and, Clarke thought, global independence made war possible so long as the nations did not partake in a rational political forum. Too many pacifists wanted to skirt that forum, and because the League entailed the responsibility of collective security and thus the possibility of a just war, it was impossible to profess a sincere pacifism and remain completely pro-League.[8]

The relationship between the pro-League groups and the pacifists could not have been anything but problematical, no matter how much their interests overlapped. There was tension over essentially every major issue after 1925. When the movement toward the Kellogg-Briand Pact began, for example, both groups became early and forceful supporters. Shotwell had a personal investment in a treaty to renounce war, since it was he who first had broached the idea with Aristide Briand, the French foreign minister. Along with Nicholas Murray Butler, Shotwell used the Carnegie Endowment to push the plan on the American public after Briand made his formal offer to conclude a nonaggression pact with the United States in spring 1927. As Shotwell had hoped, the proposal for a large, multilateral pact to renounce war stirred tremendous popular enthusiasm—Carrie Chapman Catt alone delivered 10,000 resolutions to Senator Borah from the many groups that had come to support the outlawry movement—enough that Secretary of State Frank Kellogg took control of the movement and pushed the pact to its conclusion.[9]

Shotwell, Butler, and others had sought to arouse popular opinion in favor of internationalism with the pact, but in so doing they again found themselves allied with people who wanted peace without collective security. When Levinson giddily proclaimed that "the institution of war is now dead," the pro-League liberals winced and argued that Kellogg-Briand would be mere "lip-service to peace," as George Wickersham

[8] Shotwell, *Autobiography*, 195; Clarke, *America and World Peace*, 6.
[9] Shotwell, *Autobiography*, 207–12; L. Ethan Ellis, *Frank Kellogg and American Foreign Relations, 1925–1929* (New Brunswick, N.J. 1961), 193–95; Roland Stromberg, *Collective Security and American Foreign Policy: From the League of Nations to NATO* (New York, 1963), 57.

warned, unless it led to collective security agreements and real disarmament. They were making a practical distinction here: they wanted Kellogg-Briand to stand as a prelude to American cooperation with the League; the pacifists presumed that the pact removed any need for the League. Rather than utopian pacifism, Kellogg-Briand represented a first step toward "adaptation to the real world," according to Shotwell.[10]

Accusing pacifists of embracing platitudes was a bit hypocritical coming from whose who put forth the pact in the first place, for it was nothing more than a platitude, and the pact's foremost Wilsonian supporters were clearly uneasy about the whole business. When the conservative historian Albert Bushnell Hart criticized the pact as a useless exercise in utopianism, for instance, Shotwell countered that it was instead a step toward collective security and argued that it would be enforced in an entirely realistic way because the League mechanisms that lay behind it were in the hands of objective, hard-headed scholars. Shotwell linked diplomatic realism with the scholarly search after "facts," which implied that those who belittled the pact or the League were neither scholarly nor able to reach the truth. On the other hand, he was uneasy around the pacifists. He suspected, he wrote in 1928, that the pact, with its origins in the outlawry movement, was fundamentally anti-League. By avoiding explicit connection to the League, Kellogg-Briand conceded to the isolationists' foremost demand that America avoid submission to an institutionalized process. Shotwell had to conclude that, by his own standards, the pact avoided that all-important "adaptation."[11]

On balance, Shotwell remained more optimistic about Kellogg-Briand than most of his other colleagues, no doubt because of his personal involvement. A whole range of opinion emerged on the issue. Elihu Root, maintaining his faith in public opinion, thought that Kellogg-Briand was a step forward, and his Republican colleague, George Wickersham, spoke of the pact as the "greatest" in American history. Probably the most common opinion was, as Walter Lippmann argued, that Kellogg-Briand was at least some international commitment, and given the complete failure of the internationalist agenda to that point, it was worth supporting for that lone virtue. Often attached to this tepid acceptance

[10] Shotwell, *Autobiography*, 57, 62 note; *New York Times*, 19 February 1929; and Henry Stimson's letter to the editor, *New York Times*, 21 December 1928.

[11] For the Shotwell-Hart debate, see Hart's "New Plan for an International Arcadia," *Current History* 30 (July 1929):673–77, and Shotwell's reply. For Shotwell's efforts to distinguish himself as realistic see "The Slogan of Outlawry," *Century* 116 (October 1928): 714–15; *New York Times*, 10 January 1929, 22 January 1929, and 5 February 1929.

were grumblings about the lack of any enforcement machinery, which, after all, only the League could provide.[12]

Still, the whole business of the Kellogg-Briand Pact rankled Wilsonians and encouraged them to dismiss pacifism much as they had dismissed isolationism. For those to whom the League was the mark of civilized intelligence, the pacifist and the isolationist were linked simply because American participation in the League was not foremost in the hearts of either. To reject collective security was to ignore the reality of the interdependent world, and thus the "baggy-kneed idealists" who thought peace would come without collective security revealed themselves as irrational brothers-under-the-skin to isolationists. It was no surprise to Wilsonians that William Borah took a leading role in the movement to outlaw war in the United States. As Shotwell put it with glib irony, some parts of the "peace forces" were "almost violently isolationist"; the outlawry movement was a "shoddy substitute" for the League that "made an appeal to both nationalism and pacifism, an emotional compound that was at its peak in the anti-Wilson movement." Raymond Fosdick, perhaps the most aggressive critic of outlawry and Kellogg-Briand, believed that pacifists dwelled with isolationists in a provincial land of make-believe where the tension between self-interest and the common good was obliterated with sweet rhetoric. In the real world, that tension was resolved through organic law and institutionalized processes. One had to see the outlawry campaign, conversely, as based on "the type of thinking that makes illegal the sale of cigarettes within the borders of Tennessee, or placed card-playing under the ban on trains in Texas, or fixes the maximum length of hat pins in Kansas," as Fosdick put it in a scornful allusion to the provincial basis of the idea. "It's so simple a child can understand it . . . We do not have to bother with the details of enforcement or worry over such questions as sanctions and penalties." Conceived in the spirit of Prohibition, Kellogg-Briand was "America's patented contribution to the solution of international difficulties."[13]

The strategy of casting one's opponents as provincial fools was even less fruitful against the pacifists than it had been when aimed at isolationists. Fosdick's argument hardly could explain why the outlawry idea

[12] Leopold, *Root and the Conservative Tradition*, 165; Wickersham, "Making the Pact of Paris Real," *Century* 118 (June 1929):147; *Walter Lippmann and the American Century*, 254–56; Lippmann to Philip Kerr, 2 January 1929, in Blum, *Public Philosopher*, 237–38; and Schulzinger, *Wise Men*, 39–46.

[13] Shotwell, *Autobiography*, 196; Fosdick, *Chronicle of a Generation*, 235–36.

caught on with the likes of Frank Kellogg, Coolidge's secretary of state, or with John Dewey, America's foremost philosopher. The same could be said of most pacifists in the interwar period, for they were, as a whole, from among the very sort of upper crust who were supposedly most capable of liberal reason. It was one thing to mock William Borah as a political Babbitt, but Sherwood Eddy, Kirby Page, Jane Addams, Reinhold Niebuhr (then in his younger, radical days), Dorothy Dezter, or A. J. Muste? Pacifists rested their arguments on sound understandings of how capitalism and the tensions of war were linked, on Progressive Christianity, and other foundations that were far more sophisticated than the Wilsonian analysis suggested. Fosdick's dismissive jabs not only had the quality of incivility, therefore, they were simply inaccurate.

Wilsonians paid a price for that inaccuracy in the 1930s. The pacifist position was not only sophisticated but its foremost proponents, such as A. J. Muste, were associated with various left-wing causes as well. The pacifists were closer to the popular pulse and effectively linked their view of international relations to the plight of common Americans. As we will see, the Wilsonians conversely grew more conservative during the depression and had fewer means for appealing to public opinion. At the very moment when they believed events in Europe began to make it imperative that the internationalist case be heard, Wilsonians found that public opinion was far more receptive to pacifism and isolationism. The 1930s turned into the heyday of what might rightly be regarded as popular anti-Wilsonianism. The Nye Committee sat in judgment of Wilson's war policies; the pacifist Oxford Pledge made the rounds of college campuses; the Ludlow Amendment continued to reappear in public discussion; and the Roosevelt administration conceded to public clamor with the series of annual Neutrality Acts beginning in 1935. The Wilsonians had forfeited their claims to the attention of the American public by denigrating both isolationists and pacifists, who at least respected the concerns of common Americans.

Disarmament kept Wilsonians and pacifists talking into the 1930s, but only in nervous conversation. As Charles Chatfield has written, the Wilsonians and the pacifists aligned into two blocs of activists through the decade, in which the former "supported collective security even at the risk of American involvement [in war]," while the latter "agitated for strict neutrality." The blocs were able to unite, temporarily, in cases such as the National Peace Conference, called by the Carnegie Endowment in order to build a united front after the Senate finally rejected the World Court in 1935. They continued talking to one another only out of mutual need. The pacifists, though at the height of their popularity, were in no position to turn down Carnegie money. The Wilsonians needed the pacifists' ability to touch the popular imagination; according to Chatfield, they "wanted the pacifists, but not their programs."[14]

The two blocs never united for long on any issue because they never overcame the fundamental ideological differences that divided them. The Wilsonians remained convinced that the pacifists were muddleheaded do-gooders whose recommendations always came around to isolationism. The pacifists, on the other hand, became increasingly skeptical of the League after the Manchurian crisis of the early 1930s; thereafter collective security seemed to them a new version of the preparedness campaign that preceded World War I. As A. J. Muste wrote in a 1938 debate with Clark Eichelberger, then a rising star among Wilsonians, collective security was a "gangster-versus-policeman" theory of international relations in which powers united to identify an aggressor, an act which dismissed the culpability of all nations in the breakdown of peace and ignored the failure of the industrialized world to meet basic demands for security and justice. To Eichelberger, the head of the League of Nations Association, Muste's argument smacked of the same flight from responsibility that had come to characterize too much of American liberalism. Collective security was necessary not to police the world, he countered, but because the modern reality of global interdependence required it. Nations were bound together whether Muste liked it or not, and for that reason alone they had to "respect the obligations of the Kellogg Pact and the League of Nations Covenant." As for the economic problems underlying international tensions, "they can only be corrected through an adjustment in the economic life of the world, and that is possible only through a high degree of cooperation by means of international machinery such as the League of Nations."[15]

Depression, Neoclassicism, and the Critique of the Corporate State

The critique of pacifism as a flight from responsibility should be understood not only in its relation to the similar critique of isolationism but as part of a wider view of modern political life. Increasingly after the

[14] Chatfield, *For Peace and Justice*, 101, 265.
[15] Muste, "Forth—to War?" *American Scholar* 7 (Autumn 1938):387–402; Eichelberger, "Forth—to Peace," *American Scholar* 8 (Winter 1938–1939):120–21.

onset of economic difficulties in 1929, Wilsonians began to sense that left-leaning New Deal liberals were also capitulating to irresponsibility. To the liberal left, the depression was mostly domestic and came from a maldistribution of wealth that prevented the average worker from consuming American products. Prosperity, therefore, depended on a national commitment to redistribute wealth and encourage consumption. Left-liberals sought a planned economy dedicated to economic self-sufficiency; rejecting the international division of labor, they insisted that what could not be produced naturally could be fabricated with the help of advanced science. Interdependence was therefore not an inevitable "reality," as Wilsonians insisted; as the unplanned result of free-market capitalism, interdependence was downright destructive.[16] As the left turned to economic nationalism, the moderate liberals associated with the internationalist perspective were forced to clarify what their version of the good society at home was to be. As they defined it, the idealist state rested on a neoclassical defense of the international division of labor. Wilsonians envisioned a state that was theoretically capable of reform but in practice reluctant to use its authority.

They always had embraced neoclassical economics, and as early as the 1920s they relied on this view of economics to interpret the persisting power of nationalism. Nationalism, they believed, had turned momentarily away from imperialism and refocused its attention within nations. When Ernest Minor Patterson coined one of the buzzwords of the 1930s by describing the new, symbiotic relationship of state and business as "economic nationalism," he updated the idealist critique of imperialism so that it accounted for internal political developments. Patterson argued that the industrialized nations had not learned much from the war, that the expansionist spirit merely reversed itself into an unrelenting spirit of

---

[16] I rely here on those works that Wilsonians most regularly took issue with: Charles Beard and G. H. E. Smith, *The Future Comes* (New York, 1933); *The Open Door at Home* (New York, 1934, 1935); and *The Old Deal and the New* (New York, 1940); Stuart Chase, *A New Deal* (New York, 1932); *The Economy of Abundance* (New York, 1934); and *The New Western Front* (New York, 1939); Laurence Dennis, *Is Capitalism Doomed?* (New York, 1932); Wallace Brett Donham, *Business Adrift* (New York, 1931); Jerome Frank, *Save America First* (New York, 1937); John Maynard Keynes, "National Self-Sufficiency," *Yale Review* 22 (June 1934):755–69; George N. Peek and Samuel Crowther, *Why Quit Our Own?* (New York, 1936); George Soule, *A Planned Economy* (New York, 1933) and *The Coming American Revolution* (New York, 1934); and Horace Kallen "Philosophical and Ethical Aspects of Consumer Cooperation," *Annals* 191 (May 1937):43–44.

national exclusion and protectionism.[17] Modern nationalism, therefore, was a corporatist fusion of state power and private profit that grew from the assumption that a nation's virility depended on the strength of its biggest businesses. Nationalism allied the state and the corporations in a collective defense of monopoly. "The contest is on a larger scale and whole countries are organized," Patterson wrote. "The struggle is less be-. tween individuals and groups [in] different countries, but between nations." In practice, the state protected the international expansion of business interests in exchange for the right to control the domestic economy, which nations then used to give artificial life, through tariffs and other trade restrictions, to inefficient industry. Hamilton Fish Armstrong pointed out that this collaboration allowed Mussolini to rise to power, for he not only had the help of conservatives but also of "many of the industrialists." For those who equated liberalism with interdependence and expanding loyalties, economic nationalism was transforming the state into something illiberal. The state had become, as Herbert Feis wrote, a "cave in which nations seek refuge from the lack of order in the international sphere and from the constant technical change in the economic one."[18]

Because it provided a refuge against international flux and domestic change, the state grew steadily more powerful and provided the means by which the modern dictator could rise to power. The more the state intervened in the economy the more powerful it became and the more it was in the interests of the state to foster the nationalist spirit. "The tragedy of the present world crisis," FPA president Raymond Buell insisted in 1931, "is that as conditions grow worse, the reactionary, nationalist groups in each country seem to grow stronger." The dictator, whom Wilsonians usually spoke of generically, fed on reaction and depended on its vitality. He preached the benefits of national self-sufficiency and promised a domestic prosperity utterly independent of the messy details and compromises that international trade entailed. The dictator avoided

[17] Ernest M. Patterson, "The Perils of the New Economic Nationalism," *Annals* 94 (March 1921):212; and Hamilton Fish Armstrong, "After Ten Years: Europe and America," *Foreign Affairs* 7 (October 1928):9.

[18] Patterson, "Perils of the New Economic Nationalism," 214–15; Armstrong, "After Ten Years: Europe and America," 9; Herbert Feis, "After Tariffs, Embargoes," *Foreign Affairs* 9 (April 1931):407–8; Francis Sayre, address at Ursinus College, 16 June 1934, in State Department Press Releases, Francis Sayre Papers, Library of Congress, Washington, D.C., box 15, pp. 384–85. See also William Smith Culbertson, *International Economic Policies: A Survey of the Economics of Diplomacy* (New York, 1925), 40–41, 328.

interdependence through domestic planning, which attempted to rationalize the use of available resources through clumsy trade quotas, exchange agreements, even barbaric bartering accords. Both methods only served to strengthen the dictatorship, for they brought under state control, at least theoretically, every aspect of economic life. When he needed to court public support, he merely bestowed favors on domestic industries; if necessary, as the invasions of Manchuria and Ethiopia demonstrated, the dictator could launch imperialist adventures to soothe discontent. The modern dictator brought nationalism full circle in the idealist view: where the traditional monarch had colonized the world in pursuit of raw materials, so the modern dictator turned to imperialism to hide both economic irrationality and political illegitimacy.[19]

In the Wilsonian view, any form of politics that rejected interdependence was potentially dictatorial. Fascism, communism, socialism, New Deal centralization, isolationism—they were not qualitatively different. Like the irrational politics of the past, the new "isms" sought narrow national aggrandizement at the expense of the common good. Left and right were thoroughly blurred, so that, in an utterance typical of Wilsonians in the 1930s, Raymond Fosdick warned that if Americans tried to chase prosperity down the nationalist path, "not very far ahead we shall be confronted by the sign posts that point to Fascism or Communism."[20]

In blending the "isms" together, they implied that practically any form of state economic intervention was dangerous. They agreed that the state had the right to intervene in society—here again the Hamiltonian spirit—and spoke with great conviction about the "end of laissez faire." Yet they also insisted that the depression had nothing to do with the nature of the marketplace and everything to do with state interference. Norman Davis's 1931 audience was hard pressed to see any acceptance

[19] Raymond L. Buell, *International Relations* (New York, 1925), 119–20, and "Toward Peace or War," *Forum* 85 (March 1931):157; and James Gerald Smith, *Economic Planning and the Tariff: An Essay in Social Philosophy* (Princeton, 1934), chap. 1. But especially see Henry A. Wallace, *America Must Choose* (New York, 1934). On the final point see Francis Sayre's speech to the National Peace Conference, 17 December 1935, Sayre Papers, Box 15; and William Culbertson, "Wandering between Two Worlds," 86.

[20] Raymond Fosdick, "Mr. Gerard's Dream," *Scientific American* 151 (November 1934):217. See Nicholas Roosevelt, "Economic Nationalism as It Affects the United States," *Annals* 174 (July 1934):56; Raymond Buell in Vera Micheles Dean, Bailey W. Diffie, Malbone W. Graham, and Mildred S. Wertheimer, *New Governments in Europe* (New York, 1934), viii; Alvin Hansen, *Economic Stabilization in an Unbalanced World* (New York, 1932), 362–65; James Warburg, *It's Up to Us* (New York, 1934), x, 12, 21; and "America Has Not Yet Chosen," *Vital Speeches*, 22 November 1934, 45–48; and Glenn Frank, "Notes on the Renewal of America," *Annals* 162 (July 1932):157.

of state activism in his assertion that "there is not a single basic difficulty confronting the world that is not traceable to government and which could not be removed if each and every government would only do its part in removing it."[21] There was no doing away with the basically internationalist doctrines "made by practically every economist since Adam Smith," as Raymond Buell asserted. "Because of the growing dependence of one part of the world on another, the interests of each part can best be advanced by advancing the interests of the whole." Ernest Patterson, who cautioned his colleagues that they ought not "blindly 'modernize Mill' " but "modernize economics," nevertheless argued that there was no replacement for the " 'economic man' who has been so much derided," particularly because "many lines of economic activity may be described better in classical terms than in any other way." Patterson summed up the position: "The state has intervened and *laissez faire* is profoundly modified."[22]

The only practical way of modernizing economics that Patterson could see was to develop a "world economics" that encouraged nations to cooperate. "World economics" became a cure-all for war, political regimentation, provincialism, and depression. World economics became the means for resolving the tension between legitimate state activism and the international marketplace; it provided, as they began to insist early in the New Deal, the middle way between laissez faire and regimentation.

Secretary of Agriculture Henry Wallace offered the most famous version of this argument in his pamphlet *America Must Choose*. Wallace, an Iowa native who learned the cosmopolitan ways of Washington when his father was secretary of agriculture under Harding, confronted the power of centralized government early in the New Deal when he oversaw the infamous "little-pig slaughter," the crop-destruction program designed to raise farm prices. Struck by what he called the "pain of nationalism" and the "pain of internationalism," Wallace set out to explain how the New Deal might navigate the middle course. He preferred free

[21] Norman Davis, "International Financial Problems," address before the Academy of Political Science, New York, 13 November 1931, Davis Papers, box 15, p. 6. For an early concession to the end of laissez faire see F. W. Taussig, *Free Trade, the Tariff, and Reciprocity* (New York, 1920), 3.

[22] Buell, *International Relations*, 96, 285; Patterson, *Economic Bases of Peace* (New York, 1939), 62; and *The World's Economic Dilemma* (New York, 1930), 5; see also Alvin Hansen, *Economic Stabilization in an Unbalanced World*, 141; Culbertson, *International Economic Policies*, 489; Arthur Bunce, *Economic Nationalism and the Farmer* (Ames, Iowa, 1938); and F. Cyril James, "Economic Nationalism and War," *Annals* 175 (September 1934):68.

trade, but it was impracticable given the circumstances. The market would disrupt production at home and require extensive planning in order to retire inefficient industries; it exposed people to insecurity and left them clamoring for state regulation. Nationalism, on the other hand, benefited special interests through tariffs, disrupted the market, and constantly demanded more regimentation. The only realistic approach to political economy in 1933 was to maneuver between extremes by borrowing parts of each program.[23] If Americans did not find the middle way and submit to "voluntary social discipline," then the "extreme left will join hands with the extreme right to bring about that most dangerous of all forms of government, a corrupt oligarchy, maintaining itself in power by pandering to the vices and prejudices of a bitter, perennially unemployed multitude."

To James Warburg, an expert on the money supply who had been a delegate to the London Economic Conference, Wallace's sensible ideas required that Americans recognize the "perfectly obvious": to ignore interdependence "must mean extreme regimentation and the end of democracy." Freedom depended on a "whole-hearted effort to develop an orderly program of mutually advantageous trade relationships with other nations." The "middle way" evidently depended on the reemergence of political reason, which would show itself in internationalist policies.[24]

The Marginalization of the Wilsonians

There was plenty of evidence that the Wilsonians were correct about the depression. It was an international crisis. World trade fell by 60 percent between 1929 and 1932, the world price level slid by one-third, and world unemployment soared. How could so many otherwise reasonable people fail to understand the international dimensions of the crisis? Walter Lippmann pounded out the point in the staccato prose that usually indicated his frustration: "This damnable crisis is international, whether we like it or not. It is international in spite of the fact that international bankers also think it is an international crisis. It is international in spite of Senator Johnson, Mr. Hearst, and all they have said and done to the

[23] Wallace, *America Must Choose*, 2, 18–19, 10–11, 26–27.

[24] Ibid., 15, and Henry Wallace, *New Frontiers* (New York, 1934), 15, 87, 20; "Spiritual Forces and the State," *Forum* 91 (June 1934):356; and "America—Recluse or Trader?" *Collier's*, 2 February 1935, 8; Warburg, *It's Up to Us* (New York, 1934), 154–56.

contrary. It is international even though one man likes England, but does not like France; though the other likes France, but distrusts England. It is international in spite of all prejudices, preferences, and wishes to the contrary."[25]

The real question, however, was not what caused the crisis but what to do about it, and here the Wilsonians' analysis was less sound. They clung to the neoclassical economic solutions and reverted to the tired strategy of seeking a strong statesman, someone who could hold together the national spirit without conceding to interest-group demands. They consequently ignored how painful the depression was and how badly common Americans needed an aggressive governmental response, something that they defined away as dangerous and counterproductive.

In 1932, many Wilsonians, in an early effort to take action, pushed Newton Baker for the Democratic nomination, the last time the Wilsonian "shadow wing" of the party exerted itself. Baker was the "only hope," Norman Davis believed, particularly because his political purity contrasted sharply with Franklin Roosevelt's elusiveness.[26] Baker did initiate a campaign of sorts, though it was a strange one. While his closest friends worked to make his nomination possible, Baker stood aloof, as if he intended to accept the nomination only if the convention, having found all others inadequate, implored him. A frustrated Lippmann wrote that Baker was "almost perversely unhelpful to his enthusiastic friends." Undaunted, Lippmann tried to make Baker's peculiar behavior a virtue. "There are those who cannot believe that any man who has the Presidency within his reach should sit still and do nothing to obtain it," he wrote in his syndicated column. "Difficult as it is to believe that there are such men in public life, the truth is that he is an authentic example of a man who does not seek office."[27]

Baker occasionally did act like a candidate. In mid-January, he wrote a letter to the League of Nations Association in which he made the standard internationalist points: the United States should join the League

---

[25] Quoted in Harry Gideonse, *War Debts* (Chicago, 1934), 2; see Raymond Buell, *The World Adrift* (Boston and New York, 1933), 24–25, and G. B. Roorbach, "Foreign Trade or Isolation?" *Foreign Affairs* 11 (October 1932):37–50, for more figures on the decline of trade after the 1929 peak.

[26] Davis to Baker, 7 April 1932, and Davis to Cordell Hull, 7 April 1932, Davis Papers, boxes 3 and 27 respectively; Fosdick claimed that he was a "Baker man first and last" and accused Roosevelt of "carrying water on both shoulders." Fosdick to Ellery Sedgwick, 5 February 1932, box 22, file 20430, Fosdick Papers.

[27] Baker to Lippmann, 21 December 1931, Baker Papers, box 148; Lippmann quoted in Cramer, *Newton D. Baker*, 239, and "Today and Tomorrow," 29 June 1932.

because it was an instrument both for international morality and for American economic interests. The *New York Times* printed the letter, splashing over it the claim that Baker urged immediate entry into the League. Had Baker not been a candidate, he would have ignored the very slight misrepresentation. Instead he insisted to Ralph Hayes that his position was almost the exact opposite. Where he believed that the elections of 1920 and 1924 should have been turned into referendums on the League, he now "had even graver doubt about American adhesion to the League than I ever had before." He never had wanted to take America "into the League by fiat"; his current view was that the League should be taken out of partisan politics and that there should not even be a pro-League plank in the platform.[28] Here was a new position, and, at Hayes's behest, Baker made it public several days later. It was interpreted widely as Baker's way of saying that he had entered the race, for it supposedly removed the one obstacle to his nomination, the unyielding support for American participation in the League.[29]

In itself easily dismissed as a slight concession to political expediency, Baker's stand on the League takes on a somewhat larger meaning when seen with the rest of his reluctant campaign. In a time of dire national emergency, Baker had utterly nothing to say about domestic issues. He had no solutions to the depression and already had denounced national planning as "a drastic subjection of the people to a system of compulsory and uncompensated servitude." Good Wilsonian that he was, Baker explained that he favored planning, which, in his version, began with international peace. When cooperation reigned at home and abroad, the world could anticipate a "gradual contemporaneous emancipation from the past" that would preserve wealth while creating new equality.[30] His failure to outline any response to the crisis made it easy for opponents both inside and outside the party to depict him as a friend and tool of wealthy corporate interests, which came disturbingly close to the truth. He drew campaign support from Coca-Cola's Robert Woodruff, among others others his law firm represented Cleveland's most powerful corporations, and Baker himself headed the city's Chamber of Commerce.

[28] *New York Times*, 15 January 1932, p. 17, and 16 January 1932, p. 22; Baker to Hayes 22 January 1932, Baker Papers, box 116.

[29] Cramer, *Newton D. Baker*, 241; "A New Boost for the Baker Boom," *The Literary Digest*, 6 February 1932; 8; "Newton D. Baker: Would Be President," *World's Work* 61 (March 1932):18.

[30] Newton Baker, "Is Economic Planning Possible?" *Review of Reviews* 84 (September 1931):57–59.

Both the *Nation* and the *New Republic* attacked his fondness for the rich and powerful. Baker did absolutely nothing to disassociate himself from his wealthy friends or to develop domestic programs that might undercut the criticism. The 1932 campaign, if it showed anything, illustrated that Baker had grown indifferent to general sentiment. He seemed to expect that if the public faced reality, it would choose him above all others, just as it should face the reality of world interdependence and call for American membership in the League. He based his political methods on what Robert Morss Lovett called "the genial laissez-faire of taking everyone at his own valuation."[31]

Baker's default left Wilsonian hopes in the hands of Franklin Roosevelt. He was an old associate, though familiarity bred contempt. Most of Baker's supporters had known Roosevelt for some time and had regarded him as a none-too-profound politician. Lippmann summed up their opinion when he described Roosevelt as "an amiable boy scout." At least Roosevelt would need instruction, Raymond Fosdick decided, "as far as the international situation is concerned," though this proved difficult during the election. Roosevelt's maneuvering, his refusal to be pinned down on a program, and his shifting on the tariff issue induced grimacing and hand-wringing. Particularly because he "has really been a strong advocate of the League," each departure away from internationalism brought howls of "apostasy."[32]

After the Hundred Days they warmed to Roosevelt. No single act aroused them. Having no one else, they imagined a metamorphosis. After his first meeting with the newly-installed president, Norman Davis told Fosdick "that fellow in there is not the fellow we used to know. There's been a miracle here."[33] For the most part, it was Roosevelt's decisiveness that they admired. Lippmann insisted that such presidential exertion could thwart the will of "organized minorities." Nicholas Murray Butler similarly lauded the president for providing badly needed

[31] Cramer, *Newton D. Baker,* 244–45. Robert Morss Lovett, "Newton D. Baker: The Candide of Candidates," *New Republic,* 18 May 1932, 8–11; Oswald Garrison Villard "The Shamelessness of Newton D. Baker," *Nation,* 4 July 1934, 7.

[32] Lippmann to Baker, 24 November 1931, in Blum, *Public Philosopher,* 280–81; Fosdick to Jesse Woodrow Sayre, 10 June 1932, file 20814, and Fosdick to Arthur Sweetser, 26 February 1932, box 22; Manley Hudson to Fosdick, 8 February 1932, box 22, Fosdick Papers; Francis B. Sayre to Roosevelt, 13 October 1932, Sayre Papers, box 7; Norman Davis to Walter Lippmann, 22 August 1932, and Lippmann to Davis, 25 August 1932, Davis Papers, box 35; and Fosdick's letter to the editor, *New York Times,* 8 February 1932.

[33] Fosdick, *Chronicle of a Generation,* 247.

"moral and intellectual leadership."[34] It was also possible to see the early programs as temporary measures, and generally Wilsonians were impressed more by the administration's restraint than by its programs. Though it was part of the nationalism resurgent throughout the world, wrote Raymond Buell, the New Deal retained the "underlying principles of democracy" by avoiding outright assaults on representative government or civil liberties. Butler applauded the National Industrial Recovery Act as a cooperative, popular, congressionally enacted, and "carefully planned" piece of legislation, but mostly he feared the only alternative in sight: outright dictatorship.[35] Neither Butler nor his colleagues called for a retreat from a strong centralized government, and for this reason, they enjoyed a honeymoon with the New Deal.

Wilsonians were further heartened by a few early indications that the administration intended to pursue the internationalist agenda in foreign policy. Roosevelt appointed Cordell Hull secretary of state, other Wilsonians, such as Francis Sayre, moved into the department, and still others, such as Raymond Buell, began job hunting there. Moreover, Roosevelt reappointed Norman Davis to the American disarmament team at Geneva. No one wanted to admit that Roosevelt was appeasing both the Wilsonians and Southern Democrats in choosing Hull; his short-term motives were less important than his genuine conviction that collective security was necessary, a conviction that he reenforced by naming the reliable Davis as his point man on disarmament.

The greatest praise for the president came after the approval of the Reciprocal Trade Act (RTA) in late 1933. The program was designed to coax nations to lower trade barriers by allowing the president to reduce U.S. barriers by up to 50 percent for any nation that entered such an agreement. Passed in June 1934, RTA was hailed as an administrative victory for that venerable tariff killer, Cordell Hull.[36] Already upheld as the champion of interdependence, Hull was lauded as liberalism's foremost defender. Hull kept some otherwise disgruntled liberals loyal to the Democrats, he appealed to Republicans such as Henry Stimson, and

[34] Lippmann to Felix Frankfurter, 3 March 1933, in Blum, *Public Philosopher*, 302–3. Butler to FDR, 16 May 1933, and telegram, Butler to FDR, 3 June 1933, Butler to Roosevelt, 23 May 1935, and Butler to Sol Bloom, 27 January 1936, Personal Papers file 445; also James Warburg to FDR, 9 November 1932 and 30 May 1933, Personal Papers file 540, Franklin D. Roosevelt Papers, Roosevelt Library.
[35] See Buell's preface to Dean et al., *New Governments in Europe*, vii–viii. Butler, *Between Two Worlds*, 385. See also Smith, *Economic Planning and the Tariff*, v–vi.
[36] Arthur Sweetser to Raymond Fosdick, 22 March 1933, and Fosdick to Sweetser, 17 May 1933, Fosdick Papers, box 23; Cordell Hull, *Memoirs*, vol. 1, chaps. 26–27; Francis Sayre, *Glad Adventure* (New York, 1957), chap. 12.

he even transcended mere humanity in the estimation of others. Peter Molyneaux, a Carnegie Endowment trustee and, as a Texan, one of the rare non-Eastern defenders of Hull, claimed that "every day I thank God for Cordell Hull, and I pray that more power and long life may be given him. He has held aloft the torch which has given hope to true Liberals throughout the world. . . . And because of his fidelity, chiefly because of it, there is still hope that this people may rally to the standard which he has kept from trailing in the dust and that his liberating ideals may yet save the world."[37]

What NRA was to national planners, RTA became to Wilsonians, and in the initial push for the act they argued that the RTAs constituted a New Deal for the world. The program was the international component of the New Deal, not because it would institute international planning but because it would balance the nationalist domestic program with a program for reestablishing international trade.[38] It was the answer to Wallace's challenge that America move between regimentation and laissez faire. As Raymond Buell argued, the agreements represented "a modified form of economic liberalism" upon which "political democracy in this country" depends.[39] Francis Sayre even borrowed from Wallace to entitle his defense of the Hull program. In *America Must Act*, he rehashed all the urgent warnings that "economic nationalism leads inevitably toward governmental dictatorship and strangulation of private enterprise," after which he lauded RTA as "the soundest and most practicable method" of easing the depression.[40] Some defenders of the trade agreements went well beyond Wallace; as one member of the Committee on Trade Agreements wrote, "the Hull program is intended . . . to maintain a free economy and to preserve the capitalist system"; "totalitarianism" had crept too far into America through the "light talk" of those who advocated self-sufficiency. The bottom line was that "democracy and capitalism are essentially international."[41] The act was more than a mere effort to reduce trade barriers, more than a strike against the domestic left. It was a tremendous weapon in the battle to save liberalism.

[37] Warburg to Hull, 13 October 1936, reprinted as chap. 3 in *Our War, Our Peace* (New York, 1941); Stimson and Bundy, *On Active Service*, 298–301; Peter Molyneaux, "American Trade Policy and World Peace," *Annals* 192 (July 1937):128–29; Sayre to Hull, 10 April 1940, Sayre Papers, box 4. Also Raymond Buell, *Death by Tariff*, (Chicago, 1939), 2; and *The Hull Trade Program and the American System* (New York, 1938), 21.

[38] Francis Sayre, "Tariff Bargaining," NBC radio address, 26 March 1934, Sayre Papers, box 15; Culbertson, "Wandering between Two Worlds," 84–85.

[39] Buell to Henry Stimson, 28 March 1938, Buell Papers, box 5.

[40] Francis Sayre, *America Must Act* (Boston 1936), 22, 35–36.

[41] Henry F. Grady, "The Consequences of Trade Barriers," *Annals* 198 (July 1938):35, 37–39.

It was also a strange way to go about saving liberalism. It was difficult to demonstrate how RTA benefited the general welfare, particularly because its few practical benefits went to those most deeply involved in international trade. Wilsonians were obliged, as they recognized, to offer an ideological vision just as stirring, just as capable of attracting the loyalty of depression-wracked people as were socialism and fascism. When they offered weak measures to revive international trade, they presented nothing more than the revamped version of the classical division of labor. Leaving the defense of liberalism to tariff reduction did nothing to clarify the common good and even less to inspire the public's confidence that Wilsonians had answers to the issues at hand.

Besides the RTAs, the best they could manage toward a positive liberalism was to reassert the requirements of good government—to deny power to divisive interests and to seek the general welfare—which puts them at odds with Roosevelt when he began to play mass politics through Social Security, the 1936 tax bill, and the appeal to labor. Newton Baker was the first to break with the administration over what he thought was the promotion of "sectional and group tendencies [that] look to the State as the source of well-being. The formation of coherent and vocal organizations to maintain lobbies in Washington . . . illustrates how far we have departed from our old beliefs." The administration's economic nationalism violated the old beliefs because, by definition, it conferred privileges on certain industries through tariffs and other controls. "In a word, what has happened," Nicholas Murray Butler sulked in a wistful critique of the legislative program he had commended only a year before, "is that special interest, personal ambition, and entrenched privilege have been increasingly successful in bending the national legislature to their will." By enlarging the province of the state without thwarting special interests, the New Deal merely had provided a larger public trough for the greedy to feed upon.[42] There was almost nothing about the New Deal that Raymond Buell supported by 1936, and in his view the nation was suffering from the factionalism and division that were the all-too-familiar results of modern nationalism. "Despite the cry against federal centralization," he wrote Adolf Berle, Jr., "the American people seem a less unified people than a loose confederation of conflicting regional groups."[43]

[42] Baker, "The Decay of Self-Reliance," *Atlantic Monthly* 154 (December 1934):729–33; Butler, *Between Two Worlds*, 199.

[43] "Casual Observations on the State of the Nation," 13 May 1937, Buell Papers, box 4, "National Policy Committee, March 1936–June 1947" file, pp. 1–2; Buell to Adolf

Of the prominent Wilsonians only John W. Davis took so drastic a step as to join the right-wing Liberty League, but very few defended the president, many were outspokenly critical, and still others searched for alternatives.[44] Of the anti-New Dealers, Baker and Lippmann became the most active. Baker never had liked Roosevelt, but Lippmann had, only to become disgusted with political factionalism and the appeal to group politics. By 1936 he was collecting his thoughts for what became one of the two most important statements of liberal idealism in the interwar period, *The Good Society,* and he was also considering opposing Roosevelt. He was "troubled," he wrote Baker, by the president's appeals to popular discontent.[45] Baker, sure that "the president and his advisors have lent themselves to the theory of class war," ranted that the administration had given itself to the unprincipled attempt to appeal to the masses by promising nothing more definite than "abundance." "This object I am sure is the central thought of highwaymen as well as of philanthropists," Baker howled. Roosevelt had encouraged "truculent, assertive, and selfish interests" and evidently did not care that they were "incompatible with any rational theory of permanently organized society."[46]

Both men thereafter helped to organize a group of "principled Democrats" who intended, if not to steal the nomination from Roosevelt, at least to make a stand against the corruption of national politics. Lippmann described this lot as "liberal Democrats" who had nothing in common with the Liberty League or other reactionary defenders of the status quo. The Republicans demonstrated no will to oppose Roosevelt, he wrote Lewis Douglas, and "the danger now is that the country for lack of an effective opposition won't be made to see the things that really are bad." The fight, therefore, had to be waged within the Democratic party, which was not a courageous position for Lippmann to take since he ultimately voted for Landon.[47]

Berle, 13 May 1937, Box 7, Foreign Policy Association file, and Buell to Henry Wallace, 21 June 1937, box 6, Wallace file, Adolf A. Berle, Jr., Papers, Roosevelt Library, Hyde Park.

[44] Harbaugh, *Lawyer's Lawyer,* chap. 21, and also see James Warburg, *Hell Bent for Election* (New York, 1936), and *Still Hell Bent* (New York, 1936).

[45] Lippmann to Baker, 22 January 1936, in Blum, *Public Philosopher,* 343.

[46] Baker to Lippmann, 27 January 1936, Baker Papers, box 149.

[47] Lippmann to Douglas, 16 March 1936, in Blum, *Public Philosopher,* 347; Lippmann to Douglas, 27 March 1936, ibid., 347–48; Lippmann to Arthur Page, 4 March 1936, ibid., 347; Lippmann to Berenson, 7 February 1936, ibid., 344, in which Lippmann wrote that the Republicans could do much worse than nominate Landon.

These "principled" liberals condemned Roosevelt not so much for radical commitments as for the absence of commitments, and so they took it upon themselves to restate the principles that they thought American liberalism ought to embody. In April, Lippmann sent Douglas a draft of a platform that read like the New Freedom of 1912. The 1920s, Lippmann wrote, "fostered the growth of private monopoly subsidized by exclusive privilege of tariff protection," only to be followed by a period in which various other interests were protected through "state-sponsored monopolies." Hoping to steer between reactionary big business and the New Deal, he held that both private and public forms of centralization stung "the nation as a whole" and paralyzed its progress. Lippmann then outlined his "principles": all forms of privilege had to be abolished and national policy should seek the "regulation of the economic order ... by genuinely free bargains in the open market"; decentralization of government had to be effected; fiscal responsibility should be reassumed; and an "unqualified reiteration" of the rule of law had to be made.[48]

Principled opposition, rare enough in American politics, was fine, but it got Wilsonians no closer to any real alternatives. It was doubtful in any case that they could have attracted much public support when, as it turned out, they could not even draw the support of other Democrats. Lippmann at least had hoped to engage "men like Hull and even Wallace," Carter Glass and Ogden Mills; Baker expected support from twenty-five or thirty "sufficiently leading Democrats." They failed to excite even this modest support. "One after another ... begged off," Baker complained to Ralph Hayes, "all agreeing with the soundness" of the principles while refusing to support them.[49]

Baker, Douglas, and Leo Wolman were left to declare these principles on their own in a letter to the *New York Times* in June 1936, which merely restated Lippmann's "tentative" principles of April. This "declaration of principles" was clear, moderate, and thankfully brief compared to a similar set of principles, undated and unsigned, in Baker's possession and immodestly entitled the "Declaration of Independence of 1936." In this broadside, Baker and company condemned Roosevelt for everything from granting favors to sheer dishonesty to promoting "scarcity" instead of "abundance." But it too fell hardest upon the president for pitting "group against group; debtor against creditor; employe [sic] against employer; the thriftless against the thrifty; power users against power

---

[48] Lippmann to Douglas, 16 April 1936, ibid., 348–51.
[49] Ibid.; Baker to Ralph Hayes, 10 June 1936, Baker Papers, box 117.

producers; the 'have nots' against the 'haves'—almost always the larger group against the smaller; and always with political aims favorable to himself."[50]

Excluding Lippmann and Buell, both of whom supported Landon, these Democrats cast lame votes for Roosevelt. The Republicans passed a high-tariff plank that Baker characteristically derided as "another face-saving concession for Senator Borah and his medieval Senatorial associates." Landon had his share of "common sense and practical liberalism," Baker conceded, and, to be fair, one could not expect a man who "has been preoccupied with relatively local concerns" to understand world affairs.[51] Lippmann just as lamely expected Landon to reform by November. The Republican platform was "both ignorant and reactionary," an "appeal to parochial prejudices," but Lippmann stuck with them in the end. Baker concluded simply: "I find it difficult to be a Democrat and impossible to be a Republican."[52]

The whole experience pointed up how marginal the Wilsonian wing had become in the Democratic party, and thus the falling out with the New Deal was the culmination of twenty years of political experience, especially for Baker. He was forced to admit how utterly disillusioned he was with political discourse and with the possibility of forging some sort of new consensus. He wrote Hayes that, in attempting to organize the party coup against Roosevelt, he had been inspired by Albert J. Nock's recent claim that civilization could be saved only by a determined remnant, a blatantly elitist position that summed up fairly well two decades of steady disillusionment with humanity.[53]

The Moral and Political Collapse of Liberalism

By the late 1930s, it was impossible to think, as so many idealists had believed a mere twenty years before, that a grand triumph of common-

---

[50] *New York Times*, 3 June 1936, p. 20; "Declaration of Independence of 1936," in Baker Papers, box 202, Franklin D. Roosevelt file. Douglas articulated many of these same positions in his 1935 Godkin Lectures, collected in the aptly named *The Liberal Tradition: A Free People and a Free Economy* (New York, 1935).

[51] Baker to Hamilton Fish Armstrong, 30 June 1936, and Baker to Henry Haskell, 29 September 1936, Baker Papers, box 97.

[52] Lippmann to Frank Knox, 17 July 1936, and Lippmann to William Allen White, 11 August 1936, in Blum, *Public Philosopher*, 352–53; Baker to John W. Davis, 29 September 1936, Baker Papers, box 97.

[53] Baker to Hayes, 10 June 1936.

good liberalism was humanity's immanent destiny. The failures of the League, turmoil in the Far East, the persistence of depression, fascist aggression in Ethiopia, the Spanish civil war, the increase in the demands of special interests at home, and, it is fair to say, their own failure to remake liberalism, induced an almost overwhelming sense of moral collapse. It was within this context, it should be noted, that they began to take sharp issue with the New Deal. Lippmann's *The Good Society,* as we shall see, summed up the widespread disaffection of his fellow liberals, with its contention that true liberalism had been declining since sometime in the mid-nineteenth century, when modernity began to undercut the moral and ethical basis of enlightened self-interest. Norman Davis, after reading the book, wrote: "True liberalism is certainly at a discount today. . . . The strong political current running everywhere . . . ignores that there is such a thing as the integrity of the human soul." The world was crumbling, Francis Sayre warned a commencement audience in 1935, and the cause was clear. "Civilization progresses when men share common beliefs and common faiths which are foundationed [sic] upon enduring truth. . . . A civilization in which special groups are held in restraint by force without common beliefs cannot endure. . . . A civilization which is lacking in such fundamental faiths loses its cohesiveness and its power."[54]

The sense of moral collapse was not simply a matter of ebbing élan. There were solid signs that they recognized what modernity had done to liberalism—or at least to their form of liberalism. Partly that sense had been emerging since World War I, in the concerns over technology. Even the most systematic Wilsonian examination of the problem, however, Fosdick's *Old Savage in the New Civilization,* clung to a basic confidence that political rationality would prevail and direct technology to moral ends. The experience of the 1930s called that notion into question. The best Wilsonian writings at this point had to wrestle with the causes and consequences that faced the world in light of reason's apparent demise. Lippmann did so by returning to the Enlightenment for redemptive qualities. Raymond Buell called somewhat more simply but more directly in *Isolated America* for the revivification of "moral presuppositions."

Buell became a poignant symbol for the fading idealists in the early 1940s, because he undertook a terrific personal struggle to stay faithful

---

[54] Davis to Lippmann, 20 August 1937, Davis Papers, box 35; Sayre, "Recovery," address at Bryant College, Providence, Rhode Island, 2 August 1935, Sayre Papers, box 15.

in a world he was convinced had destroyed faith—an ideological struggle intensified by an eventually fatal battle with brain cancer. In 1940 he left the Foreign Policy Association to work as editor of *Fortune's* internationalist round tables; he had abandoned Roosevelt and worked to push Hull for the 1940 nomination. When that failed, he went to work for Wendell Wilkie, less out of conviction than for lack of alternatives.

Roosevelt's victory in 1940 stiffened Buell's view that the debasement of public life was rooted in a general moral crisis in which "scientific materialism" had set loose the primary bonds between individuals, groups, and nations. Modernity had raised an economy of baffling complexity and generated an intellectual atmosphere that destroyed democracy's self-confidence and generated both international conflict and interest-group scrambling. Society had lost its moral consensus. Democracy once meant that "liberty should be exercised so as to advance moral ends, freely chosen by each individual for himself," and nineteenth-century liberalism had "rested on the idea that man was a creature of dignity [with] a rational power of choice between what we called 'good' and 'evil.' " In contrast, "scientific materialism," through Marxism and psychoanalysis, had reduced man to "nothing more than an animal," given to impulse, devoid of an inbred morality and the dignity that went with it. Where man was a mere product of environment or economics, individual action came to mean "nothing more than indulgence of the self or the exploitation of others." Modern liberalism built on scientific materialism continued to embrace individualism but jettisoned the older "moral presuppositions" that once had held individualism in check. Rather than leading to a harmonious common good, such a society lent itself to indulgent self-interest and even dictatorship. "When liberalism becomes nothing more than a competition for profit, when liberty becomes an end in itself rather than a means to an end, a spiritual miasma is produced."[55]

However deeply felt these views were, they only gave rise in Buell's case to solutions that were neither original nor well designed to arrest so complete a collapse of moral order. His best answer was "responsible competition," a sort of gentle profiteering which recalled nothing so

[55] Raymond Buell, *Isolated America*, 31–32; "Where Are the Democracies Going?" address to the Sunday Breakfast Club, Philadelphia, 2 November 1938, Buell Papers, box 7, pp. 30–31; "The Churches and the World Outside," abstract of address to the Berkshire North Association of Congregational Churches, Williamstown, Mass., 17 October 1939, box 7, p. 4.

much as Wilson's "regulated competition" of 1912.[56] He also called for a new statesmanship and rehabilitated Wilson's contention that the core of the problem lay with a "public life in America [that] so far has failed to attract the calibre of men responsible for our great intellectual and cultural progress."[57] If the nation continued to fail in that regard, Buell warned Senator Arthur Vandenberg, it could fall into a new Dark Ages. Because the political sphere could no longer be relied on as a barrier to corruption, it was left to the university to produce "real intellectual and political leadership" and "creative thinking on the problem of political philosophy and of political structure." Otherwise the world promised war, revolution, and barbarity, "made infinitely more fiendish by modern technology."[58]

Buell's ideas were open to the same objections to which internationalist economics and politics were always vulnerable. "Responsible competition" depended, first, on the willingness of business to suspend self-interest, something for which it was not widely known. Nor was there any good reason to think that a "statesman-intellectual" would be less self-interested than any other statesman. Buell's hope for a regenerated world rested on the revivication of certain "absolutist moral conceptions" that would restore a more solid foundation than the flimsy and shifting ground of liberal pragmatism or modern science. But here was the rub: how could the individual's innate sense of morality be reclaimed, how could scientific materialism be overturned, if one was determined to maintain and even strengthen the very system of industrialism that had buried those moral presuppositions and given birth to scientific materialism in the first place?

---

[56] Buell to James Gerald Smith, 23 March 1942, Buell Papers, box 5; Buell to Remsen Brial, 3 January 1944, box 1; "Balanced Abundance a Contribution to Our Democracy," address at the Annual Convention of the American Farm Bureau Federation, Chicago, 7 December 1939, box 7.

[57] Buell to Remsen Brial, p. 13.

[58] Ibid.; Buell to Vandenberg, 10 September 1944, box 6, Buell Papers.

7

The Second Chance?

The experience of the 1930s demonstrated that there was little new in the political philosophy or the practical programs of Wilsonians. The decade exposed how deeply rooted internationalism was in a static liberalism that owed considerably more to the Enlightenment than to the twentieth century. The marginalization of the Wilsonians was not simply a matter of political ineptitude or a temporary falling out of fashion. Theirs was a philosophical decline, precipitated by modernity's refusal to live up to idealist expectations.

On the surface of things, the group enjoyed a final stand, a "second chance," as Robert Divine has put it, when World War II issued in the formation of the United Nations. Wilsonians took leading roles in agitating for American aid to the Allies, in planning for postwar organization, and in defending and executing those plans once in place. But what superficially was a final victory in 1945 in fact marked the twilight of idealist hopes that enlightened self-interest could prevail. The security council veto emasculated the UN from the start, the atomic bomb bore out long-standing fears that technology might outpace ethics, and the onset of the Cold War left the world fundamentally divided according to the interests of the two great powers.

The Compromise of Collective Security

The predictable antidote to the collapse of moral absolutes lay in the institutionalization of reason in the widest possible forum, international cooperation. In the later 1930s, such a forum was no longer to be found in the League of Nations but in collective security, which in practice meant American aid to the enemies of fascism. Wilsonians hardly could have been expected to respond to the slide to war in any way other than by advocating collective security, aid to the Allies, and, eventually, American intervention in World War II.

Since the early 1920s, they had argued that collective security was the best way to achieve disarmament and neutrality. Neutrality in an interdependent world where national interests intermingled and overlapped, as Shotwell put it as early as 1926, had to mean the "prevention" of war and not simply indifference or isolation. Neutrality to them was the active prevention of war through collective security, a conception that they succeeded in insinuating into American foreign policy, for example, through the Far Eastern policies of Henry Stimson.[1]

However tentatively, Roosevelt too accepted this definition of neutrality, and his cautious moves toward collective security after 1936 brought solace in troubled times, even for those who had fallen out with the New Deal. The Quarantine Address of October 1937 was something of a triumph; Hull, Davis, and Sumner Welles worked inside the administration for a presidential renunciation of isolationism, while outsiders such as Clark Eichelberger were consulted and alerted to the content of the address. It is no wonder that Roosevelt articulated the main theme of interwar Wilsonian defense policy. "Peace-loving nations," he announced, "must make a concerted effort" to arrest the spread of "international anarchy and instability from which there is no escape through mere isolation or neutrality."[2] Wilsonians who had been bitterly critical the year before reconsidered their opposition to Roosevelt. Newton Baker remained spiteful, but he regarded the speech as unassailable and the direction of policy, thankfully in Hull's hands, as unimpeachable. James Warburg obsequiously pleaded for forgiveness in light of his aggressive criticism of the New Deal in 1936. "I was wrong and I am sorry," he wrote the president. Having thus confessed, he offered his services "in any capacity," only this time "I'll write no books." Even the crusty

---

[1] Shotwell, "An American Policy with Reference to Disarmament," *International Conciliation* 220 (May 1926): 257–58; Report of a Committee of the National Peace Conference, "A Study of Neutrality Legislation," *International Conciliation* 316 (January 1936): 18–20. Robert Divine dubs the Wilsonian definition the "new neutrality" in the best work on the neutrality debates, *The Illusion of Neutrality* (Chicago, 1962), especially 32–36, 79. On Stimson see *On Active Service*, chap. 9 and 308–16.

[2] Robert Dallek, *Roosevelt and American Foreign Policy, 1932–1945* (New York, 1979), 147–52; *New York Times*, 14 October 1937.

John W. Davis swallowed his pride and defended Lend-Lease, though he still "was out of harmony" with the New Deal.[3]

Once war erupted in Europe in September 1939 collective security advocates chose two often-used tactics: they organized and they engaged in propaganda. During the 1939 neutrality debates, members of the League of Nations Association, under Shotwell and Eichelberger, began considering what shape a revamped League or an altogether new international organization should assume, given the experience of the interwar years. Under the inelegant title the Committee for the Study of the Organization of the Peace (CSOP), Eichelberger and Shotwell organized a broadly-based group that included scholars Quincy Wright, Charles G. Fenwick, Harry Gideonse, Ernest Paterson, Eugene Staley, and Clyde Eagleton, as well as other sponsors and members who were less tied to the Wilsonian tradition such as John Foster Dulles, Alvin Johnson, and Max Lerner. Wilsonians clearly dominated the CSOP, for in addition to the many scholars from their ranks came League of Nations Association president Frank Boudreau, Des Moines *Register* editor W. W. Waymack, the journalist Malcolm Davis, Arthur Sweetser, and Virginia Gildersleeve, who was a Barnard dean and long-time patron of internationalist organizations. The CSOP met frequently over the next year, and if it failed to develop a blueprint for world peace, it nevertheless determined to fight for the construction of a new international organization.[4]

The pressure-group politics of the collective-security advocates are better known. In April 1940, Eichelberger teamed with William Allen White to organize the Committee to Defend America by Aiding the Allies (CDAAA), which they formed for the sole purpose of advocating collective security. The League of Nations Association quickly began turning local branches into units of the CDAAA, while the Council on Foreign Affairs offered less direct but nonetheless substantial help in recruiting members and speakers. Eichelberger, Shotwell, Stimson, Wright, Fenwick, Nicholas Murray Butler, Walter Lippmann, Lewis Douglas, all joined the group. Under the CDAAA, Wilsonians joined a host of other liberals. Much more than the CSOP, the CDAAA realized Shotwell's hope that the collective security movement be non-partisan and, more

[3] Baker to Ralph Hayes, 12 October 1937, Baker Papers, box 117; Warburg to Roosevelt 20 June 1940 and 8 November 1940, as well as his two pro-third-term speeches dated 14 October 1940 and 31 October 1940 in Roosevelt Papers, Personal Papers file 540. John W. Davis's remarks "In Favor of Lend-Lease" were sent as an enclosure in John W. Davis to Norman Davis, 19 February 1941, Norman Davis Papers, box 10.

[4] Clark Eichelberger, *Organizing for Peace* (New York, 1977), 111–18; Shotwell, *Autobiography*, 311–12; Divine, *Second Chance*, 30–34.

important at this point, regionally diverse. If it is impossible to know how influential the organization was, it was clear that it functioned in an atmosphere that, according to opinion polls, was increasingly sympathetic to the internationalist agenda.[5]

Whatever its success at the popular level, the CDAAA inspired and influenced the administration. The main argument that CDAAA officially advanced in 1941, that America could best avoid intervention by ensuring that the Allies were as strong as possible, was essentially the same argument used to defend the boats-for-bases deal of 1940 and Lend-Lease, the program through which the United States supplied the Allied war effort. Lippmann, in fact, had been the go-between in the boats-for-bases deal, and the CDAAA agitated hard for the passage of Lend-Lease.[6] Whether pushed by events or by internationalists, the administration was irrevocably committed to collective security by summer 1941.

That is not to say that American policy had become Wilsonian or that the Wilsonians had experienced a fateful reinvigoration. The CDAAA was an odd collection of people drawn to collective security for a wide variety of reasons: some were anti-fascist leftists; some were Anglophiles; some were nationalists who simply wanted the United States to exert power; and some probably believed the official line of the committee in 1940 and 1941 that aid to the Allies was the best way to prevent American intervention in the war.

Clashes inevitably erupted within the organization, the most important of which was the struggle between the midwestern chapters and the so-called Century Club group. Under the leadership of the aging Kansas journalist, William Allen White, the midwestern chapters wanted the CDAAA to move cautiously and to avoid inflaming their region's notorious isolationism. The Century Club group, named after the upper-eastside haven of many of the New Yorkers prominent in the CDAAA, was essentially interventionist. The relationship between the easterners and White grew increasingly tense until, in late 1941, White granted a rambling interview to Roy Howard of the isolationist Scripps-Howard chain in which he disavowed any intention of supporting American intervention and denounced the CDAAA members who did. According to Eichelberger's account, the rest of the CDAAA leadership was "stunned," and

[5] Divine, *Second Chance*, 30, 34–35, 39–40; Eichelberger, *Organizing for Peace*, chap. 9; and James C. Schneider, *Should America Go to War? The Debate over Foreign Policy in Chicago, 1939–1941* (Chapel Hill, 1989), 66–68.
[6] Steel, *Lippmann and the American Century*, 384–85; Eichelberger, *Organizing for Peace*, 150–55.

asked White to resign, a move in which the Century Club members were prominent.[7]

Such clashes, on one level, recalled the differences between the conservatives of the Carnegie Endowment and the liberals of the League to Enforce Peace before World War I. The differences between prowar liberals of the World War II generation, however, were more profound. The earlier conflicts revolved around questions of method and means, while war liberals from Root to Wilson, from Lowell to Lippmann, shared an underlying sense that internationalism fulfilled the idealist density. The second generation of war liberals was bound more by agreements on means than by a consensus on ends or by ideological conviction. The war liberals of the early 1940s comprised nothing more than an anti-fascist coalition. Collective security was merely the common ground shared by Wilsonians, for whom it was linked inherently to the advocacy of internationalism, and others for whom, as with CDAAA member Reinhold Niebuhr, it was the proper response to a world that proved that idealism was dead.

Among Wilsonians, moreover, collective security entailed subtle alterations in thinking. While they consistently asserted that the moral collapse was worldwide and included the United States, they nevertheless made the contradictory assertion that collective security was necessary because the world had split into two camps. Partly because of the objective military threat that the fascists posed, the Wilsonians increasingly described the crisis as a struggle between two clearly identifiable opponents. There stood, on the one hand, the forces of internationalism, open trade, and reason against the forces of nationalism, economic isolation, and political compulsion on the other.

This division resembled the ideological justifications of World War I. Some indeed deluded themselves that the struggle at hand lay between the forces of the past and the forces of the future, as when Shotwell cast the crisis of the mid-1930s as a contest between reactionary nationalism and "a future of anxious hope and reason."[8] It was simple enough to invoke Lincoln on the house divided, as they had during World War I. It was logical to argue that, given the dangers of fascism, to avoid collective security was to surrender to "hermit-like" isolation and "fortress

---

[7] Eichelberger, *Organizing for Peace*, 145–50; Schneider, *Should America Go to War?* 81–83; William H. Tuttle, Jr., "Aid-to-the-Allies Short-of-War versus American Intervention, 1940: A Reappraisal of William Allen White's Leadership," *Journal of American History* 56 (March 1970): 840–58.

[8] James Shotwell, *On the Rim of the Abyss* (New York, 1936), 33–34.

America."[9] It was useful to recall the fighting doctrines of World War I and point to the revival of "a new balance of power," as Charles Fenwick wrote, of "another effort to keep the peace by matching alliance against alliance; and if experience is worth anything, the results will be the same as the old balance of power brought forth."[10]

Try as they might to equate conflicts separated by a generation of tumultuous experience, they could not entirely ignore the important differences between collective security and the idealism of World War I. For one thing, they already had admitted that the political currents were running away from them, and at a time when everyone who was not a strident internationalist was cast as a backward nationalist, the term "reactionary" lost its meaning and the confidence in an immanent liberal future was undermined. Even as he reasserted the standard Wilsonian reading of history in 1936, Shotwell followed with a thoroughgoing analysis of just how marginal internationalism had become; sustaining liberal idealism, evidently, had become more a matter of "anxious hope" than of "reason."

Collective security, furthermore, was not a dissolution of alliances, a corrective to the balance of power, or a policy that, at it grandest, promoted universalism. The crisis had progressed so far by the late 1930s that Wilsonians gave little thought to employing genuinely collective diplomatic methods, and as the war began and France fell, collective security meant in practice aiding Britain. They reasserted their opposition to alliances and the balance of power only to call for a firm alliance and the reestablishment of the balance of power. If the alliance were simply a wartime necessity, so be it. They could insist that aid to Britain and unity among the Allies were essential to a hardheaded understanding of national security and thus a temporary compromise.[11] But they did not leave the matter to rest at this minimal and temporary conception. Having lost faith in the capacity of common citizens to reason, having come to believe that modern dictators combined with mass politics in the modern corporate state, collective-security advocates dispensed altogether with Wilson's distinctions between a corrupt government and its people.

[9] Stimson and Bundy, *On Active Service,* 315; Hamilton Fish Armstrong, *We or They: The World in Conflict* (New York, 1937), 45; Nicholas Murray Butler to Franklin Roosevelt, 15 August 1936, Roosevelt Papers, Personal Papers file 445; and Raymond Fosdick to Mrs. Overton Ellis, 31 May 1938, Fosdick Papers, box 25, file 22877.
[10] Charles Fenwick, "Neutrality and International Responsibility," *Annals* 192 (July 1937): 51–52; Cordell Hull, "The Spirit of International Law," *International Conciliation* 342 (September 1938): 306–7.
[11] See, for example, Stimson and Bundy, *On Active Service,* 315–16; and Sayre to James Farley, 19 October 1940, Sayre Papers, box 4.

The crisis of World War II was a struggle in which, in the oft-used phrase, "like-minded people" and "nations that care about peace and liberty" were allied. No longer were wars fought between monarchs who used mercenaries. Modern, total war was fought between nations whose populations were marshaled and whose economies were mobilized, and democracies had no choice but to match the dictators' buildup. World War II, in short, had became a collectivist war.[12] Meager room existed in such a "collaboration" for the broad democratic sensibilities that Wilson's policy had encouraged, and there was little talk this time around of making grand calls to the German people or of distinguishing the disenfranchised masses from the imperialist elite.[13]

Once the conception of the world as fundamentally divided came to dominate their perspective, the dogma of interdependence, which had provided the rationale for collective security in the first place, abruptly disappeared from Wilsonian writing. Granted, in the atmosphere of impending war there were more urgent tasks than to wax optimistic about how united the world was. Still, interdependence could have been used, if not as an excuse for battling isolationists, than at least as a rallying cry for those who thought that an interdependent world was worth fighting for. For interventionists especially, it made sense to defend American entry on behalf of the Allies along the lines that the New Nationalists had followed in the Great War: that participation in the war would teach the habits and virtues of interdependence. Few such arguments emerged, probably because the dogma of interdependence could not explain why the dictators had such staying power, nor could interdependence be reconciled with the call for like-minded nations to rise against belligerent fascists.

At the heart of the movement for collective security, then, lay an admission that the idealist conception of democratic politics no longer held much force. If, in the modern state, the common citizen was incapable of becoming the voice of enlightened reason, then neither collective security nor the Second World War had much chance of culminating in democracy's ascent. If such were the case, the entire rationale for internationalism, at least potentially, was undermined.

[12] Armstrong, *We or They*, 44. For the best Wilsonian description of the war along these lines see James Shotwell, *Lessons of the Last World War* (New York, 1942).

[13] See Francis Sayre, "Education and International Relations," Address at the University of Chattanooga, 18 April 1936, Sayre Papers, box 16, p. 1; the Armstrong memorandum of a meeting with, among others, Henry Wallace, "Notes on Conversation of May 3d," 3 May 1941, Hamilton Fish Armstrong Papers, Mudd Library, Princeton University, box 48; and Commission to Study the Organization of the Peace: Second Report, "The Transitional Period," *International Conciliation* 379 (April 1942): 149–69.

The Reckoning with Power

It was a much-chastened idealism, to say the least, that World War II–era Wilsonians kept. Perhaps it was a more mature idealism, one that accounted for humanity's imperfections and recognized the immutable tensions between self-interest and the common good. Thus humbled, most Wilsonians were prepared to acknowledge the role of power in politics and accept the possibility that international order in the postwar world might well have to concede, at least temporarily, the predominance of certain nations over others. When the CSOP proclaimed in its 1943 report that "force is inescapable in human affairs," it was not only being succinct but was forthrightly venting what we might call, borrowing Daniel Yergin's description of Roosevelt, "renegade Wilsonianism."[14]

The way in which they began to plan for the postwar world bears out such an assessment. Their writings and speeches were replete with warnings about the grim consequences of the war and the serious difficulties that lay in the future. Partly recalling the warnings against utopianism in 1917 and 1918, Wilsonians again pleaded for patience, arguing, as Shotwell did in 1944, that "the organization of peace is the most difficult task that has even been evisaged by human intelligence." Whereas the earlier generation mixed caution with faithful assertion that the organic world would flower eventually, those writing during World War II rarely mustered even that much confidence. To them, Arthur Sweetser wrote, "there is no royal road, no simple panacea or formula which will immediately eradicate the habits of centuries." A notable difference in tone crept between the two generations of wartime idealists: Wilson and his contemporaries spoke of what would happen once the League was in place; their successors, inhabitants of idealism's twilight, warned of what humanity had to do just to save itself.[15]

If the "royal roads" had disappeared, then a reformulation of internationalism was in order, which logically could have been expected to

---

[14] Committee to Study the Organization of the Peace, Third Report, "The United Nations and the Organization of Peace," *International Conciliation* 389 (April 1943): 209; Yergin, *Shattered Peace: The Origin of the Cold War and the National Security State* (Boston, 1977), 44.

[15] Shotwell, *The Great Decision* (New York, 1944), v; Sweetser, "The Framework of Peace," in Harriet Eager Davis, ed., *Pioneers in World Order: An American Appraisal of the League of Nations* (New York, 1944), 1–2. As Eichelberger wrote in 1942, the world had at its disposal the spiritual and scientific elements necessary to give "man heaven on earth instead of the hades through which he is now passing." "A Society of Nations as Wide as Possible," *The Rotarian* 61 (October 1942): 12.

lead in either of two directions. One would demand a thoroughgoing re-pudiation of national sovereignty—to demand, in other words, one world; the other would accept the balance of power in the hopes that it might hold the peace in some sort of alliance system.

Wilsonians managed the remarkable achievement of doing both and neither. On the one hand, Sweetser spoke of how future security de-pended on "an almost complete revolution in the philosophy of govern-ments and peoples" so that peace would always take priority over national sovereignty. Just as often, there came warnings about how un-realistic it was to expound "theories which at a single leap would merge the sovereign nations of today in some form of world government," as Shotwell wrote. Raymond Buell scoffed at one-worldism, with its "easy assumption that the peoples of every country are innocent, well-meaning and peace-loving."[16]

During the war they were determined to be hardheaded realists de-voted to the Allied cause, and they spoke about accepting the predomi-nance of the great powers in postwar organization. They were clear about how such conclusions ran against their own tradition and about what steps had to be taken in order to preserve as many of the original goals as possible. To account for the self-interest of great powers and still hold out hope of transcending a world built on a balance of power, Wilsonians revised internationalism in three ways: first, they insisted that a period of transition should follow the war in which the Allied powers would predominate in the regions of their greatest interest; they called for an institutionalized "regionalism" that would accommodate the relatively greater interests of each power in their respective spheres on a permanent basis; and they argued that the postwar international organization should contain a strong central council on which the pow-ers decided issues of military force and international security.

Their strategy was summed up in the notion of "regionalism," which admitted the harsh and immediate wartime facts and became central to the discussions about the postwar world. The Council of Foreign Affairs organized two different study groups to consider regionalism, and the CSOP based the essence of its recommendations on regionalist schemes. As they had done habitually in the past, meanwhile, individuals supple-mented these organized efforts with publicity efforts, magazine articles,

---

[16] Sweetser, "Framework for Peace," 10–11; Shotwell, *The Great Decision,* vi; Buell to Manley Hudson, 9 September 1943, Buell Papers, box 3.

speeches, and at least two prominent books, Sumner Welles's *Time for Decision* and Shotwell's *Great Decision.*[17]

The working success of the Grand Alliance—Britain, the Soviet Union, and the United States—deeply impressed those liberals who were defining regionalism. Not only were the Allies united in war, Eichelberger wrote, but it was only "realistic to assume that the great nations . . . will exercise a dominant influence, particularly in the period of transition and until all nations have demonstrated their capacity to cooperate."[18] So long as it seemed to be working, especially in 1943 and early 1944, no one was terribly bothered that the Grand Alliance smacked of balance-of-power arrangements. Why should they be? The main objection to regionalism, that the concept essentially endorsed balance-of-power politics, had been set aside during the collective-security debates, in light of which the Grand Alliance had to be seen as a union of "like-minded nations." Certainly the Soviet Union had its political shortcomings. But it was possible to forgive them and even to rationalize Soviet excesses, as Sumner Welles did. The "either-or" syndrome that dominated the rationale for collective security automatically gave the Soviets the benefit of the doubt. The Soviet Union was a power, it was on the right side, and therefore "differences in political philosophy," as the CSOP concluded in its 1943 report, "do not preclude international cooperation."[19]

Most writers argued that the predominance of the powers in their respective regions would be the primary feature only of a transitional stage in postwar organization, a stage both inevitable and desirable. Welles, looking back to Europe in 1919, insisted that much of the world would be destitute in the immediate aftermath of the war, and only an occupying power could provide order. In 1943 and 1944, furthermore, the various authors and committees working diligently to outline their postwar hopes could point out that the transitional period was already in effect in Africa and parts of Italy. In back of these practical considerations lurked the reality of power and the likelihood that nations just finished with a terrific war would be reluctant to surrender territory that they had taken

[17] Schulzinger, *Wise Men of Foreign Affairs*, 84–93; see the annual reports of the Committee to Study the Organization of the Peace in *International Conciliation*, especially the Third Report, 389 (April 1943) and the Fourth Report, 396 (January 1944); Welles, *The Time for Decision* (New York, 1944); and Shotwell, *The Great Decision* (New York, 1944).

[18] Eichelberger, "A Society of Nations as Wide as Possible," 57; also "Prefabricating the Peace," *Survey Graphic* 33 (September 1944): 373–75.

[19] Welles, *Time for Decision*, chap. 8; Commission to Study the Organization of the Peace, Third Report, 232.

at great cost. "There is no escaping this conclusion," Shotwell wrote, "and anything to the contrary is wishful thinking on the part of those who do not recognize the great realities of history."[20]

The problem of planning the postwar world lay in making certain that the transitional period was as smooth and as brief as possible. If the League experience taught anything, it was that the success of an international organization depended on the cooperation of the great powers, which turned on the security of the powers. The best way to ensure security was to respect the relative weight of regional interests. What this meant for the United States and the Soviet Union was clear: the Monroe Doctrine, prettified in the "good neighbor" policy, would stand, and so too would Soviet predominance in Eastern Europe. Welles was especially clear on the latter point.[21]

Beyond the transition, the main task was not simply to accept the inevitability of spheres but to figure out how to use those spheres for a long-term unification of the world. After all, as Eichelberger wrote, even after accounting for the reality of power, "everyone hopes that all nations . . . may have partnership in a universal society." "The regional approach," Raymond Buell tersely insisted, "must be combined with the universal approach."[22] With security assured, in Buell's opinion, the powers would be expected to coordinate postwar reconstruction out of "enlightened self-interest" and await the maturation of smaller states, which would "adhere" to the "firm nucleus" of one of the four powers. The arrangement could be held together, he argued, by a "four-power treaty" to provide a "20-year agreement to protect each other from aggression"; and the essential glue to the agreement would be "collective security and economic collaboration."[23] There was much talk of organizing an international police force, which would not only provide security and the "teeth" that had been omitted from the League but would offer real lessons in cooperation as well. Because Shotwell and his fellow CSOP members has come to believe that "power is and will remain the final argument of nations" ("power, not war, the distinction is vital," they wrote), the new United Nations should field a police force to which each member contributed soldiers.[24]

[20] Welles, *Time for Decision*, 370–71; Shotwell, *Great Decision*, 48–49.
[21] Welles, *Time for Decision*, 332.
[22] Eichelberger, "A Society of Nations as Wide as Possible," 57; Buell to Manley Hudson, 9 September 1943.
[23] Buell to Manley Hudson.
[24] Fourth Report, 13, 50–56.

So long as the case was made that the regional spheres would slowly dissolve in the happy atmosphere of a peaceful world ensured by secure powers, the Wilsonians could presume that they had not bastardized their long-held hopes. But they went further and argued that regionalism and great-power predominance should be institutionalized in the new United Nations, a position which took them well beyond temporary compromises. There was general agreement that regional organizations and arrangements might enhance the general efficiency of the UN by confining trivial problems to regional solutions, thereby freeing up the world body to consider the truly broad issues in which all nations had an interest. Thus emerged a notion, as Shotwell put it, of "graded responsibilities," reminiscent of Lippmann's "expanding loyalties" of 1916, in which any given issue was to be characterized by its importance to the world body. Shotwell found the precedent for regionalism not in the Monroe Doctrine or the balance or power but in the division of various responsibilities within the League of Nations, such as the labor office and the public-health agencies.[25] Arthur Sweetser, who had become deputy director of the Office of War Information, qualified Shotwell's concept when he maintained that nations should be categorized in the UN according to their strengths and responsibilities instead of the more simple grading of their power. The importance of power might even be buried under euphemism, he argued in the Council on Foreign Relations study groups. There was no need to invite "jealousy and rivalry" by referring to nations as "great," "medium," or "small," when under the notion of graded responsibilities they could be classified as "states of widest international responsibility" or "states of chief military obligations," and so on. However cast, the idea of graded responsibilities provided the rationale for insisting on permanent members of a central security council.[26]

The proposal for an executive council where the great powers could control world security seemed to synthesize traditional Wilsonianism with the recent acknowledgment of power politics. But regionalism and graded responsibilities smacked strongly of a new belief in the differentiation of interests, which made enlightened self-interest an ever-more elusive concept. To admit that there was such a thing as "graded respon-

[25] Shotwell, *The Great Decision*, 214–17.

[26] Dwight Lee to Sweetser, 27 October 1942, Sweetser to Lee, 25 October 1942 and 20 December 1942, Sweetser Papers, box 30; Schulzinger, *Wise Men of Foreign Affairs*, 84–93. On the security council, see Shotwell, *Great Decision*, 48–48, 214–17; CSOP, Fourth Report, 60–61; and Welles, *Time for Decision*, 374–77.

sibilities" was to suggest that many issues fell outside the quest for common interests, which remained the cornerstone of the faith behind internationalism. It no doubt made sense to see local border disputes or binational trade quarrels as relatively minor matters, but in suggesting that such episodes should remain outside the responsibilities of the UN or, just as important, outside the concern of the great powers, simply because they were remote, removed the very sort of issue on which the great powers might reasonably be expected to agree. If the ultimate hope behind regionalism was that it could provide a basis for long-term cooperation between the powers, it was more reasonable to expect the powers to see their interests entwined on minor issues than on ones of global security, an argument that Lippmann had used to under pin his argument in the "stakes of diplomacy" during World War I.

Shotwell and Welles alike recognized their plans as major departures from the Wilsonian agenda, even as they saw themselves committed to the tradition. The constant refrain was that all of these departures had to respect the spirit of international harmony. Regionalism was supposed to be yoked to the universalist purposes of the world body. "Nations close at hand have a more immediate interest in maintaining a good neighborhood than those at great distances," Shotwell reasoned. "But the measures which they may take for their welfare or self-protection must be in harmony with those of the United Nations as a whole, for otherwise the entire structure is weakened in proportion as the regional arrangements tend to supersede it." They continued to deny that another balance of power would result. At best, however, such assertions left the prospects for world harmony to rest on a faith in the powers' capacity to see that their ultimate interests lay in avoiding another total war. If this conclusion did not endorse a new balance of power, it did accept a balance of terror, based as it was on the assumption that the powers would see that cooperation was necessary, as Welles unambiguously insisted, to their own survival.[27]

The Second Failure

In order to claim that Wilsonianism retained any continuing vitality, it is necessary to argue that the compromises of the early 1940s were mostly temporary. In the course of the development and founding of the

---

[27] Shotwell, *Great Decision*, 215; Welles, *Time for Decision*, 378.

UN, Wilsonians were the first to see that such was not the case and to recognize that they had conceded too much to power.

They did not lack influence at crucial times. Robert Divine is right to see the years 1943 and 1944 as the highpoint of American internationalism. Public opinion was by all accounts favorable to a new world organization, and the internationalist information machine was never busier. Support for a new world organization was common to both political parties. Isolationists remained a troublesome bloc among Republicans, but the party's two leading presidential contenders, Wendell Willkie and Thomas Dewey, were internationalists, and Arthur Vandenberg, an isolationist-turned-internationalist, had become the most influential Senate Republican. Among Democrats, the issue was rarely debated. Indeed relatively young members of the party, especially J. William Fulbright, the Arkansas congressman who sponsored a 1943 House resolution committing the United States to a postwar body, potentially comprised a third generation of Wilsonians.[28]

While the Wilsonians had always been influential in Roosevelt's State Department, their wartime positions shaped—and doubtlessly were shaped by—a relative newcomer to their ranks. Undersecretary of State Sumner Welles never commanded any attention among internationalists until the late 1930s when the stylish diplomat began to emerge as Roosevelt's most trusted advisor on foreign affairs. Welles was no recent convert; he simply had not spent much time in the centers of liberalism, New York, Boston, and Washington, until the early 1930s and was therefore not well known. By 1944, when *Time for Decision* was published, he had become the conduit between internationalists and Roosevelt. The book was his testimony to the faith, beginning it as he did with a thoroughly Wilsonian interpretation of the interwar years. He fit the social mold to boot. He shared Roosevelt's aristocratic New York background, included Groton and Harvard in his pedigree, and dressed the part in hand-tailored suits and fancy walking sticks. Bred as a diplomat, he entered the foreign service in 1915 and became an expert on Latin America. He took the lead in postwar planning and was accepted into the fold by Wilsonians of longer standing, with the exception of his immediate boss, Cordell Hull.[29]

The administration official most concerned with postwar organization, Welles was also the foremost proponent of regionalism. He tried to

[28] Divine, *Second Chance*, 110–11.
[29] Ibid., 41–42.

push his agenda through the State Department subcommittee that he headed, beginning in June 1942, that was charged with developing plans for postwar organization. But Hull detested Welles and used his dogmatic universalism as a facade for opposing the undersecretary. Even Hull accepted the influence of the regionalist approach, however, when he found the Soviets warm to Roosevelt's declaration of the four-power proposal that called for the United States, Britain, the Soviet Union, and China to act as "policemen" within the respective areas of the globe.[30]

When the Allies convened at Dumbarton Oaks in August 1944 to outline the structure of the new United Nations, U.S. policy and general Wilsonian sentiment were fairly similar, and together, the administration and its supporters discovered how difficult it was in practice to reconcile power politics with universalism. Going into Dumbarton Oaks, the administration had decided to tolerate regional arrangements so long as they were in harmony with the universal organization, and it was committed to a strong Security Council in which the powers enjoyed an unrestricted right to veto. These decisions had been made in 1943, during the better days of the Grand Alliance. By the time the Allies met at Dumbarton Oaks, strains had begun to emerge between the powers. Suddenly unanimity seemed less important, and the powers, particularly the Soviet Union, which at that very moment was betraying the partisans of the Warsaw uprising, seemed less than benign. As the conference unfolded, the mounting tensions played themselves out most clearly on the question of the veto. In the early stages, the American position shifted toward the British desire to limit veto power. The argument for the limited veto was that a power should not be able to vote on issues that involved it directly and thereby veto action against itself. This had been the basic view of some U.S. delegates, and it grew somewhat stronger within the delegation as Anglo-American cooperation increased. The Soviets, however, refused to budge from their demand for the unlimited veto on the grounds that the proposed restrictions undermined great-power unity, the lack of which would destroy the fledging UN. Neither side would give, and, as Robert Hilderbrand observes, the main intention of

---

[30] Hull killed the committee when his deep dislike for Welles boiled over, and he forced Roosevelt to choose between them. The dispute was mostly personal. Hull, stiff and taciturn, resented Welles's flair, probably hated Welles because of the undersecretary's rumored homosexuality, and, above all, was jealous of his subordinate's easy access to the president. Dallek, *Franklin D. Roosevelt and American Foreign Policy*, 419–22; Hull, *Memoirs* 2:1640–48; Robert C. Hilderbrand, *Dumbarton Oaks: The Origins of the United Nations and the Search for Postwar Security* (Chapel Hill, 1990), 9–11, 18–19.

the delegates in the last days of September was simply "to end the conference as gracefully as possible."[31]

The powers did agree to a framework for the United Nations at
Dumbarton Oaks (though the issue of voting was set aside "for further
discussion"), and enough was accomplished so that the basis of the UN
charter was laid. By the time the nations met in San Francisco to convene
the United Nations in May 1945, the powers had resolved the two outstanding issues: the Russian demand for sixteen seats (one for each republic) in the General Assembly; and the procedure for Security Council
voting. Both had been subjected to compromises at Yalta, where they appeared as secondary issues, and where the Soviets, satisfied with American soft-pedaling on Eastern Europe, conceded ground on both. They
agreed to accept three seats and the American proposal—which in different forms had been floating around the State Department for some
time—to prevent the permanent members of the council from vetoing
discussion of a dispute while requiring unanimity on issues of economic
or military sanctions.[32]

The formal charter agreed upon at San Francisco reflected these compromises, but it also included planks that Wilsonians had accepted
throughout the war. Even if it was a lukewarm assertion, Article 52 did
embody the regionalist position, holding out as it did that "nothing in
the present Charter precludes the existence of regional arrangements"
that were consistent with the UN's "purposes and principles." The charter assured great-power domination of the Security Council by making
permanent members of the United States, Great Britain, the Soviet
Union, China, and France, and the scope of the charter's attention to the
council's composition and responsibilities—the section dealing with the
council is by far the largest in the document—testified to the powers'
central position in the new organization. The all-important veto was established, against considerable opposition from the smaller nations,
along the lines of the Yalta agreements.[33]

Given the positions that they had staked out between 1940 and 1944,
Wilsonians had little reason to criticize the drift of diplomacy from
Dumbarton Oaks to San Francisco. Yet from the planning conference to

[31] Hilderbrand, *Dumbarton Oaks*, 225. The above discussion rests on Hilderbrand's
work.
[32] Ruth Miller and Jeannette Muther, *A History of the United Nations Charter: The
Role of the United States, 1940–1945* (Washington, D.C., 1958), 531–37; Divine, *Second
Chance*, 264–67.
[33] Miller and Muther, *History of the United Nations Charter*, chap. 28. The charter is
reprinted as Appendix M.

the official convening of the United Nations in San Francisco their commentaries ran from disingenuous optimism to vigorous criticism to deep despair, a process that mirrored the breakdown of the Grand Alliance. Some tried to maintain a brave front, which in turn meant that initially, Wilsonians were bound to a sort of party line. Eichelberger, for one, was determined to help the administration put the best face on Dumbarton Oaks. As the official obsfucations began to roll out from the administration, Eichelberger, speaking for the League of Nations Association, eagerly provided his blessings for agreements that, as he pretentiously announced, have "embodied the traditions of the Wilsonian ideal . . . but have provided, as the result of twenty years of trial, error, and tragedy, something stronger and better." That Dumbarton Oaks improved on the mistakes of the past became something of a theme. As Raymond Fosdick told a League of Nations Association audience, Dumbarton Oaks was "significant" because it "is an attempt to build on the knowledge gained in the last twenty-five years."[34]

Most of what they had to say about the emerging plans for the United Nations rang with false optimism, which turned to unease in the months between Dumbarton Oaks and San Francisco. By March 1945, Eichelberger could defend Dumbarton Oaks merely because it was the only "official plan before the people of the world." Fosdick might have remained convinced that "human intelligence is capable of solving the unprecedented chaos which the world faces," but he had to acknowledge the charter's imperfections and warn that it was only a "first step." As he wrote to Roosevelt, it was possible to make up for the lost opportunities of 1919, "but perhaps the chance will not come again."[35]

Raymond Buell, who by then had become close to Arthur Vandenberg and shared the Republican senator's grave misgivings about the emerging world order, was more consistently critical. Though Buell endorsed regionalism, having called for a four-power arrangement only a year before, and expected the powers to draw into an increasingly harmonious

[34] *New York Times*, 12 October 1944; Divine, *Second Chance*, 232–33; Fosdick address, "The League, Dumbarton Oaks, and the Constitution," delivered 1 February 1945, in Gilchrist Papers, box 44.
[35] Eichelberger, "Dumbarton Oaks," *National Education Association Journal* 34 (March 1945): 65; Fosdick, "We Failed in 1919—Shall We Fail Again?" *New York Times Magazine*, 2 July 1944; "The Hour Is Late—We Must Not Fail," 11 February 1945; "Our Last Chance—At San Francisco," 22 April 1945; and Fosdick to FDR, 13 November 1944, Fosdick Papers, box 6. See also Huntington Gilchrist, "Political Disputes: Dumbarton Oaks and the Experience of the League of Nations," address to the Academy of Political Science, 4–5 April 1945, in Gilchrist Papers, box 54.

working relationship, he was horrified at the ramifications of the veto. The self-proclaimed "realists" who insisted that Dumbarton Oaks was a vast improvement over the old Wilsonian League because it frankly acknowledged power in international relationships held to "a very innocent view of history," because peace, in their system, depended on the good faith of the great powers.[36] Dumbarton Oaks, he grieved, established "the juridical *inequality* of states, . . . which leads small states to fear that one or more of these Giant [powers] will resort to unilateral force without restraint." The veto power simply had to be scrapped and the council converted from "an executive agency to a consultative body" that would investigate instances of aggression and consult about the addition of new members. The General Assembly needed to be strengthened by supplanting proportional voting with strict equality—one state, one vote.[37]

We need not take Buell as representative of some erupting outrage, for few others voiced their opposition quite so strongly. What makes Buell's denunciations of Dumbarton Oaks worth noting is that he could launch them without the slightest sense of hypocrisy. In addition to deriding the agreements, he ridiculed Roosevelt's policy for disguising spheres of influence with "sonorous phrasing [that] is bound to injure our own interests and lead us into war again soon."[38] Yet Roosevelt was doing nothing in 1944 that was inconsistent with the four-power notion of postwar arrangements. Buell's indignation suggests that he embraced regionalism and power politics only as an act of pure theorizing, and that as matters came to a head, he recoiled at the implications of his own reckoning with power. He reverted to an increasingly pure Wilsonianism of the sort that Reinhold Niebuhr rebuked as the muddleheaded idealism of the "purer internationalists."[39]

If Buell's heated condemnations led him away from the general drift of sentiment, he nonetheless reflected the increasing dismay of the ide-

---

[36] Buell also argued that the realists, because they advocated a sphere-of-influence diplomacy and its concomitant, a limited commitment to international peacekeeping, championed a course that would earn them many friends among American isolationists. "Should Dumbarton Oaks Be Improved?" 3 April 1945, Buell Papers, box 7, pp. 26–29.

[37] Buell to Hudson, 9 September 1943; "Should Dumbarton Oaks Be Improved?" pp. 28, 33–35, 43.

[38] Buell to Vandenberg; Buell to Landon; see also Buell to Henry Luce, "Suggested Time Inc. Program with Respect to Foreign Policy for 1945," Buell Papers, box 7, p. 11.

[39] Reinhold Niebuhr, "Is This Peace in Our Time?" *Nation*, 7 April 1945, 382–83.

alists. Time was getting short, the prevailing opinion had it; after all, the UN was the "last chance." The inadequacies of the League had to be overcome, power had to be acknowledged, of these things Buell and his fellow idealists were certain. It was entirely right to "put teeth" in the UN, as Princeton's John B. Whitton wrote in a typical essay. Yet the veto meant that the UN's force would never be used against one of the powers, only, Whitton argued, against "the ex-enemy states" and the lesser nations.[40]

Well practiced at staving off immediate failure, some Wilsonians announced that 1945 was the transition period, that point, which had been the object of much speculation and theorizing, when all things were possible but nothing was perfect. At such a point, the charter, with all its grave shortcomings, at least established the new world organization. The veto was absolutely necessary for that minimal purpose, and, as Sumner Welles argued, there was no alternative but World War III.

But then one was bound to ask why the veto had not been inserted merely as a means of ensuring a smooth transition, and the only honest answer was disconcerting. The veto, necessary for ensuring the cooperation of the powers in the transition period, had been made permanent and invulnerable to amendment; it "is the outstanding defect in the United Nations Charter," Welles wrote. "It is the one destined . . . to create the greatest difficulties in the future." That defect was of transcendent importance in 1945 because, in an atmosphere of increasing tension between the powers, "faith in the efficacy of international cooperation was never more urgently needed," and yet that faith depended, Welles contended in tones reminiscent of Buell and in sharp contrast to his own positions of the immediate past, not on the goodwill of the powers but on the determination of the rest of the world to hold the powers to account.[41] Welles and others hoped that the smaller nations would purify the tarnished new organization and help to revive faith in the common impulse toward democracy. But no amount of revived faith could alter what the United Nations had become, nor could it restore their flagging expectations. Even as they watched the birth of the UN, they sat convinced that, instead of marking the ultimate triumph of liberal de-

[40] John B. Whitton, "The Score at San Francisco," *American Mercury* 61 (September 1945): 275.
[41] Sumner Welles, "The Vision of a World at Peace," *Virginia Quarterly Review* 21 (Autumn 1945): 490, 483.

mocracy and the ideals of all right-thinking people, the organization amounted to the only possible hedge against the destruction of what remained of both.

The Bomb as the Test of Faith

This dire view begged another question. What was there to promise that the hedge itself would survive? Twenty years before the answer would have been interdependence, which the modern economy and advanced science were making irresistible. The staying power of the dictators and the apparent allure of fascism to irrational citizens, however, destroyed confidence in that foundation of world order; certainly the war itself and the collapse of the Grand Alliance only damaged it further. Under the top-heavy structure of the UN, the smaller nations had little chance to redirect the world, especially when so many of them, as Welles took pains to point out, were burdened by postwar dislocation or, particularly in Asia, engulfed in anti-colonial rebellions that seemed inevitable in the face of the powers' determination to hold on to spheres of influence.[42]

One possible candidate as successor to economic and cultural interdependence came from an ironic source, that is, modern technology in the form of the atomic bomb. Wilsonians always had been ambivalent about science: it eluded national boundaries and therefore was inherently international, but it also allowed for the production of weapons of terrific destruction. Now science had conferred upon humanity both the ultimate weapon of destruction and, potentially, the reason why no nation could aspire to exist in antagonistic isolation.

The bomb never excited bubbling optimism. Both Fosdick and Welles were quick to rebuke Albert Einstein, for instance, after the physicist argued that the bomb necessitated world government. To them, the bomb did very little to erase the faults of one-world propositions, for like all weapons, it lay in the hands of people who, in Fosdick's words, were "utterly unprepared, in terms of ethics, law, philosophy, economics, politics and government, to meet the problems which they present." Just as the outlawry movement rejected the League, so Einstein seemed to be suggesting that "all the great achievements represented by the agreement of fifty-one nations to establish the United Nations Organization must im-

---

[42] Ibid., 482–83.

mediately be scrapped." Still, as Fosdick wrote, the bomb made the discovery of new "techniques of cooperative action" all the more urgent because it brought "the possibility of complete annihiliation" for which no one was prepared. The UN made cooperative action a real possibility; his was no "idle dream," Fosdick insisted.[43]

The atomic issue could not be put aside so easily. Rather than compelling immediate world government, the bomb was the object of intense national secrecy and dangerous competition. So important had it become that the powers were determined to constrain the natural flow of scientific knowledge and maintain national monopolies, even though such attempts "have blanketed the world with a poisonous fog of suspicion and of fear," Welles warned.[44] In 1945, the primary culprit on this issue was the United States, which behind the new and increasingly anti-Soviet administration of Harry Truman had decided to use the atomic monopoly as a diplomatic lever. If the UN and the bomb were to exist in the same world, the monopoly had to be surrendered.

Raymond Buell also reached this conclusion. He recognized many of the bomb's implications as soon as he learned of the attack on Nagasaki. In a running debate with the other editors, at Time, Inc., he wrote of his hope that the bomb might generate a "revolution" in political thought similar to the military revolution that the bomb created.[45] The bomb so impressed him that he composed a detailed plan for its internationalization in which he rejected both handing the weapons over to the UN and maintaining a monopoly that surely would lead to "a new and unprecedentedly tense arms competition among the Big Three."[46] His alternative, the "Atomic Bomb Authority," would use the bomb as the heart of a genuinely international military force. Discouraged by the security-council veto, Buell wanted the bomb authority to be distinct from the useless UN, which lacked "an effective concept of the Rule of Law." His group would include no veto, and in this sense his plan prefigured the Baruch Plan that the Truman administration offered to the UN in 1946.

[43] Raymond Fosdick, "The Challenge: One World or None," *New York Times Magazine,* 2 September 1945, p. 8; Sumner Welles, "The Atomic Bomb and World Government," *Atlantic Monthly* 177 (January 1946): 39–40.

[44] Welles, "The Atomic Bomb and World Government," 39.

[45] Buell to Luce, 9 August 1945, Buell Papers, box 7.

[46] "Notes on the Atomic Bomb," Time Inc., memo, 24 September 1945, Buell Papers, box 7, pp. 2–7. On the administration's debate over internationalization of atomic bombs see Barton Bernstein, "The Quest for National Security: American Foreign Policy and International Control of Atomic Energy, 1942–1946," *Journal of American History* 60 (March 1974): 1003–44; and Gregg Herken, *The Winning Weapon: The Atomic Bomb in the Cold War* (New York, 1980).

All members would help deploy the bomb at a series of bases and encourage volunteer soldiers who would constitute "a real international force in contrast to a coalition of national contingents." In addition, the authority would monopolize manufacture of the bomb, control military research, and monitor and inspect member states for compliance. Buell looked for a truly multilateral monopoly of the bomb that was "harnessed to principles of law" and given the authority to punish aggressors.

He doubted that even Russia would refuse to enter the accord, but if she "or some other Big Power" did refuse, "the rest of us should go ahead" and proceed with the plan for cooperation. In such a case, the signers of the accord "would be justified in regarding Russia as the next threat to world peace." Russian aggression would provoke retaliation. The authority had to be prepared to resist aggression, and if it were thus resolute, "I think Russian imperialism would evaporate, and that she would become party to the agreement."[47] But Buell was more worried about American policy, which was "becoming more and more nationalistic." We had conceded the UN veto, but "now we are about as insistent upon such a veto as the Russians themselves" and off on the same pursuit of unilateral security. "The hard-boiled U.S. nationalist will condemn the proposed creation of a world monopoly of atomic power as 'impractical.' But the 'practical' course which the nationalists favor can lead only to World War III, the death of American democracy, and the suicide of the human race." He was not proposing a "world state," he wrote, but rather an organization that would leave nations sovereign while it simultaneously entwined vital national interests; the authority would solve the urgent problem of atomic weapons, avert an unprecedented arms race, and show all nations the value of enlightened self-interest. Thus "a new element will be introduced into international life," Buell pledged, "a nucleus of world stability, which today does not exist, putting limits on the competition between national power-units by creating *pooled* power, beginning with the atomic bomb. Only when some such a nucleus is created will it become possible to find durable solutions [to] all serious international problems."[48]

The editors of *Time* mocked Buell's plan. The ardent nationalist Willi Schlamm wrote that "there is not One World but Two Worlds," and "everybody who acts on the assumption that there is One World cannot fail to make a fool of himself." We should "have fun" promulgating inter-

---

[47] Buell, "Notes on the Atomic Bomb," pp. 8–12.
[48] Ibid., 12–14. The emphasis is Buell's.

national agreements of any and all kinds. But "all we can do is make the One World to which we belong so strong and prosperous that the other One World has not a fraction of a chance if, as and when it tried another bit of expansion."[49] Buell responded that Schlamm distrusted any international authority and his embrace of a bipolar world matched Russian imperialism with American imperialism. The only value in a western bloc was the security it offered, a dubious virtue in the age of atomic weapons. Buell was not "prepared to give up eastern Europe, Poland, and eastern Germany to the totalitarian world as a permanent proposition. But this certainly would happen under your program." All that remained, he concluded, was to make one last but sincere effort to deal with Russia on a "**world** scale" and "create a workable international authority or we are all sunk."[50]

If he departed from Fosdick and Welles in his distrust of the UN, Buell nevertheless argued that the bomb could teach lessons in international cooperation only if the will to cooperate existed, and thus, in the end, the argument came back around to an element of idealist faith, the faith, in this case, that the prospect of atomic destruction would generate the necessary action. Like economic and cultural interdependence, the bomb fused the interests of varied peoples and competing nations in disregard to any petty attachments.

Yet the interdependent world was, according to the old dogma, the very real instrument of unvarnished liberal good, of economic progress and cultural and intellectual advance. It was standing proof of reason's beneficence. Not so with the bomb, for it was the ominous product of technology's darker side and was not exactly a beacon for a liberal future of peaceful abundance. Even in Buell's vision, the bomb was nothing more than a bludgeon hanging over humanity's collective head. Grasping for this last shred of hope, Buell reached for reaffirmation that conflict would be overridden regardless of humanity's stupid propensity for self-destruction, only to invest his faith in something that was clearly associated with that propensity. Because the bomb was a product of science, the amorality of which Wilsonians long had brooded over, it was hard to see how anyone could expect the device to choose correctly which direction to shove humanity. One is hard pressed to see in this thinking the sort of satisfaction that should accompany a sense of final victory. Instead there is panic in Buell's work, the frenetic gathering of faith that

[49] Schlamm memo, "Concerning Ray Buell's Notes on the Atomic Bomb," Buell Papers, box 7, p. 3.
[50] Buell to Schlamm, 26 September 1945, Buell Papers, box 7, p. 2.

the dying perform when facing the ultimate confrontation with fate (Buell was, in fact, succumbing to cancer). There is the sense of faith merely asserted, quite detached from the messy details of the real world. Nor was he alone. Just as Francis Sayre had demanded the reimposition of "enduring truths," just as Buell fell back on overarching "moral presuppositions" in his rebuke against modern politics, so was it necessary, according to Eichelberger, to "foresee a world in which all nations, no matter what their regional responsibilities and their cultural differences, are bound by certain fundamental moral laws and by the desire to develop among all nations better economic and social standards."[51] What began as a process of coming to terms with the reality of power ended in a reassertion of purely idealistic virtue that had no anchor in the real world.

Cold War Critics

James Warburg shamelessly reneged on the promise he made to Franklin Roosevelt in 1940 that he would not write any more books. From 1944 to 1952, Warburg published eight of them, each serving as part of a running critique of American Cold War policy.[52] Throughout the period, he traveled extensively in war-torn Europe, worked as a roving reporter for the internationalist Chicago *Sun* syndicate, and returned to the U.S. regularly to speak on international affairs. His efforts made him the most persistent Wilsonian critic of the Cold War, if not the most original or influential. While there were those who were a bit of both—Lippmann, Sumner Welles, Raymond Buell, Henry Stimson—it was Warburg who most clearly connected the Cold War to the collapse of liberal reason. As he explained in *Faith, Purpose, and Power* (1950), he "grew up, as did many present-day 'liberals', in the firm belief in a rational world—in the belief that 'reasonable' human beings . . . would conciliate their conflicting desires and opinions *through reason,* and so reach a working agreement for the common good. One cannot have lived through the last twenty years of world history . . . without recognizing

[51] Clark Eichelberger, "Plans for World Security," *Virginia Quarterly Review* 20 (Autumn 1944): 596.

[52] *Foreign Policy Begins at Home* (New York, 1944); *Unwritten Treaty* (1945); *Germany—Bridge or Battleground?* (New York, 1947); *Put Yourself in Marshall's Place* (New York, 1948); *Last Call for Common Sense* (New York, 1949); *Faith, Purpose, and Power* (New York, 1950); *Victory without War* (1951); and *How to Co-exist without Playing the Kremlin's Game* (Boston, 1952).

that recent history has in part, and perhaps only temporarily, invalidated the assumptions of nineteenth-century 'liberalism'." Warburg continued to believe that reason would prevail; in his view, the totalitarian threat was not permanent. "The world can, in time, be peacefully united." He chose to believe "that man is capable of mastering the machines he has created, instead of becoming enslaved and destroyed by his own inventions; and that the limits of what is 'attainable' are largely set by what we believe to be attainable." It was possible, accordingly, to construct "an affirmative American policy . . . based upon a consensus of reason [that] must also be fortified by a common impulse."[53]

To Warburg and others, the Cold War was only secondarily related either to totalitarianism or to the Soviet-American diplomatic confrontation. It was a crisis in faith, which could be reversed, as Raymond Fosdick put it, only through "acts of faith for a time of peril." The modern world itself ultimately generated the postwar difficulties and would have done so, Warburg wrote, if "Marx and Lenin had never lived or written." The real causes of strife were technological advance and global interdependence, the economic and political disruptions that followed the war and the collapse of colonialism, and the destruction of the traditional balance of power. As he had since the 1920s, Fosdick chose to emphasize the ambiguities of technological transformation. Atomic predominance had given rise to "a sense of omen," a cynical mood of "purposelessness" among Americans. The real danger was not the Red Army but "that this morbid attitude will dominate our thinking, jeopardizing whatever future can be salvaged, and corroding the vivifying hope and the sense of promise which over long ages have brought meaning and dignity to human life."[54]

People who had been lamenting the collapse of a common moral system since the 1930s might predictably interpret the Cold War as a crisis of faith. At the same time, their view has a strange quality of originality to it, for no other reason than that it was so thoroughly out of step with Cold War liberalism. Wilsonians distanced themselves from nearly all of their contemporaries: they denounced nationalists, and yet continued to shy away from the one-worlders; they decried the Truman administration's tendency to blame all problems on aggressive Soviet expansion and yet believed Henry Wallace was naive. Perhaps what distinguished them the most was that they were observers of the international scene who by

[53] Warburg, *Faith, Purpose, and Power*, x–xii.
[54] Warburg, *Last Call for Common Sense*, 29–32; Fosdick, *Within Our Power* (New York, 1952), 2–3.

and large had a good deal more experience than those who made Cold War policy. They offered the very thing most lacking in that policy: perspective. Only John Foster Dulles, secretary of state under Eisenhower, could boast as much experience in the field as Lippmann, Stimson, or Fosdick; Warburg and Welles had been insiders longer than Averell Harriman, James Byrnes, or Dean Acheson and were certainly more intimately knowledgeable about Rooseveltian policy making. To these seasoned observers, Russian behavior was not qualitatively different from the unprincipled nationalist policies of the past, and far from necessitating a drastic reorientation of American policy, postwar problems recommended only a reaffirmation of internationalism.

Experienced observers could not help but see a drift away from internationalism after 1945, which meant that their criticism fell mostly on Harry Truman. The new president, Welles remarked, entered office without "the familiarity with modern history, the grasp of international affairs, [or] the innate flair for foreign relations possessed by his predecessor." The inexperienced president was forced to rely on those advisors nearest him, who were no better equipped to handle diplomacy at such delicate times. Edward Stettinius, Truman's first secretary of state, was in Welles's view much like Truman: a man with all the good intentions in the world but one nonetheless "devoid of any knowledge of international relations." Nor did it help matters that Truman replaced Stettinius with James Byrnes, whose only substantial experience, Welles pointed out, had been in domestic affairs. Welles conceded that Byrnes learned quickly, but not quickly enough to avoid disasters at the first two conferences of his tenure, the vitally important September meeting in London and the December talks in Moscow. Byrnes mismanaged his delegation, bungled the vital issue of atomic power, and unnecessarily inflamed superpower tensions. Welles concluded that "in one of the most critical moments of world history," the American secretary of state "had only the most tenuous comprehension of the currents and crosscurrents of international affairs."[55]

The Truman dilettantes, above all, lacked a sense of perspective. As Welles admitted, men like Stettinius were perfectly well-intentioned. It was simply hard to imagine that newcomers could appreciate the magnitude of the task at hand. Having had no role in shaping wartime diplomacy, they were in no position to understand the implicit arrangements of Yalta, and they expected immediate results. Here the Wilso-

[55] Sumner Welles, *Where Are We Heading?* (New York, 1946), 53, 63–66.

nians were well prepared to counsel patience. They had been speaking about the importance of the "transition period" since the beginning of postwar planning, and now that it had come, the Truman administration seemed determined to move recklessly through it, disregarding the oft-spoken need for the powers to feel secure before democratic order could be restored. As Lippmann wrote, "the death of Roosevelt was followed by the disappearance of almost all the key men who had played a leading part in shaping the high strategy of the war, and had known first hand the issues which had been resolved in order to organize successfully the military coalition of the United Nations."[56]

As Cold War tensions mounted and nationalism became more prominent within American policy, the administration's drift became aggressive and globalist and, according to Wilsonian critics, matched nationalism with nationalism. The powers practiced a "me-too approach," Vera Micheles Dean wrote, so that, for example, British activity in the Mediterranean or American salivation over the Pacific islands invariably provoked Russian territorial demands. The administration was hypocritical when it condemned Russian imperialism as a serious threat to security when power-grabbing was the order of the day. American policy was built on a self-fulfilling prophecy in which, in Warburg's words, "the more Western policy became obsessed with the necessity of containing Soviet expansion, the more negative became its effect, and the greater became the vacuum into which Soviet pressure could penetrate."[57]

The American attempt to maintain an atomic monopoly after the Japanese surrender was an even more glaring example of how nationalism and amateurish diplomacy made a mess of things. It is well known that in his last days as secretary of war, Henry Stimson warned Truman that to "negotiate with [the Russians] with this weapon rather ostentatiously on our hip" would only serve to heighten "their suspicions and their distrust of our purposes."[58] Not only was Stimson's reasoning similar to Raymond Buell's, but others mounted a critique of U.S. atomic policy beyond 1945. Welles argued the following year that the monopoly had issued from postwar hysteria in the democracies and from the evidently self-interested demands of "many high-ranking officers of the Army and Navy." Pressured by such hysteria, Byrnes had gone to the London con-

---

[56] Walter Lippmann, "A Year of Peacemaking," *Atlantic Monthly* 178 (December 1946): 39.

[57] Vera Micheles Dean, *The United States and Russia* (Cambridge, 1946), 132–34; Warburg, *Put Yourself in Marshall's Place,* 9.

[58] Stimson and Bundy, *On Active Service,* 642–44.

ference "hopelessly unprepared" and with little appreciation for the bomb's diplomatic implications. London, to which Byrnes did indeed carry the bomb on his hip, devolved into "one of the most disastrous international conferences of modern times." The mere attempt at keeping the monopoly "created an immediate gap of suspicion and of misunderstanding" between the powers. In 1948, Warburg looked back on the events surrounding the first uses of the bomb with much the same criticism as New Left historians writing in the 1960s. "Opinions vary" on the extent to which Truman revealed the atomic secret to Stalin at Potsdam, where Truman settled the terms by which the Russians would enter the Pacific war. But "the fact is . . . that the two bombs were dropped in circumstances which could suggest that at least part of the purpose was to bring about surrender before Russia could rightfully claim any part in the victory."[59]

Among the most important lasting problems with atomic diplomacy was that it stole from the United Nations an important source of authority at a time when the agency badly needed a symbol of power. The attempt to maintain the monopoly not only generated predictable superpower tensions but gravely weakened the fledgling UN, which, after all, was supposed to be strengthened slowly through the transitional period. The Baruch Plan, through which the administration offered to internationalize atomic technology under the auspices of a UN agency set up outside security council control, was insufficient to undo the damage done in late summer 1945 and was not a particularly disinterested proposal in any case. For as Dean pointed out, the Russians promptly saw the plan as "a backdoor attempt to evade the veto"; the U.S., furthermore, "made it plain that it would not give up manufacture of atomic bombs, or destroy existing stockpiles."[60]

Atomic diplomacy grew out of negative nationalism, these critics believed, and thus presaged the containment policy, of which they were similarly critical. Whereas Lippmann argued that any policy based on George Kennan's "Mr. X" would mire the U.S. down in long-term and expansive commitments to unreliable allies, Warburg countered containment in more immediate terms. Mr. X refused to consider the possibility

[59] Welles, *Where Are We Heading?* 67; Warburg, *Put Yourself in Marshall's Place*, 7. The standard New Left treatment is Gar Alperovitz, *Atomic Diplomacy: The Use of the Atomic Bomb and the American Confrontation with Soviet Power* (New York: Vintage, 1965).

[60] Dean, *United States and Russia*, 269–75.

that Soviet conduct might be inspired to some degree by "an actual fear . . . of attack by the United States" and ignored how the bipolar world bound the two superpowers in antagonisms. Most of all, Kennan wrongly assumed that the conflict was "irreconicilable," an assumption which rested on the delusion that the U.S. was always right and which absolved the U.S. of the responsibility for altering its own conduct in search of solutions, of ignoring, in other words, the very essence of diplomacy.[61]

Negative policies that abjured diplomacy thwarted any serious attempt to settle outstanding issues in Germany and riveted American attention on Eastern Europe with unjustifiable intensity. If the four-power approach to postwar settlement was going to work anywhere, Warburg argued, surely it had to work in Germany. Well into 1947, however, each power continued to rest in its own zone, and even if each had reasonable intentions, the division of Germany prevented any true recovery. Germany, Warburg wrote, was like "a very sick patient . . . in the hands of four doctors." Indeed, as Lippmann maintained, it was unprecedented that, after a great war, the victors should not treat with the vanquished. More to the point, no true world recovery could begin until Germany, the heart of Europe, recovered. Instead of coming to terms, the Americans and English chose to base the "whole great business" of world settlement on Eastern Europe. Together, Lippmann wrote, the Americans and the English, "armed only with the Yalta Declaration, were attempting to take by frontal assault the main positions held by the Red Army. These positions are looked upon by all Russians as the British look upon the Low Countries, as we look upon the Caribbean region—as vital to the security of Russia against invasion. [They] picked the one region of the globe where the Soviet Union was the strongest, and we most nearly impotent." Warburg added that the Truman administration was proceeding on the dubious assumption that Eastern Europe had been composed of democratic, independent nations, when in fact "Rumania, Bulgaria, Hungary, and Yugoslavia were ruled by feudal squirearchies which exploited their predominantly peasant populations." True, Czechoslovakia and Finland were democracies that Russia was poised to crush, but even here the most rational approach would be to encourage economic development in Eastern Europe, first through the revival of Ger-

[61] Warburg, *Put Yourself in Marshall's Place*, 38–39.

many and second through American policies that ignored the "iron curtain."[62]

No one was recommending that the administration give Eastern Europe up for lost. Over time, trade between east and west would promote democracy and, presumably, lessen Soviet insecurity. Such developments demanded a positive policy promulgated with a forceful vision of what the world should be. The administration proceded to lay out such a forceful vision of the future in the Truman Doctrine speech, but it was hardly rosy; in asking for $400,000,000 in aid to Greece and Turkey in April 1947, Truman depicted the world as the battleground of two "ways of life," the antithesis of the positive vision that the Wilsonians awaited. Warburg was convinced that Truman had fallen into the Churchillian trance, and like Churchill, sought to unite "English speaking peoples—a sort of latter-day 'master race' "—"shades of the man with the little mustache!" Dean was more circumspect but still claimed that the U.S. seemed determined to "become heir of the British Empire."[63]

To Warburg, the Marshall Plan presented the first indication that the administration was willing to try a new approach to the international crisis. It was, he believed, "a return to reason" that discarded the two misconceptions of the Truman Doctrine: that "Communism" was the primary threat to the West, rather than misery and insecurity, and that an "idea" could be contained. There was much to like about the plan for European recovery. It focused on tangible economic problems rather than on uncertain military possibilities, and removing economic insecurity might alleviate the principal cause of political irrationality in Europe. It was a program with vision that addressed the desire for a productive future; it was multilateral, in that it was submitted to the various European nations for approval; and it was designed to enhance global interdependence—or so Warburg, and Lippmann too, hoped.[64]

Those hopes relied on the extent to which the administration would work in good faith to enlist the Soviets in the program or, failing that, make it possible for Eastern European nations to participate. But the administration based its aid on a system of American oversight and shaped

[62] Warburg, *Germany—Bridge or Battleground?* 119, 2–4, and *Last Call for Common Sense*, 26–27; also *How to Co-exist*, 116–25; Lippmann, "A Year of Peacemaking," 37; Dean takes the same line of reasoning in *United States and Russia*, 161–74.
[63] Warburg, *Put Yourself in Marshall's Place*, 9; Dean, *United States and Russia*, 158–61. Lippmann argued along similar lines that Truman's ideological proclamation was too sweeping and vague to make good policy. Steel, *Lippmann and the American Century*, 438–39.
[64] Warburg, *Put Yourself in Marshall's Place*, 27–28.

the program so that the Soviets would refuse to join. The administration's hope that the Eastern Europeans would shun the Soviets and join the plan was based on wishful thinking instead of a clear understanding of the political and military realities of the region, and thus when the Soviets refused to participate, the Eastern Europeans were condemned to follow them.[65] Warburg accordingly came to think that the Marshall Plan could not transcend the context out of which it was developed. "Submerged in the surrounding atmosphere of the Truman Doctrine and diverted from its original purpose by the cold war against the Soviet Union," the plan was doomed. It could never be truly global, and it therefore did not enhance interdependence. It did nothing to bring a larger sense of peace and security at home, for whatever its economic benefits to Western Europe, the arms race continued to drain the nation's resources.[66] The end result of the Marshall Plan was quite the opposite of what the Wilsonians, and at least some administration officials, expected. Rather than promoting economic integration, it amounted to the first major step toward consolidating the division of Europe.

The development of a western defense alliance rendered the division of Europe all but irreversible; with NATO, the Wilsonian hopes of a "second chance" were completely lost. NATO, Warburg insisted, "raises the question whether we have not reached the point in our present policy at which the cold war ceases to be a method of seeking a peace settlement and becomes, instead, merely the preparation for an atomic war which is tacitly assumed to be inevitable." Lippmann railed against NATO as an example of how containment generated superfluous alliances.[67] Here was a rather surprising position for an alleged defender of the balance of power, and for that matter, for anyone who had once commended the alliance of "like-minded nations" in the late 1930s. NATO, one could argue, was nothing more than a revived version of collective security. To counter such inconsistency, both Warburg and Lippmann noted the indiscriminate collection of "weak and dubious allies," in Lippmann's words, to whom the Atlantic Pact was proposed, hardly the "like-

---

[65] John Lewis Gaddis, *Strategies of Containment: A Critical Appraisal of Postwar American National Security Policy* (New York, 1982), 37–38; Michael Hogan, *The Marshall Plan: America, Britain, and the Reconstruction of Western Europe, 1947–1952* (New York, 1987), 38–45.

[66] Warburg, *Last Call for Common Sense,* 128–33.

[67] Lippmann and Warburg also thought it was a bad idea to rearm Western Germany that soon after the war. Warburg, "An Alternative Proposal," *Nation,* 19 March 1949, 332; and *Faith, Purpose, and Power,* 43, 68–78; Steel, *Lippmann and the American Century,* 458–61.

minded" friends that collective security envisioned. There was nothing particularly democratic about an alliance that was casting "flirtatious eyes" at Franco's Spain, nor could anyone take seriously the claim that NATO would be used to strengthen the UN.[68] NATO did not qualify as a regionalist alliance. Writing in *Foreign Affairs,* Hamilton Fish Armstrong admitted that because the UN was in no position to protect any of its members from aggression by one of the powers, NATO was a not-unreasonable response to a state of international "unprepardness." But in such a state of chaos, prudence recommended against anything provocative, which was certainly the way that the Soviets would interpret a western defense alliance. It would be better, Armstrong argued, to propose a general nonaggression pact, an elaborate Locarno.[69] In a follow-up essay in April 1949, Armstrong reiterated the wartime belief that local conflicts could be dealt with through regional arrangements but argued that the powers transcended regions. Their interests were so broad as to leave them with universal obligations, and to be committed to regionalism was to accept limits on responsibility.[70]

Because it accepted the global responsibilities to which the Truman administration had pledged itself and yet sought to tie American intentions to the UN, Armstrong's argument ultimately hung on U.S. benevolence. Indeed the entire Wilsonian critique of American Cold War policy rested less on differences on ends than on matters of motive and spirit. Obviously they could not condemn Truman liberals for seeking to extend America's international involvement. It was impossible for them to criticize American attempts to rebuild the world economy, because any efforts in that direction necessarily would enhance interdependence. Committed as they always were to liberal capitalism, they hardly could have opposed programs aimed at rebuilding that system.

But agreement on ends ought not to obscure the differences between Wilsonians and Truman globalists. To the Wilsonians, Truman and his colleagues were pursuing internationalist ends either for self-interested reasons or in a unilateral quest to make the world conform to American capitalism. As Warburg put it, Truman had determined to remake the world in the image of America and thus defined democracy and justice as

[68] Steel, *Lippmann and the American Century,* 459; Warburg, "An Alternative Proposal."

[69] Hamilton Fish Armstrong, "Coalition for Peace," *Foreign Affairs* 27 (October 1948): 1–16.

[70] Hamilton Fish Armstrong, "Regional Pacts: Strong Points or Storm Cellars?" *Foreign Affairs* 27 (April 1949): 352–68.

that which prevailed in or was good for the United States. Truman's globalism showed that "we have not really given up our isolationism; we have merely turned it inside out. . . . We are willing to be citizens of the world, but only if the world becomes an extension of the United States. . . . We instinctively seek to adapt the world to ourselves, rather than ourselves to the world around us."[71] As in their criticism of NATO, this line of reasoning sounds curious coming from those who once predicted the coming of the "United States of the World." It was the sort of position that was much easier for someone to take when out of power. Still, their critique had the virtue of perspective. The root problem, Warburg claimed, was not so much that Americans had lost their sense of morality as that the march of industrial development had expanded the area, both in a geographic and a social sense, over which liberal morality had to govern, and a "discrepancy" had developed between the now-vast expanse of ideals and the capacity of the individual to live up to those expanded ideals. When the sense of morality expanded and gave rise to social reform as well as to internationalism, it ironically undercut the immediate forms of moral authority: the church, the family, and the individual. Moral attenuation created a national conscience that was moralistic rather than moral, and when taken to foreign affairs, this moralism led to globalism.[72]

The foremost casualty of moral confusion was the idealist sense of vision, to which Warburg and others constantly referred as a positive sense of the future. Without moral vision, the international arena became the conflict-ridden battleground of superpower struggle, and at home, Americans increasingly cowered in fear of the future. The realist anticipation of inevitable conflict created a garrison state, if not in fact, surely as a state of mind. The United States had become, Warburg lamented, "a nation armed to the teeth, yet constantly looking over its shoulder or under the bed for hidden enemies." The garrison state could not "succeed in harnessing its productive energy to reconstruction and peace," and the preparation for conflict undermined the capacity to commit the nation to the positive programs that alone would eliminate the true sources of conflict. As the hunt for hidden enemies proceeded, so the possibility for moral vision waned. Here lay the explanation for the Red Scare, which amounted to a national movement against anything that smacked of positive and progressive purpose. Raymond Fosdick put it in a way that re-

[71] Warburg, *Faith, Purpose, and Power,* 9.
[72] Warburg, *How to Co-exist,* 90–105.

called the old critiques of isolationism and economic nationalism: "Fear breeds an instinctive hostility to growth, and in anxious hours men tend to cling to the shelter of the present or to put their faith in nostalgia for the past. . . . The illusion that security can be found in immobility . . . is perhaps the most dangerous form of imbalance which plagues the minds of men."[73]

The antidote to fear and insecurity, the only alternative to Cold War, they argued, was a positive program based on a commitment to Wilsonian ends. Their "middle way" ran, this time, between appeasement and aggression. Indeed the less attention given the superpower conflict, the better. It made more sense to seek ways to encourage interdependence. The U.S. should commit itself to a global open door, for example, not, Warburg maintained, out of economic self-interest but because it was "an essential prerequisite to world peace." If trade encouraged political liberalization, all to the good, and if it encouraged liberalization in Eastern Europe, then it made sense to work for more direct trade with the Soviets as well. Beyond mere trade, Fosdick and Warburg called on the United States to commit itself to a broad political and economic vision of uplift for the Third World based on commitments to political justice. Above all, American policy should build upon the common interests of the superpowers. Both had an interest in avoiding war, given the stakes involved. Both could enjoy benefits from trade. And, at least Warburg maintained, both had ideological commitments to equality and freedom from oppression. When all was said and done, "in spite of all evidence to the contrary," as Fosdick wrote, "the things that divide the world are trivial as compared with the things that unite it."[74]

Fosdick's claim was, to say the least, debatable. The elements of commonality to which he and Warburg pointed were either intangible, like the "passionate desire for peace," or wishful thinking, as was the age-old dream of global free trade. Contrary to Fosdick's claim, the legitimately practical appeals to common interests that Wilsonians had made in the past—to the reality of interdependence, to the existing machinery of international organization, even to the power of technology—seemed entirely irrelevant to the Cold War. The Cold War was fought on the presumption that interdependence was unnecessary. When he called for the open door as a necessary instrument of peace, Warburg himself ad-

[73] Warburg, *Last Call for Common Sense*, 48; Fosdick, *Within Our Power*, 27–33.
[74] Dean, *United States and Russia*, 262–63; Warburg, *Germany—Bridge or Battleground?* 248–52, *Faith, Power, and Purpose*, 136–41, and *Last Call for Common Sense*, 46–47; Fosdick, *Within Our Power*, 57–58, 80.

mitted that international trade was not actually vital to American economic well-being.[75] The old appeals to international organization were even less powerful. The United Nations was impotent from the start, and no one in power sincerely cared to make it otherwise. Even the most optimistic assessment could go no farther than Hamilton Fish Armstrong when he proclaimed that at least the UN had "set a standard of civilized behavior." Technology, once hailed as the principal force for progress, held out only the comparatively modest hopes of improvement in world agriculture and public health.[76] No person with any pretense to the practice of reason in 1950 could follow Raymond Buell and hope that the mere existence of the bomb would compel nations into cooperation.

The exhaustion of past promises left Wilsonians in the Cold War in much the same position that Buell was in when he died in 1946. Unable to base their alternatives on tangible, practical guides, they were reduced to calling for acts of sheer faith. Henry Stimson called President Truman to such an act when he gently chided him on the issue of the atomic monopoly: "The chief lesson I have learned in a long life is that the only way you can make a man trustworthy is to trust him." Arthur Sweetser, who revived his idea of an internationalist news bureau after World War II, rested his hope on such acts when he told a commencement audience in 1951 that the future of the world hung on "the spirit" with which young people took their place in the world, "whether hope or fear, courage or defeatism, consecration or resignation." Sweetser may have taken inspiration from his old friend Raymond Fosdick, who struck the same note when he warned that "the moral defeatism which is creeping through this country today should be challenged by men and women of high faith who do not and will not accept the sterile doctrine that we are in the grip of emotional forces we cannot control. . . . We are not so riddled with unbelief and impotence," Fosdick concluded, "that we are going to surrender now." Surrender, perhaps not. But this line of appeal—one cannot quite call it "reasoning" any longer—completed the stumbling toward metaphysics that Buell had begun and was a sure indication that little was left to Wilsonians but appeals to "high faith."[77]

---

[75] Warburg, *Germany,* 248.
[76] Armstrong, "Regional Pacts," 366; Warburg, *Common Sense,* 56; Fosdick, *Within Our Power,* 105–7.
[77] Stimson and Bundy, *On Active Service,* 644; Sweetser, "World Organization: Retrospect and Prospect," address at Gettysburg College, 3 June 1951, Sweetser Papers, box 30; Fosdick, *Within Our Power,* 22.

PART II

IDEALISTS IN A REALIST WORLD

8

The Dialectic of Realism and Faith

When the Wilsonians retreated to metaphysics in the face of circumstances they could not explain, they conceded liberalism to liberal realists. By and large people who were slightly younger and removed from direct or substantial experience with Wilson and the Great War, the realists counted as their forming experiences not the Progressive Era but a world depression, the bomb, and the Holocaust. From their perspective, liberal idealism in general and Wilsonianism in particular—realists consistently confused the Wilsonians with do-gooders—simply could not come to grips with the malevolence of human nature, and in a time of great international crisis, idealism thus was dangerously naive. The Cold War was no time for Pollyanna.

Such, at any rate, was the picture of liberal idealism that George Kennan, Reinhold Niebuhr, and Hans Morgenthau drew in the mid-1940s and thereafter. There was some substance to the characterization, at least in that realists believed that idealism's reliance on humanity's better instincts was unwarranted. Indeed the origins of liberal realism lay in the effort to transcend the idealist dependence on faith in a world that made it hard to believe in transcendent truths. Rooted in both the pragmatic revolt and the increasing power of social science, liberal realism widened into an assault not just on dogma but on habit, naivete, and dilettantism, all with the purpose of distinguishing "fact" from habit or mere "opinion." "Fact," according to the first realists, was truth turned up through diligent investigation and searching criticism, as opposed to opinion, which was nothing more than a set of unexamined beliefs. Kant had it backwards, the realists believed: truth inhered in experience, not in the formalist realm of "true Being."[1]

In the Progressive Era, realism emerged among muckrakers, Progressive social scientists, and the prewar New Nationalists, all of whom expected that fact would shed light on the darker recesses of society and corrode entrenched irrationalities with the solvent of practical truth. Because the distinction between fact and opinion clearly helped to justify expert rule, it attracted social scientists, especially after World War I, who argued that if democracy were to work, each citizen would have to embrace scientific method, appreciate the complexities of modern government, and understand the contingency of truth. The depression slowed realist development, though it by no means destroyed the realist perspective. But World War II provided the context out of which realism emerged to dominate the next generation of liberals. Two world wars, a protracted world depression, the Holocaust, and the atomic bomb reinforced the doubts about human rationality that had generated realism to begin with. The Cold War, meanwhile, provided an accommodating political and intellectual atmosphere for the realist view that politics was a battle of competing interests.[2]

By the mid-1940s, realists began to argue that modern industrial society had generated such chronic instability that the individual citizen had become rootless and irrational, and was prepared to follow any demagogue who held out the promise of recovering a golden age. Not only was political truth relative in such a context but the search for it was potentially totalitarian. Without fixed truths, it made little sense to speak about a "common good," and liberal society, realists argued, could

---

[1] The following can stand as the benchmark works of the post–World War II shift in liberalism: Theodor Adorno et al., *The Authoritarian Personality* (New York, 1950); Reinhold Niebuhr, *The Children of Light and the Children of Darkness* (New York, 1944); Daniel Bell, ed., *The Radical Right* (Garden City, 1964); William Kornhauser, *The Politics of Mass Society* (Glencoe, Ill., 1959); Seymour Martin Lipset, *Political Man: The Social Bases of Politics* (Garden City, 1959); John Kenneth Galbraith, *American Capitalism: The Theory of Countervailing Power* (Boston, 1951); Robert Dahl, *Who Governs?* (New Haven, 1961); Hans Morgenthau, *Scientific Man vs. Power Politics* (Chicago, 1946) and *Politics among Nations*, 3rd ed. (New York, 1960); and Arthur Schlesinger, Jr., *The Vital Center* (Boston, 1949).

[2] Christopher Lasch, *The New Radicalism in America* (New York, 1965), 262–65; Raymond Seidelman and Edward Harpham, *Disenchanted Realists: Political Science and the American Crisis, 1884–1984* (Albany, 1985), 111–26; Westbrook, *John Dewey and American Democracy*, 280–86. Donald B. Meyer and David Ricci show in their respective works on American Protestantism and the political science discipline that the realist perspective continued to develop quietly in the 1930s. See *The Protestant Search for Political Realism* (Berkeley, 1960) and *The Tragedy of Political Science* (New Haven, 1984).

achieve nothing more than to balance competing interests through "countervailing pressure" in hopes of keeping society working on a minimal level of civility. If such a strategy were necessary in domestic politics, it was all the more essential to the dangerous realm of international relations. The realist understanding of the balance of power appeared most forcefully in the writings of George Kennan and Hans Morgenthau, who argued that national interests were slippery concepts at best that usually defied rational pursuit even when clearly understood; statesmen could do nothing more than define national interests according to each circumstance, develop flexible policies, and prepare for the worst.

At least to some degree, the behavior of American liberals in the Cold War should be understood as a function of these assumptions. Regardless of Soviet behavior, American liberals, beginning in the immediate aftermath of Roosevelt's death in April 1945, prepared themselves for conflict. From Harry Truman's famed confrontation with Soviet Foreign Minister Vyacheslav Molotov and the attempt to sustain the atomic monopoly, through the development of Kennan's Containment in the Truman Doctrine and the Marshall Plan, Cold War liberals were guided by realism.

The onset of the Cold War more than any single element brought force to the realist perspective. Hence, by the time it developed into the predominant strain of political thought among mainstream liberals, realists had mounted a philosophy that portrayed the common citizen as instinctively irrational, and liberal reason therefore became the impulse of well-educated, cosmopolitian elites who were given to skepticism, were scientific by temperament, and were certain only that truth was practically relative. Political order, given these "realities," could be maintained only by the regulation of clashing interests, no claim of which was more just than another.

Walter Lippmann and the Realists

In contrast to the many other liberal opponents of Wilsonianism—Progressive Era pluralists, isolationists, pacifist do-gooders, the New Deal left—liberal realists engaged Wilsonians in a competition for predominance in mainstream liberalism, which implied that the two strains shared more than most cared to admit. Especially as the Wilsonians grew more doubtful about reason's universality and the realists became more dependent on social science, each grew similarly elitist. Realism and idealism were both responses to the crisis of reason; they were partners in the dialectic of liberalism's confrontation with modernity. Once the second chance became nothing but a bitter dream, no Wilsonian with any hope of becoming influential in liberal America could tout idealist positions consistently. For that matter, no idealist with any pretense to being a serious thinker could avoid confronting the challenge of realism thereafter.

Walter Lippmann's career shows as much. Lippmann was very much a part of the modernist revolt against nineteenth-century liberalism, the history of which he read as a period of destructive laissez faire and facile individualism. Reading back through his Progressive tracts, *A Preface to Politics* and *Drift and Mastery,* is like reading popularized versions of Freud and Nietzsche applied to politics. Taken together, they represented Lippmann's critique of the unvarnished optimism and simplistic assumptions of Progressive reformers.

For our purposes, however, they are better seen as precocious efforts at coming to terms with modernity's heady implications, and it is easy to read into those works the stuff of nascent realism. In mocking the Progressive desire to root out vice, which he saw as an unquenchable aspect of human nature, Lippmann called attention to the prominence of irrationality, as opposed to reasoned self-interest, in human behavior. It was a general irrationality that caught Lippmann's attention and not just a symptom of the common folk's ignorance. Irrationality lingered everywhere people clung to old beliefs even though modernity had blown the foundations of traditional ideals to bits. Insofar as a means of philosophical discipline existed, it lay in scientific method, "the irreconcilable foe of old bogeys," he wrote in *Drift and Mastery.* "The scientific spirit is the discipline of democracy, the escape from drift, the outlook of free men. Its direction is to distinguish fact from fancy, its enthusiasm is for the possible, its promise is the shaping of fact to a chastened and honest dream."[3]

Democracy, in his mind, was a process of flouting habit and rejecting amateurism, and this conception encouraged Lippmann first to search for his "stern commander" and later to advocate intervention in the war, even though this course brought him, as we have seen, into line with mainstream internationalism. As a member of Colonel House's "Inquiry," the committee commissioned with the task of drawing up the Fourteen Points, Lippmann got the opportunity to apply the search

[3] Walter Lippmann, *Drift and Mastery* (New York, 1914), 276.

for facts to practical political life. Once he committed himself to Wilson's war effort, however, he did so whole-heartedly, and he invested as much hope in its outcome as any idealist. Though he initially called for intervention in the war as an act of national interest, by 1918 he clearly hoped that the revolutionary events of the war would issue in a democratic victory, and at this point he seemed to embrace the Wilsonian definition of democracy based on anti-imperialism and liberal politics.

When the dire reports of compromise began to filter out of Versailles, Lippmann condemned Wilson in terms that leave the impression that he was adrift, uncertain which liberal impulse to follow. To begin with, he violated one of the first rules of realism when he criticized Wilson's diplomacy without having any real information at his disposal. His stint as a "special assistant" to Newton Baker in the War Department left him, like many others, to interpret events from a distance. Lack of knowledge did not discourage him from launching a strident critique of Wilson in the *New Republic* in which he simultaneously called for an urgent reconstruction of political order in Central Europe and accused Wilson of participating in an anti-Bolshevik effort under the auspices of the League. The United States would do better to return to isolation. "I presume that you hardly believe that this is either a just or workable peace," he wrote Newton Baker, "and I suppose that you keep your faith in the future by hoping that the League of Nations can modify the terms and work out a genuine settlement. I can't share that belief. . . . It seems to me to stand the world on its head to assume that a timid legal document can master and control the appetites and the national wills before which this Treaty puts such immense prizes."[4] His critique was realist, after a fashion, but only months before he had been excited by the prospects of Versailles. He considered himself a "hard-headed realist," but when he proposed that Wilson leave Paris, he was suggesting that the president leave himself without options. It was uncharacteristically shabby of him to accuse Wilson of trying to build a facade of "unreality" around the conference and to scorn the president's defenders as naive idealists who had "entered a monastery where they contemplate ecstatically the beatitudes of the League of Nations."[5]

[4] "The Political Scene," *New Republic*, 22 March 1919, Supplement; Lippmann to Baker, 9 June 1919, in Blum, *Public Philosopher*, 117–19.
[5] Lippmann to Frankfurter, 28 July 1919, *Public Philosopher*, 123. After he made peace with the Wilson legacy, Lippmann admitted that the president had little leverage at Versailles. See "The Intimate Papers of Colonel House," *Foreign Affairs* 4 (April 1926): 383–93.

Lippmann's disillusionment with Wilson was not permanent, but his sense of having been sobered was. He was the first prominent Wilsonian to translate the war experience into doubts about the public's political aptitude. The first three books that he published during the 1920s in one way or another recalled the bitter experience of the war, as when, for instance, in *Liberty and the News* (1921) and the much more important, *Public Opinion* (1922), he considered the implications of propaganda for the democratic process. Particularly in *Public Opinion,* Lippmann argued that the new reality of modern life rendered traditional conceptions of democracy obsolete. It is plain enough, furthermore, that this work was not only a coming-to-terms with war but was of a piece with his Progressive tracts. The search for the "stern commander" culminated in the elitist implications of *Public Opinion* and the frank elitism of *The Phantom Public,* where he made a case that modern democracy had to rely on expert guidance.[6]

To rest on the conclusion that his work was moving clearly toward realism misses the tensions that plagued him and that cut to the heart of the liberal conundrum. The tensions in his work lay not so much in the questioning of democratic values, something he certainly thought necessary, as in his struggle with the collapse of faith in objective truth. On this issue Lippmann had written before; *Public Opinion* nevertheless was his first systematic attempt to confront a relentlessly relativistic world. A look at wartime events, he argued, showed that the modern world was too far-flung and too complex for the traditional democrat to know what was going on, and therefore the individual's capacity to make reasoned judgments was compromised. In some cases, battlefield developments ran in one direction, official interpretations, based on misinformation and bureaucratic self-interest ran in another, and the response of the public's alleged representatives to the information ladled out went in yet another. Wartime events illustrated that "the real environment is altogether too big, too complex, and too fleeting for direct acquaintance," he wrote, "and we have to reconstruct it on a simpler model before we can manage it."[7] Between the citizen and fact had arisen, in his famous term, a "pseudo-environment," a reconstructed mental area where, through combining biases, presumptions, and information, the citizen managed to interpret a given event.

[6] D. Steven Blum, *Walter Lippmann: Cosmopolitanism in the Century of Total War* (Ithaca, 1984), 55.
[7] Walter Lippmann, *Public Opinion* (New York, 1922), 11.

The working assumption behind the "pseudo-environment" was an internationalist one in which momentous events were either functions of urban complexities or transpired far from the insular world that the typical American inhabited. Global interdependence thus posed the fundamental challenge to democratic theory, which traditionally had upheld, and when necessary retreated to, the ideal of a "self-contained community," much as in Jefferson's agricultural society. Jefferson was a good example, Lippmann claimed, that traditional democratic theorists ignored the "unseen environment" because their faith in the all-knowing citizenry could not account for such a realm. "The democratic tradition is therefore always trying to see a world where people are exclusively concerned with affairs of which the causes and effects all operate within the region they inhabit. . . . The environment must be confined within the range of every man's direct and certain knowledge."[8] Traditional democracy, devoted by necessity to the concept of the small republic, was therefore inherently "subjective," isolationist, and anti-progressive. This line of reasoning was similar to the emerging Wilsonian critique of isolationism, and Lippmann clearly influenced Baker, Fosdick, and others.

Far more than building a case for the League of Nations, he was confronting the modern epistemological crisis head-on. It was precisely this purpose that distinguishes *Public Opinion* as an attempt to analyze the liberal place in the modern world and separates it from the Wilsonians' anti-isolationist polemics or the contemporary realist critique of democracy, however much it shared with both. Having concluded ten years before that the Kantian distinction between experience and *a priori* truth was untenable, he attempted here to overcome the dualisms of both Kant and the Progressives. The bridge between "fact" and "opinion" was the pseudo-environment, the construction of which was, in his mind, a constant human need. The pseudo-environment preceded modern complexities; it was that area where "conditions" met "human nature." He maintained the realist distinction between "fact," which was, literally, the "truth," and "opinion," which, as a "moralized and codified version of the facts," was the region of stereotypes and a priori reasoning. The pseudo-environment was where the two met, for better or worse.[9]

Though the pseudo-environment was necessary, it was vulnerable to corruption from obsolete democratic traditions and to basic human shortcomings. The first threatened the pseudo-environment because, as

[8] Ibid., 170–71.
[9] Ibid., 16.

with Jefferson, traditional democrats resisted the interdependent realities of modern life; the second threat—a web of avarice, short-sightedness, well-intentioned stupidity, in short, irrationality—inevitably seeped into the pseudo-environment so long as steps were not taken to seal that realm against it. Both threats combined in the form of the "self-centered man," who, as a traditional democrat, continued to hold to the parochial interests of the "self-contained community" and yet who, as a modern citizen, chased after symbolic leaders or joined interest groups. The self-centered man clung to the pretense that he mattered and that his self-interest coincided with the common good. Both were nonsense, in Lippmann's view. In fact, only group leaders, politicians, and functionaries actually governed, "a very small percentage of those who are theoretically supposed to govern" according to democrats. Everyman was no leader and had to rely, therefore, on interest groups to represent him. Collective politics was not a symptom of "the perversity of human nature," Lippmann contended. Organized efforts were one of the few ways by which "people can act directly upon a situation beyond their reach." In combining elite leadership and interest groups, Lippmann clearly presaged the interest-group theories of Robert Dahl and Seymour Martin Lipset, for like these later realists, Lippmann believed that the "specialized class" of leaders "whose interests reach beyond the locality" would be more worldly and therefore more realistic than the self-centered man.[10]

To leave *Public Opinion* at this point would be to miss Lippmann's own uncertainties and, I think it is fair to say, his hopes. The book is not an ugly attack on popular capacities, as was his next book. While Lippmann concluded that the self-centered man could apprehend objective truth only by overcoming terrific obstacles, he resisted the descent into relativism. Indeed one of his complaints about traditional democratic theory was that its parochial vision was subjective. Coming to terms with the wider world, even if it required a "specialized class" of experts, was a means of instilling objective truth into the pseudo-environment. He had not lost faith in reason, which even the skeptical Lippmann believed usually resulted in the acquisition of truth over time. Unfortunately the machinery was not in place for the principle of universal reason to work well as a means for governing, since, again, the individual citizen could not know all the facts. However essential "the method of reason" was, "our rational ideas in politics are still large, thin gen-

[10] Ibid., 16, 164, 145–47.

eralities, much too abstract and unrefined for practical guidance." Determined to pull together abstraction and reality, Lippmann insisted that solutions to the modern predicament be immediate and workable. As a matter of short-term practicality, "the only prospect which is not visionary is that each of us in his own sphere will act more and more on a realistic picture of the invisible world, and that we shall develop more and more men who are expert at keeping those pictures realistic." Reason had its limits, but we could do no better than to rely on it, along with experts, in spite of its shortcomings.[11]

In *The Phantom Public* (1925), Lippmann went headlong toward realism. Current events had done little to dissuade him that the elitist strain in *Public Opinion* was incorrect. The clashes at the 1924 Democratic convention, the scattering of liberals into the LaFollette campaign, the persistent Republican refusal to move toward the League, all convinced him that, if anything, *Public Opinion* was insufficiently anti-democratic.

He took on democratic theory at its most basic level. In advancing the prospects of citizen as "omnicompetent" ruler, Lippmann insisted, democratic theory put forth an "unattainable ideal." It was not just the complexities of life that pushed the ideal away from realization but the basic indifference and incompetencies of people, who were moved only by their own interests to act on particular issues, and even then they often acted irrationally. Democratic theory asked the impossible, for its conception of citizenship was so far beyond human capacities that, Lippmann wrote, "I have not happened to meet anybody, from a President of the United States to a professor of political science, who came anywhere near to embodying the accepted ideal of the sovereign and omnicompetent citizen."[12] So much the worse that democratic theory asked the impossible of the weak, the ignorant, and the self-interested. There was simply no redeeming either citizen or theory. The proposition, advanced by so many well-intentioned liberals, that education could stand as "the remedy for the incompetence of democracy," was "barren," because teachers could not possibly supply all the student needed to know about the world—so much for his call in *Public Opinion* for a public that kept its assumptions "realistic." There was too much evidence that the "public" did not want to know the facts, that it was content to dwell in the backwaters so long as its rulers did not rock the boat. "We must assume," he wrote, "that a public is inexpert in its curiosity, . . . that it dis-

[11] Ibid., 195–97, 202, 260.
[12] Walter Lippmann, *The Phantom Public* (New York, 1925), 38–39, 20–21.

cerns only gross distinctions, is slow to be aroused and quickly diverted, . . . and is interested only when events have been melodramatized as a conflict."[13]

If the omnicompetent citizen was a delusion, any faith in universal reason was similarly bankrupt. Declaring bankruptcy on this account bound Lippmann to take the further step and foreclose on the faith in objective truth. Modern political organization, which grew out of "the conflict of standards," stood as proof that "there are too many moral codes" that represented only "local standards" even if they made pretenses toward universal application.[14]

Overcoming the distinction between fact and opinion by discarding fact as a political element altogether, Lippmann now contended that politics ran on two different sorts of opinion. The first was general opinion, which, through such manifestations as voting, expressed vague feelings on merely symbolic levels. General opinion rarely effected genuine action, and even here it was "degraded" to the point at which it merely shaped the alternatives open to leaders. Specific opinion, conversely, was the self-interest that drove leaders of particular groups to act decisively on matters of importance to them. Opinion of this sort was the essence of modern politics, for it shaped the give-and-take of action, the cajoling and bargaining that comprised law and policy making. Within the process, "there is only one common interest: that all special interests shall act according to settled rule." Lippmann's polity was built on interest-group politics, therefore, and insofar as it worked, it achieved nothing more grand "than that two conflicting interests have found a modus vivendi" best described as "a slightly antiquated formulation of the balance of power among the active interests in the community." Modern liberal politics thus could boast only that the interest-group process "makes the conduct of men somewhat rational and establishes a kind of unity in diversity."[15]

The Phantom Public was full-blown realism and was therefore open to the criticisms most easily leveled at realists, the first of which is that it surrendered the faith in respectable leadership. Whatever else his vices,

[13] Ibid., 38–39, 26–28, 64–65. Note how similar this conception of democracy is to George Kennan's, for whom democracy was "uncomfortably similar to one of those prehistoric monsters with a body as long as this room and a brain the size of a pin: he lies there in his primeval mud and pays little attention to his environment; he is slow to wrath—in fact, you practically have to whack his tail off to make him aware that his interests are being disturbed." Kennan, *American Diplomacy* (Chicago, 1951), 66.
[14] Lippmann, *Phantom Public*, 30–31.
[15] Ibid., 46–48, 106, 98–101.

the expert of *Public Opinion* was theoretically capable of disinterestedness on behalf of the common good. In *The Phantom Public*, Lippmann supplanted his experts with a new cadre of "insiders," the movers and shakers who did the bargaining of politics and were too seamy to have fit comfortably in the gentlemanly garb of disinterestedness. Lippmann accepted his insiders' irresponsibility and ignored the possibility that their bureaucratic self-interest lay in keeping their own constituents ignorant and dependent. If the tangible interests of the citizen were diluted as they flowed upward through levels of organization, so power was diluted as it trickled down, thus leaving citizens impotent not because they were ignorant but because the mechanisms of power lay in the hands of elites.

As Lippmann described him in *The Phantom Public*, everyman would not have known what to do with power even if he had it, a position which rested on his confusion of reason with knowledge and unreason with irrationality. The form of reason that he believed appeared in the expert or the insider was functional; it was that rational process by which people made specific decisions based on their immediate calculations, and if reason was simply this means to a definite end, then the crisis of knowledge debilitates the faith in reason, since action is dependent on "knowing" precisely. If reason is understood, conversely, as a practical sensibility, as something similar to common sense, or as the instinctive capacity for skepticism by which the citizen can know a liar when one appears, then the crisis of knowledge does not destroy the faith in reason. Practical reason might be understood, in contrast to Lippmann's functional reason, as a humility before the past and as a sense of responsibility to the future. As Thomas Spragens points out, Enlightenment liberals expected reason to provide not certainty but moral vision, and that sense of reason's potential is lost in *The Phantom Public*.[16]

The Quest for Certainty

Open to such criticisms, *The Phantom Public* was a less meaningful work than *Public Opinion*. The book's sole strength was its exploration of the basic epistemological problem that Lippmann had raised in the

[16] This broader conception of reason is not far from Hannah Arendt's use of the term "judgment," by which she rendered reason akin to foresight and prudence as a sort of thinking with public consequences constantly in mind. See Spragens's comment about "moral vision," *The Irony of Liberal Reason*, 67–69; Margaret Conovan, *The Political Thought of Hannah Arendt* (New York, 1974), 111–13.

earlier work: in an age of eroding faith, how does one organize a liberal polity? It was by no means an easy question, and none of the foregoing criticism quite comes to grips with it.

Conceivably Lippmann's balance-of-power politics was the best answer. We might grant him this much, were it not that John Dewey was offering contemporaneous alternatives to Lippmann that answered the realist critique of democracy. In *The Public and Its Problems* (1927), *Individualism Old and New* (1930), and *The Quest for Certainty* (1930), and his work in general, Dewey considered the problem of knowledge and the citizen as Lippmann had posed it. While conceding that modern complexities threatened the political capacities of the citizen, Dewey maintained that it was a mistake to dismiss democratic theory. Modern conditions did undermine traditional individualism, but not traditional democracy, and Dewey insisted that the two be distinguished. Democracy remained relevant because modernity did not destroy the capacity of the individual to reason, which was universal and could be built up through inculcating scientific method and critical thought among citizens. Dewey was not about to resurrect a defense of absolute truth, but he did build his position on the assumption that reason was an innate capacity, and he believed that citizens could make their way through modern chaos to something like the common good by applying critical thought to the problems at hand. The problem of knowledge in the modern world was formidable, but not necessarily incapacitating.[17]

In light of Dewey's work, Lippmann's conception of balance-of-power politics appears, if not cynical, at least picaresque. If Lippmann really held to it, one would expect him to have accepted with greater good humor the public developments that quickly seemed to confirm his dire view of democracy, not least the Scopes trial, which brought to a head the ongoing struggle between the rural fundamentalist wing of American society and the urban cosmopolitans. Had he been consistent, Lippmann would have interpreted the fundamentalist crusade, not as as some impending majoritarian tyranny, but as a self-interested campaign of Bible salesmen determined to maintain their share of the textbook market. Instead, as Ronald Steel writes, Lippmann "churned out a stream of impassioned editorials" condemning the fundamentalists for, among other things, attempting to establish a state religion. He was working on a double standard, then, in which he lorded his clearheaded understanding

[17] John Dewey, *The Public and Its Problems* (New York, 1927), *Individualism Old and New* (New York, 1930), and *The Quest for Certainty* (London, 1930); Westbrook, *Dewey and American Democracy*, 293–300.

of politics over the provincial democrats, only to react with condescending indignation when some democrats had the effrontery to organize themselves and take political action. If politics boiled down to a competition between interests with no common element or goal other than an agreement on the rules of the game, then consistency required that Lippmann match his heated denunciations of the "semi-literate priestridden and parsonridden people" of Tennessee with at least some doubt about whether cosmopolitans were the guardians of enlightenment.[18] He was guilty of changing the rules almost as soon as he laid them down; political truth was relative, he argued in *The Phantom Public*, and yet he set up his own standards of truth.

His behavior throughout the Scopes business pointed up—and perhaps reminded him—how disjointed his realist theorizing and his practical political activity had become. Maybe the most curious aspect of his realist work in the 1920s was its detachment from his practical activity, a strange situation for a "realist." In theory he lauded the roguish insider and the virtues of interest-group competition; in practice he was a Wilsonian. He joined the Council on Foreign Relations, and after joining the New York *World* in 1922, became the nation's foremost commentator on foreign affairs. He continued to search for the great statesman, whether in Newton Baker, John W. Davis, or Dwight Morrow. He supported the World Court and opposed protectionism. He criticized isolationism, especially William Borah (though he tried, with some success, to cultivate the isolationist leader). Lippmann shared the general Wilsonian distrust of the outlawry movement and Kellogg-Briand. Like Stimson, Shotwell, Norman Davis, and others, he held high hopes for the success of the disarmament process, seeing especially naval disarmament as the key to long-term international stability. Indeed he greeted the London Disarmament Conference in January 1930 by proclaiming it a "stupendous vindication . . . of the idealism of 1919," a sign that "no government any longer dares to deny its responsibility to the community of states." Such sentiments were difficult to square with the realist critique of reason and truth, for Lippmann's internationalism, like the impulse generally, continued to move along traditionally liberal presumptions.[19]

We need to see his realist work in the 1920s as a combination of exploration, elitist invective, temporizing, and qualification of his idealism.

---

[18] Steel, *Lippmann and the American Century*, 216–19; Lippmann to Learned Hand, ca. 8 June 1925, in Blum, *Public Philosopher*, 176.

[19] Steel, *Lippmann and the American Century*, 252–56.

By the end of the decade, he began to synthesize his qualified idealism with his political activity.

He began his swing away from realism in the Barbour-Page lectures delivered at the University of Virginia in spring 1928 and collected in *American Inquisitors*. There he broached the possibility that, whatever the absurdity of their position, the fundamentalists had a firmer grasp than the smug modernist intelligentsia did on a part of human nature that realism could neither relieve nor account for: the need to believe in a settled and predictable truth. Relying on a series of classical dialogues, Lippmann posed Bryan against Jefferson (with Socrates as mediator), fundamentalist against modernist, and patriot against scholar, faith against reason. He assured his listeners that he was merely playing devil's advocate in favor of reason, but it was not so clear that he had quenched his own need for a solid faith.[20]

In his concluding remarks, Lippmann has his teacher reassert the critique of democracy to Socrates, as if to give realism the last word, but the weight of the discussion is on the shortcomings of modernism, which "is the religion of elites." The foremost problem with modernism, and, Lippmann implies, with Dewey's faith in scientific method, is that it leads inexorably to relativism. "The conclusions reached by reason are not final," he has Jefferson proclaim. While modernists would be perfectly happy with this state of affairs—indeed a contentment with Dewey's scientific method and the resulting relativism defined the modernist, according to Lippmann—it could hardly satisfy the need for a clear moral code.

With this problem in mind, his antagonists reverse roles, and the fundamentalist toys with realism. When the modernist suggests that each citizen can define his own moral code, the fundamentalist asks how anarchy is to be averted. "You have got to have some faith in the common-sense and decent instincts of your fellow men," comes the reply. The fundamentalist turns realism on its head and reminds the modernist that "your natural man is a natural barbarian, grasping, selfish, lustful, murderous. Your psychoanalysts will tell you that. The religious teachers knew it long before. . . . They called it original sin." Relativistic reason, with its shifting conclusions and acceptance of flux, could not command the "transformation of will" necessary to transcend original sin precisely

[20] Walter Lippmann, *American Inquisitors* (New York, 1928), 11.

because there was nothing left to afix the will to, and thus "even if the modernists could agree upon a moral code, they could not inculcate morality."[21]

American Inquisitors was a tentative return to idealism and thus presaged Lippmann's more important attempt to negotiate between faith and modernity, *A Preface to Morals*. *Preface* had almost nothing to do with Wilsonianism, advocating as it did humanistic asceticism as an antidote to anomie. But the book was nothing if not an attempt to rediscover the basis on which faith and reason could be united under modern conditions.

Lippmann addressed the book to those who were neither fundamentalists nor modernists and who therefore fell between the poles of dogma and unbelief. He aimed at the like-minded—or the similarly uncertain. In a more formal presentation of the ideas he had advanced in the *American Inquisitors,* he contended that modernity made it impossible for any thinking person to believe in an almighty God and yet the basic need for certainty, for a coherent means of ordering one's relation to the rest of the world, remained. Modernity was an imperious but insufficient sovereign. "Certainty itself," he maintained, "is dissolving not merely for an educated minority but for everyone who comes within the orbit of modernity." Modernity dissolved not just accepted truths but the very possibility of having faith in any new dogma. "The modern world is haunted by the realization . . . that it is impossible to reconstruct an enduring orthodoxy, and impossible to live well without the satisfactions which an orthodoxy would provide."[22]

Neither fundamentalism nor modernism offered relief. Given the state of modern knowledge, at this point defined by Einstein, one could not accept the reality of an omnipotent God and still claim to be reasonable. On that point, Lippmann probably did not expect much argument. He was even more critical of the modernists, from whom he no doubt anticipated criticism. The "children of the great emancipation," as he derisively called them, embraced the smug assumption that they could do away with the omnipotent God and simply whip up a suitable alternative to soothe the soul. They did not stop to think that believers invested their faith in God in the first place because He was a sovereign whose reign was completely independent of human contrivance. When modern theo-

[21] Ibid., 39, 42–43, 55–57.
[22] Walter Lippmann, *A Preface to Morals* (New York, 1929), 19–20.

logians such as Henry Emerson Fosdick conceived of God in man's image rather than the other way around, they rendered unto man what had been God's.[23]

Modern believers wanted to believe, they simply could not. Modernists could not recreate a religion that upheld a superior God, nor did the other disciplines to which they were attached, such as they were, offer solutions. Lippmann dismissed Dewey's faith in scientific method as a means to certainty because its business was hypothesizing, the very opposite of dogmatics. The habit of the scientist, Lippmann rightly pointed out, was to assume that there was no such thing as a fixed and impermeable truth. In these terms science and religion were irreconcilable, for the former was based on "a denial of the premises of faith," and even if the two sides worked out a "policy of toleration," the scientific enterprise would make the arrangement "inherently unstable." Lippmann had no patience with the attempts to frame science to meet the popular need for faith, especially the "pseudo-religions" of Darwinism and psychoanalysis. Where these movements gained a popular hearing, it was necessary for true scientists to make clear that the premises on which the movements were built were open to question and therefore to change. Likewise, if an honest and well-meaning scientist sat down to judge the evidence of Genesis, the very act of passing judgment would destroy "certainty, as the devout understand it . . . ; verity, as they understand it, would be gone; objectivity, as they imagine it, would be gone." Faith and reason worked at cross purposes, and thus it was enormously difficult to reconcile "the human desire for a certain kind of universe with a method of explaining the world which is absolutely neutral in its intention."[24]

His quest, nonetheless, was to achieve a reconciliation. The problem was that religion absorbed the need to believe but misdirected it toward dogma, which he regarded as thoroughly subjective, because unprovable. Reason had access to truth, on the other hand, but only in limited and incomplete ways. The only solution under these circumstances was a strict humanism that quieted the soul through subordinating the will to moderation and self-discipline and yet that arrived at settled understandings of objective truth through reason. The "ascetic principle" was that introspection and controlled gratification provided the basis for an orderly society based on a knowledge of and reasoned adjustment to facts.

[23] Ibid., 35–42, 53–54.
[24] Ibid., 123–32.

The humanist solution had many things to recommend it, Lippmann argued. First, it incorporated the valuable "truths" from the past's "great teachers," including theologians and religious figures. The "greatest religious teachers were not religious men," because they did not accept the "theocratic principle" that God was a sovereign king and religion "a matter of commandments and obedience, reward and punishment." Thinkers as diverse as Aristotle, the Christian prophets, Buddha, and Spinoza all "placed their emphasis upon the conversion, the education, and the discipline of the human will." If this were so, then there was no conflict between the truths of the past and the truths of modern science. Psychology might not provide certainty, he wrote, but it taught, much as had the "great teachers," that maturity came through subordinating desires to reality. Likewise the scientific method reflected the spirit of disinterestedness and sacrifice. Scientific method, he claimed, was "high religion incarnate"; as far as it goes "it translates into a usable procedure what in the teaching of the sages has been an esoteric insight. Scientific method can be learned. The learning of it matures the human character."[25] Lest he concede ground to Dewey, he quickly added that scientific method, like the insights of the "sages," was mostly lost in popular application and thus provided no new defense, as Dewey believed, of democracy. "The multitude," he wrote, was no better able to grasp the lessons of scientific rigor than it had the "wisdom" of the sages.[26]

The conceptions of science and reason that emerge in *Preface to Morals* are peculiar ones. The practical uses of science, whether the applied science of the technocrats or the democratic science of Dewey, are factored out, and science becomes a moral discipline in its own right. Reason itself becomes less a means to an end than an ideal, a conception completely at odds with the functional reason of Lippmann's realist writings. Where science becomes an ideal, the scientist ascends to the realm of Being, and reason flies with him. Lippmann came close to imitating Nietzsche's strategy of escaping the swamp of idealism by seizing hold of the superior individual; his scientist is Nietzsche in a lab coat, the new high priest. If Lippmann's intent was to criticize modernism, following Nietzsche was a dubious strategy. Where reason itself is detached from daily affairs, it completely loses its political content. So too, where the scientist is conceded heaven, it is impossible to question that which scientists produce.

[25] Ibid., 194–95, 172–75, 180–83.
[26] Ibid., 237–40.

Lippmann, in effect, tried to counter Dewey's critique of realism by relying on an idealism every bit as elitist as his realism. Again Dewey got the better of him. In *Individualism Old and New,* the philosopher attacked the new "humanism" that "proposes restraint and moderation, exercised in and by the higher volition of individuals, as the solution of our ills." That intellectuals had come to believe that it was necessary to adopt any such strategy was itself testimony to the "disintegration of individuality." "But a sense of fact, as well as a sense of humor," Dewey wrote, made it difficult to see how intellectuals had the power to reorient society and address the true causes of disintegration simply through a series of personal decisions. Because Lippmann refused to criticize technocracy even though he conceded that technological flux was at the root of the problem, he continued to avoid Dewey's argument that practical reason offered the best solution to reorienting the individual. Lippmann conceivably could have argued that Dewey's practical reason did nothing to address the anxiety of the soul and the need to merge intellect and faith. But in dismissing practical reason Lippmann ignored the one human activity that, properly conceived, combines practical reason, scientific method, and an ascetic devotion to high standards: craftsmanship. Instead of trying to elude spiritual anxiety by escaping to an ivory tower, Lippmann would have done better to return to the practice of individual work, which, as Dewey argued in his defense of vocational education for example, was a universal human need associated with the impulses of productivity and curiosity and yet was quite receptive to the discipline of critical thought. Elitist by habit and increasingly determined to return to Enlightenment liberalism for his ideals, Lippmann could not transcend the boundaries of traditional individualism. As Dewey wrote, in the absence of serious criticism of the social order, "the urging of some higher personal will, whatever that may be, is itself only a futile echo of just the old individualism that has so completely broken down."[27]

It is true that one can read some measure of realism into Lippmann's discussion of politics in *Preface to Morals,* insofar as he dealt with the issue. The complexities of modern life had broken down old loyalties to family, tribe, church, and state and had burdened the citizen with a multiplicity of interrelated interests, just as the modern nation existed within an interdependent community. Interdependence recommended moderation on the part of citizens and nations, lest their complex interests be

---

[27] Dewey, *Individualism Old and New,* 67–68. See Dewey's various comments on work, craftsmanship, and scientific method in *The School and Society,* ed. Jo Ann Boydston (Carbondale, Ill. 1980), especially 7–13, 92–93.

damaged. "Responsible men of affairs," he wrote, recognized "the necessity of not pressing any claim too far, of understanding opposing points of view, of seeking to reconcile them, of conducting matters so that there is some kind of harmony in a plural society."[28]

Even here he was moving away from a defense of interest-group politics, and we must take note of changes in tone and emphasis, subtle as they were. Multiple interests as they appear in *Preface to Morals* encourage interdependence, whereas in the realist writings they constitute nothing more elaborate than a society of tense compromise held together by a minimal agreement on the rules of the game. The state, as he describes it, is the embodiment of authority and law. He thus returned to a more traditionally liberal conception of the state, which carried with it overtones of Wilson's concept of organic law. There was no going back to the traditional notion of the omnicompetent citizen, but the orderly and harmonious society nevertheless relied on the statesman, who in contrast to the "politician," a mere seeker after "the special objects of particular interests," guided society by "elucidat[ing] the confused and clamorous interests" and "penetrat[ing] from the naive self-interest of each group to its permanent and real interest." The statesman was the political analogue to the sage in theocratic society and the scientist in a technocratic one; he worked, often "in advance of his constituents," from "insight which comes only from an objective and discerning knowledge of the facts, and a high and imperturbable disinterestedness."[29]

We need only recall Wilson's remarks on "the ideal statesman" to recognize where Lippmann's quest for certainty led. It had taken him through an immature Progressive modernism, to idealism during the war, to a dissatisfying realism, and finally to a conclusion that blended faith and reason in a way that sustained the sense of objective truth and the common good in spite of modern flux. The quest for certainty took Lippmann firmly to idealism, and thus the book was not so bleak as most of its readers seemed to think.[30] When he wrote that modern liberals must abide by "the belief that the duty of man is not to make his will conform to the will of God but to the sure knowledge of the conditions of human happiness," he necessarily affirmed his own faith in a form of reason that was no longer merely functional and implicitly accepted a view of the future that recovered the moral vision of traditional

[28] Lippmann, *Preface to Morals*, 268–71.
[29] Ibid., 268–71, 281–83.
[30] See Steel, *Lippmann and the American Century*, 263–64.

liberalism. In this sense, *Preface to Morals* presented a view less pessimistic than the realist world of irreconcilable interests and competitive
clashes.[31]

The Good Society

Lippmann's political direction in the 1930s must be understood in
light of this intellectual odyssey. As in the 1920s, his oscillation from one
liberal strain to the other was more extreme than that which moved other
Wilsonianians. More extensively than most, Lippmann acknowledged
the need for emergency measures in 1933 and praised President
Roosevelt as a master of public life. Yet he opposed the nationalist bent
of the New Deal, which he believed spurred the growth of interest-group
politics, and when he turned on Roosevelt he did so with an intensity all
the greater for having flirted with the New Deal.

   At times, Lippmann wrote and spoke as if the depression had forced
him to the liberal left. In the 1934 Godkin Lectures, his most systematic
defense of the New Deal, he argued that collectivism was inexorable and
that we had to make the best of it by encouraging a "compensated economy" of "free collectivism." Relying on the novel ideas of John Maynard
Keynes, Lippmann claimed that the government could use its resources
to ensure balance in a society run, on the whole, by private individuals.[32]
His application of Keynesianism resembled his use of Freud twenty years
before. Obviously there is the similar attraction to, and rapid application
of, a novel doctrine, and just as in the Progressive years, it is possible to
see these modernist influences pulling him to the left. Just as he used
Freud for *Preface to Politics,* Lippmann seized Keynes as a practical tool
with which he might think through unprecedented problems; modernism's allure continued to be its immediate usefulness.

   Keynes provided a medium that allowed Lippmann to gloss over his
otherwise conventional economic views. For the most part, he called for
the "middle way," just as other Wilsonians did, which charted between
self-sufficiency and "a truly international world with truly international
markets."[33] Self-sufficiency promised to protect people "against the vi-
cissitudes of international trade" and rapid technological change but

[31] Lippmann, *Preface to Morals,* 137.
   [32] Walter Lippmann, *The Method of Freedom* (New York, 1934), 46, 57–59; see Steel,
Lippmann and the American Century, 305–6, for Keynes's influence on Lippmann.
   [33] Lippmann to William Allen White, 22 April 1932, and Lippmann to Arthur Salter,
28 April 1932, in Blum, *Public Philosopher,* 288–89.

could not be had without regimentation. Internationalism sanctioned individual freedom, but under that sanction lay the "anonymous compulsion of the markets" that tore at human security and social stability.
Perhaps more than other Wilsonians, he was willing to see both paths as
inadequate to the task at hand and to consider the respective positions,
"in any rigorous sense, incompatible with our reality."[34]

It is easy to explain his support for the Hundred Days' legislation, the
abandonment of gold, and Roosevelt himself. Lippmann urged Congress
to allow the president any power he might need to deal with the emergency, and when Roosevelt simply took what power he wanted, Lippmann was impressed. The "amiable boy scout" with the "weaseling
mind" had matured into a "kindly and intelligent man." Roosevelt captured Lippmann's allegiance because of his willingness to take command, to liberate himself from myths like the gold "fetish." The
president surely had the dash and resolve that Lippmann admired in public men. Like Nicholas Murray Butler, Lippmann admired Roosevelt's
statesmanship. Indeed he urged that the president be given greater power,
he explained to Felix Frankfurter, only after "I had been satisfied as to
the essential wisdom with which he would use such authority."[35]

The New Deal itself, furthermore, established important forms of economic authority. In his view, the nation faced two fundamental problems: a complicated private economy incapable of self-regulation, and a
self-conscious electorate. The state had to take an active role in society if
only to prevent the economy and the masses from destroying one another. Lippmann contended that because the state now assumed responsibility for national life, it had to be freed from narrow interests and had
to "look upon the economy as a national establishment for which it is
responsible and not as a mere congeries of separate interests which it
serves, protects and regulates"—so much for the realist's interest-group
competition. Centralization put distance between the administration
and special interests, and the middle way was ensured through the guidance of some automatic aid, in this case, the complexities of modern
capitalism.[36]

[34] Lippmann, *Method of Freedom*, 207, 209–10, 212; Lippmann to Robert Wood, 1
August 1933, in Blum, *Public Philosopher*, 311.
[35] Quoted in Steel, *Lippmann and the American Century*, 301. Lippmann wrote Bernard Berenson that "my only fear as regards his leadership is that he has undertaken too
many things. . . . But he is amazingly confident, and his political insight has so far proved
to be uncanny." Lippmann to Berenson, 23 March 1935, in Blum, *Public Philosopher*, 327.
[36] Lippmann to Frankfurter, 3 March 1933, in Blum, *Public Philosopher*, 302–3; Lippmann, *Method of Freedom*, 28, 78–79, 76, 74.

190 Idealists in a Realist World

Lippmann became a critic of the New Deal suddenly and for reasons that are not altogether clear. He claimed in 1938 that he really had not changed his views: he supported the New Deal as an emergency program but opposed it when Roosevelt tried to make it permanent.[37] It was a reasonable explanation. Roosevelt's populism also coincided with the worsening international scene. Lippmann wrote Hamilton Fish Armstrong in 1935 that he was as certain as ever that "permanent peace through collective securities would require essentially free trade." With nationalism rampant, "I have ceased hoping for permanent peace and now have reduced my hopes to the idea of long periods of tranquility such as the world knew in the Victorian Age." If peace depended on free trade but nationalism was still "world-wide, cumulative, and irresistible," as he remarked to John Davis, something had to give. No specific episode turned him against Roosevelt, but his public break began when he conspired with Baker and Douglas in spring 1936, continued on through the 1936 election in which he backed Landon, and culminated in his treatise *The Good Society* the next year.[38]

The book was much more than a compilation of his election-year frustrations with Roosevelt. He intended it as a comprehensive piece that related "domestic and foreign relations organically one to the other," and the result was the best summary of contemporary Wilsonianism.[39] There was the disdain for the wealthy and powerful who believed in crass social Darwinism. There was the opposition to "irrational" theories of planning that drove coercive government. There was the knowledge that natural law had little place in technocratic society, joined with a frantic attempt to excavate it anyway. There was, finally, the contention that only the international division of labor and world interdependence could bring peace.

Lippmann began *The Good Society* on the defensive and described a political scene in which fascists, communists, progressives, liberals, and nationalists of all sorts were determined to "collectivize" the world. If right and left were indistinguishable in contemporary politics, then the past and present were akin as well; what liberals fought in the eighteenth century, they would have to fight again in the twentieth. It should be un-

---

[37] Steel, *Lippmann and the American Century*, 321–22.

[38] Lippmann to Armstrong, 30 March 1935, in Blum, *Public Philosopher*, 329–30; and Lippmann to Davis, 1 July 1935, ibid., 337–38. Walter Lippmann, *An Inquiry into the Principles of the Good Society* (Boston, 1938, originally published September 1937).

[39] Lippmann to Hamilton Fish Armstrong, 9 November 1935, in Blum, *Public Philosopher*, 341.

derstood, he wrote, "that the collectivist movement is a tremendous re-action in human affairs, that on the main line which western society has advanced it is carrying mankind backward and not forward."[40]

Lippmann thought that the immediate resurgence of economic nation-alism resulted from Versailles, yet he located its origin more deeply. Sometime in the middle of the nineteenth century, western liberals quit seeking freedom and resumed an old preoccupation with "organization, authority, and collective power." At that point, business sought tariffs, radicals organized workers, and even reformers looked "to the capture of the sovereign power." Having won the day against monarchy, liberals grew complacent and traded the philosophy of freedom for a facile jus-tification of the status quo, namely, the doctrine of laissez faire. "Latter-day liberals" such as Spencer and Mill assumed that law could be limited, that there could exist a small sphere of law and order and a larger sphere of freedom and anarchy.[41] But this was not possible, as-serted Lippmann, because all civilized life was governed by consensus ei-ther rooted in common habit or based in law. When they conceived of a "realm of freedom" in which property and contract ran free of public restraints, the latter-day liberals grew insensitive both to the self-serving inclinations of the powerful and to the underlying power of the state.[42] Indeed laissez-faire liberals never dismantled the state, they merely used it to protect certain interests, and the predictable reaction against that liberalism sent newly organized groups rushing to exploit state power for selfish ends. The more special privilege drove politics, the more potent the state became. Along with tariff privileges and restrictive laws, along with the ubiquitous assumption that the state provided the abundant life, came greater regimentation.

In the historical context of creeping collectivism came World War I, Versailles, and the "subsequent failure to restore the international econ-omy." The world's failure after the war drove the Germans and the Ital-ians to imperialism and, more important, to militarize their economies. Much the same happened in Russia. The war taught collectivists that the only way to plan a modern economy was to demand absolute compliance and crush any dissent. The only difference between communists and fas-cists, therefore, was that the Bolsheviks were driven to the militarized economy by civil war, and the Germans frankly declared their intentions of using military might to have their way. War, he concluded in his sec-

[40] Lippmann, *The Good Society*, 16–17, 11.
[41] Ibid., 46–47, 184–86.
[42] Ibid., 188–90.

tion on collectivist planning, "is where all planned economies have originated and must in the very nature of things originate. . . . There is only one purpose to which a whole society can be directed by a deliberate plan. That purpose is war, and there is no other."[43]

His middle way of "free collectivism," in light of this argument, must have been just so much musing, for now he held that wherever the state grew, economic progress was retarded, no matter how democratic state organization and control was. Even "humane" collectivists such as George Soule and Stuart Chase regularly appealed to the war experience, hoping to create enthusiasm and to prove that planning could work. That well-intentioned men could speak glibly of forming "general staffs" of planners showed that war was an inherent part of all planning. When they appealed to patriotic enthusiasm, planners admitted that planning by other means had failed. Lippmann knew that "humane" collectivists shunned regimentation. Left in control of state power, they usually proved wary of using it; sincerely interested in the plight of the dispossessed, they usually proved easy targets for group pressure. Because they were not authoritarians, the collectivists, like the classical liberals, opened the state up to the introduction of special interests; "gradual collectivism," as he put it, brought "the polity of pressure groups."[44]

Barraged by the pressure groups that they helped to create, the liberal collectivists had no way of discerning the common good. Their goal was to create special privilege and force the state to decide which among the many competing privileges were most worthy. This was the lesson of the New Deal, where the state cultivated chosen groups, labor and farmers especially, and conferred on them collective rights only because someone in the administration was convinced that the general welfare depended on farmers and workers. There was simply no firm test to measure which interests were more important to the general welfare, and thus the ultimate control of state favors was left to whoever happened to control the state at any given time. There was no objective measure of justice, no embodied truth. Moreover, the entire system of special privilege restricted the production of wealth, and that was the one thing that the whole society had a stake in. Organization froze society both politically and economically, Lippmann declared; the organized society "must imitate the mollusk, which, though it can neither walk, swim, nor fly, and

[43] Ibid., 64, 86, 89–90.
[44] Ibid., 111–12.

has only meagre ambitions, does seem to enjoy a reasonably well-protected and stable existence."[45]

His gripe was not that organizational complexity was dangerous. Interdependence, after all, was by nature organized and complex. Rather, its intentions aside, liberal collectivism created fragmentation and retreated from unity. Connecting the collectivists to the "polity of pressure groups" was therefore critical to his argument. "Democratic collectivism" was the antithesis of the good society, because it unwittingly forced citizens to seek out some organization to represent them and thus it encouraged them to project their loyalty to the interest group rather than to the common good. The rise of the domestic interest group paralleled the rise of nationalism abroad, and groups, like nations, girded up to protect their members from the larger world. Thus collectivism obstructed interdependence, for by encouraging divisive interests, it dissolved the natural bonds that once led people away from parochialism and toward, presumably, internationalism.[46]

Expanding loyalties were the opposite of collectivist organization and had to be reaffirmed in order to salvage the mess of the 1930s. Lippmann argued that such a reaffirmation depended on relearning the lessons of Enlightenment liberals, the first of which was that the division of labor not only produced wealth but locked people into an interdependent world. This was precisely what had happened in the eighteenth century, he claimed, when the intellectual and scientific Enlightenment eroded the power of monarchs by creating an international division of labor. "It was by a stupendous liberation of the minds and spirits and conduct of men that a world-wide exchange of goods and services and ideas was promoted," he wrote, and this supplanted petty principalities with the nineteenth-century "commonwealths." The isolated individual, the "self-sufficing household," and the petty state, all had disappeared in the West and could be found, if at all, only in backward nations; the division of labor, he asserted, forced "the most revolutionary experience in recorded history."[47]

Not that the history of liberal capitalism was unblemished. The division of labor, he recognized, destroyed parochial attachments and created enormous wealth, but it also had destroyed the objects of security, the church, the family, and assured status. The industrial revolution

[45] Ibid., 111–12, 121–23, 35–38.
[46] Ibid., 140.
[47] Ibid., 20.

thus brought with it "progress and poverty," "democracy and insecurity," "the interdependence of nations and their fiercely competitive imperialism."[48] The flaw in the system, he assured his readers, was purely technical and was to be found in the discrepancy between labor mobility and capital mobility: especially in the complex industrial economy, workers could not move easily to where they could best exploit the market. Anxious to distinguish himself from the typical defender of the status quo, Lippmann argued that the state had a right to undertake reforms that allowed equal participation in the division of labor and equal access to the wealth that it produced. The state should allow labor to organize, administer weights and measures, and even develop a system of social insurance to "indemnify" those injured by technological progress. All of these reforms, he felt sure, were "deeply consistent with the classical heritage and with the liberal tradition," because they all worked against privilege and remained true, therefore, to the liberal ideal of freedom.[49]

Lippmann thereby managed to rejoin individual freedom, the free market, and internationalism and equate progress with expanding political and cultural loyalties. The market should be free not in order to protect the status quo or because it was a worthy end in itself, but in order to strengthen the division of labor, which then deepened human associations and expanded political loyalty. Thus the burden of the whole argument fell on the international division of labor: it allegedly would guarantee economic prosperity, restore psychological security, and emancipate people from parochialism. The division of labor seemed omnipotent and undeniable. Despite all of his hand-wringing about the power of collectivism, he declared that no one could reverse the industrial revolution. Nations were "committed to the new mode of production, to the division of labor among interdependent communities and individuals. . . . They can no more reverse the industrial revolution by an act of will and by political coercion than they could return from manufacture to handicraft, from settled agriculture to a pastoral economy."[50]

The division of labor held the key to everything but practical political consensus. Lippmann suggested that modern liberals could find the basis for the common good in "a common law which defines the reciprocal rights and duties." The practical choice for society lay between regula-

---

[48] Ibid., 20, 161–67, 171–72.
[49] Ibid., 222–24, 234.
[50] Ibid., 205.

tion by common agreement or by "arbitrary sovereign commands."[51] With this he made his most suggestive contribution to the attempt to sustain idealism, for he forthrightly excavated natural law, the ingrained acceptance by the public that some "higher law" compelled citizens to put the common good above their selfish interests. Just as Wilson had, Lippmann went back beyond the age of laissez faire to find a liberalism worth reviving, one that was based on the natural regulation of society by the common acceptance of public duty. Even with a free division of labor, "a free and ordered society, resting chiefly on persuasion rather than on coercion, on the pacific adjudication of human conflicts, . . . is inconceivable in theory and unworkable in practice unless in the community there is a general willingness to be bound by the spirit of a law that is higher and more universal than the letter of particular laws."[52]

The combination of natural law and the international division of labor amounted to an attempt to revive flagging faith and was a systematic description of the objective and certain political truth that he had looked to in *A Preface to Morals*. Lippmann in 1937 argued essentially what Grotius had argued three hundred years before: that even if higher law had no objective basis in fact, it could still provide the basis for a just society if people chose to believe. Yet there remained a modernist tension, an indication that faith alone was insufficient, because, after all, he did not expect natural law, political consensus, and objective truth to be reborn by themselves; he looked to the division of labor to revive and sustain them. If anything is clear about Lippmann's thinking in *The Good Society*, it is that realism held little attraction for him. It is as if this book and *The Phantom Public* were written by two different authors.

The argument was nothing less than a Wilsonian synthesis, which meant that the fundamental contradictions that plagued liberal idealism caught the author's idealism as well. The division of labor of which he was enamored was a product of the corporation and mass production, not of human instinct for association, and to embrace the result he had at least to tolerate the creator. To accept the division of labor as inexorable and virtuous led to the delusion that neither technology nor capitalist imperialism threatened the rest of the world, and he was forced to restate his earlier view of imperialism as a "pathological disease . . . but a transient phenomenon." Lippmann could not admit the coercive nature of the international division of labor, because he would have been

---

[51] Ibid., 205, 272–73.
[52] Ibid., 335.

unable to make moral distinctions between Wilsonian interdependence and collectivist complexity, and the whole elaborate defense of idealism would have come undone.

An impressive book, *The Good Society* came out rather too late to attract the attention of fellow Wilsonians who were increasingly obsessed with collective security. Newton Baker reviewed the work and wondered whether Lippmann was not on a futile intellectual quest. Lippmann had spent more than twenty years detailing and describing the intellectual chaos of modernity, Baker wrote, and "in the meantime the people of the world have become as confused as he was." The prescriptions for the good society and the warnings against totalitarian planning were well and good but "inconsistent with the present purposes of the world." Like it or not, the world was bellicose and war impended, and in such an atmosphere any talk of the good society was mere gibberish. Instead of warning against the encroachments of the state, Baker implied, Lippmann should prepare for war. "It would have been enough if he had said baldly that the present world is organized on the theory of war, [and] that the future world should be organized on the theory of peace." The only choice that faced people now, Baker asserted, was whether they would fight on the side of despotism or of freedom. As for his friend Lippmann, "the next few years may set his book entirely aside, to be reviewed again when the war is over."[53] In this case, Baker proved prophetic.

The Public Philosophy

When he turned toward diplomatic realism in the late 1930s, as he did in his two oft-noted wartime books, Lippmann was answering Baker's call to arms.[54] His renewed defense of balance-of-power diplomacy, like many of his earlier intellectual swings, was more a response to the urgent crises of the moment than a well-conceived philosophical position. Indeed both *U.S. Foreign Policy* (1943) and *U.S. War Aims* (1944) were the type of brief that he used to make quick points. The Anschluss, Munich, and the Nazi-Soviet pact reinforced Lippmann's dwindling optimism about Western society, encouraged him to take Baker's advice, and

[53] Newton Baker, "The Good Society for the Future," *Atlantic Monthly* 160 (November 1937): 612, 614–16.
[54] Walter Lippmann, *U.S. Foreign Policy* (Boston, 1943); *U.S. War Aims* (Boston, 1944).

brought him to push the mainstream arguments for aid to the allies. As we have seen, his fellow Wilsonians were doing likewise, and no discussion of Lippmann's diplomatic writings should miss the point that he moved in tandem with other Wilsonians when he called for the alliance of like-minded states and tried to balance the realities of power with internationalism.

Without a doubt, he increasingly laced his defense of collective security with realist rhetoric about limited national interests and spheres of influence. Lippmann began *U.S. Foreign Policy* with something of a confession, which allowed him to parade as a converted realist. The reader would find, he explained, that his views on international politics had changed considerably over the years; his new opinions "represent what I think I have learned, not what I always knew."[55] He learned specifically that Wilsonian diplomacy was too idealistic and imprecise. Wilson had trafficked in "legalistic and moralistic and idealistic" justifications for American intervention in World War I, all of which were misleading, for intervention was necessary to long-term national security. Wilson should have justified intervention on this straightforward ground, Lippmann asserted, not only because it was the real reason for war but because it was an explanation that Americans probably would have understood. Many Americans "recognized intuitively" that the United States either had to defend the allies or face a victorious Germany made all the more powerful by its subjugation of those powers and its alliance with Japan. "Because this simple and self-evident American interest was not candidly made explicit," he contended, "the nation never understood clearly why it entered the war. As time went on, the country was, therefore, open to every suggestion and insinuation that the nation had fought for no good reason at all." Misled by vague diplomacy, Americans were almost justified in their interwar isolationism and at the very least had never been taught by American statesmen the essential reality of international politics: that nations must and do heed their own security interests.[56]

These diplomatic failures went beyond Wilson himself and could be found in the general aversion to alliances and in the illusion that nations would behave like the original American colonies had—both stock Wilsonian tenets. Lippmann had no objection to the existence of and the commitment to the League, but he now argued that the League could have enjoyed strength only if it were based upon a primary alliance be-

[55] Lippmann, *Foreign Policy,* xiii.
[56] Ibid., 33–38.

tween Britain and the United States. Recalling his 1919 essay "The Political Scene," he insisted that the League could enforce peace only if and when the Allies resolved to protect their mutual security interests underneath its banner. Not only Wilson but "all good and true men" denied the virtues of alliances, and with no core of aligned power, the League was incapacitated from the start.[57] In place of primary alliances, the Wilsonians called for a League of Nations "brought together by consent" as the original thirteen American colonies had been, and they erred when they claimed that distinct nations, "juridically equal but otherwise unequal," would evolve into a harmonious union without a core of organized power to ensure the security of each state. During its lifetime, the League had relied on "moral indignation" to tame national self-interest and was thus committed to "a radical error about the behavior of nations."[58]

Because nations sought security before they pursued enlightened interests, the defining task of foreign policy was to ensure security through the rational calculation of and proper balance among security needs, international commitments, and the available means. In a world composed of several powers, no nation could enjoy isolated security, nor could one nation conquer the world alone, as the Axis alliance demonstrated. For the United States, these axioms demanded an unbreakable alliance with Great Britain and France—the Atlantic Community, he called it. Geography, history, capitalism, and liberalism all bound these nations together into an organic core.[59]

In practice, American war aims had to look to an international order within which the powers would be secure, a position not qualitatively different from that which underlay the Wilsonian arguments for a strong UN security council. For as long as any one power was insecure, peace was threatened. Such a postwar order was complicated, Lippmann agreed, by the problematic nature of the Soviet-American relationship. He predicted that the Soviets naturally and legitimately would seek to control Eastern Europe. Matching Sumner Welles in forthrightness, he explained that "we have to look at these things as the most pessimistic

[57] Ibid., 73–75; *U.S. War Aims,* 160, 176–77.

[58] Lippmann, *Foreign Policy,* 72–73; Lippmann to Stringfellow Barr, 9 December 1941, in Blum, *Public Philosopher,* 411; Lippmann to the *Nation,* 29 June 1943, ibid., 439; Lippmann to Jacques Maritain, 1 July 1943, ibid., 440; Lippmann to Grenville Clark, 19 September 1944, ibid., 453; and "After Geneva: The Defense of the Peace," *Yale Review* 28 (June 1938): 650–58, 662–63.

[59] Lippmann, *Foreign Policy,* 6–7, 100–101; *U.S. War Aims,* chap. 7 for his discussion of the Atlantic Community.

and suspicious Russian might see them." Even with the vast differences between the Soviets and the United States, there should be no real cause for open conflict. In the realist order, conflict would break out when one regional power encroached on the region of another power, and the vital interests of the two great powers were so far apart that there was no good reason for tension.[60]

Lippmann envisioned, in other words, regionalism. His point was not that the powers could afford to do away with international organization, only that regional blocs should precede and protect such an organization. The blocs already stood in fact, Lippmann argued, and the only way to overcome tension was "by perfecting these regional groupings." There were four natural regions that would comprise the realist order: the Atlantic Community; the Russian "Orbit"; East Asia; and the "Moslem and the Hindu nations of North Africa, the Middle East, and Southern Asia."[61] He stopped short of his older claim that "expanding loyalties" would bring the blocs together but still believed that the blocs could participate in an international association. In an order based on regional blocs, "the true constituents of the universal society would not then be seventy-three political molecules, likely to split into no one knows how many atoms; the universal society would be the association of the great communities of mankind."[62]

In spite of the lingering current of hope, Lippmann's wartime books gained for him a reputation as America's foremost realist. Because renegade Wilsonianism had become the order of the day, the most one can say is that Lippmann's position was more aggressive than that of other Wilsonians. But there was no genuine difference between them. The reception of the books bears out such an assessment, for there was no indignant outcry from injured Wilsonians, who paid little attention to them in print. In no way can his work be read as a defense of the belief, so common to Cold War liberals, that conflict between the powers was an inevitable fact of life. Lippmann believed that conflict grew from insecurity, just as insecurity in domestic life led to radicalism and demagoguery; and just as the state had to accommodate the elemental needs of its citizens, so the international order had to accommodate the security needs of the great powers. True, he was pessimistic, but he did not repudiate Wilsonianism. He continued to believe that nations would seek

[60] Ibid., 121, 132.
[61] Ibid., 157–58.
[62] Ibid., 188–92.

a harmonious order once security was assured. He believed that secure regional blocs would lend themselves to a wider international order.

The postwar Lippmann held to the essential Wilsonian hope of international peace and the more modest faith in the efficacy of diplomacy, lingering hopes which turned him into a Cold War critic. Though given to occasional anti-Soviet outbursts, he nevertheless sustained the most important criticism of Cold War diplomacy among mainstream thinkers.[63] His 1946 attack on the Truman administration's foolish preoccupation with Eastern Europe remains one of the sharpest analyses of the postwar failure of American diplomacy. So too his long answer to Kennan's "Mr. X" article so clearly exposed the shortcomings in the containment policy that Kennan agreed more with Lippmann than with his own essay.[64] In his own estimation, the Cold War left him feeling as though he were "swimming up Niagara Falls," and the current was running against him most forcefully on the issue of negotiating with the Russians. Lippmann stubbornly insisted that the two superpowers could come to terms, and if his position was less than optimistic, he still reminded American Cold Warriors that the most basic assumption of diplomacy was that negotiation and compromise were possible. At bottom, the difference between Lippmann and Truman liberals was his lingering hope at least for a modus vivendi through diplomacy; in contrast, the official line was, as Dean Acheson remarked during the Truman Doctrine crisis, that "it is a mistake to believe that you can, at any time, sit down with the Russians and solve questions."[65]

The prevailing mood in Cold War diplomacy, which presumed that conflict was inevitable, was not only one approach to diplomatic difficulties, it had its analogue in domestic thought, where realism was emerging in the critique of mass politics and in interest-group theory. Just as he criticized Cold War policy, so did Lippmann make one last attempt at mediating between the realist and idealist impulses of liberalism. *The Public Philosophy* was clearly no simple reaction against the currents of the Cold War, he began it, in fact, quite soon after having finished *The Good Society*.[66] As in his earlier works, Lippmann em-

[63] He exploded after the invasion of Czechoslovakia, for instance. Steel, *Lippmann and the American Century*, 450–51.

[64] Lippmann, "A Year of Peacemaking," 35–40; *The Cold War* (Boston, 1947); and Steel, *Lippmann and the American Century*, chap. 34.

[65] Lippmann's comment about the basic premise of diplomacy appears in Lippmann, *The Cold War*, 60–61. Acheson is quoted in Yergin, *Shattered Peace*, 275.

[66] Steel, *Lippmann and the American Century*, 491–92.

braced some of the current ideas that surrounded him; in this case, he sounded themes similar to those of Hannah Arendt or David Riesman when he worried over the "deracinated masses" who ran in the "lonely crowd." He continued to laud the virtues of a strong executive; he was suspicious of politicized masses; he reiterated the old distinction between a republic and a democracy; and he returned, ultimately, to liberal reason as the fundamental solution to modern decline.[67]

Lippmann began his treatise with a description of the "obscure revolution" of World War I, that historic watershed which rocked the complacent liberal belief that governing was easy and that governments should be weak. Pressed by the chaos of war, "their authority to bind and their power to command" exhausted, governments surrendered "the executive power of decision over the strategical and the political conditions for concluding the war" to public opinion. The consequences were momentous, because the concession of executive power undermined the capacity of states to wage war rationally and, more important, constituted a "functional derangement between the mass of people and the government." Recalling *Public Opinion*, he wrote that this derangement encouraged people to avoid difficult decisions and to seek narrow, immediate ends. In foreign policy, popular opinion said "no" to every hard decision: no to adequate preparation in peacetime; "no" to new taxes; and "no" to intervention in a developing conflict.[68] What applied in foreign policy applied to domestic life as well, where the average citizen allowed the government to opt for the "soft" choices. "That is why governments are unable to cope with reality when elected assemblies and mass opinions become decisive in the state," Lippmann wrote, "when there are no statesmen to resist the inclination of the voters and there are only politicians to excite and to exploit them." Where mass politics prevailed, the apparently inevitable result was "insolvency," factionalism, assaults on liberty, and war. The old distinctions between republics and democracies still made sense, he claimed. For there was a difference between the people as a community and the people as a mass of conflicting interests attempting to exercise political leadership. Modern democracy had devolved into the latter, and the "executive had become enfeebled."[69]

With such an analysis, Cold War liberals would not necessarily have disagreed. They too demonstrated little faith in "the people," whom they

---

[67] Walter Lippmann, *The Public Philosophy* (Boston, 1955), 111–12.
[68] Ibid., 9, 12–14, 19.
[69] Ibid., 45–46, 32, 55.

regarded as irrational, "other-directed," and "pseudo-conservative." But Lippmann did not call for government by expert rule, much less for limiting politics to the representatives of organized interests. His solution was to reassert a broader sense of community and reaffirm objective standards of political morality and obligation. Where his Cold War peers saw rational politics as the give and take of interest-group competition, as in fact he had in the 1920s, Lippmann now argued that political reason was marked by the willingness of citizens to put aside "private and special interests" for the public good. Far from leading to the regularized clash of interests, liberal reason encouraged concessions to community standards. Where no public consensus existed, he wrote, liberty was nothing but the freedom to hold personal beliefs without "public significance." When rationality and morality became matters of self-interest and personal choice, "then the citadel is vacant . . . , and all the defenders of freedom have to defend in common is a public neutrality and a public agnosticism."[70] The alternative to political unbelief, with its attendant fragmentation was, again, a rediscovery of higher law. It was not simply a matter of recovering the "will to believe," for of such will "there is no lack. The modern trouble is in a low capacity to believe in precepts which restrict and restrain private interests and desire." The problem was not that the modern world had done away with an "anthropomorphic God" but that it had done away "with the recognition that beyond our private worlds there is a public world to which we belong."[71]

He had come far since *A Preface to Morals,* far enough that he should have seen that his answer was no answer at all, for it did not explain how public commitments were to be reinvigorated. Even his contention that there existed "two realms" that had to be balanced, one private, the other public, got him no closer. For this only begged the same question: how was the balance to be kept? Lippmann's answer was wholly inadequate, and, indeed, his was the inadequacy not only of his reformulated Wilsonianism, but of twentieth-century liberalism as a whole. In the common spirit of idealists and realists, Lippmann contended that the task of restoring political rationality, whatever form that rationality took, fell to the intellectual, to the modern statesman, to the philosophers and the theologians—to the "defenders of civility."[72]

The mature Lippmann thus is best understood as the bridge between the idealists of the World War I generation and the realists of the fol-

[70] Ibid., 42, 113, 176.
[71] Ibid., 114, 176.
[72] Ibid., 177–81.

lowing generation. In their similar suspicions that mass movements, far from asserting a rational moral consensus, only advanced totalitarianism, Wilsonians and postwar liberals were more alike than either would have cared to admit. But to the end Lippmann remained an idealist. His own conclusion was that "it is not possible to reject this faith in the efficacy of reason and at the same time to believe that communities of men enjoying freedom could govern themselves successfully."[73] After the grueling intellectual and political odyssey through which he had lived, perhaps just this sort of conclusion makes Lippmann the foremost idealist of them all.

[73] Ibid., 134.

9

A Tradition
in Disrepute

The Wilsonian critics of the Cold War were reasonable and sincere, but they are the forgotten critics of American foreign policy, forgotten because they were falling from official grace at the time, and their expressions of liberal faith seemed too innocent to be taken seriously. Very early in the period, it was painfully clear that they were losing influence. His prolific works notwithstanding, James Warburg found himself speaking mostly before audiences of one-worlders, an audience of the second choice, not the second chance. Hamilton Fish Armstrong's internationalism was increasingly out of step with the Cold War bent of the CFR, and while presidents still read Walter Lippmann, he wrote increasingly as an outsider; one need only read Ronald Steel's account of Lippmann's heated rivalry with Lyndon Baines Johnson to appreciate the point. Within the Truman administration, the lone old hand, Henry Stimson, was edged out of power after his impertinent proposal for the internationalization of the bomb. Some continued on as always. Clark Eichelberger used the United Nations Association, the successor to the League of Nations Association, as a vehicle for publicity; hardly missing a beat, the Foreign Policy Association poured forth the same dry, explanatory pamphlets about UN functions as it had about the league. With the UN in New York, it was both more convenient and politically acceptable for Americans to serve in some capacity, and Francis Sayre, for one, took the opportunity to engage in UN humanitarian work, as did Huntington Gilchrist. They were merely going through the motions.[1]

---

[1] Note the addresses in Warburg's *Last Call for Common Sense;* Steel's description of Truman and Lippmann, *Lippmann and the American Century,* 457; and Schulzinger, *Wise*

Intellectual and political traditions do not simply disappear, of course, and the Wilsonian heritage remained even into the arch-realist period of Kennedy liberalism. Where it lingered, it did so in ways that pointed up its displacement. In foreign affairs, Wilsonianism, as we have seen, encouraged a genteel opposition to American policy that began in a trenchant Cold War critique, lingered in a sort of chronic distress over the exercise of unilateral power, and reemerged in a defense of international liberalism. In domestic politics its absence was more complete, yet it persisted in the 1950s and 1960s, largely through the singular character of Adlai Stevenson, who, though he demonstrated that idealism could be compelling if packaged correctly, also showed that idealism in a realist age was quite out of place, respectable and entirely civilized, to be sure, but nonetheless out of place.

Declassé Wilsonianism

Just as the long process of Wilsonian decline was reaching its end, the shell of the tradition began to reappear in the career of Adlai Stevenson, who was more strongly associated with Wilsonianism in the minds of the interested public than any other individual after World War II. An "egghead" to his right-wing detractors, he was to admirers such as Herbert Muller "a good Wilsonian Democrat."[2] His public life invited such depictions: he had gone to Washington as one of the countless young New Deal lawyers; became an internationalist among isolationists in Chicago; served under Secretary of the Navy Frank Knox during the war; acted as a delegate to the founding conferences of the UN at San Francisco and London; and, finally, assumed the UN ambassadorship in the Kennedy administration. His political inclinations reinforced that activity, for he viewed politics as service to the commonweal, was ambivalent about the fruits of technology, and kept his faith in the long-range prospects of liberalism.

Stevenson's Wilsonianism was not philosophically rigorous. His reputation as an intellectual in politics was a cultivated image. He was not dull; he was simply no thinker. As a Princeton man, he no doubt heard the same lectures as Raymond Buell, but he majored in the gentleman's

---

Men of Foreign Affairs, chap. 5; on Stimson see Godfrey Hodgson, *The Colonel: The Life and Wars of Henry Stimson, 1867–1950* (New York, 1990), 359–66.

[2] Herbert J. Muller, *Adlai Stevenson: A Study in Values* (New York, 1967), 37.

"C." Nor did he read widely in internationalist writings any time after leaving Princeton, though he was familiar with Lippmann and Warburg and probably skimmed an occasional issue of *Foreign Affairs.* "He complained that he never had time to read" the many books he kept about him, one friend recalled, but "the fact is that he did not want to read a book." John Kenneth Galbraith has called Stevenson's intellectual image an "amiable fraud. . . . There could be doubt as to whether, after becoming governor of Illinois, he ever read a serious book. . . . No one was so relentlessly admiring of mine; he was always about to read them."[3]

Stevenson's liberalism was partly hereditary. His maternal great-grandfather had befriended a young Abraham Lincoln and, family legend has it, proposed the Lincoln-Douglas debates. His paternal grandfather had been vice-president under Grover Cleveland during the second term, and he provided Adlai with early memories of Sunday dinners that always included history and family lore. Stevenson relished the latter especially; his embittered ex-wife once claimed that the Stevensons "must have Chinese blood in them, they all worship their ancestors so." According to Herbert Muller, Stevenson's father, Lewis, kept alive the young man's interest in Democratic internationalism, once taking his son to visit Wilson and, after college, Norman Davis. Born and bred in the Democratic party, he touched upon the tradition there, and his connection with it was doubtlessly sustained during a lifetime devoted to the party.[4]

There was also a social component to Stevenson's convictions. Wilsonianism was an appropriate tradition for a man who spent his life both craving social and political success and wishing for personal isolation. Nothing if not respectable and always alert to social status, he nonethe-

[3] John Bartlow Martin, *Adlai Stevenson of Illinois: The Life of Adlai Stevenson* (Garden City, 1976), 473; John Kenneth Galbraith, *A Life in our Times: A Memoir* (Boston: Houghton Mifflin, 1981), 288.

There is no reason to doubt that he sincerely embraced the general outlines of Wilsonianism. But in his convictions he was something like Franklin Roosevelt, whose basic beliefs Paul Conkin once described as so vague "as to be almost meaningless except as a type of verbal assurance." Whereas firm but absolute convictions "proved invaluable political assets" for Roosevelt, because, free from doubt, he was able to communicate "an assurance so deplorably absent in events," Stevenson's Wilsonianism served him well only in the short term and probably was a handicap in national politics. If Roosevelt's self-confidence reassured Americans in the midst of depression, Stevenson's persistent advocacy of international law and world cooperation in the midst of the Cold War dismayed liberal realists and amounted to treason in the eyes of the right wing. Paul Conkin, *The New Deal* (New York, 1975), 7–10.

[4] Muller, *A Study in Values*, 25–31; Martin, *Stevenson of Illinois*, 129.

less was never long comfortable anywhere. Incessantly in search of acceptance, he never found permanent satisfaction with any one set of friends and never developed deep bonds of friendship, at least not with anyone other than married women who, because of their obligations, could extend affection but were limited in their opportunities to press demands. What could be more appropriate to a such a man than a set of convictions that was entirely respectable but musty and out of place in both prewar Chicago and postwar Washington? Like Stevenson's famous tattered shoe, Wilsonianism was the symbol of detached gentility.[5]

Stevenson's prominent downstate family, with its pedigree that included the Daughters of the American Revolution, had done well since its arrival in Illinois in the mid-nineteenth century. But Stevenson's parents did not have inexhaustible means. By birth, Stevenson lacked both the old wealth of Roosevelt and the Brahmin connections of the nouveau riche Kennedy, which helps explain why he lacked the former's self-confidence and the latter's brashness. The family had no national prominence, but worse as a matter of status, its prestige was rooted in downstate Illinois. His people could not even claim a Chicago heritage, which would not have mattered except that his parents were gregarious and bred in him a love of polite society that was unquestionably an important part of his life. Conquering Chicago became something of a goal. After graduating from Northwestern Law, where he landed after failing at Harvard, he began to rise in the city's social circles; having come up short in the east, he became one of the most eligible bachelors in Chicago. He dabbled in intimate relationships before finally marrying an unstable young women whose lone virtue, that she was from one of the city's most illustrious families, outweighed the prospect of a loveless future.[6]

He was discontented almost from the beginning of his arrival among the city's elite and was no sooner included than he looked for an escape. He never quite fit into Chicago society, for he was more serious and politically-minded than his friends, most of whom, it bears mention, were just as habitually Republican as he was Democratic. He left Chicago for a stint in the New Deal Agriculture Department where he

---

[5] In this sense, Stevenson was peculiarly like Wilson, whose closest male acquaintance was not a friend but an advisor, Edward House. Stevenson's social life is amply described throughout John Bartlow Martin, *Adlai Stevenson and the World: The Life of Adlai E. Stevenson* (Garden City, 1977).

[6] See Martin, *Stevenson of Illinois*, chaps. 1–3.

worked, ironically, under George Peek, a family friend, economic nationalist, and bitter enemy of Cordell Hull. Though he stayed in Washington barely a year, there is no hint that Stevenson left for philosophical reasons, which one might have suspected of a "good Wilsonian Democrat."[7]

Within a year and with no apparent sense of ideological inconsistency, Stevenson began his career as Chicago's leading internationalist, a career he embarked on initially as a distraction from Lake Forest's frivolity. He first joined the local Council on Foreign Relations in 1930, at a time when, according to one colleague, "the Council was an elite group. It was the fashionable thing to do." When he returned to Chicago after working with Peek, he returned as well to the council and became its president. "It was a very rapid rise for him," recalled a friend, Harriet Welling. He did his job so well that, as another acquaintance explained, "there wasn't anybody who was anybody who didn't go to the Council luncheons—it was the same as the Chicago symphony." To his credit, Stevenson worked to broaden the organization's base. "We tried to get the Council off the society page and on to the news pages," according to Welling, though the very notion that the council was society news points up the character of the organization as Stevenson joined it.[8]

So here was Stevenson, a downstater among the Chicago elite, a Democrat among Republicans, and now an internationalist in the isolationist midwest. He continued to hobnob with the Chicago crowd, but he also searched for ways to stand out, and leading the council sufficed. There was always something high-minded about the work; it was more than a socially acceptable use of extra energy. Like Jane Addams, another well-to-do Chicagoan who was not content to squander her time at coming-out parties, Stevenson was bored with the predictable prospects that lay before him. He never enjoyed law; its virtue was that it paid well. The council was his vehicle of self-actualization. It was his Hull House. The council also brought him into contact with a new set of people, particularly the editors and reporters around the internationalist Chicago *Daily News*, Frank Knox's paper, and, somewhat later, intellectuals from the University of Chicago such as Quincy Wright, Paul Douglas, and Walter Johnson. The council necessitated some public speaking, even if often in the form of introducing other speakers, and it was through this

[7] Ibid., 103–13.
[8] Ibid., 97–98, 125–26.

work that Stevenson began to hone his unique oratorical skills. The same cannot be said for his ideas, which were rarely honed or unique.[9]

When he became chairman of the Chicago CDAAA in June 1940, he stepped into a position that forced him to decide to what extent he was willing to disengage himself from Lake Forest. The fight over aid to the Allies was, as we have seen, most bitter in Chicago, and he paid a price for his defense of aid. He believed, at least at first, that aid to the Allies was indeed the best policy for keeping the United States out of the European war.[10] Stevenson's position became particularly strained during the controversy over William Allen White's leadership, after it became clear that many in the CDAAA really intended to push for intervention. Though mentioned as a possible successor to White, he believed that the committee should not mislead the public if in fact its members were interventionists, and he argued that the headquarters should be in the midwest where the debate was most intense. The Century Club group pushed him aside. It was his first brush with the eastern foreign policy elite, among whom he was comfortable enough but who "never really accepted him," as John Bartlow Martin puts it.[11]

The immediate result of his internationalist work was that he began to look beyond Chicago and attach himself to national issues and national leaders, an attachment symbolized in his move to Washington to work under Knox in July 1941. As Knox's wartime assistant, Stevenson undertook a variety of tasks. He was almost peripatetic; he was clearly restless. He endured the obligatory drudgery of wartime work, because he expected appointment as an undersecretary of the navy. That possibility fell through when Knox died in April 1944 and James Forrestal replaced him. Forrestal and Stevenson were not friendly, and the root of their difficulties was that Forrestal, the Wall Street lawyer who later became one

[9] Ibid., 97–98. Stevenson spoke in support of Hull's RTAs during the 1936 election, and, in denouncing Republican "isolation and narrow nationalism," in prescribing "wholesome international commerce" as "the best antidote for regimentation and discontent," in pointing to a "middle road," Stevenson showed nothing more than that he probably had read Francis Sayre's pamphlets. Adlai Stevenson, "The Reciprocal Trade Agreement," address at Carleton College, 23 October 1936, in *Ethic for Survival: Adlai Stevenson Speaks on International Affairs, 1936–1965*, ed. Michael H. Prosser (New York, 1969), 33–34.

[10] Stevenson, "Aid to America Will Keep Us Out of War," address to the League of Women Voters, 4 October 1940, in *Ethic for Survival*, 41–51; Schneider, *Should America Go to War?* 77–80.

[11] Schneider, *Should America Go to War?* 83–84; Martin, *Stevenson of Illinois*, 164–65, 169–70, 183–84.

of Truman's principal Cold War advisors, thought that Stevenson was soft.[12] Stevenson drifted for several months thereafter, until he joined with George Ball and several others in the Strategic Bombing Survey, an important study group that discovered that the widespread bombing campaigns, which had included civilian areas, had been something less than "surgical." Interesting and important, the survey was nonetheless temporary.[13]

Stevenson found himself back in Chicago in early 1945 when Archibald MacLeish and Edward Stettinius convinced him to join the American delegation to the San Francisco conference. There was a certain logic to Stevenson's attendance there. He had been on the internationalist side of things since the mid-1930s, he was known as an idealist, and as a prominent midwestern Democrat he brought a unique combination of virtues to a delegation that was chosen more for domestic political purposes than for knowledge of international organization. He may have been appealing because he had not played a part in the prewar planning for the UN. He never even had spoken consistently about the issue. Not that he was indifferent; he simply had not given much attention to world organization. At first he played coy with MacLeish, begging off in order to get family matters in order. But he went, spent two months as the liaison to the press, and at some point in San Francisco discovered that UN work could be stretched into other appointments. He insinuated himself into the American delegation to the UN Prepatory Conference in London, which met that fall, though he explained to his law partner that he had "succumbed to considerable pressure to go to London," presumably from the State Department.[14]

The path that eventually would have him dubbed "the First Gentleman of the World," the personfication of American commitment to international cooperation in the postwar world, began as a career move, and a paltry one at that, since it carried no permanent position and served mostly to get him out of Chicago and away from the home and friends that he loved but could not tolerate for any length of time.

It certainly was not a deeply felt, searching conviction that drove him. Stevenson's view of the UN's founding had all of the profundity of Chamber of Commerce boosterism. At a time when genuine Wilsonians, even the optimists, were watching the collapse of their dreams, Stevenson praised the delegates and the charter. "There was no cynicism, no com-

[12] Martin, *Stevenson of Illinois*, 220–22.
[13] See George Ball, *The Past Has Another Pattern* (New York, 1982), 42–48.
[14] Martin, *Stevenson of Illinois*, 234–41.

placency, and no resignation" at San Francisco, he told the Chicago Bar Association. The charter, he proclaimed, "is not only a long advance from the League of Nations, it is also a much more flexible and democratic document than the Dumbarton Oaks proposals." Reports of disagreement were exaggerated. Of course the delegates discussed the issues on which they disagreed. Why waste time discussing those matter they agreed on? He asserted that the veto was not a serious flaw, but his explanation of the security council's function showed how little he understood it. He ignored the importance of allowing one nation to flout the will of the others and instead focused on the demand for unanimity, which, he claimed, "does not invest [Council members] with any new rights, and the formula proposed for taking action . . . made the operation of the Council *less* subject to obstruction than under the League of Nations Council." His description was disingenuous and bore little relation to realities in San Francisco. At least he could have employed the Wilsonian arguments, to which he surely had access, that the veto was necessary in the transitional phase. He evidently was being neither evasive nor lazy; he believed the charter was the very best possible and had no working knowledge of Wilsonian arguments to the contrary. As late as the 1960s, even as he admitted that the organization was less than perfect, he still recalled San Francisco as "a beginning. It was the morning—fresh with new hope."[15]

Throughout the 1940s, Stevenson showed a desire for public service, mostly State Department work, but he would not have been happy as a functionary. Such a career, particularly in the State Department, could have provided a comfortable, serene life, but not one of much movement or acclaim. Stevenson's gregarious nature pushed him toward more. He returned to Chicago in 1946 and began to plan a run for the Senate when, as it turned out, his ambitions and his temperament suited the needs of the Cook County Democratic machine, which convinced him to run as the "good-government candidate" in the 1948 Illinois gubernatorial election.[16] Naturally repulsed by any dealings with the Chicago machine, Stevenson found that his distaste could be turned to political advantage. Though the Chicago machine provided the infrastructure of

[15] Adlai Stevenson, "The United Nations: Collaboration Based on Self-Interest," address to the Chicago Bar Association, 28 June 1945, in *Ethic for Survival,* 55–61; "Let None Mock Its Strength," address to the San Francisco chapter of the American Association for the United Nations, 23 October 1961, in *Looking Outward: Years of Crisis at the United Nations,* ed. Robert L. and Selma Schiffer (New York, 1963), 133.
[16] Martin, *Stevenson of Illinois,* 260–81.

his campaign, he ran as a "good-government" candidate who promised to battle the interests and diminish patronage in state government. His theme—"I am not a politician; I am a citizen"—could have been Wilson's gubenatorial message.[17]

The most curious thing about Stevenson was that his oft-professed disinterestedness was in perfect keeping with the tensions between his yearning for acceptance and his instincts for disassociation. It may be that contemporary electoral politics offers the ultimate means of ascent and acceptance; especially in the imperial presidency, an executive election brings with it extraordinary attention and, potentially, unparalleled adulation. For someone so inclined, modern politics can assuage, if not satisfy, the most deeply felt urges for belonging. The curious thing about Stevenson, as John Kenneth Galbraith insightfully suggests, is that he approached this business backwards. Instead of claiming that he was an outsider who wanted in, Stevenson spoke as if he wanted no part of power. He "was committed," Galbraith writes, "to picturing not his strength in contending with harsh circumstance but his frailty, not his certainty but his doubts, not his wisdom but the immeasurable extent of what he needed to know."[18] He chased after the ultimate form of acceptance by insisting that he did not want to be accepted.

The strategy worked against a scandal-plagued incumbent in Illinois, and Stevenson assumed that it would work as well on the national level. There is little question that he wanted the Democratic nomination of 1952, and yet the more attention he enjoyed, the more diffident he grew. The more prominent politicians and intellectuals began to collect around him, the more he fretted over the magnitude of the task. He ran an extraordinary primary campaign, reminiscent of Newton Baker's non-candidacy of 1932, yet was a more determined candidate backed by more influential supporters against less substantial competition. Truman himself began grooming Stevenson for the nomination as early as 1949, but Stevenson remained noncommittal up to the convention. He left more or less subtle hints that he would accept a convention draft, and when the draft emerged he accepted it with the characteristic plea that "I have not sought the honor you have done me." As in his gubenatorial run, his reluctance served political purposes in that, as John Bartlow Martin and others have suggested, it allowed him to distance

[17] Ibid., 135–36, 281–92.
[18] Galbraith, *A Life in Our Time*, 288.

himself as far as possible from the unpopular Truman and to run as his own man.[19]

It might have been shrewd political judgment, as Martin sees it, but it also put Stevenson at odds with the prevailing liberalism of his day. His backers, Truman first and then the intellectuals who came to support him after the nomination, were successively disturbed to discover that Stevenson was not a liberal—at least by the prevailing Cold War categorizations. In one March 1952 meeting with Truman, Stevenson "almost defiantly and angrily" contended that he supported none of the Democrats' stock positions. He believed that it was unnecessary to repeal the anti-labor Taft-Hartley bill, he opposed federal aid to education and national health care, and he did not think the South should be pushed on civil rights. Even when the health of the party was at stake, Stevenson could not put aside his antipathy to interest groups, and he had confrontations with both labor and Jewish groups, the Democratic Party's biggest financial backers. "We felt," Galbraith recalls, that "he was insufficiently committed to the constituency and the policies that had brought the magnificent string of Democratic victories." Stevenson, meanwhile, bemoaned the pressure. "I get so sick of the everlasting appeals to the cupidity and prejudice of every group," he wrote Archibald MacLeish. "There is something finer in people; they know that they *owe* something too. I should like to try, at least, to appeal to their sense of obligation as well as their avarice."[20]

He gradually surrendered to the firm instruction of the realist intellectuals, who, hoping to play the part of the "vital center," gathered regularly to "help [Stevenson] overcome his upbringing," as Arthur Schlesinger, Jr., put it. In the 1956 presidential campaign, Stevenson ran on a platform that included public housing, a raised minimum wage, greater emphasis on civil rights, and social security increases. "Much less troubled by the liberal heresies than he had been four years before," Galbraith writes, Stevenson spoke not of what people "owed" but the language of postwar liberalism, the language of economic and social claims. Like Wilson in 1916, he came to see that appeals to interest groups were not incompatible with the common good. "The government of the democracy," he assured a UAW audience while chiding the Eisenhower administration for its cozy relationship with corporate America, "must trust *all* the people it serves, . . . and its obligation can

[19] Martin, *Stevenson of Illinois*, 403, 558, 566–68.
[20] Ibid., 540, 629–30, 653, note 10; Galbraith, *Life in Our Times*, 295.

not be to any special interest but to all the people." Serving the common welfare included speaking to the interests of the elderly, labor, farmers, and consumers.[21]

He made his appeals to interest groups—and no doubt salved his conscience thereby—by arguing that the economically wasteful and morally stupefying effects of the Cold War made it necessary for those groups to demand their government's attention. By 1956 he had come out against the draft as inefficient and outrageously expensive and argued that defense spending was taking money better spent on education, health, and welfare. Complacent defenders of Republican policy, he insisted, exploited the Cold War as an opportunity for self-indulgence, an excuse "to defend every abuse, every self-interest, every encrusted position of privilege in the name of love of country." Like automobile tail fins, those symbols of superfluous abundance, the Cold War had deadened the national spirit. Americans could fight the Cold War more effectively (and more cheaply) through a revived spirit, through pushing forward a "vision of the open society fulfilling itself in an open world. . . . This gives our country a universal validity."[22]

His call for infusing containment with an idealist spirit bridged the gap between the realists and his own tradition, but it also obliged him to offer concrete proposals by which American policy might be redirected. He seized on the issue of disarmament after prodding from the intellectuals and, once he made the issue his, inflated it with characteristic elaboration. He argued that Secretary of State Dulles's brinksmanship "put too many of our eggs in the atomic and hydrogen basket" when prudence probably called for a more flexible foreign policy. Moreover, the powers should ban the above-ground testing of nuclear weapons that had become dangerous health and environmental hazards. There was no excuse for balking on a test ban; as he pointed out, above

---

[21] See Galbraith, *Annals of an Abiding Liberal*, ed. Andrea D. Williams (Boston, 1979), 299, where he doubts that Stevenson ever became a "liberal." For the 1956 campaign see Stevenson, *The New America* (London, 1957), where the speech to the UAW is printed as "Single-Interest Government," 251–55. The Finletter Group included something of a mix of Stevenson liberals, George Ball, Chester Bowles, and Stevenson himself, and realists such as Galbraith, Schlesinger, Seymour Harris, George Kennan, Paul Nitze, and Leon Kesyerling. See Martin, *Stevenson and the World*, 82–89.

[22] Adlai Stevenson, "Crusades, Communism, and Corruption," address to the Democratic National Committee Southern Conference, Miami, 7 March 1954, in *What I Think* (New York, 1956), 64–71; "Draft, Disarmament, and Peace," address in Youngstown, Ohio, 18 October 1956, in *New America*, 60–61; "The Hard Kind of Patriotism," *Harper's* 227 (July 1963): 33–34.

ground testing could be detected and inspections were not a problem. On this reasoning, the candidate called for a unilateral halt to testing as a sign of good faith.[23]

Stevenson became more substantive through the 1956 election, though his supporters have tended to look at the 1956 campaign as a pale imitation of 1952.[24] There was less nonpartisanship in 1956, but then he was running against the Eisenhower record, as Arthur Schlesinger and Seymour Harris pointed out, instead of in defense of an incumbent Democrat. Some of his closest advisors agreed that it worked to his disadvantage to have the campaign center on his disarmament and draft proposals. George Ball regretted that Stevenson knew little about the issues and retreated to obviously desperate claims of environmental catastrophe when he charged that the nation's milk supply was contaminated. Still, his platform as a whole contained ideas and proposals that liberals very soon made stock positions, not least the idea of "flexible response," which became the Kennedy approach to foreign policy.[25]

Flexible response is but one example that the realists took more from Stevenson than they returned. They came to him in the first place because he was a refreshing alternative to the otherwise pervasive banality of American politics; they admired his political poetry, his fine bearing, his consistent criticism of American materialism. His descriptions of a world beyond the Cold War provided them with an antidote against their own pessimism. And he was an elitist to boot. Irving Howe saw that "Stevenson made it possible for the liberal intellectuals to see themselves as both realists and idealists at the same time: they could sanction a theory that American liberalism meant little more than the proper regulation of a division of the social spoils while yet invoking, through Stevenson's soaring rhetoric, a vision of that good society which once, long ago, had some actual relationship to liberal politics." Howe was right to argue that "Stevenson was the first of the liberal candidates in the post-Wilson era who made no effort to align himself with the plebian tradition or with plebian sentiments; Stevenson was the candidate whom the intellectuals, trying hard to remove plebian stains, admired most." It was his sense of alienation, "of separation from his audience," that "made Stevenson seem an emblem of the intellectual

---

[23] Martin, *Stevenson and the World*, 207; "H-Bomb," television broadcast, 15 October 1956 and "H-Bomb: Program Paper," 29 October 1956, in *New America*, 51, 46; see Schlesinger and Seymour Harris, introduction to *New America*, xvi–xvii.

[24] See Murray Kempton, "Stevenson: The Saddest Story," *Spectator*, 23 July 1965.

[25] Stevenson, *New America*, xiv–xix; Ball, *The Past Has Another Pattern*, 145–48.

condition."[26] They shared, in other words, a sense of repulsion, almost as if they wanted to be noble losers—indeed Murray Kempton eulogized Stevenson in just that fashion in 1965.[27] One wonders whether a Stevenson victory might have presented as many difficulties as defeat, for it would have meant that the public was not so doltish as liberals wanted to believe.

Both the intellectuals and Stevenson yearned for victory, of course, so much so that the relationship dissolved after the 1956 loss. Galbraith decided to embrace John F. Kennedy as early as 1957, and Schlesinger gradually moved in that direction thereafter. Kennedy was Stevenson's opposite in the most important ways: he was a realist hiding behind an idealist's mask, and he was a winner. So close were the two men in form and place, however, that the intellectuals simply picked up the Stevenson message of 1956, especially the emphasis on an inspired "New America," and handed it to Kennedy. There is little question that Stevenson's appeal to renewed commitment, to social reform, and even to youth made Kennedy's rise to prominence possible. That was something of a shame, for Kennedy was a natural realist whose political gift was his capacity for idealistic rhetoric—a far more dangerous arrangement of impulses and talents than that which was found in Stevenson.

The Problem of Idealism in a Realist World

Although the high idealism of Kennedy liberalism owed much to Stevenson's path-breaking in the 1950s—the Inaugural Address is sufficient testimony—Kennedy liberals assumed that espousing idealist ends when working on the inside was fatal to one's career. They admired intelligence, toughness, brawn, and for lack of a more formal word, panache. The administration's ranks swelled with realist intellectuals: Walt W. Rostow, Robert McNamara, McGeorge Bundy, Schlesinger, and Galbraith. Brash and self-confident, they believed they could accomplish anything.[28] In this atmosphere, it became increasingly difficult to sustain idealism, and those who tried had either to reformulate their views, as J. William Fulbright did, or be pushed to the margins, as Stevenson was.

[26] Irving Howe, "Stevenson and the Intellectuals," in *Steady Work* (New York, 1966), 209–13.

[27] Kempton, "Stevenson: The Saddest Story," 100.

[28] Thomas G. Paterson, "Bearing the Burden: A Critical Look at JFK's Foreign Policy," *Virginia Quarterly Review* 54 (Spring 1978): 193–212.

It is illuminating to compare Stevenson's Cold War career to that of Fulbright, the Arkansas senator who gained national notoriety as the leading congressional opponent of the Vietnam War. Like Stevenson, whom he looked to as a mentor, Fulbright was raised in a well-to-do family far from the center of internationalism. His provincial upbringing in Little Rock appears to have encouraged an interest in foreign relations, as if the subject spoke to an early desire to transcend the constraints of Little Rock. A Rhodes Scholar and one-time president of the University of Arkansas, Fulbright also was regarded as an intellectual in politics, though he was a more genuinely thoughtful man than Stevenson and more openly paradoxical. As Daniel Yergin has written, he assumed the role of the "urbane peace prophet" in Washington and "plain old Bill Fulbright" talking of "cotton and chickens" to his Arkansas constituents; mentor of the antiwar movement, he was also a signer of the Southern Manifesto.[29]

Fulbright by all rights should have become a leader among a third generation of Wilsonians. In his first important act as a freshman congressman he sponsored the 1943 House resolution calling for American membership in the UN. Far more strongly than Stevenson, Fulbright was willing to stand with the Wilsonian critics of the early Cold War against Truman's nationalistic drift. At the very least, as he explained on a nationwide radio broadcast in 1946, destructive nationalism would lead to barbarity unless people found a way of reviving "rules of conduct applicable to all peoples." If anything, he came closer to advocating one world than most Wilsonians.[30]

The dual momentum of Cold War events and party politics pushed both Stevenson and Fulbright to a standardized defense of American policy. Fulbright's position underwent a rapid change in 1946 when he faced up to Soviet imperialism, and through the 1950s, as Eugene Brown has written, he consistently spouted Cold War dogma.[31] Stevenson's Cold War rhetoric occasionally took on the blanket condemnations that grow from unexamined ideals. To him, the Soviets were not enemies so much as outright heretics. "While the anti-Christ stalks around, organized communism seeks even to dethrone God from his central place in the universe," he intoned during the 1952 campaign. "It attempts to up-

---

[29] Daniel Yergin, "Fulbright's Last Frustration," *New York Times Magazine*, 24 November 1974, 14.

[30] J. William Fulbright, "The Outlook for Peace," *Vital Speeches*, 1 April 1946, 358–60; and quoted in Eugene Brown, *J. William Fulbright: Advice and Dissent* (Iowa City, 1985), 26.

[31] Brown, *Fulbright*, 27–28, 40–42.

root everywhere it goes those gentle and restraining influences of the religion of love and peace."[32] Yet each man maintained his integrity. For
Fulbright, showing the obligatory anti-Communist ardor was a means of
counterbalancing his lonely opposition to Joseph McCarthy. He had
been the only senator to vote against appropriating money for McCarthy's special investigating committee—"his style and manner and what
he said offended me," Fulbright later explained—and however overrated
McCarthy's electoral influence, his wrath could not have done "plain old
Bill Fulbright" any good in Arkansas.[33] Much the same held for Stevenson. John Kenneth Galbraith is undoubtedly right to argue that, especially for a Democrat tainted by even the slightest association with Alger
Hiss, "departing from official Cold War belief in 1952 would have
brought charges of naivete if not outright disloyalty." Stevenson too
spoke out against McCarthy, which was probably one reason why the
liberals fell in behind him.[34]

In light of the pressures on public figures to hold to anticommunist
dogma, Stevenson's attempt at breaking the political mold took some
courage, and he set an example that Fulbright admittedly followed in
his similarly noteworthy opposition to the Vietnam War. Their adherence to an independent course was rooted in two conditions: both believed that the nation was losing its earlier commitment to liberal ideals;
and, more important, both shared a sense that their ideals left them essentially disenfranchised public figures with little choice but to take independent stands.

In the first case, even as they imitated the Cold Warriors, both men
simultaneously worried that the nation was losing its moral vision.
Stevenson set the example in the wake of the 1956 defeat; his speeches
and writings thereafter sound more honestly idealist. He continued to regret American materialism and regarded interest-group politics as the
public expression of the unfortunate national obsession with gain. "Interests deserved representation," he wrote in 1961, and the compromises
of contervailing power make for healthier social conditions than stifling
unity imposed from above by single-party rule. "But the national purpose is more than a sum of these compromises." Realism was better than
communism, he implied, but a truly liberal society required "an extra di-

---

[32] Martin, *Stevenson of Illinois*, 324; Stevenson, "First Fireside Speech," talk on WGN
radio, 29 September 1952, in *Ethic for Survival*, 168; also "America under Pressure,"
Harper's 223 (August 1961): 21–24; and "The Hard Kind of Patriotism," 31–34.
[33] Yergin, "Fulbright's Last Frustration," 14, 78.
[34] Galbraith, *Life in Our Times*, 297.

mension of vision to see beyond our inner circle of interest." The problem was that "there is a danger of this element of vision vanishing almost wholly from our political life."[35] Fulbright insisted that the absence of vision at home undermined foreign policy at a time when the foremost issues grew out of anticolonial uprisings. "It is not our affluence, or our plumbing, or our clogged freeways that grip the imagination of others," he maintained several months after the Bay of Pigs fiasco, but our values and our principles, and we would do better in the world to stick by them. The Cold War had been such an intense preoccupation over the years, Fulbright maintained, that important resources were diverted to the military establishment, and the nation had become convinced that its technological prowess ensured security. This complacency led Americans to equate foreign policy with "automobiles, televisions, and refrigerators: they work in a predictable and controllable manner, and on the rare occasions when they break down, any good mechanic can put them back in working order."[36]

Both men expected Kennedy to awaken national idealism and ease their growing disenchantment over the Cold War. Both, in fact, hoped to become secretary of state. While Kennedy admired Fulbright, his opposition to civil rights, a political necessity in Arkansas, made his appointment to State impossible. He had to settle for the chair of the Senate Foreign Relations Committee, a position to which he had ascended in January 1959 and which he considered a subordinate position, powerful though it was.[37] Stevenson, meanwhile, begrudged Kennedy the presidency and probably assumed that Kennedy would welcome him as secretary of state. He was too much an idealist for the Kennedy liberals, however, and Kennedy offered him an appointive booby prize, the UN ambassadorship. Like Fulbright, Stevenson was left in a marginal position, and he was not pleased. He accepted the position only after being assured that he would have a voice in policy making, that he would run the UN embassy, and that the administration would use the UN as the center of a policy that paid greater attention to the developing world. Kennedy offered these assurances and claimed that he needed him in New York, that the world would listen to the United States because it

[35] Stevenson, "The Political Relevance of Moral Principle," address at Constitution Hall, Washington, D.C., 18 January 1959, in *An Ethic for Survival*, 248–49.

[36] J. William Fulbright, "Recent Events and Continuing Problems," *Vital Speeches*, 1 August 1961, 617; "The Cold War: Its Effect on American Life," ibid., 1 May 1964, 423–24; and "Evaluation of Our Society," ibid., 15 June 1963, 520–22.

[37] See Steel, *Lippmann and the American Century*, 523–24; Martin, *Stevenson and the World*, 560; Arthur M. Schlesinger, Jr., *1000 Days* (Boston, 1965), 134–36.

would listen to Stevenson. They were phony assurances. Kennedy knew
that the UN was the political equivalent of being put out to pasture. He
wanted nothing more than an "official liar," as he was reputed to have
described Stevenson during the Bay of Pigs disaster.[38]

There was something particularly fitting about Stevenson's arrival as
UN ambassador. The cosmopolitan post marked his final escape from
small-town provincialism, his final arrival. It brought considerable acclaim, but in its diffuse formality, it was acclaim free of important demands or dramatic consequences. Stevenson enjoyed the trappings and
appearances of the powerful insider, yet he was safely irrelevant, unbur-
dened by substantive obligations, and unaccountable for events. Never
certain of his place anywhere, he came to rest in a world of unreality.
Living in the Waldorf high above the city, he seemed, as John Bartlow
Martin writes, "almost a great statesman without a constituency, a great
personage but nothing more, a ceremonial figure."[39] Small wonder that
he should surround himself with sychophantic women, to whom he was
similarly without obligations, or that he should strike his closest friends
as painfully lonely even though his social life was frenetic. Stevenson was
trapped and knew it.

It was just as fitting that Stevenson should come to Turtle Bay at a
time when the UN was beginning to feel the effects of the insurgent
Third World. The newly independent African nations took their membership with some pride, and because both of the superpowers were determined to win over the new nations, the body became a Cold War
public-relations forum. His job, as he saw it, was to uphold liberal internationalism, to remind the UN that America was the only true anti-
colonial power. He had no doubt that if debate swung on democratic
values, the United States would come out the leading nation. His job was
to convince the developing world that Wilson had been right and that
their best interests were protected by American principles: law, democracy, and "the integrity of an international body rising above international rivalries into the clearer air of international morality and
international justice." The United States did not necessarily need the
UN, but the weaker nations surely did: "My own country is in the fortunate position of being able to look out for itself and its own interests,
and look out it will. But it is for the vast majority of states that the
United Nations has vital meaning and is of vital necessity." He excelled

[38] Martin, *Stevenson and the World,* 558–65.
[39] Ibid., 590.

at the task, because he believed all of what he argued, even if he knew that nothing he said was of real importance in Washington or Moscow.[40]

He was so good at what he did that the new administration expected him to cover for the botched and ill-conceived invasion of Cuba. Though he was briefed on the impending invasion, Stevenson was not given many details. Instead the State Department provided a speech based on the CIA cover story that Cuban Air Force defectors undertook the hostilities, which he dutifully presented, unaware that it was a fabrication. When the real story broke, Stevenson did appear as the official liar. He should have resigned. The affair demonstrated the UN's lack of credibility as well as Kennedy's intention to keep him out of the policy-making process. But he stayed on, in part because the administration was only in its first months and in part because Kennedy quickly made conciliatory gestures by inviting Stevenson to act as point man for the Alliance for Progress and asking his advice on Laos.[41]

In the long run, Kennedy's gestures only made Stevenson's position more painfully obvious. He felt less obliged to be respectful, and he spoke loosely at times of the president's inexperience, among other things. The more Stevenson hung about the administration, the more he clashed with those who enjoyed real influence, and they were realists almost to a man—Dean Rusk, McGeorge Bundy, and Paul Nitze. To them the UN was little more than a public-relations show, and Stevenson a mere dreamer.

They clashed most directly during the Cuban missile crisis, when Stevenson argued against various exertions of force to which the administration had committed itself. He recommended instead a diplomatic onslaught that focused on the Organization of American States and the UN and that held out the possibility of American withdrawal from Guantanamo Bay and from Turkish missile bases. Stevenson arrived into the secret discussions late, after the rest of Kennedy's advisors had dismissed what he was proposing. His performance reinforced their dislike for him, and they dismissed Stevenson as naive and, worse, redundant. Improperly briefed, he was at a disadvantage going in, but then again, as George Ball recalls, Stevenson entered the discussions from "the United Nations shadow world, where compromise was the invariable formula

---

[40] Stevenson, "Shall the United Nations Survive?" address to the Security Council, 15 February 1961, *Vital Speeches*, 15 March 1961, 323–24; "The United States and China," address in the General Assembly, 1 December 1961, ibid., 1 January 1962, 167–70.

[41] Martin, *Stevenson and the World*, 622–37.

for solving all problems." No doubt the realists saw Stevenson exactly in this way. But this is less a criticism of Stevenson than of the realists, who dismissed the diplomatic approach because they had so little regard for diplomacy in the first place. Stevenson probably would have received the same treatment had he been on hand originally.[42]

Stevenson managed to turn the crisis into something of a personal victory, but it was a bitter one. When Soviet ambassador Valerian Zorin waffled on the direct question of whether the Soviets had put missiles in Cuba, Stevenson announced that he would wait "until hell freezes over" for a honest answer. Kennedy wired his appreciation, and even his Republican Lake Forest friends were proud of him. But was this hardly seems like a great victory for an idealist who hoped for peaceful development and the end of the Cold War. Nor did it mark any seizure of influence on his part; Stevenson was not making policy but was acting as a mouthpiece. He could not take much real satisfaction in the course of events, though no doubt the favorable publicity was nice.[43]

Then in December 1962, the publicity turned ugly when Stewart Alsop and Charles Bartlett published an account of the missile crisis meetings in which they described Stevenson's call for a diplomatic approach. Alone, the information would have been harmless—it was essentially accurate—but the journalists quoted one of Stevenson's "nonadmirers," as Alsop described the source, to the effect that the UN ambassador "wanted a Munich." It was a scurrilous comment, given Stevenson's UN performance on the issue, but one that might be expected to turn up in a story by journalists with a long-standing grudge against Stevenson. For that reason too, it should have passed over quickly. Bartlett, however, was the president's friend, which set the Washington press corps, "desperate for something to write about," according to Alsop, to speculating that Kennedy planted the story in order to undercut Stevenson. The administration could not claim that Stevenson had not taken such a line, and Stevenson, who believed that Kennedy was behind the story, put out not-so-subtle hints that he intended to resign.[44]

Again he did not, which might be the saddest part of the whole strange affair. He told a friend that it was a personal matter; he could not quit,

---

[42] Ibid., 721–23; Ball, *The Past Has Another Pattern*, 294–96.

[43] Martin, *Stevenson and the World*, 732–36.

[44] Ibid., 740–47; James A. Welcher, "The Brothers Alsop and Adlai Stevenson," *The Progressive* 27 (March 1963): 14–18. Kennedy may have shaped the story. According to Alsop, he saw a piece before publication and recommended several changes, though not necessarily dealing with Stevenson. Stewart Alsop, *The Center: People and Power in Political Washington* (New York, 1968), 190–91.

lest it look as if he were dumped. In part it was political; it would cause a split in the party.[45] The Cuban missile crisis befit his whole peculiar career, for it marked both Stevenson's finest hour and his worst moment as UN ambassador. The former came when he stood up as a tough-talking Cold Warrior; the latter transpired because he recommended a course that his colleagues considered idealistic.

Fulbright exhibited more staying power, but only because he was more determined to remain an influential insider. Whereas Stevenson believed he was Kennedy's equal in most ways and superior on all remaining counts, Fulbright was content to assume the role of congressional advisor on foreign policy. He was acting the part when he opposed the Bay of Pigs invasion on the grounds that intervention against Fidel Castro would violate the Organization of American States charter and cause considerable trouble in the UN. If it succeeded, the United States would be obliged to prop up the new government; if it failed, there would be a terrific temptation to use American troops. The nub of his argument was that Castro was not a sizable threat. Castro was, in his memorable phrase, "a thorn in the flesh, . . . not a dagger in the heart." Beyond such practical considerations, there were principles at stake. Intervention "is of a piece with the hypocrisy and cynicism for which the United States is constantly denouncing the Soviet Union in the United Nations and elsewhere. This point will not be lost on the rest of the world—nor on our own consciences." He was half right in this summation. The point was not lost on the world, but the realists missed it entirely. When he made his case before the Kennedy advisors, according to Schlesinger, "he left everyone in the room, except me and perhaps the President, wholly unmoved."[46]

The Bay of Pigs alerted Fulbright's attention to the possibility that the administration was too enamored of military solutions, too eager to prove itself, and perhaps too inexperienced. But he did not become an immediate critic or an embittered, marginalized advisor. So long as he sought influence, just so long did he continue to support American policy.

He had to juggle ideals and aspirations, an act which was particularly evident regarding American policy in Vietnam, which he supported until it became clear that he had no influence whatsoever. The issue left him constantly in a logical or political bind. In a much-publicized speech to

---

[45] Martin, *Stevenson and the World,* 747.
[46] Schlesinger, *1000 Days,* 235–36.

the Senate in March 1964, for example, he laid out an argument against containment, only to end the speech with a long justification of American policy in Vietnam, which, as William Berman rightly observes, "seemed out of character with the rest of the speech." Later that year he guided the Gulf of Tonkin resolution through the Senate, a mistake he later regretted. He claimed that he supported the resolution because "I was confident that President Johnson would use our endorsement with wisdom and restraint" and because he did not wish to rock the boat on the eve of a presidential election. As Berman argues, however, Fulbright also assumed this position because Johnson continued to flatter him with attention: "Encouraged by Johnson to believe that his advice was still welcome, Fulbright felt he had no choice [but to refrain from criticism] if he wanted to retain his effectiveness at the White House." He forced himself into the untenable position of supporting the administration while trying to find the kinds of ideas and interpretations to which Johnson policy makers would respond. In that squeeze, both logic and ideals eluded him. When his colleague Wayne Morse asked why the matter of Vietnam could not be taken to the UN, Fulbright responded that, in this case, the "rules of law" did not apply. He could defend policy in Vietnam only at the cost of reason, and for someone who considered himself a reasoning statesman that was quite a high cost.[47]

As the American commitment in Vietnam grew, Fulbright gradually lost patience, and in so doing he lost influence. He called his famous Foreign Relations Committee hearings on Vietnam, which made him a national symbol of reasoned opposition to the growing disaster of the war, only after it was abundantly clear that Lyndon Johnson no longer cared to listen to him.[48] The hearings made it obvious that Fulbright enjoyed some institutional power, but it was not the sort of influence that he preferred and it tended mostly to call attention to his removal from the policy-making center.

In articulating his objections to American policy, Fulbright fell back to some extent on his internationalism. Yet he certainly did not return completely. For one thing, there were far too few genuine internationalists around to serve as compatriots. Stevenson himself was the best argument against relying too much on internationalist strategies of dissent. He recognized that the old internationalist arguments had lost their power.

---

[47] Fulbright, *The Arrogance of Power* (New York, 1965), 51–52, and "Old Myths and New Realities," *Vital Speeches,* 15 April 1964, 388–94; William C. Berman, *Fulbright and the Vietnam War: The Dissent of a Political Realist* (Kent, Ohio, 1988), 16–17, 39.
[48] Berman, *Fulbright and the Vietnam War,* 51–58.

He looked back to Versailles as "perhaps the high-water mark of democracy in world history," for there, "out of the ruins of the old European order, British and American statesmen devised the League of Nations—a radically new idea for the creation of a world-wide community of law." "The great paradox of this century is that the divisive force of nationalism appears to have reached its historical peak at precisely the time when developments in science and military technology have unified the world in the physical sense and established the need for political units far beyond the existing frontiers." Fulbright concluded that the UN was merely a reflection of this reality; it had the necessary pretensions to building a world community of law and yet it was marred by the undeniable power of nationalism. He discounted it as a viable institution not because he was contemptuous of its purposes but because it could not achieve them, and consequently, he recommended, like the past advocates of collective security, a "concert of free nations" comprised of the western democracies.[49]

Convinced that the substance of Wilsonianism had been discredited, he moved to the realism of Morgenthau and Kennan. It seems a strange turn for someone whose instincts were clearly in the other direction, but it is necessary to understand that by the mid-1960s, Kennan and Morgenthau both had become opponents of the very policy that their doctrines had encouraged. How these two theorists became opponents of policy conducted in their name is too tangled a story for us to unravel here, but suffice it to say that their opposition to Vietnam was the liveliest and most intellectually rigorous available to establishment critics such as Fulbright.[50] Fulbright gradually measured his understanding of events by their standards. Growing apprehension over the Far East goaded him to believe that peaceful coexistence with the Soviets was

[49] J. William Fulbright, "For a Concert of Free Nations," *Foreign Affairs* 40 (October 1961): 3–9, 12–15.

[50] Between them, Kennan and Morgenthau had become the leading authorities on foreign affairs outside of official circles by 1960, and they influenced Fulbright and others through their constant testimony to congressional committees if not through their writings. In general, both thinkers grew steadily disenchanted with American policy from the Korean War onward. Among their main points: the United States had foresaken any real diplomatic efforts to ease tensions; it had come to rely far too much on nuclear weapons; and it had given into a moralistic impulse that had resulted in a greatly inflated sense of national interests. The problem with U.S. diplomacy, to put it in a rather ironic way given the similar criticisms that Warburg and Fosdick had made of Truman, was its globalism. For Morgenthau's views see his *Vietnam and the United States* (Washington, 1965); on Kennan see Gaddis, *Strategies of Containment*, 238–39, 260; and Walter Hixson, *George F. Kennan: Cold War Iconoclast* (New York, 1989), 228–30.

both possible and necessary. Kennan's ideas resounded in his claim that a rigid moralism that "confused freedom and democracy . . . with capitalism, federalism, and the two-party system" had left American policy rigid. Americans were conducting their foreign policy under the illusion that they had the truth, to which others had to conform. Unable to admit to a diverse world and a relativist morality, Americans could not reconcile "fact and perception," and consequently "action becomes irrelevant and irrational."[51]

Fulbright's dismay with national moralism provided the thesis of his famous tract, *The Arrogance of Power*. Fulbright began by dismissing rational interests as the principal motivations behind foreign policy and argued that one had to look at psychological explanations for why nations chose certain paths. Behind foreign policy, he wrote, lay "the ordinary hopes and fears of the human mind." The will to power was rarely a calculating one. Nor was it a consciously ruthless one, and such was particularly the case with the United States. Naturally blessed and historically fortunate, the United States had gained unparalleled wealth and power and yet remained innocent and naive; these national traits encouraged the well-meaning yet moralistic, arrogant yet blundering behavior that had carried the nation into Vietnam. Indeed there were "two Americas," he concluded: the imperialistic, crusading, and puritanical nation of Teddy Roosevelt and Woodrow Wilson; and the humble, just, and self-critical nation of Abraham Lincoln and Adlai Stevenson. "I prefer the America of Lincoln and Adlai Stevenson," he wrote as if there were any doubt, "and I prefer to see my country in the role of sympathetic friend to humanity rather than its stern and prideful schoolmaster."[52]

Like Lippmann, Fulbright demonstrated his lingering debt to his internationalist ideals of world cooperation even as he criticized them. If the UN promised little hope, he argued, the Cold War nevertheless could be dissolved through small and practical exercises in cooperation—intellectual and cultural exchanges, the open door—all of which could be counted on to build internationalist habits. "The reconciliation of East and West is primarily a psychological problem," he concluded, "having to do with the cultivation of cooperative attitudes and of a sense of having practical common objectives." The Fulbright Program for

---

[51] Fulbright, "Old Myths and New Realities," 388–94.
[52] Fulbright, *Arrogance of Power*, 4–11, 245–57.

scholarly exchange is ample testimony to that commitment.[53] If he seized on the realists' arguments to mount effective analyses, it seems that he began to recover internationalist ideals as he gained confidence and a more solid sense of independence. It was as if he was fully aware that talk about international law, world cooperation, and the United Nations automatically caused eyes to glaze over and evoked the cynicism of the policy-making elite. When he no longer cared what the president and his advisors thought, his instincts resurfaced.

If he departed from Stevenson's example of trying to uphold Wilsonianism, he nonetheless continued to share his mentor's peculiar position in public life: an outsider who seemed to many to be inside, a loyal opponent of American policy whose idealism made it impossible to place him on a political spectrum that, in the chaos of the 1960s, was itself fragmenting. Admirers and enemies alike misunderstood the basis of his dissent. Some antiwar protesters nearly deified him. But it is hard to imagine that Fulbright, always the self-conscious and proper gentleman, had much in common with the New Left. His detractors too misjudged him, as did the one who described Fulbright's thinking as "a new and embittered crypto pacifism-isolationism."[54]

As for Stevenson, there was an almost poetic symmetry in his decline. To his contemporaries, he represented Wilsonianism, but it was a shallow, ritualistic Wilsonianism. So too the United Nations had become shallow and ritualistic, and thus together the man and the institution deserved one another. He remained in his post until his death in 1965, partly in the vain hope that Johnson would have to rely on him for advice, but mostly because the UN was the end of the line for him. He remained to voice uneasiness over Vietnam and the intervention in the Dominican Republic, but to little effect. He was never the same after the missile crisis, according to his old friend and long-time associate George Ball. "History had passed him by," Ball thought. "He talked about leaving the UN but he had no place to go." Ball went further:

> His role had become ritualistic. From then on he knew he was not going to have an impact on foreign policy—which was what was most important to him. Washington was a force of its own and he was not part of it. He was a member of the Cabinet but not really. . . . It was an unhappy life, certainly

[53] Ibid., 204–5.
[54] Quoted in Tristram Coffin, *Senator Fulbright: Portrait of a Public Philosopher* (New York, 1966), 14.

not his finest hour. I loved Adlai but by the time he died I felt he was almost a caricature of himself—a hollow man. He was going through the motions. . . . [His women friends] gave him adulation—they gave him the best food in New York—he went to every first night—it was an unhealthy business. So then he finally fell over and died.[55]

Idealism and the Contemporary World

There is a certain irony in the careers of Fulbright and Stevenson, in that realism itself was passing from predominance among American liberals just as the two were being pushed from influence. The great upheaval of the 1960s brought the realist "establishment" into disrepute, and the catastrophe of Vietnam sealed its political demise. We will put off consideration of the effects of the 1960s on domestic liberalism for the moment; in international affairs, the failure of American military solutions in Vietnam, the development of true Soviet military parity, and the self-assertion of the Third World all served to elevate the importance of public relations as a means of protecting and extending national interests, as a means, in other words, of policy making. The Cold War became a competition of gestures, and there was some reason to begin reconsidering the usefulness of internationalist rhetoric and, along with it, the importance of the United Nations, to American policy making.

Daniel Patrick Moynihan—one-time reform liberal turned domestic policy advisor to Richard Nixon turned diplomat—tried to make something of this point, in various ways, in the mid-1970s. The Cold War had frozen the United Nations out of any truly important role in the world, he recollected after his stint as UN ambassador in 1975, and the organization had nothing better to do than fuss with social and humanitarian work. "The huge irony," according to Moynihan, was that "just as the United Nations was being thus written off," its humanitarian work "came to be of enourmous moment to its new members, now categorized as the Third World. At issue was nothing less than the legitimacy of Western political systems and democratic beliefs that the UN charter embodied. This is to say, the low politics of the UN became the highest, most consequential politics of all."[56]

Surely Moynihan was exaggerating. For had he been right, then to ignore the United Nations would have been an act of shocking indifference

---

[55] Quoted in Martin, *Stevenson and the World*, 748.
[56] Daniel P. Moynihan, *A Dangerous Place* (New York, 1978), 11.

to fundamental national interests. If Moynihan is given to rhetorical excess, he nonetheless caught a development that had eluded the realists but that Stevenson and Fulbright had been talking about in the 1950s and Warburg and Fosdick before them: that regardless of the Cold War, the post-colonial world would have to reckon with the less developed nations. Unlike Stevenson, whose ideas were perverted into a interventionist strategy, unlike Fulbright who made the point as part of a plea to open relations with China, Moynihan transformed it into a fighting faith.

In his mind, the challenge of the post-colonial world was intimately related to the Cold War and, accordingly, the UN recommended itself as a strategic battleground, even if it was mostly a stage for rhetorical tirades. His thinking had a certain appeal, especially to Henry Kissinger. It redeemed the UN from the quivering hands of do-gooders; it met the developing and less developed nations on the theoretically neutral ground of high principle; and, most important, it promised a certain amount of revenge—or if not revenge, a smug sense of vindication—against the Third World tendency to tweak the American nose after Vietnam. Moynihan offered not just an analysis but a program, specifically rendered in an essay in *Commentary* in March 1975, and that is what convinced Kissinger, then foreign policy czar under President Gerald Ford, that the Harvard professor would make a splendid UN ambassador.

In the essay that caught Kissinger's eye, Moynihan argued that the rhetoric of interdependence was as strong as it had ever been, but that it had shifted from a rhetoric that encouraged cooperation to one that demanded obligations—obligations, that is, on the part of the wealthy nations to share with the less fortunate. On the face of it, this demand for a redistribution of international wealth smacked of communism, but it owed much more to British Fabianism, to an ethic of leveled wealth, fellowship, and anti-Americanism of a haughty, genteel sort. The Third World might be socialist but not totalitarian; its impulses were anti-American but had been learned from the London School of Economics, not the Stalin School for the Toilers of the Far East. It was time that American diplomats quit behaving as if the demands that issued from international Fabians were either inherently just or expressions of legitimate anti-colonialism. They served the self-interest of the espousers and were based on imported doctrine, every bit as much a heritage of colonialism as economic underdevelopment. The United States should "go into opposition," Moynihan urged. "It is time we grew out of our initial—not a little condescending—supersensitivity about the feelings of new nations." Return to the UN Moynihan's message went, but discard flimsy do-goodism. Here "was an idea foreign policy could *use*,"Moynihan has boasted in explaining its reception in the State Department. The old policy "went on interminably about 'damage limitation.' I had come along with a different view."[57]

If Moynihan's call for UN diplomacy had the virtue of utility about it, it is possible to see the Wilsonian instincts underlying his analysis of international Fabianism; at least he wished to give the Third World the benefit of the doubt. He is also well aware that Wilsonianism awaits salvaging out of a depressing past. Like Fulbright, he sees Versailles as the crucial turning point in liberal history, that "sorrowful enough memory" when Wilson "seemed to embody, and in that sense unify, the hopes of the peoples of the 'civilized' world." Moynihan too marks 1919 as the highpoint of American prestige and liberal power: "No man in the history of the world . . . so engaged the passions and the hopes of mankind as Wilson did in those months of 1918 and 1919." While he has misread parts of Wilson's career—Moynihan mistakes Wilson as "Calvinist" and overestimates his affection for the working man—he certainly understands that Wilson's vision of world order anticipated humanity prevailing through the "Holy Ghost of Reason," a vision which rested on faith and which therefore is generally considered irrelevant to contemporary politics.[58]

Wilson's vision was twofold, in Moynihan's estimation: it sought self-determination, "accompanied by a rhetoric of personal freedom"; and it called for an institution that would "sufficiently contain" the movements for self-determination by recognizing their legitimacy. The first half of the vision largely has been achieved, he believes. Unfortunately the second part of the vision has not gone so well, and its failure has been enough to induce Americans to "act as if Wilson were wrong." Policy makers from those at Versailles to Kennedy carried on a "corrupt Wilsonianism" that wavered between moralism and interventionism, and the only alternative to arise was Kennan's view that equated Wilsonianism "with dangerous nonsense, the prattle of soft and privileged people in a hard and threatening world." Even among those who should have been expected to uphold Wilsonianism, the vision faded, a point brought home to Moynihan when in 1979 he gave a talk on the virtue of international law at the Council on Foreign Relations. "My talk was not well

[57] Daniel P. Moynihan, "The United States in Opposition," *Commentary* 59 (March 1975): 43; *A Dangerous Place*, 50.
[58] Daniel P. Moynihan, *On the Law of Nations* (Cambridge, 1990), 1–2.

received," he writes, "nothing notable in itself, save that this was the Council on Foreign Relations, where what I had said was once doctrine, . . . the standard fare of Wednesday afternoon teas. . . . A friend suggested that the audience thought I had been defending the war in Vietnam."[59]

He clearly has considered his own view of diplomacy as part of the Wilsonian legacy, but he has failed to explain why, if the assault on reason had come from liberals themselves, and American liberals at that, it made any sense to mount a defense of reason through confrontations with Third World representatives in General Assembly debates. He may have sensed that it would be futile to attempt a liberal revival through the UN, for he was less than enthusiastic about taking the ambassadorship there. "I had seen Stevenson humiliated. [Arthur] Goldberg betrayed. Ball diminished. [James] Wiggins patronized. [Charles] Yost ignored. Bush traduced. [John] Scali savaged," he recalled. "For my part, I had twice said no to the post." Nor did he believe that Kissinger cared about the UN, "save on the odd occasion [when] it caused him trouble." Moynihan assumed the post on two conditions, both of which suggest how much Stevenson's career weighed on his mind: first, "I would not be lied to"; second, at those times when the truth could not be told, he "expected to be warned."[60]

Still the post was not without its importance in Moynihan's view of things. His tour in India and a widened knowledge of Third World politics convinced him that a major front in the battle for liberal reason lay in international relations. "As liberal internationalism seemed more and more to fail abroad," he believed, "the same corruptions of doctrine appeared in international dialogue" that, as we shall see, he believed had perverted American politics; there was the same Orwellian double-talk, the same irrationality, the same drive toward self-destruction. Moynihan directly equated what he considered the post-Vietnam failure of liberal nerve with the decline of the Wilsonian vision. The concept of liberty was being lost, he believed, and it needed to be reasserted for "it no longer speaks for itself." Once he decided to accept the post, in any case, he was bound to exaggerate its importance.[61]

He anticipated strident debate when he went to New York. He "was not looking for a fight," he claims in his UN memoirs, but he "would not back off from one, and might even relish one if someone else chose to

[59] Ibid.; and Moynihan, *Counting Our Blessings* (Boston, 1980), 41, 8, 19, 11, 14.
[60] Moynihan, *A Dangerous Place*, 3, 59, 66–68.
[61] Ibid., 21, 69–71; *Counting Our Blessings*, 52–53.

start it." By this same account, even he was not prepared for competitors quite so aggressive as those he confronted. The thesis that the Third World was Fabian, a view no doubt drawn from his experience in India, had comforted him in 1975; after a year at work he had lost that comfort. "Such has been the success of Communist arms, Communist intrigue, Communist treachery in Asia and Africa that the reputation of democracy in those regions has all but collapsed." In Africa particularly, many of the less developed countries were not "socialist" so much as nations with rulers who used centralized economic controls to organize state power; they were "state-capitalist regimes of a most depressing order" that, rather than delivering socialism, "simply deprived people of freedom." The effect on the UN, in Moynihan's appraisal, was to produce an authoritarian majority in the General Assembly, which while not predominantly communist, ranked political freedom alongside imperialism and capitalism as enemies to be fought. By implication, that meant that Moynihan's "opposition" was not just constructive parliamentary banter but a contribution to the Cold War, the very thing his original thesis seemed to argue against.[62]

He was poised to take up the fight in autumn 1975 in response to the movement among nonaligned nations to equate Zionism with apartheid, the one notable issue of his UN tenure. Clearly the move was a direct affront to American interests, for the arraignment of Israel as a racist nation went along with a parallel movement to have her expelled from the UN and thus amounted to an assault on a crucial U.S. ally.

For Moynihan, the issue symbolized all that was dangerous about international relations, certainly all that he was personally alert to. The term racism as a derogatory swipe at opponents had become more fashionable as the number of Third World nations in the UN had increased, he believed, and it was rhetorically linked to imperialism as a particular threat to the self-determination of the weaker states. To brand Israel as racist was to imply that it was akin both to South Africa and the odious Western imperialism of the past; it linked African states to the Arabs as racial allies in what Moynihan saw as a fundamentally anti-Western way. The nations behind the resolution, he argued repeatedly, were despotic or worse and had no right to criticize anyone else's human-rights records. The accusation itself was a totalitarian bastardization of language and, hence, an assault on objective truth that could only diminish,

---

[62] Moynihan, *A Dangerous Place*, 101, 55–56, 113–15; and "A Diplomat's Rhetoric," *Harper's* 2252 (January 1976): 41; Frances Fitzgerald, "Warrior Intellectuals," *Harper's* 252 (May 1976): 50.

he insisted during his General Assembly speech against the resolution, the odium of the word racism and invite similar perversions of human rights. "Many of the members of the United Nations owe their independence in no small part to the notion of human rights," he maintained in tones reminiscent of Stevenson. "How will the small nations defend themselves, on what grounds will others be moved to defend and protect them, when the language of human rights . . . is no longer believed and no longer has a power of its own?" He suspected, moreover, that the Soviets instigated the whole business as a means of punishing Egypt for taking nonalignment seriously and was appalled but hardly surprised that many American liberals had sat supinely by and watched the movement develop.[63] Taken as a whole, the issue symbolized liberal decline, the ultimate elevation of irrationally against the formalism of reason.

In retrospect, Moynihan exaggerated the threat that the resolution posed either to Israel or the United States, just as he exaggerated the general threat that the rise of the Third World presented. The origins of the resolution, at least on the Arab side, lay more in clear diplomatic interest than in any abstract assault on reason. As Frances Fitzgerald pointed out, the Arab states wanted primarily to force Kissinger and the Israelis back into the process of negotiating a West Bank withdrawal. If the resolution marked any Cold War victory for the Soviets, furthermore, it did so only on the level of symbolism, an advantage that less contentious diplomacy would have undermined.[64]

The whole affair was counterproductive. The resolution only diminished the Israeli respect for the UN and obviously did nothing to encourage a West Bank withdrawal. Nor did it turn Egypt away from its policy of accommodation with Israel, which reached its high point at Camp David. American prestige in the Third World was so dismally low that not even Moynihan could do so much damage as he was given credit for, and thus he was denied the satisfaction of having "given hell" to anyone who truly cared. If that were not chastisement enough, the British representative in New York, Ivor Richard, launched an attack that Moynihan believed was inspired, if not directed, by Kissinger himself, who evidently no longer thought it in his interests to have hell raised at Turtle Bay. Moynihan does not consider his time in New York counterproductive—quite the contrary. In his view, the stand that the U.S. mission made over the Zionism issue tapped into a popular zeal for human rights

[63] Moynihan, *A Dangerous Place*, 159–81, 198.
[64] Fitzgerald, "Warrior Intellectuals," 51.

in America, helped push it to the forefront of discussions over how to shape foreign policy, and eventually resulted in its emphasis in the Carter administration's foreign policy.[65]

That too, however, he exaggerated. President Jimmy Carter did emphasize human rights, but the roots of the emphasis do not lead back to much of anything that would indicate or encourage ideological revival. Human rights emerged as a Democratic platform plank in 1976, because it was the only foreign-policy stance on which the McGovern Democrats and the Jackson Democrats (Moynihan was counted among the latter) could agree. It was curious that Moynihan should use it as grounds for compromising with the sort of pusillanimous liberals whom he believed had been running from liberal ideals since the 1960s. Perhaps he believed that out of this deal would come a consistent human-rights policy, but there is a strong hint that party considerations overrode even his determination to defend the West. "We'll be against dictators you don't like the most," Moynihan claims to have said to Sam Brown, the McGovernite with whom he was hashing out the plank, "if you'll be against the dictators we don't like the most."[66]

It is difficult to find much pure idealism underlying the human-rights doctrine. Moynihan had demonstrated how it might be used as a means for waging the Cold War, and the prospect of "taking the ideological initiative," as one Carter aide put it, appealed to some. Carter himself had never given much thought to using human rights as a foundation for policy. Most insiders agree that it was an approach that had an immediate appeal to Carter's deep Christian convictions, and it was as good a general approach to the Third World as any alternative. Others saw in human-rights doctrine a foreign policy that could unite the nation, presumably on the theory that if Democrats could agree on it, everyone could. It also had the unmentioned virtue of being cheap, for not only did if offer a solid excuse to cut aid to offending nations, but, like all true gestures, it promised nothing in the way of developmental aid.[67] The official embrace of human rights as a basis of policy had a peculiarly futile quality about it from the start. It was not long before the predictable breakdown of the compromise left some administration officials demanding a hard line against the Soviets and others working hard to sus-

---

[65] Moynihan, *A Dangerous Place*, 212–25.

[66] Moynihan, "The Politics of Human Rights," *Commentary* 64 (August 1977): 22–24.

[67] Ibid., 23; Gaddis Smith, *Morality, Reason, and Power: American Diplomacy in the Carter Years* (New York, 1986), 27–33; Joshua Muravchik, *The Uncertain Crusade: Jimmy Carter and the Dilemmas of Human Rights Policy* (Lanham, Md., 1986), 7–17.

pend aid to such states as Argentina. The predictable complaints arose that the administration was pressing hard against some nations and not others, while various other observers could not even agree on where the inconsistencies lay. As for Moynihan, he believed that Secretary of State Cyrus Vance was determined to gut the approach by turning it into a mere humanitarian program run by the middling bureaucrats to whom obscurity and inconspicuousness were basic career principles. Vance relegated human rights to a matter of "departmental routine," he lamented, and "if the foreign service prevails, the Secretary of State will soothe the Soviet Union and only challenge Ecuador."[68]

Having taken pride in his role in establishing human-rights doctrine, Moynihan keenly felt its demise, so keenly, in fact, that he believed Carter's failure to sustain the doctrine in the UN had caused the administration's unraveling and led, indirectly, to Ronald Reagan's 1980 victory. Instead of following his example, the UN mission under Carter reverted to the policy of avoiding confrontation, of denying that other nations were hostile and thus of denying reality itself. When the Camp David Accords were met in the United Nations by new resolutions variously denouncing Israel (particularly Resolution 465, which condemned Israel as an outlaw sate), the United States voted with "the jackals," as Moynihan calls the resolutions' supporters. Coming as it did on the eve of the New York primaries, the administration's actions allowed Edward Kennedy to steal a victory there and begin his divisive attempt to unseat Carter. The result was Ronald Reagan's victory, and with it an administration that kept the human-rights bureaucracy but guided it by the specious distinction that there was a difference between totalitarianism and authoritarianism and put it under Eliot Abrams, whose means to human rights included covert war in Central America.[69]

The end could not have been more dismal for Moynihan, for neither liberalism nor the Democratic party succeeded. Probably he had hoped for too much. It was never clear, even in the Carter administration, that the most important policy makers were prepared to take the United Nations seriously enough to put much energy into defending the charter. Carter turned to the UN much as Kissinger had, when it suited him. The blunder on Resolution 465 may well have been due as much to indifference as to cowardice, though that hardly would exonerate the adminis-

[68] Moynihan, "Politics of Human Rights," 22–24; Muravchik, *The Uncertain Crusade,* 113–16.
[69] Daniel P. Moynihan, "Joining the Jackals," *Commentary* 71 (February 1981): 23–31.

tration in Moynihan's eyes. Certainly the Reagan administration, which turned to unilateralism with a vengeance, hardly promised a revival of Wilsonianism. Moynihan appears to have been tilting at windmills as much as Stevenson was, only with greater flourish. He seemed to have been carried along in the faith that Wilsonianism could be revived through sheer exhortation.

Precisely because he knows that a Wilsonian revival is a mere hope without a similar revival of the conditions that made it once believable, his recent post-Cold War defense of world order based on law is interesting. For now, one can argue, the only obstacle to a liberal world order is the revival of doctrine, the Cold War obstacles to interdependence having been removed. If in recent memory, Moynihan suggests, international law has not been very effective at controlling conflict, "yet to observe a U.S./Soviet team supervising the dismantling of a Pershing II missile is, at the very least, to introduce the thought that it might be becoming more effective than it has been." In light of these events, no one could argue that Wilson had been wrong. He might have been flawed, perhaps a bit too zealous in his optimism, but he was not "wrong to think that there was something better ahead than Auschwitz and Hiroshima." If before the Berlin Wall fell, "real men did not cite Grotius," perhaps now those attracted to Wilsonianism might come out of the closet.[70]

It is necessary, he maintains, to jar the official American memory so that it remembers what international law is and that it once was the core of American foreign policy. "In the annals of forgetfulness," he quips, "there is nothing quite to compare with the fading from the American mind of the idea of the law of nations." The amnesia itself was a long-running affliction, but it was at its worst in the Reagan years. The invasion of Grenada, the mining of Nicaraguan harbors, the Iran-Contra fiasco—all were violations of law undertaken by dogmatists whose devotion to higher ideals neglected to take note of the highest ideal, respect for law. The roots of the Reagan policy, he writes, lay in the emergence of intellectuals, "notably a new generation of young conservatives trained on the *National Review* and the mutated historicism of the *Wall Street Journal* editorial page," in addition to "displaced Democrats" such as Jeane Kirkpatrick, who believed that "world Communism had commenced a new offensive against the West." The Reaganites convinced themselves that the battle against this new offensive was all-

---

[70] Moynihan, *On the Law of Nations*, 11, 8, 99, 100, 13.

important and that a small thing like international law ought not to get in the way. Whereas Kennedy, for instance, at least had the decency to claim that his violations of international law were not truly violations, the Reagan administration actually took the line that international law was optional, something to be adhered to when convenient.[71]

A cynic reading Moynihan might point out that he was once one of these "displaced Democrats," that he too seemed to think at one time that the Soviets had figured out how to extend unprecedented influence in the Third World, and that he too acted as if history were on the side of the totalitarians.

But new circumstances make new distinctions possible or in this case, old distinctions can reemerge. However convenient Moynihan's argument, it is in keeping with his cultivated Wilsonianism, which in essence always distinguished him from nationalists such as Scoop Jackson and Jeane Kirkpatrick. The Cold War had the continuous effect of cutting out the liberal center, and thus centrists have had no way of marking themselves off from the right wing; this helps explain why people like Moynihan have been dubbed "neoconservatives." Moynihan's recent book is an attempt to reassert the liberal center. International law, he hopes, will establish the ground rules for a world order based on self-determination and theoretical equality between nations that renounce the use of violence. No one should be so foolish as to think that international conflict will end, but the point is to construct a set of objective guides to international behavior and thus restore the soul as well as the substance of liberalism: "And so we return to the Wilsonian project, but with a new emphasis."[72]

Moynihan's book might turn out to be the first in a revival of liberal idealism, one based on the long-awaited union of ideals and reality. Certainly the much-admired global economy has withstood the political horrors of the century and continues to hold out the structural basis for a liberal world order, just as liberals internationalists expected. It will be a strong temptation for liberals to see the twentieth century as a mere interlude in the march of world progress, a nightmarish one to be sure, but an interlude nonetheless. Perhaps the renewed vision will be infectious. Even George Kennan has given some thought to the matter. When Moynihan recently asked him, no doubt with a certain degree of self-satisfaction, what the collapse of the Soviet bloc meant to

---

[71] Ibid., 123–24, 132–37.
[72] Ibid., 13.

"the Wilsonian project," Kennan explained that while he "was long skeptical about Wilson's vision," recent events led him "to think that Wilson was way ahead of his time."[73] If the father of diplomatic realism can reach such a conclusion, how much easier will it be for others to do so?

But as Moynihan's own career shows, the idealist alternative to realism has been badly compromised and if the collapse of the Soviet Union and the triumph of global capitalism provide an environment for a renewed confidence in interdependence, it is not clear that it can bring back the Enlightenment element of faith.

Instead, some might accept the global marketplace as an end in itself, as, for example, Francis Fukuyama does in his recent, popular work, *The End of History.* Fukuyama has gone beyond Moynihan to insist that liberalism has not only prevailed in the struggle against totalitarianism, it has prevailed over history itself. Communism has collapsed because of the homogenizing power of the high-tech marketplace and of what he calls the "desire for recognition," the fundamental human craving for public acclaim, softened under present-day liberalism into a desire to have our individual dignity recognized. The end of the Cold War represents the ultimate combination of those two forces. Here rests Fukuyama's provocation, which did so much to excite Washington when his original essay was published in 1989: humanity has reached the point in both its technological and political existence at which "we simply cannot picture to ourselves a world that is *essentially* different from the present one, and at the same time better." The "liberal *idea*" has won; "there is now no ideology with pretensions to universality that is in a position to challenge liberal democracy, and no universal principle of legitimacy other than the sovereignty of the people." Ipso facto, Wilson is avenged.[74]

We need not pore over the details of Fukuyama's argument here—one of the foremost problems with his book, in fact, is its lack of serious detail—and others already have begun to call him out on his application of a derivative Hegelianism. At least it ought to be noted, as one reviewer has written, that Fukuyama has chosen some odd philosophical mentors, Hegel and Nietzsche, on whom to base a homage to liberalism.[75] It is

[73] Quoted in ibid., 151.
[74] Francis Fukuyama, *The End of History and the Last Man* (New York, 1992), 200, 45–46.
[75] Alan Ryan, "Professor Hegel Goes to Washington," *New York Review of Books*, 26 March 1992, 8.

similarly easy to note Fukuyama's waffling: his uneasiness with consumer abundance and his unquestioning awe of technological development; his upbeat message is tempered by recurring concessions that plenty of cause for conflict remains. It is easy to see Fukuyama's indifference to anything approaching a theory of international relations. It is easy to scoff at his extraordinary claims.

But it is those grand claims that call our attention to the book and invite the speculation that it might be to post-Cold War officialdom what Kennan's "Mr. X" was in 1946, or perhaps more modestly, provide what Moynihan's "U.S. in Opposition" provided. Fukuyama is far less specific about how to construct a foreign policy than Kennan was, and his failure to lay out guidelines for policy makers lessens his chances for real influence. Of course the very liberal victory that he applauds also makes it less urgent that some innovative approach to policy be embraced, in contrast to the grim days of 1946 and 1947.

While Fukuyama is alert to the general outlines of idealism's twentieth-century collapse, much as he is generally conversant with Western political philosophy, he sees World War I and the rise of totalitarianism more as causes than as consequences of reason's demise. Liberalism lost ground not because of its own faults but because it suffered from a lack of confidence, manifested in "the almost universal belief in the permanence of a vigorous, communist-totalitarian alternative to Western liberal democracy."[76] He does not bother to consider the contributions of liberals themselves to the twentieth-century catastrophe beyond that failure of nerve, which means, in turn, that liberals have won the day by default. Not really to blame for the enervated condition of their ideals yet unwilling to stand up for themselves, liberals can only have prevailed because, in the end, totalitarians were even weaker.[77]

A world ruled by phlegmatic liberals, whom even Fukuyama admits lack the will to die for their honor, might be safe, perhaps even more generally prosperous. A world in their hands would be decent but not very exciting. Nor is there anything in Fukuyama's idealist vision that promises any real democracy. His understanding of democracy is superficial, assuming as he does that almost everything that is not totalitarian is democratic: "A country is democratic if it grants its people the right to choose their own government through periodic, secret-ballot, multiparty elections, on the basis of universal and equal adult suffrage. It is

[76] Fukuyama, *The End of History,* 7–8.
[77] Ibid., 12.

true that formal democracy alone does not always guarantee equal participation and rights. . . . But once we move away from a formal definition, we open up the possibility of infinite abuse of the democratic principle. In this century, the greatest enemies of democracy have attacked 'formal' democracy in the name of 'substantive' democracy."[78] He merely restates here the self-serving definition on which American Cold War dogma rested, which might be one explanation for why Fukuyama makes sense in Washington.

Such a definition makes it is easy to be optimistic about the future, and Fukuyama sees the democratic wave washing everywhere he chooses to look. He thinks that the Pacific Rim is either democratic in fact or about to be. Though he concedes that some Asian nations might try to blend formal democracy with "a new Asian authoritarianism," he dismisses the possibility that such a system would "be the harsh totalitarian police state with which we have become familiar." Things are looking up in Latin America, and even South Africa has begun to dismantle apartheid, though the rest of Africa is rather laggard. Only the realm of Islam stands out as undemocratic, and it is the exception that proves the rule. Many of the Islamic nations crave capitalist consumer goods, a desire which, in international relations, certainly should outweigh the limited appeal that Islam has outside the Middle East and near East Asia.[79]

Democracy in the sense of citizens participating in rational discourse and meeting their obligations to grant others a hearing, or democracy in the sense of people being able to control the things that matter in their lives—their work, their communities, their spiritual life—would fall under his idea of potentially subversive conceptions of democracy. We could grant him the force of this point and admit that searching for "substantive democracy" is indeed a slippery slope, except that he is numb to the way his formal democracy has been gutted of its substance. The democratic basis of formal democracy, of liberalism itself, had been the assumption that the individual was capable of exercising self-interested reason in concert with the common good. To say that formal democracy is the best we can do is no less a pessimistic capitulation than Cold War liberalism was.

His conception of democracy as the formal process of voting and electioneering is the companion, furthermore, of his support for technological change. In his view, modern science and the technological

---

[78] Ibid., 43.
[79] Ibid., 243, 13–15, 112.

transformation that it produces are the principal forces behind what he calls "directional history," the linear progression toward his liberal end. It is the force behind the homogenization of the world. Like the invisible hand, technology takes on a life of its own that is dragging the world in a singular direction regardless of human will. It confers decisive military advantage on those nations that have the most of it, and all nations want it. It provides creature comforts and consumer abundance, and all people crave it. It drives the marketplace, and in order to deal in the marketplace, people have to accept its dominance.

These positions were all standard Wilsonian assumptions, though there is no evidence that Fukuyama knows of earlier think-tank idealists who proclaimed the Wilsonian equivalent of the end of history. He could have done with a reading of Raymond Fosdick, for in studying someone who tried for thirty years to reconcile liberalism and technology, he might have understood that complacent acceptance of the latter undermines the former, though in a more subtle way than it undermines fundamentalist religion, traditional societies, and the like.

His embrace of the technocratic ethos compromises the new idealism in two serious ways. First, it is by no means clear that the technological society provides general prosperity; increasingly, even in the United States, the opposite seems the case. The two-tiered economy, where well-paid technocratic elites literally fence themselves off from everyone else, is a direct result of that technological change that Fukuyama endorses. The related growth of the service economy, and along with it the proliferation of unskilled, part-time jobs, demonstrates that labor in the postindustrial economy will retain its meaning only for the technocratic elite.[80] For more and more people, technological advance destroys the dignity of work by destroying work itself, and in so doing destroys the activity that does more to combine the "desire for recognition" with individual control over one's circumstances than any single human endeavor. But Fukuyama's chapter on work relates the desire for recognition not to the control of one's labor, not to the devotion to craft, but to the Weberian work ethic.

Without coming to terms with technocracy, he cannot see that the end of the Cold War is best understood as the culmination of the movement toward fragmentation that began around World War I. In his view, ethnic consciousness is irrational and archaic and will be filtered out in the

[80] See Robert B. Reich, *The Work of Nations: Preparing Ourselves for Twenty-First Century Capitalism* (New York, 1991); and Bennet Harrison and Barry Bluestone, *The Great U-Turn: Corporate Restructuring and the Polarizing of America* (New York, 1988).

process of modernization. Nationalism, especially ethnic nationalism, will go the way of religion; it will become a personal commitment, sustainable only to the extent to which it becomes tolerant of other cultures.[81] Were ethnic conflict limited only to the former Soviet satellites it might be possible to accept the optimistic view that such conflicts as the Yugoslavian civil war are temporary matters of readjustment. But what of the rest of the world? What of Africa, or South Africa, for that matter, where the dismantling of apartheid has ignited simmering ethnic conflicts among blacks, where conservatives are making a case for a white homeland? Canada cannot even quell the separatist pressures of Quebec. In the United States, racial animosities seem to grow more intractable as the nation's culture becomes more homogenized. These conflicts are not temporary maladjustments but indications of modern society's dialectic, which any Hegelian ought to grasp: where technocracy rules, interdependence and fragmentation coexist.

The End of History illustrates the costs that the Cold War has exacted on liberal thought as the intellectual-political elite seems determined to practice it. Idealism may resurface as international conditions change, but the official new idealists have no commitment to common-good liberalism, a conception of society that the whole episode of the Cold War battered beyond the point of redemption for American elites. What is left is democracy as Fukuyama defines it: formal democracies committed to rationality but perfectly able to accommodate the diluted irrationality of ethnic politics and other forms of separatism. It is liberal formalism built not on reason but on a relativism that flourishes beneath the technocratic umbrella. Hegel himself was a relativist, according to Fukuyama, because his view of history "gives an account not only of the progress of knowledge and institutions, but of the changing nature of man himself." Indeed "modern man is the *last* man," Fukuyama writes, because "he has been so jaded by the experience of history" that he cannot accept absolutes any longer.[82]

Democracy at the end of history is a formality rather than an ideal, which rests not on deference to the common good but on the assumption that voting and party organization constitute democracy. In this sense, the new idealism truly is Hegelian, for "the best we can do" is the omnirationalist state that can be indifferent to or indulgent of political irrationality. Fukuyama's reception becomes intelligible in this light, for

[81] Fukuyama, *End of History*, 200–202, 270–73.
[82] Ibid., 62–64, 306–7.

there is an underlying sympathy between the new idealism and the official mind-set that constitutes the city of Washington. As the national tide of anti-Washington sentiment continues to rise (overrated perhaps as an electoral phenomenon but ominpresent as sentiment), as the nation's infrastructure and urban centers continue to collapse, and as public life itself continues to decay, Washington more and more resembles the merely formal democracy that Fukuyama claims is the best we can do. Washington as a power center has become a functional ideal enmeshed in "pure Being," detached from the increasingly disappointing reality that the rest of the nation stumbles through. It is an appropriate condition for those who hold power in anticipation of the two-tiered future. As Hegel would have had it, only they are "free."

10

Idealism in the Age of the New Politics

Partly in response to the official cynicism of the Cold War generally and of the Vietnam War specifically, political idealism resurfaced during the 1960s. Its resurgence was also connected inherently to the civil rights movement and the spirit of the Great Society reform program. The so-called New Politics that has since defined American liberalism was therefore anti-realist and reformist, and one might think that the post-realist liberalism of the New Politics would mark the idealists' revenge.

The idealism of the 1960s was of the "do-gooder" variety, however, while the main ideological thrust of New Politics liberalism drove even further toward group politics and relativism while doing too little to tackle the power of technocracy. Because the New Politics rejected the universal values of idealism, it is best understood as the progeny of realism, even though the realists represented the establishment against which the New Politics rebelled. Having destroyed a priori thinking through the "end-of-ideology" campaign, realists made it extremely difficult to construct coherent political alternatives and thereby channeled legitimate animosity toward cultural rebellion. Having institutionalized technocratic thinking in the universities, they invited assaults on those institutions when the war exposed the corruption of science. Having preached a structuralist morality that undermined the universalistic basis of idealism, they encouraged the relativism of contemporary liberals that at times seems willing to rid itself of a commitment to reason altogether. As Thomas Spragens has written of the student rebellion, the "complacent skepticism of middle-aged 'pragmatists'" in the late 1950s and 1960s created a "moral vacuum" that "established both the occasion and the argumentative terms for a youthful and often romantic rebellion. . . . You have convinced us of the impotence and irrelevance of reason in ethical and political affairs, the rebels might well have said; now don't turn around and tell us to 'be reasonable.' "[1] In somewhat the same way, American politics so narrowed the options of many activists that the only path by which to pursue legitimate causes reasonably lay along interest-group lines. For all of these reasons, the practitioners of the New Politics embraced the core of the liberalism that they sought to rebel against.

If liberal idealism provided the grounds for countering realism, therefore, it could be used similarly as a basis for criticizing the New Politics—its self-refuting relativism, its encouragement of fragmentation and group politics, its rejection of Enlightenment traditions. Even if it provides only a minority view, and a very obscure minority at that, the Enlightenment ideal in a sense furnishes the common basis for the ideas of figures such as Daniel Moynihan, Theodore Lowi, Jr., Orlando Patterson, and Thomas Spragens, Jr. In the twilight of the twentieth century, the New Politics has aged considerably, and the perspective that comes from age has tempered the best of recent writers toward considering the universalist implications of liberalism and conceding that some general claims, some sense of formal ideals, must be retained in order to make sense of the world. Escaping the Enlightenment has just not been so easy as the postmodern rebels assumed.

Idealism and Domestic Life

A long look at the career of Daniel Moynihan raises the question of whether diplomacy is his love and domestic politics his avocation or the other way around. In *A Dangerous Place*, his United Nations memoir, he explains: "Foreign service had been my only ambition as a young man, but in 1949 I failed the English composition portion of the Foreign Service examination. I didn't know much about anything in 1949, but I knew that I wrote as well as the people who flunked me, and I decided

---

[1] Spragens, *Irony of Liberal Reason,* 309. Spragens quotes Alasdair MacIntyre to the same effect: "The pragmatism of the attitude involved in the end-of-ideology thesis leaves precisely those whom it seeks to educate vulnerable to almost any ideological appeal by its failure to criticize social wholes. . . . The implicit nihilism of so much student attack on institutions is the natural outcome of the defense of the institutions of the status quo as the only possible ones."

it was best to stay away."[2] He did not seek out foreign policy positions once in politics; his first important job was as assistant secretary of labor under Kennedy. Nor did he write much on foreign policy until the 1970s. Instead he wrote, or helped write, on domestic affairs, focused most of his energies on issues related to public welfare, and indulged his tandem propensities to write about himself and to think of himself as an outsider, a renegade determined to uphold sanity in the midst of the growing madness.[3]

Like "plain old Bill Fulbright," Moynihan has cultivated a dualistic public image: he carries himself with the affect of upper-crust breeding and yet "presents himself," in Fred Barnes's words, "as a regular Democrat who serves the interests of an alliance of Jews, Catholics, ethnics, and labor."[4] There is something of the political climber in Moynihan, as there was in Stevenson, and when his ambitions were frustrated even though he had played by the rules, Moynihan too fell back on idealism to mark off his distance from fellow liberals. Like Fulbright and Stevenson he presents himself as an intellectual in politics, and his admirers agree. "In the sense of an educated man," the journalist George Will has said, "one conversant with the great ideas, the large issues of the twentieth century, he is it."[5] If Moynihan actually has made part of his living as an intellectual, he never has had much use for the scholarly life. Nor is his writing particularly scholarly: his favorite subject is himself.

Moynihan hails from a world unlike that of Fulbright and Stevenson. His upbringing was modest, Irish Catholic, and urban. His roots run back to mass politics and academic realism. He has called himself a "Kennedy Democrat," a fair self-assessment, inasmuch as he was among that first generation of urban ethnics to assimilate into the WASP bastions of national politics and academia.[6] For Moynihan, assimilation meant politics beyond the city limits and entailed a commitment to the prevailing habits of university intellectuals. Politics, in short, was a companion of social science.

---

[2] Moynihan, *A Dangerous Place*, 44.

[3] James Traub, "Liberal? Conservative? Or Just Pat?" *New York Times Magazine*, 16 September 1990, 78–79. My discussion of the Great Society and Moynihan's career in the Johnson administration is drawn from Nicholas Lemann, *Promised Land: The Great Black Migration and How It Changed America* (New York, 1991); Allan Matusow, *The Unravelling of America* (New York, 1984); and Moynihan's *Maximum Feasible Misunderstanding* (New York, 1969).

[4] Fred Barnes, "Pat Moynihan, Neoliberal," *New Republic*, 21 October 1981, 15–18.

[5] Quoted in Traub, "Liberal? Conservative?" 79.

[6] Barnes, "Pat Moynihan," 15; Fitzgerald, "The Warrior Intellectuals," 47.

Moynihan's career began in realism, in a world, figuratively and literally, beyond the melting pot, which of course was the title of the first important piece of social science with which he was associated. *Beyond the Melting Pot*, the 1963 study of New York City politics on which Moynihan was the secondary author behind Nathan Glazer, was an important book, for among other things it presaged the fragmentation of late-1960s politics in ways that the authors dared not imagine. Their thesis was direct: ethnic diversity was a permanent fact of life in New York City; the melting pot was a myth. American society did not have the power to erase ethnic differences, primarily because ethnic groups had become interest groups. Rather than a means for ensuring survival during the gradual process of assimilation, the ethnic group had emerged to block the culmination of that process.[7]

One would think that here lay the basis for criticizing ethnic politics, which, in fact, the book provided later in the decade. But in 1963 both men were still too close to their own upbringings in the city. Besides, the work was the sort that appealed to New Frontier intellectuals: it addressed urban politics, described groups that were different from the suburban middle class, and debunked a mainstay of American mythology. Most important, the book carried a rigid tone of social-science neutrality. "We had never in any event celebrated ethnicity," Moynihan wrote later, "we had merely described it."[8] They had not criticized ethnicity either, and in the absence of such criticism, the book stood not as a critique of American politics but as the sort of neutral study upon which the realists in the Kennedy and Johnson administrations hoped to base their ambitious reforms.

For Moynihan, social science was both an occupation and a means to career advancement. It was in this dual spirit that he put together his notorious report on the state of the poor, urban black family. As Nicholas Lemann recently has shown, the Moynihan report was a product of bureaucratic turf wars, the spoils of which were Great Society programs. Rooted in Chicago School of Sociology assumptions about ghetto youth, as well as Oscar Lewis's "culture-of-poverty theories," Lyndon Johnson's poverty program was an episode of social science applied to

---

[7] See especially, Nathan Glazer and Daniel Patrick Moynihan, *Beyond the Melting Pot: The Negroes, Puerto Ricans, Jews, Italians, and Irish of New York City* (Cambridge, 1970), 16–17. I work from the second edition of the book because, for reasons I will touch on below, its much expanded introduction, which almost constitutes a new book in itself, illuminates the authors' mounting dismay over the interest-group wrangling of New York politics.

[8] Moynihan, *A Dangerous Place*, 65.

policy. Both strains of analysis had a narrow middle-class perspective and rested heavily on the view that poor people lived in a more or less maladapted subculture. Some critics charged that these theories were fundamentally forms of cultural imperialism—charges often leveled at Lewis in particular. In the hands of people like Richard Cloward or Richard Boone, however, social science justified the political radicalization of the poor in the community-action program on the grounds that cultural barriers could be overcome if the poor learned to assert themselves. The radical social scientists, as good Kennedy liberals, were contemptuous of Washington bureaucracies and fought to have the poverty program placed entirely under Sargent Shriver in the new Office of Economic Opportunity. As Lemann shows, it was in an attempt to capture programs for the Labor Department that Moynihan wrote the "Report on the Negro Family" in spring 1965.[9]

The public reception accorded the Moynihan report—or actually rumors of what the report contained—is an old story. Moynihan's description of the dissolving urban black family evoked a storm of bitter criticism; Lemann calls the report "probably the most refuted document in American history."[10] Some of the criticism resulted from the haphazard way the report was written, some from the fragmentary way it was released to the public. The most bitter criticism accused Moynihan of "blaming the victim," in the phrase coined by William Ryan, a New York liberal whose interpretation of the report was so skewed that one doubts whether Ryan ever read it. Some civil-rights leaders lambasted Moynihan as a "subtle racist" pandering a "new racism." Other critics, feminists and black nationalists most prominently, seized on his description of the female-headed family as "pathological"; the former charged that Moynihan was guilty of patriarchal bias, while the latter claimed that the matrifocal family was rooted in African culture. Buried in an avalanche of criticism, Moynihan was isolated within the administration. Initially Johnson intended to devote an entire conference to the problems of the family, but by the time the conference met in fall 1965, Berl Bernhard, the conference chief, felt compelled to open the proceedings by announcing that he "had been reliably informed that no such person as

[9] Lemann, *Promised Land*, 170–77; Matusow, *Unravelling of America*, 197–98. Lee Rainwater and William L. Yancey, eds., *The Moynihan Report and the Politics of Controversy* (Cambridge, 1967) includes the report itself and representative examples of commentary.
[10] Lemann, *Promised Land*, 177.

Daniel Patrick Moynihan exists."[11] His attempt to employ social science in the cause of career advancement backfired, for as he noted in a somewhat different context, "even worse than to be blamed in Washington is to be ignored."[12]

There were certainly sound criticisms of the report. It probably understated illegitimacy in the white community and failed to acknowledge white women's greater access to contraception; Moynihan also failed to note with sufficient rigor that births out of wedlock were rising among whites as well, which might have led to the conclusion that the family crisis was more a matter of urban poverty than of race and culture. No fair reading can conclude that Moynihan blamed blacks themselves, for he went out of his way to blame America's racism and the heritage of slavery for the disintegrating family.

Lost in the furor surrounding the report was how much it shared with the theories that lay behind the community-action programs. Moynihan's hope was to turn the poverty program into a traditional, New Deal sort of jobs package, which almost certainly would have been more effective in fighting poverty than the community-action program. But the report nevertheless focused on culture in essentially the same fashion as Oscar Lewis or the Chicago sociologists did in their work. There was little in the report that signaled a sense of class relations between poor people and American capitalism; the gist instead was that the black family was in crisis because it was black, just as, in the estimation of liberal social sciences, racial conditions drove youths to juvenile delinquency, drug abuse, and any number of other vices. Moynihan pointed out the class distinctions within the African-American community mostly to insinuate some measure of optimism into the document and to head off the predictable criticism that he was lumping all blacks together in one big, pathological mass. That class differences existed among African-Americans should have encouraged an analysis that focused more on economic than on racial issues, but the trend among liberals was decisively away from class analysis, and that was the way Moynihan chose to go.

Even his use of the term "pathological" was far more rooted in current academic usage than his critics then—and since—appreciated. Lemann

---

[11] Ibid., 154–55, 172–79.

[12] Daniel P. Moynihan, "The Professors and the Poor," *Commentary* 46 (August 1968): 19. Moynihan was refering to the fate of OEO here, but the sense of his own fate having been similar is easy to see. See also Moynihan, *Maximum Feasible Misunderstanding*, xvii, where he speaks of the extent of his exclusion from Washington.

notes that Kenneth Clark, who hardly could be accused of cultural imperialism, used the term in *Dark Ghetto* and surmises that Moynihan took it from him. Yet Clark was not the only sociologist to use it. Eliot Liebow used it in *Tally's Corner,* and Herbert Gans employed it to refer to "lower-class" Italian families in *The Urban Villagers.* Moynihan was just as likely to have absorbed the term from Gans, who was associated with the Cambridge school of urban sociologists, Leonard Duhl, Glazer, and others. Whatever its origin, the term's connotation reveals much about social scientists as policy makers. For they applied it to the same sort of people whom earlier generations of liberals considered the "deserving poor"—the widowed, the deserted, those truly at loose ends. Seen in this light, the term had a less odious meaning than Moynihan's critics understood. It also demonstrated a transformation of liberal assumptions. In the older construct, the deserving poor were to be helped because they could not help themselves; they were the biblical poor who would always be with us. Applying the term "pathological" to them, whatever else it showed by way of psychology's influence on other academic disciplines, implied that the deserving poor could be cured of their condition, presumably through a dose of cultural therapy. They were not fate's unfortunates; they were temporarily maladjusted, awaiting only the right measure of liberal largess to be applied by the well-intentioned and properly informed policy maker. Moynihan's description of the poor black family as pathological was the necessary prerequisite to government action on their behalf and was in perfect keeping with the spirit of the Great Society. Those who railed at Moynihan as a "new racist" waging a war of cultural imperialism missed the point. The report is better understood as an example of how postwar social scientists sought to arrogate to themselves the role of people savers.

It was against this arrogation that Moynihan rebelled after it became clear to him that he was no longer in good standing within the administration, and in so doing he necessarily departed from his social-science roots. In his account of the Great Society, he criticized the connection between social scientists and reform by remarking on the unprecedented nature of the relationship. The Great Society was a product, he suggested, of white middle-class social scientists who had little firsthand knowledge of the groups they decided needed help, and the discrepancy between those engineering reform and those who were the projected beneficiaries grew as Kennedy liberals decided that to be poor mainly meant to be black: "At no time did any Negro have any role of any consequence in the drafting of the anti-poverty program." Consequently the reforms heightened the expectations of the poor without understanding very well what was needed to improve their condition. The community-action programs sounded good but were fundamentally illogical; obviously those at the top never really wanted to empower those at the bottom. The predictable result was that the poor, with the bit of power that modest attention brought, railed at the lack of real improvement, which only convinced the Johnson administration to cut its commitment to antipoverty programs, which only encouraged Congress to attack the existing programs, which generated more rage.[13]

The self-defeating nature of the Great Society, he maintained, grew from the collective mentality of social scientists, who, instead of using their methods to bring skeptical discipline to government, engaged in self-indulgent boat-rocking, indifferent to the disorder they caused.[14] Moynihan's criticism was not of social science but of social scientists, and not of them as a political elites so much as a politicized group. He was most bothered that social scientists had sneaked deftly into the political process as an identifiable group, plying their own ideological interests and encouraging other groups to engage in conflict.

His critique of the Great Society was therefore closely connected to his growing distress over the pluralism of the New Politics, particularly what he called the "new racialism," the tendency of groups to engage in political action not just to further group interests but to antagonize others. This distress underlay the other infamous episode in Moynihan's political career, the so-called "benign neglect" memo that he wrote for his new boss, Richard Nixon. He had been encouraging Nixon to push a guaranteed minimum income plan through Congress, and in so doing he had argued that the federal government could do more to help poor blacks by developing substantive economic programs while the "race issue" was left to benefit from "benign neglect." "We may need a period," he wrote, "in which Negro progress continues and racial rhetoric fades."[15] Just as with the work on the black family, Moynihan's position was assailed by liberal critics, the civil-rights establishment, and the *New York Times,* and just as with the earlier controversy his position looks sounder than the critics' in retrospect.[16]

---

[13] Moynihan, *Maximum Feasible Misunderstanding,* 98, 169–77.

[14] Ibid., 191–92.

[15] Quoted in Carl Gershman, "A Bum Rap," *New Republic,* 10 April 1976, 19. See also Traub, "Liberal? Conservative?" 79–80; Moynihan, *A Dangerous Place,* 64–65. For a critique of Moynihan's guaranteed income plan, see Gus Tyler, "The Politics of Pat Moynihan," in Lewis A. Coser and Irving Howe, eds., *The New Conservatives: A Critique from the Left* (New York, 1973), 181–92.

[16] Daniel P. Moynihan, "The New Racialism," *Atlantic* 222 (August 1968): 35–40.

The main point here is that Moynihan was quite clear about the origins of the new racialism: they lay in the liberal attempt to empower groups by imposing reform from above. He was not opposed to reform; he was opposed to reformers. To him, reform should flow from the demands of those groups who wanted the benefits. As he wrote repeatedly, the main problem with the New Frontier reforms was that they were based on scholarship "that involves the dissection of unusually unsuccessful groups by representatives of unusually successful ones. While more and more of the billowing literature on poverty and race relations in the United States centers on the conditions of black persons in a white society, less and less of it is actually the work of Negro scholars. This must be repeated. *less.* It was not ever thus." Indeed, he writes, there had been a thriving and vital tradition of scholarship on blacks by blacks before the 1950s. Thereafter whites "took over the subject, newly *en vogue,* much as they took over the Federal houses in Georgetown and on Capitol Hill."[17] He never said as much, but what he implied was that reform had become deracinated, deprived of its vital roots in the ethnic traditions of those whom reform was supposed to benefit.

Intellectuals themselves, in a sense, were deracinated, which is why he insisted on criticizing them as a social group. By Moynihan's account, liberalism had gotten derailed when, in the aftermath of World War II, the intellectuals had their essential tradition of "liberal rationalism" swept from under them. Worse, "the nineteenth-century faith in secular individualism . . . had brought mankind into a zone of disaster from which its eventual emergence was problematic at best."[18] The result was a preoccupation among social scientists with alienation that demonstrated nothing so much as the intellectuals' own yearning for community. This quest, in turn, led to the supposition that power should be decentralized, a belief that emerged full-blown among the Kennedy reformers and underlay the commitment to community action.[19] The deracination of the intellectuals, in Moynihan's interpretation, was a result of the collapse of reason. Here is why he approved of social science and supported reform, so long as they were not united. The reform impulse was to come from interest groups; it was the intellectuals' job to apply reason so as to judge the necessity of reform and mediate between groups.

[17] Moynihan, "Professors and the Poor," 27.
[18] Moynihan, *Maximum Feasible Misunderstanding,* 7.
[19] Ibid., 8–17; "The New Racialism," 36–38.

This position was not initially an idealist one, for it did not occur to Moynihan that the intellectuals had foresaken their role as reasoned advisors until liberalism itself had devolved into the politics of rage and irrationality in the late 1960s. But in his essay the "New Racialism," and in his collaboration with Glazer on the introduction to the second edition of their book, Moynihan did begin to argue that liberalism was better off when its agenda was founded on two central tenets: strong government and, as he put it, "the complete disappearance of ethnic characteristics."[20] In the meantime, he began his career in the international arena, where he devoted himself to his ideal role as intellectual, whose job was to return to the traditions of liberal reason. To do less would be to remain rootless, adrift, unhinged.

When Moynihan left his place as a domestic policy advisor for the international arena, he made good on that lingering aspiration to work in the foreign service. But it was also a symbolic flight from what liberalism had become under the New Politics: an amalgam of new interest groups—civil-rights activists, women's-rights activists, gay-rights activists, environmentalists, intellectuals who habitually mark themselves off from the rabble, and cultural radicals of various sorts—bound together by post-structuralist liberalism.

It made sense then that an idealist critique of liberalism as it existed in 1970 would have taken issue with the New Politics as well as with realism. In the second edition of *Beyond the Melting Pot,* Moynihan and Glazer distanced themselves from both when they pointedly warned that ethnic politics was becoming tribalistic and dangerous. Their new introduction transformed the book. Where earlier they had presented ethnic politics as a fact of life, they had now concluded that this fact was a distinctly unhealthy one. They argued that traditional members of the Roosevelt coalition in New York, lower-class Jews and working-class Catholics most notably, no longer could identify their interests with blacks and Hispanics with whom they were logically bound by class and with whom they shared the common experience of immigration. The contemporary scene destroyed any sense of shared interests, much less shared destiny, because upper-class groups and intellectuals, for their own reasons, had built an unlikely alliance with the groups that they decided ought to be identified as particularly oppressed. The city's politics consequently had become obsessed with the categories of race and ethnicity, and in such a scene there were no winners.

[20] Ibid., 36.

For Moynihan, the new introduction served as a way of breaking his ties with the interest-group politics of his past. Interest-group theory never accounted for the destructive consequences of group conflict, which Moynihan had come to see as potentially disastrous. The alternative was to reassert a sense of collective well-being based on more-or-less traditional individualism. "The city should not be a federation of nations," the authors wrote. "Public action should operate not on the basis of group membership but on the basis of individual human qualities. It has been the curse of this country for so long that this did not happen in fact, and that Negroes—and other groups, in lesser degree—were excluded from even-handed public action. We must not now move to another extreme, in which a sense of injustice is implanted in other groups."[21] After having his say, Moynihan fled for the rarified air of the diplomatic corps. He never got around to explaining how and by whose standards "even-handed public action" is to be developed.

The work of Theodore J. Lowi, which shares much of—indeed anticipated—Moynihan's dismay over political fragmentation, offers more along these lines, because Lowi has been more consistently critical of the technocratic inclinations of social scientists. Like Moynihan, Lowi had intellectual roots planted firmly in liberal realism; he studied under Robert Dahl at Yale in the very heart of interest-group theory. The entire body of his work in the 1960s both testified to the enormous influence that Dahl had on his thinking and represented Lowi's effort to challenge that influence. When he chose Dahl's language to speak of liberal realism as the philosophy of "pluralism," he showed that he was on intimate terms with the beast that he set out to fight, far more so than those who struck out against establishment liberalism without quite knowing exactly how the establishment worked.

On one matter Lowi agreed with Dahl: interest-group politics was the order of the day in American life. Lowi began to distance himself from Dahl in his first book, *At the Pleasure of the Mayor* (1964), though he hid his indignation over interest-group politics until the penultimate chapter, almost as if to hold his fire until he paid the Dahl perspective due homage with a suitably arid discussion of the way the New York City mayor delivers patronage appointments. His first intention was to demonstrate how the processes of appointment and patronage in New York had changed over time, essentially from a late-nineteenth-century machine system to a modern, more technocratic process. In the midst of

[21] Glazer and Moynihan, *Beyond the Melting Pot,* lxxxv.

this transformation, New York's mayors increasingly relied on interest groups as recruiters of administrative talent, and, Lowi maintained, the power of interest groups widened accordingly.[22]

Lowi's New York was much like the city of *Beyond the Melting Pot.* The city never really eradicated ethnic differences; if anything, politicians' increasing reliance on interest groups kept people from assimilating thoroughly. The more ethnicity became a "primary variable in the political calculus," the more politicians ensured that their administrations were duly balanced; appointments became a process of appeasing all groups or, at the very least, making "token efforts on behalf of other groups." The appeal to ethnicity was a direct result of the decline of the party system, which itself resulted from the increasing need for technocratic skill in government administration. Over the sixty years of his study, Lowi found that the "number and types of characteristics that leaders felt they must accommodate" increased because the process encouraged competing politicians to court ever more marginal groups. The predictable result was that politicians "help perpetuate traditional ethnic and religious groupings."[23]

Lowi's gripe with ethnic politics was not that it defied the melting pot but that it tended to frustrate both social justice and governmental effectiveness. Unlike the traditional machines, interest groups could not carry the burden of ensuring social and economic mobility for an entire group. If anything, the usefulness of interest-group politics in ensuring the upward mobility of whole groups seemed inversely related to the strength of the interest-group process. Economic advance made it less necessary for people to rely on political jobs as a source of mobility, and those who gained appointments because they represented certain groups were usually elites who probably did not need such jobs anyway.[24] More important from Lowi's view, interest-group politics turned government from a distinctive and tangible entity to a diffuse and ungainly collection of mere "agencies." One could not accurately speak of a "power structure" any longer; there was only an arena that contained a process, and at stake was the effectiveness of popular control. Specialized administrators who ran isolated agencies dealt only with the particular groups whose self-interest was involved, and consequently the power of the electorate was diminished. In the past, "the power of the masses could over-

[22] Theodore J. Lowi, *At the Pleasure of the Mayor: Patronage and Power in New York City, 1898–1958* (New York, 1964), 8–14.
[23] Ibid., 33–34, 119, 216–17, 46, 44.
[24] Ibid., 217, 46–49.

whelm the power of status and wealth, but only seldom does it appear to be a match for the authority of esoteric knowledge and the intensity of specialized, subject-matter interest."[25]

In laying out such concerns in a tentative way, *At the Pleasure of the Mayor* presaged Lowi's much better known and more systematic attack on interest-group liberalism, *The End of Liberalism* (1969). He began where he had left off in the earlier book with the blunt assertion that modern liberal government was incapable of either effective action or justice. He extended his historical overview of liberal development and argued that traditional liberal society and its modern variant were distinguished by two very different public philosophies. In the former, capitalism as a philosophy of social and political organization prevailed; a deep fear of public power limited the scope of the state and engendered the complacent belief that the invisible hand would maintain order. Yet when it produced industrialization and urbanization, capitalism created a society too complex to be governed by "informal institutions." Technocratic society relied less on production than on administration and, accordingly, undermined the faith in the invisible hand as the guarantor of social order. The capitalist economy did not disappear, but liberal economics as a public philosophy and as a measure of legitimation did. The older public philosophy was not "wrong" so much as it simply became "at some undetermined point," presumably around the turn of the century, "irrelevant and erroneous . . . because capitalist ideologues became disloyal to the intellectual spirit of liberal economics."[26]

Disloyalty against classical liberalism swelled from within the ranks of capitalists and liberal intellectuals. Modern industry required "administration," Lowi maintained, which necessitated the growth of regulated activity. Well before the rise of the welfare state, corporations in industry after industry organized themselves as bureaucracies and regulated their industries through trade associations. This self-regulation was not an outgrowth of monopolistic industries; he pointed out that the most aggressive and best organized trade associations had emerged in highly decentralized industries—real estate, medicine, and pharmacy. This

---

[25] Ibid., 217–18.

[26] Theodore J. Lowi, *The End of Liberalism: The Second Republic of the United States* (New York, 1979), xvi, 10, 21, 14, 6. As with *Beyond the Melting Pot,* I work here from the second edition of Lowi's classic so to gain the advantage of the new introduction. This edition includes his sardonic "Constitution of the Second Republic of the United States" and discusses how the 1970s confirmed his original positions. Lowi airs a certain bit of satisfaction, for he was able to point out that interest-group liberalism survived the 1960s, even if liberal reformers did not.

mixture of capitalist economics, internal administration, and organized regulation within markets was responsible for the curious and ill-conceived nature of modern liberalism: it produced organized interests that operated under the faulty assumption that the invisible hand would continue to work, not to regulate markets but to regulate the bargaining that organized interests conducted in the quest for self-regulation.

For Lowi, contemporary pluralists turned traditional liberalism on its head. Whereas James Madison, for example, feared factions though he regarded them as inevitable, modern pluralists "turned the Madisonian position from negative to positive; that is, government is good because many factions do compete for its favor." Because power was plural, the state was not qualitatively different from any other source of power, which was another way of reducing the state itself to an interest group and was one step away from arguing that government should work the same as, indeed in the service of, organized interests.[27]

When the state set out to adjust and regulate the modern economy, it did so by responding to the wishes of interest groups, encouraging the unorganized to organize, and constructing governmental procedure so that bargaining determined who got what. "Groups become virtuous," he wrote, and "they must be accommodated, not regulated."[28] If problems arose, liberals assumed that they could be settled not according to law, much less according to moral dictates, but by proceeding with the happy assumption that it would all work out in the end. Modern liberals routinely dealt with problems, Lowi charged, by simply "defining them away."[29]

Taken together, technocracy, pluralism, and the bargaining process amounted to a new public philosophy: interest-group liberalism. "It is liberalism," as Lowi defined it, "because it is optimistic about government, expects to use government in a positive and expansive role, is motivated by the highest sentiments, and possesses a strong faith that what is good for government is good for the society." Interest-group liberalism assumed that "the role of government is one of insuring access to the most effectively organized, and of ratifying the agreements and adjustments worked out among the competing leaders."[30] This formulation logically meant that what was good for interest groups was good for society, and it took nimble manipulation to convince the body politic that

[27] Ibid., 24–28, 32–36.
[28] Ibid., 36.
[29] Ibid., 44.
[30] Ibid., 51.

this formulation was sound. For the cynical and the well organized, on the other hand, interest-group liberalism held a healthy appeal. It provided the blueprint by which the state could expand to accommodate its modern responsibilities regardless of constitutional barriers. It offered politicians the perfect excuse not to be leaders: "It transformed access and logrolling from necessary evil to greater good." Above all, it created the illusion of democracy and hid the fundamentally coercive power of the state.[31]

A half-century of liberal reform in reality was no reform at all. Reform itself was mere sleight of hand. To Lowi, Franklin Roosevelt was the master magician, because the New Deal laid down the unwritten guidelines of interest-group liberalism. There was no better example of how the process worked than in the case of agriculture. One of the most decentralized of industries, utterly incapable of self-regulation, agriculture pressed itself on the federal government and on the Democratic party in particular. In the spirit of cooperative democracy, the New Deal reached out, helped organize the otherwise scattered bits of the industry, and essentially allowed farm interests to regulate themselves thereafter. What went for agriculture went for industry as well; labor and business were not only given the National Recovery Administration but were symbolically welcomed into the corridors of legitimate government in the form the cabinet posts for Commerce and Labor.[32]

What of real reforms, those determined efforts to do justice to the poor and the disenfranchised? Lowi was mostly silent about the civil rights movement, though he does suggest that, as a well-organized and basically successful effort to force government to grant justice to southern blacks, it was the exception that proved the rule.[33] No one with any sense of real justice could deny that much to what was indeed an exceptional movement, though Lowi might have done well to consider why it was so extraordinary. He drew his attention instead to the anti-poverty programs of the Great Society, which advanced an essentially new conception of poverty in order to justify the programs that the Kennedy and Johnson liberals were determined to implant. According to Lowi, liberalism always had recognized the problem of poverty but addressed it as an inevitable part of society. The "old welfare" held to the axiom that the best society could manage was to alleviate the plight of the

[31] Ibid., 52–56.
[32] Ibid., 68–84.
[33] Ibid., 253.

poor.[34] Under Kennedy, however, liberals decided that "alleviation was for sissies"; poverty, they decided, could be eliminated. The only way they knew to approach the task of eliminating it, however, was by organizing it, or better put, by paying local authorities to encourage the poor to organize and regulate themselves. Community-action programs, in their decentralized administration, their vague extension of power, and their aimlessness, constituted "the most systematic expression of interest-group liberalism."[35] Much as Moynihan had argued, Lowi contended that community action raised hopes with promises that could not be fulfilled, and the inevitable result was the rise of black militancy and the collapse of the Great Society. The most tragic consequence of the War on Poverty was "that so many black leaders took [it] as their own." By accepting Great Society funds, they embraced the process of "indemnifying damages" rather than seeking justice and in so doing squandered the moral power of the civil rights movement.[36]

The poverty program and the civil rights movement showed that the pluralist state could not achieve justice because it was fundamentally impotent. Echoing Lippmann's *Good Society*, Lowi maintained that interest-group liberalism was an open invitation for private interests to invade the state, and the only possible result of that invasion was a decline in the power of the state. It was a glaring myth that the more the state grew, the more powerful it was. The opposite was true: the more the state grew, the more it became diffuse and prone to failure. Having conceded power to "personalized fealties" in what was essentially a "feudal pattern," the state conceded its authority as well. "A most maladaptive political formula, it was almost inevitably going to produce a crisis of public authority even though its short-run effects seem to be those of consensus and stabilization."[37]

Restoring authority depended on political strategies that would limit state action. It was always better to have no program than a bad one, Lowi believed. Liberal restoration depended more fundamentally on a strict separation of the public and private spheres and the establishment

---

[34] Even the New Deal accepted the inevitability of a population of variously incapacitated people who deserved care, and Lowi credited the New Dealers for that bit of traditionalism. He lauded the Social Security Act, for instance, because it was dedicated to caring for the infirm, the widowed, and the aged, was aimed at clearly identified groups, and was carried out with "notable legal integrity." Ibid., 200–205.

[35] Ibid., 207–12.

[36] Ibid., 236.

[37] Ibid., 50, 68, 44.

of law as the measure of legitimacy. Interest-group liberalism was hostile to law, because law was the opposite of bargaining; the hostility to law was also a hostility to universal standards, which is why the pluralist state could be amiably amoral. Justice, he implied, depended on, perhaps was even defined by, the setting down of universals, a position that he could take only if he revived the idealist conception of objective truth. He was not frank about attempting that revival—he seemed a bit embarrassed that it needed to be revived—but it underlay his advocacy of "juridical democracy."[38] Nothing less than a rejection of liberal pragmatism, juridical democracy was an *a priori* conception of equality under law. Government would know its limits, administrators would know the rules, and, more important, citizens would know where the coercive power of the state began and ended. Only that way did the powerless have any protection against the powerful, and the state itself would have the clearly defined power that effective planning required.

It was certainly a unique argument at the time, and it put him at odds with both realists and the New Politics. He further distinguished himself from both groups in a mostly forgotten but nonetheless fine short book, *The Politics of Disorder* (1971). The tone of the book, which departed from the stodgy, restrained professionalism of his earlier writing, reflected the temper of the nation in the aftermath of the Cambodian invasion and Kent State (not to mention the student extremism of his own campus, Cornell University). Against those critics who had called juridical democracy unrealistic, he reasserted that democracy run according to rule-of-law "constrasts in the extreme from the pluralist practice of policy-without-law." In realist eyes, he wrote, he was "guilty of an unpardonable sin. I had not committed a social science. Far worse, I had committed a civics. It is plainly unsophisticated to argue that formalisms are more than humbug. . . . I had not anticipated the fact that those nurtured on pluralism as an ideology, whose entire political lives had been enveloped in the governmental principles of delegation and manipulation . . . would find formal democracy totally unreal, alien, and even offensive."[39]

Where the New Left was attacking the establishment liberal, Lowi assaulted the "political man," the realist technician who had unwittingly brought the nation to its ugly condition. "Political man is a hypercivilized man, a political dandy," Lowi asserted. He "is basically the polit-

---

[38] "The need to define juridical democracy," he wrote, "is to me a measure of the decline of law and of legitimate government in the United States." Ibid., 298.

[39] Theodore J. Lowi, *The Politics of Disorder* (New York, 1971), xviii.

ical version of organization man. If he is a brilliant thinker, that only makes him a better technician." Political man was so enmeshed in his administrative functions, so narrow in his vision of what is to de done, and so self-important that he had no time to consider justice or morality. He hated ideology, because he thinks that "ideology is moralizing on a grand scale." His ideal was process, not moral commitment: "If we were all political men and the Eichmann trial had been in the United States, Eichmann's most effective defense would have been that he had not formulated extermination policy, that he took the job to keep a *real* Nazi from getting it. . . . We would have treated Hitler as evil not because his ideology was evil but because he was an ideologist who did not believe in compromising."[40]

After simplifying the anti-realist argument of *The End of Liberalism*, Lowi turned on the New Left. Advocates of the New Politics seemed determined to do little more than restate the liberal obsession with decentralization, even though it might be called participatory democracy. The term sounded nice, but in practice Lowi was sure it would be as ineffectual as all forms of liberal decentralization and would succumb, in the end, to the power of interest groups. The degree to which the New Politics only mirrored the problems of the liberal establishment was best seen in campus radicalism. He was not unsympathetic to students, who rebelled against what the technocrats had left them: morally bankrupt institutions that were deeply politicized regardless of the official attempts at feigned neutrality. Yet student assaults against the university too often took the form of demands for participation as administrators, which usually ended when they were bought off with bureaucratic bits that they could call their own. University politics was disturbingly similar to national politics, as administrators conceded power along increasingly decentralized institutional appendages. All that student radicals were learning was how to play the bargaining game.[41]

The New Politics also carried overtones of romantic rebellion and anti-rationalism and had reasonableness, if not reason itself, on the run. Within the university, liberals seemed to have lost their commitment to reasoned judgment, an act which entailed discriminating between a just cause and nonsense. University liberals dealt summarily with threats from the right: "If a delegation of students were to call upon a social science department chairman to demand a better presentation of Chris-

---

[40] Ibid., xii–xv.
[41] Ibid., 67, 125–26.

tianity, they would be sent away with a firm lecture on the evils of in-
terfering with who teaches what." But judgment escaped academicians
when the left came knocking: "The liberal, after years of identifying with
the left, quite frankly cannot distinguish a good demand from a bad one.
He is ready to abandon organized knowledge itself if that seems to be the
only manner of proving that no one can outlib him, for the voices of the
left remove his bearings." In the process of fumbling for direction, university liberals conceded to the "totalitarian strain" of the student movement. It was not a matter of right or left. It was that the students were
demanding a new orthodoxy in the institutions that guilty liberals were
all too ready to hand them.[42]

The Politics of Disorder provided Lowi with the opportunity to distance himself from both his colleagues and the New Politics, but he failed
to make much clearer what exactly he meant by "juridical democracy."
He reiterated his hope that it would be understood simply as the "rule of
law" and expanded his claim for its importance: "I am now coming to
the conclusion that it is democracy itself. Properly understood, democracy is juridical, or it will not remain democratic or vital very long."[43]
His expanded claims only made precise definition more elusive and inevitably invited criticism.[44] He never has been more precise than to say
that juridical democracy limited government action to cautious, gener-
alized programs run strictly according to clearly defined rules. Such a
clarification did not explain what was democratic about juridical democracy. In the absence of rigorous explanation, Lowi could not allay suspicions that he was advocating a new version of elitist idealism, not
unlike Lippmann's; he left his readers cause to worry that those in power
would set the rules and guide government, that the common good meant
whatever was good for the status quo.

If his conception is not well defined, Lowi's juridical democracy
clearly is built around his objections to pluralism as a vision of the good
society.[45] Lowi conceives the state as a formalist one, as some critics have
pointed out: juridical democracy has to grow out of a public consensus
on the part of the citizenry about the legitimate role and limits of the
state. He therefore presupposes that a rational citizenry, even one organized in various interest groups, can hash out that consensus, which in

---

[42] Ibid., 158–59, 162.

[43] Ibid., 60–61.

[44] See Robert C. Grady, "Interest-Group Liberalism and Juridical Democracy," *American Politics Quarterly* 6 (April 1978): 213–35.

[45] "We cannot rid ourselves of [factions]," he writes elsewhere. "We would not want to
if we could. . . . The cure for factions is worse than the disease." Theodore J. Lowi, *Private Life and Public Order: The Context of Modern Public Policy* (New York, 1968), vii.

turn presupposes that reasoning citizens can grope toward an agreement on the common good. Assuming the existence of such a thing as a "public philosophy," whether as classical liberalism, pluralism, or juridical democracy implies that, in his view, people do share values and therefore agree about what constitutes truth. He could not have defined juridical democracy closely and still have carried on the pretense that public debate underlay prevailing conceptions of justice; to define it would have been a contradiction in terms. But he owed it to himself to lay out more solid fortifications in defense of reason, particularly against the insidious attacks from technocratic rationalism. Juridical democracy becomes not so much elitist, Raymond Seidelman and Edward J. Harpham have written, as "a utopian longing."[46]

Lowi came closest to that necessary confrontation with technocratic thought in his consistent criticism of his own profession, political science, for its cheap tramping after political influence, its innate conservatism, and, perhaps most important, its realism.[47] The profession assaulted idealism, in Lowi's view, through its narrow focus on decision making and on isolated events; in its refusal to consider the influence of ideas and values, the profession demonstrated the worst and most unrealistic aspects of realism. Political scientists originally combined pluralist theory with administrative processes, and they therefore bore a good deal of blame for cloaking interest groups with ideological legitimacy. He could not have been more critical of his own profession than to accuse it of having taken a leading role in creating modern liberalism. Like Moynihan, he did not renounce the applicability of social science to government altogether. His tentativeness encouraged instead such unpromising strategies as his attempt to juxtapose classical economics against modern political science. The former had the virtue, as he saw it, of being almost entirely a priori—"perhaps the closest thing to pure theory at the societal level in all the social sciences." Classical economists knew the limits of their theory's applicability; and because they advanced a theory about the state even as they tried to argue it away, they offered something that constituted a systematic philosophy.[48]

He applauded classical economics for its consistency and substance but missed entirely the way in which laissez faire's own conception of reason led logically to the narrow rationalism that drove political sci-

[46] Seidelman and Harpham, *Disenchanted Realists*, 201.
[47] Lowi, "Decision Making vs. Policy Making: Towards an Antidote for Technocracy," *Public Administration Review* 30 (May/June 1970): 314–25; Ricci, *The Tragedy of Political Science*, 19–20, 188–89; Seidelman and Harpham, *Disenchanted Realists*, 209–13.
[48] Lowi, "Decision Making vs. Policy Making," 315.

ence. He rightly saw political science as a form of legitimation for modern liberalism and knew that classical economics played the same role in nineteenth-century liberalism. But he failed to note the similar contributions to a rationalistic view of reason that bound the two. Just as he too readily praised liberal economics, so also he consistently has never reached beyond, as Seidelman and Harpham put it, "a plea for the fusion of expertise, science, and political reform." Critical of his colleagues, he nonetheless has directed his efforts at saving them from themselves.[49]

On Salvaging and Democratizing Reason

Lowi's idealism presents itself as a counterweight to post-structuralism, the defining philosophy of our day. As such his work stands out as a rather lonely but necessary fortification against the rejection of universalism, that post-structuralist act which Orlando Patterson has denounced as nothing less than "intellectual treachery." Like Lowi, Patterson sees the New Politics as an organized repudiation of the best parts of the liberal tradition, its commitment to universal standards of right and justice, and like him concludes that the "cultural and symbolic demands" of organized interests are easily met but do nothing to establish justice. Black nationalism is a case in point. "It was ridiculously easy for the establishment to respond [to nationalist demands] by changing the color of a few faces in the ads for the 'Pepsi generation', by introducing a few network shows in which the traditional role of blacks as clowns and maids was updated . . . , by publishing a spate of third-rate books on the greatness of the African tradition, by the glorification of blacks roots, and, most cruel of all, by introducing into the curriculum of the nation's colleges that strange package of organized self-delusion which goes by the name of Afro-American studies." In Patterson's view, the retreat into ethnicity diverts attention from the urgent need to build black progress by addressing the community's economic marginality. Hence organized ethnic politics "simply plays into the hands of the American establishment."[50]

In contrast to Lowi, Patterson has attempted to come to terms with the entire modern debacle of liberalism by confronting and conceding the blows to universalism that technocracy has dealt. He sees the problem

---

[49] Seidelman and Harpham, *Disenchanted Realists*, 209.
[50] Orlando Patterson, *Ethnic Chauvinism: The Reactionary Impulse* (New York, 1977), 153–55.

for exactly what it is: a problem of holding faith in a faithless age. One solution to the fragmentation of our political life is to "reject modernity altogether, including its rewards, and return to the preindustrial culture that is more favorable to faith. For those for whom this is still possible and so choose, I have no complaint. Unfortunately, in the perverse manner of human beings, most of us want it both ways. We demand the rewards of industrial civilization but we are not prepared to worship at its shrine. We still want the solace of the old gods and the old faith."[51] His solution is to uphold reason, embrace modernity and control the latter with the former. He recommends that we reclaim the Enlightenment and factor out its imperfections: its excessive rationalism; its easy optimism about human progress; its bourgeois selfishness; its empiricism. Doing so has two profound virtues. It would reestablish "universal culture" and with it standards of justice that society is obliged to meet; and it would also constitute, in the act itself, a democratic choice that represents a lesson in the application of reason. Rather than turning back to the preindustrial age, he looks to "a modern humanistic socialism" in which the universal ideals of justice and equality provide the bases for further choices.[52]

I am well aware of the arguments to be made against such positions as Patterson, Lowi, or Spragens, have taken. No doubt they all are examples of thinkers whom Richard Rorty would chide as captives of the Enlightenment. This is not the place to take up an examination of Rorty or other post-structuralists, though it is important that they not be dismissed. Rorty's "post-modern bourgeois liberalism" is intended as an answer to the tyranny of universals, and in insisting that everyone accept the contingency and "historicity" of their values he calls us to both honesty and humility. Because Rorty probably has taken post-structuralism to its limits, it is illuminating that at those limits the polity looks very much like the realists' interest-group battleground. "All you need" for a reasonably civil society, he reassures us, "is the ability to control your feelings when people who strike you as irredeemably different show up at City Hall. . . . When this happens, you smile a lot, make the best deals you can, and after a hard day's haggling, retreat to your club." But even here Rorty himself cannot quite escape the Enlightenment project and recently has had to concede that if nothing else, we must accept contingency as universal. His own intellectual integrity has led him to a

---

[51] Ibid., 278–79.
[52] Ibid., 286–87.

defensive distinction between contingency and relativism—he certainly cannot be driven by any real danger to post-structuralism, which seems solidly established—which in turn finds him almost embarrassingly speaking of himself as a "freeloading atheist" who willingly upholds Judeo-Christian concepts of human rights and human dignity even though he recognizes such an act as philosophically groundless.[53]

Leaving aside the question of whether Rorty's is not an anti-philosophy, I must still point out that even this wee bit of civility rests on the prior assumption that the hagglers will have cause to smile when it might be just as easy and more effective to shoot the irredeemably different. Even if justice is indefinable, we can only protect ourselves against the war of all against all (which heretofore interest-group liberals have avoided) if we make an attempt to set the ground rules for political participation, law, and the distribution of wealth. And this, in turn, requires a previous sensibility, which we might understand as the impulse to sit down and work out those ground rules in the first place.

I agree with Orlando Patterson, who maintains that the recovery of that broader conception of reason cannot be left to liberals, who cannot disassociate themselves from capitalism by definition or from technocracy by habit. But I am still troubled by Patterson's democratic socialism primarily because he assumes that a revolutionized economic order will obviate the need for faith, and in a strange sense Patterson the universalist meets Rorty the post-structuralist. Like Lippmann, I am not sure we can ever rid ourselves of our need to believe, and as a consequence, I believe we should try to elucidate exactly what part of our political being is built on that admittedly vague and indefinable impulse.

Thomas Spragens's recent work recommends itself along all these lines. Spragens has argued in both of his major books that Enlightenment liberalism contained more than the seeds of utilitarianism, narrow rationalism, and technocracy. Rather it advanced a "capacious" definition of reason that meant more than just mathematical precision; it was better defined as "practical reason," through which the citizen calculates with moral ends and the common good in mind.[54] In *The Irony of Liberal Reason,* he maintains that practical reason had to compete from the first with another conception of reason that increasingly linked truth to scientific absolutes—moral Newtonianism, as he calls it. The connection of

[53] Richard Rorty, *Objectivity, Relativism, and Truth: Philosophical Papers* (New York, 1991), 1:202, 209. See also his *Contingency, Irony, and Solidarity* (New York, 1989).

[54] He lays out this argument directly in the introduction to *Reason and Democracy* (Durham, 1990).

truth with science at once elevated the purveyor of scientific truth and increasingly buried the reasoning citizen in the automatic workings of nature and later of the marketplace.[55] The failure of the Wilsonians lay in their uncritical return to the Enlightenment, which amounted to an effort to recapture a youth unsullied by experience. Spragens returns critically, and that critical return leaves him neither slavishly committed to an Enlightenment revival nor completely willing to depart from the modern world. Hoping to avoid a confrontation with the contradictions embedded in their tradition, the Wilsonians avoided coming to terms with the rationalist ideal and paid for that evasion by capitulating to modernity. Spragens confronts the contradiction forthrightly and successfully distances himself from modernity even as he admits that modernity cannot be ignored.

Technocracy has littered the world with too much for its influence to be eradicated, one of the consequences of which, Spragens suggests, is that we can never completely overcome relativism. To put the matter another way, we never again can know absolutes (which is why the postmodern claim that justice is indefinable is not merely glib); to claim otherwise would be to invite a new round of "moral Newtonianism." The humble admission that our knowledge is "fallible and imperfect," however, neither diminishes the power of reason nor undermines the pursuit of the common good, if, that is, one conceives of reason as a method of approaching the common good rather than as a means of producing infallible truth. Spragens finds philosophical support for his version of liberal reason in curious places: the philosophy of science and the philosophy of language, both of which have done their fare share to advance relativism. Karl Polyani and Robert Merton, Spragens writes, offered a conception of the scientific enterprise that provides a useful model for politics. Scientists see themselves as a community of individuals engaged in a common endeavor; they are dedicated to the disinterested pursuit of a common end through individual activity; and they inherently tolerate dissent and recognize that what they accept as truth today may not be true tomorrow. In an even more natural, less obtrusive way, Spragens argues, one can draw from post-Wittgensteinian ideas about language and understand speech as a common commitment to certain rules employed in an effort at mutual understanding. The upshot of both lines of thought, he believes, is that people are indisputably capable of reasoned behavior in pursuit of a common end, and these insights can

[55] Spragens, *Irony of Liberal Reason*, 93–109.

underscore a new way of conceiving the political sphere that recognizes modern sensibilities and still recovers the original liberal commitment to practical reason.[56]

Conceived thus, a renewed commitment to a politics of the good in no way implies the revival of an embedded elite responsible for dictating truth to the rest of society. Quite the contrary, Spragens assures us. Only interested citizens willing to partake in acts of "collective judgment" through revived forums of public debate can define the common good. State action, furthermore, which has been the vehicle for technocratic control in the twentieth century, must only take the form of "general imperatives" precisely because the power to shape community will lie in the hands of citizens. Spragens helps make clearer what Lowi meant by juridical democracy: the state should remain the disinterested center of law (and therefore compulsion) while citizens debate the course and needs of their society under its general rules. Liberal reason thus comes down to a substantive and democratic ideal: "The human good is the rationally desirable flourishing of human life. Because we can effectively deploy our cognitive powers both to illuminate the nature of human wants and needs and to understand the circumstances within which these wants and needs must be pursued, it makes sense to say that the human good is at least to some degree knowable. Moreover, since we are . . . animals destined to live in association with our fellows, there will be elements of commonality in what is rationally desirable for the individual members of any given society."[57]

In a revivified public sphere where what people think actually matters, it is not inconceivable that citizens would choose to reestablish the common-law definition of the corporation, restrain capital flight, put limits on technological displacement, insist on measuring environmental costs against the benefits of new products, or in a hundred other ways restrict property rights by insisting that the common good comes first. It is not inconceivable that in a world where what they think matters, citizens can reach some understanding about how society's benefits can be distributed with justice. It is not inconceivable that citizens in such an environment might even commit the greatest of all heresies against contempory liberalism and devise a means of keeping pornography a purely private matter, and accomplish that restraint without recourse to the censor.

[56] Ibid., 93–97, 103–8, 112, 119.
[57] Ibid., 168, 196–97, 185–86.

To create such an environment, we should not return to Wilson, or Lippmann, or Lowi, but to John Dewey, whose understanding of reason exalted the scientific method of critical thought of which, he believed, people were universally capable. In its rich association with the activities of work and play, Dewey's conception of reason relates as much to common sense as to the common good, as much to daily life as to high politics, and as much to decency as to debate. Reason as common sense finds political resources in the most immediate circumstances of people's lives, and thus provides them a way to undercut the elitist inclinations of both idealists and realists. Reason as critical thought, meanwhile, not only disabuses people of dogma, as Dewey always insisted, but protects them from unleashed technology by allowing them to know scientific pretentiousness when they see it. And reason as basic decency implies that we are all obliged to accept the good faith and the reasonableness of our fellow citizens. In the last days of a miserable century, Dewey's conception of the good society stands out as the best we can do, and we ought to have enough faith in ourselves to manage that much.

Bibliography

Primary Sources

Manuscripts

Hamilton Fish Armstrong Papers. Mudd Library, Princeton University, Princeton, New Jersey.
Newton D. Baker Papers. Library of Congress, Washington, D.C.
Adolf A. Berle Papers. Franklin D. Roosevelt Library, Hyde Park, New York.
Raymond Leslie Buell Papers. Library of Congress, Washington, D.C.
Norman H. Davis Papers. Library of Congress, Washington, D.C.
Abraham Flexner Papers. Library of Congress, Washington, D.C.
Raymond Blaine Fosdick Papers. Mudd Library, Princeton University, Princeton, New Jersey.
Harry Augustus Garfield Papers. Library of Congress, Washington, D.C.
Huntington Gilchrist Papers. Library of Congress, Washington, D.C.
Hapgood-Reynolds Family Papers. Library of Congress, Washington, D.C.
Warren G. Harding Papers. Ohio Historical Society, Columbus, Ohio.
David Starr Jordan Papers (microfilm). Stanford University Library.
Walter Lippmann Papers. Sterling Memorial Library, Yale University, New Haven, Connecticut.
Theodore Marburg Papers. Library of Congress, Washington, D.C.
Franklin Delano Roosevelt Papers. Franklin D. Roosevelt Library, Hyde Park, New York.
Elihu Root Papers. Library of Congress, Washington, D.C.
Francis Sayre Papers. Library of Congress, Washington, D.C.
Arthur Sweetser Papers. Library of Congress, Washington, D.C.
William Howard Taft Papers. Library of Congress, Washington, D.C.
Henry A. Wallace Correspondence (microfilm). University of Iowa Library.
Henry A. Wallace Papers. Franklin D. Roosevelt Library, Hyde Park, New York.

Books

Adorno, Theodor, et al. *The Authoritarian Personality*. New York: Harper & Row, 1950.

Armstrong, Hamilton Fish. *Peace and Counterpeace from Wilson to Hitler: Memoirs of Hamilton Fish Armstrong*. New York: Harper & Row, 1971.

——. *We or They: The World in Conflict*. New York: Macmillan, 1937.

——. *When There is No Peace*. New York: Macmillan, 1939.

Arendt, Hannah. *The Origins of Totalitarianism*. 1951; New York: Harcourt Brace Jovanovich, 1973.

Baker, Newton D. *Frontiers of Freedom*. New York: George Doran, 1918.

——. *Why America Went to War*. New York: Harper, 1936.

Baker, Ray Stannard. *Woodrow Wilson and World Settlement*, 3 vols. Garden City, N.Y.: Doubleday, 1922.

Ball, George W. *The Past Has Another Pattern*. New York: Norton, 1982.

Beard, Charles, and G. H. E. Smith. *The Future Comes*. New York: Macmillan, 1933.

——. *The Old Deal and the New*. New York: Macmillan, 1940.

——. *The Open Door at Home*. 1934; New York: Macmillan, 1935.

Bell, Daniel, ed. *The Radical Right*. Garden City, N.Y.: Doubleday, 1964.

Bonsal, Stephan. *Suitors and Supplicants: The Little Nations at Versailles*. New York: Prentice-Hall, 1946.

Bourne, Randolph. *War and the Intellectuals: Collected Essays, 1915–1919*, ed. Carl Resek. New York: Harper and Row, 1964.

Buell, Raymond Leslie. *Death by Tariff*. Chicago: University of Chicago, Public Policy Pamphlet, No. 27, 1939.

——. *The Hull Trade Program and the American System*. New York: World Affairs Pamphlet, No. 2, April 1938.

——. *International Cooperation*. Columbus, Ohio: Educational Printing House, 1933, Modern Problems Pamphlet, No. 16.

——. *International Relations*. New York: Henry Holt, 1925.

——. *Isolated America*. New York: Knopf, 1940.

——. *The Native Problem in Africa*, 2 vols. New York: Macmillan, 1928.

——. *The Washington Conference*. New York: Appleton, 1922.

——. *The World Adrift*. Boston and New York: Foreign Policy Association and World Peace Foundation, Public Policy Pamphlet, No. 1, 1933.

Bunce, Arthur. *Economic Nationalism and the Farmer*. Ames, Iowa: Collegiate Press, 1938.

Butler, Nicholas Murray. *Between Two Worlds*. New York: Scribner's, 1934.

——. *The Faith of a Liberal*. New York: Scribner's, 1924.

——. *The Family of Nations*. New York: Scribner's, 1938.

——. *Is America Worth Saving? Addresses on National Problems and Party Policies*. New York: Scribner's, 1920.

——. *Scholarship and Service*. New York: Scribner's, 1924.

——. *True and False Democracy*. New York: Scribner's, 1915.

———. *Why Should We Change Our Form of Government?* New York: Scribner's, 1912.

———. *A World in Ferment: Interpretations of the War for a New World.* New York: Scribner's, 1917

Chase, Stuart. *The Economy of Abundance.* New York: Macmillan, 1934.

———. *A New Deal.* New York: Macmillan, 1932.

———. *The New Western Front.* New York: Harcourt Brace, 1939.

Clarke, John H. *America and World Peace.* New York: Henry Holt, 1925.

"Cosmos." *The Basis of a Durable Peace.* New York: Scribner's, 1917.

Croly, Herbert. *The Promise of American Life.* New York: Macmillan, 1909; Indianapolis: Bobbs-Merrill, 1975.

Culbertson, William Smith. *International Economic Policies: A Survey of the Economics of Diplomacy.* New York: D. Appleton, 1925.

———. *Reciprocity.* New York: Whittlesey, 1937.

Dahl, Robert. *Who Governs? Democracy and Power in an American City.* New Haven: Yale University Press, 1960.

Davis, Harriet Eager, ed. *Pioneers in World Order: An American Appraisal of the League of Nations.* New York: Columbia University Press, 1944.

Dean, Vera Micheles. *The United States and Russia.* Cambridge: Harvard University Press, 1948.

Dean, Vera Micheles, Bailey W. Diffie, Malbone W. Graham, and Mildred S. Wertheimer. *New Governments in Europe.* New York: Thomas Nelson and Sons, 1934.

Dennis, Laurence. *Is Capitalism Doomed?* New York: Harper, 1932.

Dewey, John. *German Philosophy and Politics.* New York: Henry Holt, 1915.

———. *Individualism Old and New.* 1930; New York: Capricorn, 1962.

———. *The Public and Its Problems.* New York: Henry Holt, 1927.

———. *The Quest for Certainty.* London: George Allen & Unwin, 1930.

Donaldson, John. *International Economic Relations: World Economy and World Politics.* New York: Longmans, Green, 1928.

Donham, Wallace Brett. *Business Adrift.* New York: Whittlesey, 1931.

Douglas, Lewis. *The Liberal Tradition: A Free People and a Free Economy.* New York: D. Van Nostrand, 1935.

Eichelberger, Clark. *Organizing for Peace.* New York: Harper & Row, 1977.

Fenwick, Charles G. *International Law.* 1924; New York: Appleton, 1934.

Fisher, Irving. *America's Interest in World Peace.* New York: Funk & Wagnalls, 1924.

Fosdick, Raymond B. *Chronicle of a Generation.* New York: Harper, 1956.

———. *Letters on the League of Nations,* ed. Arthur S. Link. Princeton: Princeton University Press, 1966.

———. *The Old Savage in the New Civilization.* New York: Doubleday, Doran, 1929.

———. *Within Our Power.* New York: Longmans, Green, 1952.

Frank, Jerome. *Save America First.* New York: Harper, 1937.

Fukuyama, Francis. *The End of History and the Last Man.* New York: Free Press, 1992.

Fulbright, J. William. *The Arrogance of Power.* New York: Vintage, 1965.

Galbraith, John Kenneth. *American Capitalism: The Theory of Countervailing Power.* Boston: Houghton Mifflin, 1951.

——. *Annals of an Abiding Liberal,* ed. Andrea D. Williams. Boston: Houghton Mifflin, 1979.

——. *A Life in Our Times: A Memoir.* Boston: Houghton Mifflin, 1981.

Gideonse, Harry. *War Debts.* Chicago: University of Chicago, Public Policy Pamphlet, No. 4, 1933.

Glazer, Nathan, and Daniel Patrick Moynihan. *Beyond the Melting Pot: The Negroes, Puerto Ricans, Jews, Italians, and Irish of New York City.* Cambridge: M.I.T. Press, 1963, 1970.

Goldsmith, Robert. *A League to Enforce Peace.* New York: Macmillan, 1917.

Hansen, Alvin. *Economic Stabilization in an Unbalanced World.* New York: Harcourt Brace, 1932.

——. *Full Recovery or Stagnation?* New York: Norton, 1938.

Hill, Helen. *Foreign Trade and the Worker's Job.* Boston and New York: World Peace Foundation, Popular Pamphlets on World Problems, No. 1, January 1935.

Hobson, J. A. *Imperialism: A Study.* New York: J. Potts, 1902.

Howe, Frederic Clemson. *The Only Possible Peace.* New York: Scribner's, 1918.

——. *Privilege and Democracy in America.* New York: Scribner's, 1910.

——. *Why War?* New York: Scribner's, 1917; Seattle: University of Washington Press, 1970.

Hudson, Manley O. *Current International Co-Operation.* Calcutta: Calcutta University Press, 1927.

Hull, Cordell. *The Memoirs of Cordell Hull.* New York: Macmillan, 1948.

——. *The Restoration of International Trade.* Washington, D.C.: Government Printing Office, 1935.

Jordan, David Starr. *Ways to Lasting Peace.* Indianapolis: Bobbs-Merrill, 1916.

Kallen, Horace. *The League of Nations.* Boston: Marshall Jones, 1918.

——. *The Structure of Lasting Peace.* Boston: Marshall Jones, 1918.

Kornhauser, William. *The Politics of Mass Society.* New York: Free Press, 1959.

Laski, Harold. *Studies in the Problem of Sovereignty.* New Haven: Yale University Press, 1917.

League to Enforce Peace. *Enforced Peace: Proceedings of the First Annual National Assemblage of the League to Enforce Peace.* New York: League to Enforce Peace, 1916.

——. *Win the War for Permanent Peace: Addresses at the National Convention of the League to Enforce Peace, in the City of Philadelphia, May 16th and 17th, 1918.* New York: League to Enforce Peace, 1918.

Lippmann, Walter. *American Inquisitors.* New York: Macmillan, 1928.

——. *The Cold War.* Boston: Little, Brown, 1947.

——. *Drift and Mastery.* New York: Mitchell Kennerly, 1914.

——. *An Inquiry into the Principles of the Good Society.* Boston: Little, Brown, 1937, 1938.

——. *Method of Freedom.* New York: Macmillan, 1934.

——. *The Phantom Public.* New York: Macmillan, 1925.

——. *A Preface To Morals.* New York: Macmillan, 1929.

——. *Public Opinion.* New York: Harcourt Brace, 1922.

——. *Public Philosopher: Selected Letters of Walter Lippmann,* ed. John Morton Blum. New York: Ticknor & Fields, 1985.

——. *The Public Philosophy.* Boston: Little, Brown, 1955.

——. *The Stakes of Diplomacy.* New York: Henry Holt, 1915.

——. *U.S. Foreign Policy: Shield of the Republic.* Boston: Little, Brown, 1943.

——. *U.S. War Aims.* Boston: Little, Brown, 1944.

Lipset, Seymour Martin. *Political Man: The Social Bases of Politics.* Garden City, N.Y.: Doubleday, 1959.

——, and Earl Raab. *The Politics of Unreason: Right-Wing Extremism in America, 1790–1970.* Chicago: University of Chicago Press, 1978.

Lowell, A. Lawrence. *Public Opinion and Popular Government.* New York: Longmans, Green, 1913.

Lowi, Theodore J. *At the Pleasure of the Mayor: Patronage and Power in New York City, 1898–1958.* New York: Macmillan, 1964.

——. *The End of Liberalism: The Second Republic of the United States.* New York: Norton, 1979.

——. *The Politics of Disorder.* New York: Basic Books, 1971.

Mantoux, Paul, et al. *The World Crisis.* New York: Longmans, Green, 1938.

Marburg, Theodore. *The League of Nations,* 2 vols. New York: Macmillan, 1917.

Miller, David Hunter. *The Drafting of the Covenant,* 2 vols. New York: 1928.

Morgenthau, Hans. *Politics among Nations,* 3d ed. New York: Knopf, 1960.

——. *Scientific Man vs. Power Politics.* Chicago: University of Chicago Press, 1946.

Moynihan, Daniel Patrick. *Came the Revolution: Argument in the Reagan Era.* New York: Harcourt Brace Jovanovich, 1988.

——. *Counting Our Blessings.* Boston: Little, Brown, 1980.

——. *A Dangerous Place.* Boston: Little, Brown, 1978.

——. *On the Law of Nations.* Cambridge: Harvard University Press, 1990.

Mumford, Lewis. *Men Must Act.* New York: Harcourt Brace, 1939.

Myers, Denis P. *Handbook of the League of Nations Since 1920.* Boston: World Peace Foundation, 1930.

Niebuhr, Reinhold. *The Children of Light and the Children of Darkness.* New York: Charles Scribner, 1944.

Patterson, Ernest Minor. *The Economic Bases of Peace.* New York: Whittlesey, 1939.

——. *The World's Economic Dilemma.* New York: Whittlesey House, 1930.

Patterson, Orlando. *Ethnic Chauvinism: The Reactionary Impulse.* New York: Stein and Day, 1977.

Peek, George N., and Samuel Crowther. *Why Quit Our Own?* New York: D. Van Nostrand, 1936.

Rainwater, Lee, and William L. Yancey, eds. *The Moynihan Report and the Politics of Controversy.* Cambridge: M.I.T. Press, 1967.

Redfield, William C. *Dependent America.* Boston: Houghton Mifflin, 1926.

Root, Elihu. *Addresses on International Subjects,* ed. Robert Bacon and James Brown Scott. Cambridge: Harvard University Press, 1916.

——. *Experiments in Government and the Essentials of the Constitution.* Princeton: Princeton University Press, 1913.

——. *Men and Policies.* Ed. Robert Bacon and James Brown Scott. Cambridge: Harvard University, 1925.

Rorty, Richard. *Contingency, Irony, and Solidarity.* New York: Cambridge University Press, 1989.

——. *Objectivity, Relativism, and Truth: Philosophical Papers,* vol. 1: New York, Cambridge University Press, 1991.

Sayre, Francis. *America Must Act.* Boston: World Peace Foundation, World Affairs Pamphlet No. 13, 1936.

——. *Glad Adventure.* New York: Macmillan, 1957.

Schlesinger, Arthur M., Jr. *The Vital Center: The Politics of Freedom.* Boston: Houghton Mifflin, 1949.

Scott, James Brown. *James Madison's Notes of Debates in the Federal Convention of 1787 and Their Relation to a More Perfect Society of Nations.* New York: Macmillan, 1918.

Seymour, Charles. *Letters from the Paris Peace Conference,* ed. Harold B. Whiteman, Jr. New Haven: Yale University Press, 1965.

Shotwell, James T. *The Autobiography of James T. Shotwell.* Indianapolis: Bobbs-Merrill, 1961.

——. *The Great Decision.* New York: Macmillan, 1944.

——. *On the Rim of the Abyss.* New York: Macmillan, 1936.

——. *What Germany Forgot.* New York: Macmillan, 1940.

Smith, James Gerald. *Economic Planning and the Tariff: An Essay in Social Philosophy.* Princeton: Princeton University Press, 1934.

Soule, George. *The Coming American Revolution.* New York: Macmillan, 1934.

——. *A Planned Society.* New York: Macmillan, 1933.

Spragens, Thomas A., Jr. *The Irony of Liberal Reason.* Chicago: University of Chicago Press, 1981.

——. *Reason and Democracy.* Durham: Duke University Press, 1990.

Stevenson, Adlai. *An Ethic for Survival,* ed. Michael Prosser. New York: William Morrow, 1969.

——. *Looking Outward: Years of Crisis at the United Nations,* ed. Robert L. Schiffer and Selma Schiffer. New York: Harper & Row, 1963.

——. *New America,* ed. Seymour Harris and Arthur Schlesinger, Jr. London: Rupert Hart-Davis, 1957.

——. *What I Think.* New York: Harper & Row, 1956.

Stimson, Henry L., and McGeorge Bundy. *Democracy and Nationalism in Europe.* Princeton: Princeton University Press, 1934.

——. *On Active Service in Peace and War.* 1947; New York: Harper, 1948.

Streit, Clarence K. *Union Now.* New York: Harper, 1940.

Summers, Robert E., ed. *Dumbarton Oaks.* New York: H. W. Wilson, 1945.

Sweetser, Arthur. *The First Ten Years of the League of Nations.* New York: Carnegie Endowment for International Peace, 1930.

——. *The League of Nations at Work.* New York: Macmillan, 1920.

——. *The League of Nations in World Politics.* Washington, D.C.: American Council on Public Affairs, 1941.

——. *The Practical Workings of the League of Nations.* New York: Carnegie Endowment for International Peace, 1929.

——. *What the League of Nations Has Accomplished.* New York: League of Nations Non-Partisan Association, 1924.

Taft, William Howard. *America Can't Quit.* New York: League to Enforce Peace, 1919.

——. *Taft Papers on the League of Nations,* ed. Theodore Marburg and Horace Flack. New York: Macmillan, 1920.

Taft, William Howard, and William Jennings Bryan. *World Peace: A Written Debate between William Howard Taft and William Jennings Bryan.* New York: George H. Doran, 1917.

Taussig, F. W., *Free Trade, the Tariff, and Reciprocity.* New York: Macmillan, 1920.

Tippett, Charles. *Autarchy: National Self-Sufficiency.* Chicago: University of Chicago Press, Public Policy Pamphlet, No. 5, 1934.

Veblen, Thorstein. *An Inquiry into the Nature of the Peace and the Terms of Its Perpetuation.* New York: Macmillan, 1917.

Wallace, Henry A. *America Must Choose.* New York: Council on Foreign Relations, 1934.

——. *New Frontiers.* New York: Reynal & Hitchcock, 1934.

Warburg, James. *Faith, Purpose, and Power.* New York: Farrar & Straus, 1950.

——. *Foreign Policy Begins at Home.* New York: Harcourt Brace, 1944.

——. *Germany—Bridge or Battleground?* New York: Harcourt Brace, 1947.

——. *Hell Bent for Election.* New York: Doubleday, Doran, 1936.

——. *How to Co-Exist without Playing the Kremlin's Game.* Boston: Beacon, 1952.

——. *It's Up to Us.* New York: Knopf, 1934.

——. *Last Call for Common Sense.* New York: Harcourt Brace, 1949.

——. *Our War, Our Peace.* New York: Farrar & Straus, 1941.

——. *Peace in Our Time?* New York: Harper's, 1940.

——. *Put Yourself in Marshall's Place.* New York: Simon & Schuster, 1948.

——. *Still Hell Bent.* New York: Doubleday, Doran, 1936.

——. *Unwritten Treaty.* New York: Harcourt Brace, 1945.

——. *Victory without War.* New York: Farrar & Straus, 1951.

Welles, Sumner. *Time for Decision.* New York: Harper, 1944.

——. *Where Are We Heading?* New York: Harper, 1946.

Weyl, Walter. *American World Policies.* New York: Macmillan, 1917.

——. *The End of the War.* New York: Macmillan, 1918.

——. *The New Democracy.* New York: Macmillan, 1912.

Whitton, John B., ed. *The Second Chance: America and the Peace*. Princeton: Princeton University Press, 1944.
Wilson, Woodrow. *Division and Reunion*. New York: Longman, Green, 1894.
———. *The Papers of Woodrow Wilson*, ed. Arthur Link et al. Princeton: Princeton University Press, 1966–.
Young, John Parke. *The International Economy*. New York: The Ronald Press, 1942.

Articles

Baker, Newton D. "Beyond the Bread Lines." *Saturday Evening Post,* 17 December 1932, 21.
———. "Can Uncle Sam Do Our Good Neighboring?" *Saturday Evening Post,* 13 October 1934, 23.
———. "The Decay of Self-Reliance." *Atlantic Monthly* 154 (December 1934): 726–33.
———. "The Good Society for the Future." *Atlantic Monthly* 160 (November 1937): 612–16.
———. "Human Factors in a Depression." *New Outlook* 161 (November 1932): 19–20.
———. "Is Economic Planning Possible?" *Review of Reviews* 84 (September 1931): 57–59.
Beard, Charles. "National Politics and War." *Scribner's Magazine* 97 (February 1935): 65–70.
Buell, Raymond. "The Crux of the Situation." *The Weekly Review,* 10 September 1921, 229–31.
———. "The Development of Anti-Japanese Agitation in the United States." *Political Science Quarterly* 37 (December 1922): 605–38, and 38 (March 1923): 57–81.
———. "Toward Peace or War." *Forum* 85 (March 1931): 153–59.
Chittenden, H. M. "Questions for Pacifists." *Atlantic Monthly* 116 (August 1915): 158–69.
Dean, Vera Micheles. "The San Francisco Conference." *Foreign Policy Reports* 21 (July 1945): 110–25.
Dewey, John. "On Understanding the Mind of Germany." *Atlantic Monthly* 117 (February 1916): 251–62.
Eichelberger, Clark. "Dumbarton Oaks." *National Education Association Journal* 34 (March 1945): 65.
———. "Forth—To Peace." *American Scholar* 8 (Winter 1938–1939): 120–22.
———. "The Pact and the U.N." *Nation,* 19 March 1949, 329–31.
———. "Plans for World Security." *Virginia Quarterly Review* 20 (Autumn 1944): 591–99.
———. "Prefabricating the Peace." *Survey Graphic* 33 (September 1944): 373–75.
———. "A Society of Nations as Wide as Possible." *Rotarian* 61 (October 1942): 12, 57.

Eliot, Charles W. "National Efficiency Best Developed under Free Governments." *Atlantic Monthly* 115 (April 1915): 433–41.

Elliott, William Y. "This Economic Nationalism." *Atlantic Monthly* 152 (October 1933): 424–34.

———. "A Time for Peace?" *Virginia Quarterly Review* 22 (Spring 1946): 167–78.

Fosdick, Raymond B. "Mr. Gerard's Dream." *Scientific American* 151 (November, 1934): 246–47.

———. "One World or None," *New York Times Magazine*, 2 September 1945, 8, 35–36.

———. "Our Foreign Policy in a Looking Glass." *Atlantic Monthly* 148 (August 1931): 137–48.

———. "Our Last Chance: At San Francisco," *New York Times Magazine*, 22 April 1945, 8, 41.

———. "We Failed in 1919—Shall We Fail Again?" *New York Times Magazine*, 2 July 1944, 14, 42.

Fulbright, J. William. "The Cold War: Its Effect on American Life." *Vital Speeches*, 1 May 1964, 423–24.

———. "Evaluation of Our Society." *Vital Speeches*, 15 June 1963, 520–22.

———. "Old Myths and New Realities." *Vital Speeches*, 15 April 1964, 388–94.

———. "The Outlook for Peace." *Vital Speeches*, 1 April 1946, 358–61.

———. "Recent Events and Continuing Problems." *Vital Speeches*, 1 August 1961, 617.

Gauss, Christian. "Can America Live Alone?" *Scribner's Magazine* 94 (August 1933): 71–77.

———. "The End of Nationalism." *Scribner's Magazine* 93 (May 1933): 266–71.

———. "Recovery—A Longer View." *Scribner's Magazine* 92 (December 1932): 333–37.

Hart, Albert Bushnell. "A New Plan for an International Arcadia." *Current History* 30 (July 1929): 673–77.

Jordan, David Starr. "Unrest and Progress." *Independent*, 8 August 1912, 310–14.

Kallen, Horace. "Democracy vs. the Melting Pot: Part One." *Nation*, 18 February 1915, 190–94.

———. "Democracy vs. the Melting Pot: Part Two." *Nation*, 25 February 1915, 217–20.

Kempton, Murray. "Stevenson: The Saddest Story." *Spectator*, 23 July 1965, 100.

Keynes, John Maynard. "National Self-Sufficiency." *Yale Review* 22 (June 1934): 755–69.

Lippmann, Walter. "After Geneva: The Defense of the Peace." *Yale Review* 28 (June 1938): 649–63.

———. "The Setting for John W. Davis." *Atlantic Monthly* 134 (October 1924): 530–35.

———. "A Year of Peacemaking." *Atlantic Monthly* 178 (December 1946): 35–40.

Lovett, Robert Morss. "Newton D. Baker: The Candide of Candidates." *New Republic*, 18 May 1932, 8–11.

Lowell, A. Lawrence. "A League to Enforce Peace." *Atlantic Monthly* 116 (September 1915): 392–400.

Lowi, Theodore J. "Decision Making vs. Policy Making: Toward an Antidote for Technocracy." *Public Administration Review* 30 (May/June 1970): 314–25.

Mead, George H. "The Psychological Basis of Internationalism." *Survey*, 6 March 1915, 604–7.

Moynihan, Daniel Patrick. "The Democrats, Kennedy, & the Murder of Dr. King." *Commentary* 45 (May 1968): 15–29.

———. "A Diplomat's Rhetoric." *Harper's* 252 (January 1976): 40–43.

———. "Joining the Jackals." *Commentary* 71 (February 1981): 23–31.

———. "The Liberals' Dilemma." *New Republic*, 22 January 1977, 57–60.

———. "The New Racialism." *Atlantic* 222 (August 1968): 35–40.

———. "Party and International Politics." *Commentary* 63 (February 1977): 55–59.

———. "The Politics of Human Rights." *Commentary* 64 (August 1977): 19–26.

———. "The Professors and the Poor." *Commentary* 46 (August 1968): 19–28.

———. "The United States in Opposition." *Commentary* 59 (March 1975): 31–45.

Muste, A. J. "Forth—To War?" *American Scholar* 7 (August 1938): 387–402.

Niebuhr, Reinhold. "Is This Peace in Our Time?" *Nation*, 7 April 1945, 382–84.

Patten, Simon. "Economic Zones and the New Alignments of the National Sentiments." *Survey*, 6 March 1915, 612–13.

Patterson, Ernest Minor. "American Cooperation in International Affairs." *Contemporary Review* 140 (October 1931): 438–45.

———. "An Approach to World Economics." *American Economic Review* 21 (March 1931), supplement, 142–49.

Perry, Ralph Barton. "What Is Worth Fighting For?" *Atlantic Monthly* 116 (December 1915): supplement, 142–49.

Potter, Pitman B. "Universalism versus Regionalism in International Organization." *American Political Science Review* 37 (October 1943): 850–62.

Root, Elihu. "Tampering with the Constitution." *Independent*, 9 March 1911, 497–501.

Shotwell, James T. "Disarmament Alone Is No Guarantee of World Peace." *Current History* 30 (September 1920): 1024–29.

———. "The Movement to Renounce War as a Diplomatic Weapon." *Current History* 27 (October 1927): 62–64.

———. "Setting the Pattern for Peace." *Rotarian* 63 (August 1943): 8–10.

———. "The Slogan of Outlawry." *Century* 116 (October 1928): 713–20.

Stevenson, Adlai. "America under Pressure." *Harper's* 223 (August 1961): 21–24.

———. "The Hard Kind of Patriotism." *Harper's* 227 (July 1963): 33–34.

———. "Shall the United Nations Survive?" *Vital Speeches*, 15 March 1961, 323–24.

——. "The United States and China." *Vital Speeches,* 1 January 1962, 167–70.
Stimson, Henry. "The Basis of Military Training." *Scribner's Magazine* 61 (April 1917): 408–12.
Taussig, F. W. "Wanted, Consumers." *Yale Review* 23 (March 1934): 433–37.
Villard, Oswald G. "The Shamelessness of Newton D. Baker." *Nation,* 4 July 1934, 7.
Wallace, Henry A. "America—Recluse or Trader?" *Collier's,* 6 February 1935, 7–8.
——. "Spiritual Forces and the State." *Forum* 91 (June 1934): 352–56.
——. "The Tyranny of Greed." *Collier's,* 6 October 1934, 7–8.
——. "We Are More than Economic Men." *Scribner's,* 6 December 1934, 321–26.
Warburg, James. "An Alternative Proposal." *Nation,* 19 March 1949, 331–33.
——. "America Has Not Yet Chosen." *Vital Speeches,* 22 November 1934, 45–48.
Welles, Sumner. "The Atomic Bomb and World Government." *Atlantic Monthly* 177 (January 1946): 39–42.
——. "The Vision of a World at Peace." *Virginia Quarterly Review* 21 (Autumn 1945): 481–96.
White, William Allen. "Unity and American Leadership." *Yale Review* 32 (September 1942): 1–17.
Wickersham, George W. "Making the Pact of Paris Real." *Century* 118 (June 1929): 141–47.
Wood, Leonard. "Heat Up the Melting Pot." *Independent,* 3 July 1916, 15.

Secondary Sources

Adler, Les, and Thomas Paterson. "Red Fascism: The Merger of Nazi Germany and Soviet Russia in the American Image of Totalitarianism, 1930s–1950." *American Historical Review* 75 (April 1970): 1046–64.
Adler, Selig. *The Isolationist Impulse: Its Twentieth-Century Reaction.* New York: Free Press, 1957.
Alperovitz, Gar. *Atomic Diplomacy: The Use of the Atomic Bomb and the American Confrontation with Soviet Power.* New York: Vintage, 1965.
Ambrosius, Lloyd. *Woodrow Wilson and the American Diplomatic Tradition.* Cambridge: Cambridge University Press, 1986.
Bailey, Thomas. *Woodrow Wilson and the Great Betrayal.* 1944; Chicago: Quadrangle, 1963.
Barnes, Fred. "Back to Liberalism," *New Republic,* 11 October 1982, 15–16.
——. "Pat Moynihan, Neoliberal." *New Republic,* 21 October 1981, 15–18.
Bartlett, Ruhl. *The League to Enforce Peace.* Chapel Hill: University of North Carolina Press, 1944.
Bendiner, Elmer. *A Time for Angels: The Tragicomic History of the League of Nations.* New York: Knopf, 1975.

Berman, William C. *William Fulbright and the Vietnam War: The Dissent of a Political Realist*. Kent, Ohio: Kent State University Press, 1988.

Bernstein, Barton. "The Quest for National Security: American Foreign Policy and International Control of Atomic Energy, 1942–1946." *Journal of American History* 60 (March 1974): 1003–44.

Birdsall, Paul. *Versailles Twenty Years After*. New York: Reynal & Hitchcock, 1941.

Blau, Joseph, ed. *Social Theories of Jacksonian Democracy*. New York: Hofner, 1947.

Bledstein, Barton. *The Culture of Professionalism: The Middle Class and the Transformation of Higher Education in America*. New York: Norton, 1976.

Bloomsfield, Arthur I. "Adam Smith and the Theory of International Trade." In *Essays on Adam Smith*, ed. Andrew Skinner and Thomas Wilson, 466–74. Oxford: Clarendon Press, 1975.

Blum, D. Steven. *Walter Lippmann: Cosmopolitanism in the Century of Total War*. Ithaca: Cornell University Press, 1984.

Borg, Dorothy. *The United States and the Far Eastern Crisis of 1933–1938*. Cambridge: Harvard University Press, 1964.

Brick, Howard. *Daniel Bell and the End of Ideology*. Madison: University of Wisconsin Press, 1986.

Brown, Eugene. *J. William Fulbright: Advice and Dissent*. Iowa City: Iowa State University Press, 1985.

Brown, Thomas. *Politics and Statesmanship: Essays on the American Whig Party*. New York: Columbia University Press, 1985.

Burner, David. *The Politics of Provincialism: The Democratic Party in Transition, 1918–1932*. New York: Norton, 1967.

Chatfield, Charles. *For Peace and Justice: Pacifism in America, 1914–1941*. Knoxville: University of Tennessee Press, 1971.

Coffin, Tristram. *Senator Fulbright: Portrait of a Public Philosopher*. New York: E. P. Dutton, 1966.

Cole, Wayne S. *Roosevelt and the Isolationists, 1932–45*. Lincoln: University of Nebraska Press, 1983.

Collini, Stefan. *Liberalism and Sociology: L. T. Hobhouse and Political Argument in England, 1880–1914*. Cambridge: Cambridge University Press, 1979.

Cooper, John Milton. *The Warrior and the Priest: Woodrow Wilson and Theodore Roosevelt*. Cambridge: Cambridge University Press, 1983.

Craig, Gordon. *Germany, 1866–1945*. New York: Oxford University Press, 1978.

Cramer, C. H. *Newton D. Baker: A Biography*. Cleveland: World, 1961.

Cyr, Arthur. *Liberal Party Politics in Britain*. New Brunswick, N.J.: Transaction, 1977.

Dallek, Robert. *Franklin D. Roosevelt and American Foreign Policy, 1932–1945*. New York: Oxford University Press, 1979.

Dangerfield, George. *The Strange Death of Liberal England*. New York: Smith & Haas, 1935; Capricorn, 1961.

DeBenedetti, Charles. *The Peace Movement in American History.* Bloomington: Indiana University Press, 1980.

Divine, Robert A. *The Illusion of Neutrality.* Chicago: University of Chicago Press, 1962.

———. *Second Chance: The Triumph of Internationalism in America during World War II.* New York: Atheneum, 1967.

Dorfman, Joseph. "The Role of the German Historical School in American Economic Thought." *American Economic Review* 45 (May 1955): 17–28.

Douglas, Roy. *The History of the Liberal Party, 1895–1970.* London: Sidgwick & Jackson, 1971.

Downing, Lyle, and Robert B. Thigpen. "A Liberal Dilemma: The Application of Unger's Critique of Formalism to Lowi's Concept of Juridical Democracy." *Journal of Politics* 44 (February 1982): 230–246.

Dubin, Martin David. "The Carnegie Endowment for International Peace and the Advocacy of the League of Nations, 1914–1918." *Proceedings of the American Philosophical Society* 123 (December 1979): 344–68.

Duff, John B. "The Versailles Treaty and the Irish-Americans." *Journal of American History* 55 (December 1968): 582–98.

Eksteins, Modris. *Rites of Spring: The Great War and the Birth of the Modern Age.* Boston: Houghton Mifflin, 1989.

Elcock, Howard. *Portrait of a Decision: The Council of Four and the Treaty of Versailles.* London: Eyre Methuen, 1972.

Ellis, L. Ethan. *Frank B. Kellogg and American Foreign Policy, 1925–1929.* New Brunswick, N.J.: Rutgers University Press, 1961.

———. *Republican Foreign Policy, 1921–1933.* New Brunswick, N.J.: Rutgers University Press, 1969.

Epstein, Joseph. "Adlai Stevenson in Retrospect." *Commentary* 46 (December 1968): 71–83.

Fitzgerald, Frances. "The Warrior Intellectuals." *Harper's* 252 (May 1976): 47–54.

Fleming, Denna Frank. *The United States and the World Court.* Garden City, N.Y.: Doubleday, 1945.

Floto, Inga. *Colonel House in Paris: A Study of American Policy at the Paris Peace Conference.* Princeton: Princeton University Press, 1980.

Forcey, Charles. *Crossroads of Liberalism: Croly, Weyl, Lippmann, and the Progressive Era, 1900–25.* New York: Oxford University Press, 1961.

Fowler, W. B. *British-American Relations, 1917–1918: The Role of Sir William Wiseman.* Princeton: Princeton University Press, 1969.

Freeden, Michael. *Liberalism Divided: A Study in British Political Thought, 1914–1939.* Oxford: Clarendon Press, 1986.

Fussell, Paul. *The Great War and Modern Memory.* New York: Oxford University Press, 1975.

Gaddis, John Lewis. *Strategies of Containment: A Critical Appraisal of Postwar American National Security Policy.* New York, Oxford University Press, 1982.

Galambos, Louis. "The Emerging Organizational Synthesis in Modern American History." *Business History Review* 44 (Summer 1970): 279–90.

——. "Technology, Political Economy, and Professionalization." *Business History Review* 57 (Winter 1983): 471–93.

Gardner, Lloyd. *Safe for Democracy: The Anglo-American Response to Revolution, 1913–1923*. New York: Oxford, 1984.

Gershman, Carl. "A Bum Rap." *New Republic*, 10 April 1976, 19.

Gerson, Louis L. *The Hyphenate in Recent American Politics and Diplomacy.* Lawrence: University of Kansas Press, 1964.

Gilbert, Bentley Brinkerhoff. *David Lloyd George, A Political Life: The Architect of Change, 1863–1912*. Columbus: Ohio State University Press, 1987.

Glad, Betty. *Charles Evans Hughes and the Illusion of Innocence*. Urbana: University of Illinois Press, 1966.

Goldman, Ralph M. *Search for Consensus: The Story of the Democratic Party.* Philadelphia: Temple University Press, 1979.

Graham, Otis. *Encore for Reform: The Old Progressives in the New Deal*. New York: Oxford, 1967.

Grampp, William D. *The Manchester School of Economics*. Stanford: Stanford University Press, 1960.

Haber, Samuel. *Efficiency and Uplift: Scientific Management in the Progressive Era, 1890–1920*. Chicago: University of Chicago Press, 1964.

Harbaugh, William. *Lawyer's Lawyer: The Life of John W. Davis*. New York: Oxford University Press, 1973.

Hartz, Louis. *The Liberal Tradition in America*. New York: Harcourt, Brace, 1955.

Haskell, Thomas. *The Emergence of Professional Social Science: The American Social Science Association and the Nineteenth-Century Crisis of Authority*. Urbana: University of Illinois Press, 1977.

Hawley, Ellis. *The Great War and the Search For a Modern Order*. New York: St. Martin's Press, 1981.

Herken, Gregg. *The Winning Weapon: The Atomic Bomb in the Cold War*. New York: Knopf, 1980.

Herman, Sondra. *Eleven against War: Studies in American Internationalist Thought, 1908–1921*. Stanford: Hoover Institution Press, 1969.

Hildebrand, Robert C. *Dumbarton Oaks: The Origins of the United Nations and the Search for Postwar Security*. Chapel Hill: University of North Carolina Press, 1990.

Himmelberg, Robert F. "Business, Antitrust Policy, and the Industrial Board of the Department of Commerce, 1919." *Business History Review* 42 (Spring 1968): 1–23.

——. "The War Industries Board and the Antitrust Question in November 1918." *Journal of American History* 52 (June 1965): 59–74.

Hixson, Walter. *George Kennan: Cold War Iconoclast*. New York: Columbia University Press, 1989.

Hodgson, Godfrey. *The Colonel: The Life and Wars of Henry Stimson, 1867–1950*. New York: Knopf, 1990.

Hoff Wilson, Joan. *American Business and Foreign Policy, 1920–1933.* Lexington: University of Kentucky Press, 1971.

Hofstadter, Richard. *Age of Reform.* New York: Vintage, 1955.

———. *The American Political Tradition and the Men Who Made It.* New York: Knopf, 1948.

Hogan, Michael J. *The Marshall Plan: America, Britain, and the Reconstruction of Western Europe, 1947–1952.* New York: Cambridge University Press, 1987.

Hoogenboom, Ari. *Outlawing the Spoils: A History of the Civil Service Reform Movement, 1865–1883.* Urbana: University of Illinois Press, 1961.

Horwitz, Martin J. *The Transformation of American Law, 1780–1860.* Cambridge: Harvard University Press, 1977.

Howe, Daniel Walker. "The Decline of Calvinism: An Approach to Its Study." *Comparative Studies in Society and History* 14 (1972): 306–27.

———. *The Political Culture of the American Whigs.* Chicago: University of Chicago Press, 1979.

Howe, Irving. *Steady Work.* New York: Harcourt Brace & World, 1966.

Huff, Robert. "Frederic C. Howe: Progressive." Ph.D. dissertation, University of Rochester, 1966.

Josephson, Harold. *James T. Shotwell and the Rise of Internationalism in America.* Cranbury, N.J.: Associated University Presses, 1975.

Kaplan, E. Ann, ed. *Postmodernism and Its Discontents.* London: Verso, 1988.

Katz, Friedrich. *The Secret War in Mexico: Europe, the United States, and the Mexican Revolution.* Chicago: University of Chicago Press, 1981.

Kennan, George. *American Diplomacy.* Chicago: University of Chicago Press, 1951.

———. *Soviet-American Relations.* 2 vols. Princeton: Princeton University Press, 1956.

Kernak, Sterling J. "Woodrow Wilson and National Self-Determination along Italy's Frontier: A Study in the Manipulation of Principles in the Pursuit of Political Interests." *Proceedings of the American Philosophical Society* 126 (1982): 243–300.

Kloppenberg, James. *Uncertain Victory: Social Democracy and Progressivism in European and American Thought, 1870–1920.* New York: Oxford University Press, 1986.

Kuehl, Warren. *Hamilton Holt, Journalist, Internationalist, Educator.* Gainesville: University of Florida Press, 1960.

———. *Seeking World Order: The United States and International Organization to 1920.* Nashville: Vanderbilt University Press, 1969.

LaFeber, Walter. *The New Empire: An Interpretation of American Expansion, 1860–1898.* Ithaca: Cornell University Press, 1963.

Landes, David S. *The Unbound Prometheus: Technological Change and Industrial Development in Western Europe from 1750 to the Present.* Cambridge: Cambridge University Press, 1969.

Langer, William L., and S. Everett Gleason. *The Challenge to Isolation: The World Crisis of 1937–1940 and American Foreign Policy.* 2 vols. Gloucester: Peter Smith, 1970.

Lasch, Christopher. *American Liberals and the Russian Revolution.* New York: Columbia University Press, 1963.

———. *The New Radicalism in America.* New York: Random House, 1965.

Lawson, R. Alan. *The Failure of Independent Liberalism.* New York: G. P. Putnam, 1971.

Lederer, Ivo J. *Yugoslavia at the Paris Peace Conference: A Study in Frontier-making.* New Haven: Yale University Press, 1963.

Lemann, Nicholas. *The Promised Land: The Great Black Migration and How It Changed America.* New York: Knopf, 1991.

Leopold, Richard W. *Elihu Root and the Conservative Tradition.* Boston: Little, Brown, 1954.

Leuchtenberg, William. *Franklin D. Roosevelt and the New Deal, 1932–1940.* New York: Harper & Row, 1963.

Levin, N. Gordon. *Woodrow Wilson and World Politics: America's Response to War and Revolution.* Princeton: Princeton University Press, 1968.

Levy, David. *Herbert Croly of the New Republic: The Life and Thought of an American Progressive.* Princeton: Princeton University Press, 1985.

Link, Arthur. *The Higher Realism of Woodrow Wilson and Other Essays.* Nashville: Vanderbilt University Press, 1971.

———. *Wilson.* 5 vols. Princeton: Princeton University Press, 1947–65.

———. *Woodrow Wilson: Revolution, War, and Peace.* Arlington Heights, Ill.: Harlan-Davidson, 1979.

———, ed. *Woodrow Wilson and a Revolutionary World.* Chapel Hill: University of North Carolina Press, 1982.

Lord, Russell. *The Wallaces of Iowa.* Boston: Houghton Mifflin, 1947.

Lustig, R. Jeffrey. *Corporate Liberalism: The Origins of Modern American Political Theory, 1890–1920.* Berkeley: University of California Press, 1982.

Maddox, Robert J. *William E. Borah and American Foreign Policy.* Baton Rouge: Louisiana State University Press, 1969.

Maizlish, Stephan, and John J. Kushma, eds. *Essays on American Antebellum Politics.* College Station: Texas A & M University Press, 1982.

Marchand, C. Roland. *The American Peace Movement and Social Reform, 1898–1918.* Princeton: Princeton University Press, 1972.

Martin, John Bartlow. *Adlai Stevenson and the World: The Life of Adlai E. Stevenson.* Garden City: Doubleday, 1977.

———. *Adlai Stevenson of Illinois: The Life of Adlai E. Stevenson.* Garden City: Doubleday, 1976.

Matusow, Allen J. *The Unravelling of America: A History of Liberalism in the 1960s.* New York: Harper & Row, 1984.

Mayer, Arno. *The Political Origins of the New Diplomacy, 1917–1918.* New Haven: Yale University Press, 1959.

———. *The Politics and Diplomacy of Peacemaking: Containment and Counterrevolution at Versailles 1918–1919.* New York: Knopf, 1967.

Meyer, Donald B. *The Protestant Search for Political Realism.* Berkeley: University of California Press, 1960.

Morgan, Kenneth O. *The Age of Lloyd George.* New York: Barnes & Noble, 1971.

———. *Consensus and Unity: The Lloyd George Coalition Government, 1918–1922.* Oxford: Clarendon Press, 1979.

Morison, Elting E. *Turmoil and Tradition: A Study in the Life and Times of Henry L. Stimson.* Boston: Houghton Mifflin, 1960.

Mulder, John M. *Woodrow Wilson: The Years of Preparation.* Princeton: Princeton University Press, 1978.

Muller, Herbert J. *Adlai Stevenson: A Study in Values.* New York: Harper & Row, 1967.

Muravchik, Joshua. *The Uncertain Crusade: Jimmy Carter and the Dilemmas of Human Rights Policy.* Lanham, Md.: Hamilton Press, 1986.

Noble, David F. *America by Design: Science, Technology, and the Rise of Corporate Capitalism.* New York: Oxford University Press, 1977.

Nore, Ellen. *Charles A. Beard, An Intellectual Biography.* Carbondale and Edwardsville: Southern Illinois University Press, 1983.

O'Grady, Joseph P. "Irish-Americans, Woodrow Wilson, and Self-Determination." *Records of the American Catholic Historical Society* 74 (1963): 159–73.

Osgood, Robert. *Ideals and Self-Interest in America's Foreign Relations: The Great Transformation of the Twentieth Century.* Chicago: University of Chicago Press, 1953.

Paterson, Thomas G. "Bearing the Burden: A Critical Look at JFK's Foreign Policy." *Virginia Quarterly Review* 54 (Spring 1978): 193–212.

Pells, Richard. *The Liberal Mind in the Conservative Age: American Intellectuals in the 1940s and 1950s.* New York: Harper & Row, 1985.

———. *Radical Visions, American Dreams: Culture and Social Thought in the Depression Years.* New York: Harper & Row, 1973.

Persons, Stow. *The Decline of American Gentility.* New York: Columbia University Press, 1973.

Pomerance, Michla. "The United States and Self-Determination: Perspectives on the Wilsonian Conception." *American Journal of International Law* 70 (1976): 1–27.

Posey, John Philip. "David Hunter Miller and the Far Eastern Question at the Paris Peace Conference, 1919." *Southern Quarterly* 7 (1969): 382–84.

———. "David Hunter Miller and the Polish Minorities Treaty, 1919." *Southern Quarterly* 8 (1970): 163–76.

Rappaport, Armin. *Henry L. Stimson and Japan, 1931–33.* Chicago: University of Chicago Press, 1963.

Ricci, David. *The Tragedy of Political Science.* New Haven: Yale University Press, 1984.

Rochester, Stuart. *American Liberal Disillusionment in the Wake of World War I.* University Park: Pennsylvania State University Press, 1974.

Rogin, Michael P. *The Intellectuals and McCarthy: The Radical Specter.* Cambridge: M.I.T. Press, 1967.

Russell, Ruth B., and Jeanette E. Muther. *A History of the United Nations Charter: The Role of the United States, 1940–1945.* Washington, D.C.: Brookings Institution, 1958.

Rutland, Robert A. *The Democrats from Jefferson to Carter.* Baton Rouge: Louisiana State University Press, 1979.

Schlesinger, Arthur M., Jr. *The Age of Roosevelt.* 3 vols. Boston: Houghton Mifflin, 1957–1960.

———. *1000 Days.* Boston: Houghton Mifflin, 1965.

Schmidt, Hans. *The United States Occupation of Haiti, 1915–1934.* New Brunswick, N.J.: Rutgers University Press, 1971.

Schneider, James C. *Should America Go to War? The Debate over Foreign Policy in Chicago, 1939–1941.* Chapel Hill: University of North Carolina Press, 1989.

Schorske, Carl E. *German Social Democracy, 1905–1917: The Development of the Great Schism.* Cambridge: Harvard University, 1955.

Schroeder, John H. *Mr. Polk's War: American Opposition and Dissent, 1846–1848.* Madison: University of Wisconsin Press, 1973.

Schulzinger, Robert. *The Making of the Diplomatic Mind: The Training, Outlook, and Style of United States Foreign Service Officers, 1908–1931.* Middletown, Conn.: Wesleyan University Press, 1975.

———. *Wise Men of Foreign Affairs: The Council on Foreign Relations.* New York: Columbia University Press, 1984.

Schwabe, Klaus. *Woodrow Wilson, Revolutionary Germany, and Peacemaking, 1918–1919.* Chapel Hill: University of North Carolina Press, 1985.

Seidelman, Raymond, and Edward Harpham. *Disenchanted Realists: Political Science and the American Crisis, 1884–1984.* Albany: State University of New York Press, 1985.

Siegel, Frederick F. *Troubled Journey: From Pearl Harbor to Ronald Reagan.* New York: Hill & Wang, 1984.

Singal, Daniel. "Beyond Consensus: Richard Hofstadter and American Historiography." *American Historical Review* 89 (1984): 976–1004.

Smith, Daniel M. "National Interests and American Intervention, 1917: A Historiographical Appraisal." *Journal of American History* 52 (June 1965): 5–24.

Smith, Gaddis. *American Diplomacy during the Second World War, 1941–1945,* 2d ed. New York: Knopf, 1985.

———. *Morality, Reason, and Power: American Diplomacy in the Carter Years.* New York: Hill & Wang, 1986.

Sproat, John. *"The Best Men": Liberal Reformers in the Gilded Age.* New York: Oxford University Press, 1968.

Steel, Ronald. *Walter Lippmann and the American Century.* Boston: Little, Brown, 1980.

Stephanson, Anders. *Kennan and the Art of Foreign Policy.* Cambridge: Cambridge University Press, 1989.

Stephensen, Wendell. "The Influence of Woodrow Wilson on Frederick Jackson Turner." *Agricultural History* 19 (October 1945): 249–53.

Sternsher, Bernard. *Rexford Tugwell and the New Deal.* New Brunswick, N.J.: Rutgers University Press, 1964.

Stillman, Richard J., II. "Woodrow Wilson and the Study of Administration: A New Look at an Old Essay." *American Political Science Review* 67 (March–June 1973): 582–88.

Stone, Ralph A. *The Irreconcilables: The Fight against the League of Nations.* Lexington: University of Kentucky Press, 1970.

Stromberg, Roland. *Collective Security and American Foreign Policy: From the League of Nations to NATO.* New York: Praeger, 1963.

Tansill, Charles C. *America and the Fight for Irish Freedom.* New York: Knopf, 1957.

Thompson, J. A. "Woodrow Wilson and World War I: A Reappraisal." *Journal of American Studies* 19 (December 1985): 325–48.

Thompson, John M. *Russia, Bolshevism, and the Versailles Peace.* Princeton: Princeton University Press, 1967.

Thorsein, Neils. "The Political and Economic Thought of Woodrow Wilson." Ph.D. dissertation, Princeton University, 1981.

Traub, James. "Liberal? Conservative? Or Just Pat?" *New York Times Magazine,* 16 September 1990, 78–79.

Tuttle, William H. Jr. "Aid-to-the-Allies Short-of-War versus American Intervention, 1940: A Reappraisal of William Allen White's Leadership." *Journal of American History* 56 (March 1970): 840–58.

Tyler, Gus. "The Politics of Pat Moynihan." In *The New Conservatives,* ed. Lewis Coser and Irving Howe, 181–92. New York: Meridian, 1976.

Unterberger, Betty Miller. *The United States, Revolutionary Russia, and the Rise of Czechoslovakia.* Chapel Hill: University of North Carolina Press, 1989.

Van Tassel, David D. "From Learned Society to Professional Organization: The American Historical Association, 1884–1900." *American Historical Review* 89 (October 1984): 929–56.

Watson, David R. *Clemenceau: A Political Biography.* London: Eyre Methuen, 1974.

Weisenberger, Francis P. "The Middle-Western Antecedents of Woodrow Wilson." *Mississippi Valley Historical Review* 23 (1936–37): 375–84.

Welcher, James A. "The Brothers Alsop and Adlai Stevenson." *The Progressive* 27 (March 1963): 14–18.

Westbrook, Robert B. *John Dewey and American Democracy.* Ithaca: Cornell University Press, 1991.

Whittmore, Richard. *Nicholas Murray Butler and Public Education, 1862–1911.* New York: Teachers College Press, 1970.

Williams, William Appleman. "The Legend of Isolationism in the 1920's." *Science and Society* 18 (Winter 1954): 1–20.

Wilson, Trevor. *The Downfall of the Liberal Party, 1914–1935*. Ithaca: Cornell University Press, 1966.

Yergin, Daniel. "Fulbright's Last Frustration." *New York Times Magazine*, 24 November 1974, 14, 76–94.

———. *Shattered Peace: The Origins of the Cold War and The National Security State*. Boston: Houghton Mifflin, 1977.

Index

Ambrosius, Lloyd, 62–63
American Civil War, 4, 35, 55–56
American Committee to Negotiate the Peace (ACNP), 62, 82, 100
Anti-pluralism, 45–52
Anti-Semitism. *See* Jewish questions
Arendt, Hannah, 75–76, 179n16, 201
Armstrong, Hamilton Fish, 115, 137, 162, 165, 204
Atomic bomb, 131, 150–54, 158, 214–15

Baker, Newton D., 47, 173, 181, 196; on German technocracy, 59–61; and the Democratic party, 88–90, 119–21; relationship with Lippmann, 89, 119, 125–27, 173, 196; view of public opinion, 90, 103–4; opposition to the New Deal, 124–27, 132
Baker, Ray Stannard, 62, 69n14, 72, 74–75, 77, 80–83
Ball, George, 210, 221, 227–28
Bay of Pigs invasion, 221–23
Benes, Edvard, 65, 67
Bledstein, Barton, 18
Bok, Edward, 94
Bok Peace Prize, 94
Bolshevik Revolution, 63–67, 76
Borah, William, 98, 101, 111, 181
Bourne, Randolph, 8
Bryan, William Jennings, 32–33, 54n30, 182
Buell, Raymond Leslie, 17; *Isolated America,* 128; on William Borah, 101; early support of the New Deal, 122; on

economic nationalism, 115–17; applause for RTA, 123; moral disillusionment, 124, 128–30; suspicions of one-worldism, 139; defense of regionalism, 140–41; condemns UN veto, 148–49; plan for multilateral control of the bomb, 150–54; death from cancer, 154
Butler, Nicholas Murray, x, 10, 40, 109, 133; argument for internationalism, 15–17; view of political authority, 46–47; on the New Deal, 121–24
Byrnes, James, 156, 157–58

Carnegie Endowment for International Peace, 10, 94, 109, 112, 133, 135
Carter, Jimmy, 234–35
Catt, Carrie Chapman, 108, 109
Century Club, 134–35, 209
Chatfield, Charles, 112
Clarke, John H., 88, 93, 108–9; *America and World Peace,* 95
Clayton Anti-Trust Act, 27
Clemenceau, Georges, 63, 76–77
Cohalan, Daniel, 70
Cold War, 7, 131, 217–18, 222, 233, 236, 237, 242; Wilsonian critique of, 154–65; and liberal realism, 169–71, 200, 204
Collective security, 132, 135–37. *See also* Kellogg-Briand Pact; Protocol for the Pacific Settlement of Disputes; Shotwell, James
Committee to Defend America by Aiding the Allies (CDAAA), 133–37, 209